Bargaining and Market Behavior

This second Cambridge University Press collection o   pers by Vernon L. Smith, a creator of the field of experimental economics, includes many of his primary authored and coauthored contributions on bargaining and market behavior written between 1990 and 1998. The essays explore the use of laboratory experiments to test propositions derived from economics and game theory. They also investigate the relationship between experimental economics and psychology, particularly the field of evolutionary psychology, using the latter to broaden the perspective in which experimental results are interpreted. The volume complements Professor Smith's earlier work by demonstrating the importance of institutional features of markets in understanding behavior and market performance. Specific themes investigated include rational choice, the notion of fairness, game theory and extensive form experimental interactions, institutions and market behavior, and the study of laboratory stock markets.

Vernon L. Smith is Regents' Professor, McClelland Professor, and Research Director of the Economic Science Laboratory at the University of Arizona. He received his doctorate from Harvard University and has also taught at Purdue and Brown Universities and the University of Massachusetts. Professor Smith is the author or coauthor of more than 200 professional papers and books on experimental economics, finance, capital theory, and natural resource economics, including *Papers in Experimental Economics* (Cambridge University Press, 1991). He serves or has served on the editorial boards of the *American Economic Review, The Cato Journal, Journal of Economic Behavior and Organization, Journal of Risk and Uncertainty, Science, Economic Theory, Economic Design, Games and Economic Behavior, and Journal of Economic Methodology.*

Professor Smith is past president of the Public Choice Society, the Economic Science Association, the Western Economic Association, and the Association for Private Enterprise Education. He is a Distinguished Fellow of the American Economic Association and a Fellow of the Econometric Society, the American Association for the Advancement of Science, and the American Academy of Arts and Sciences. Professor Smith has also been a Ford Foundation Fellow, a Fellow of the Center for Advanced Study in the Behavioral Sciences, and a Sherman Fairchild Distinguished Scholar at the California Institute of Technology. He holds an honorary doctorate from Purdue University.

Vernon Smith was elected a member of the National Academy of Sciences in 1995. He has served as a consultant on the privatization of electric power in Australia and New Zealand and has participated in numerous high-level public- and private-sector discussions of energy deregulation in the United States, including the National Electric Reliability Council in 1997.

Bargaining and Market Behavior

Essays in Experimental Economics

VERNON L. SMITH
University of Arizona

CAMBRIDGE
UNIVERSITY PRESS

CAMBRIDGE UNIVERSITY PRESS
Cambridge, New York, Melbourne, Madrid, Cape Town, Singapore, São Paulo

Cambridge University Press
The Edinburgh Building, Cambridge CB2 2RU, UK

Published in the United States of America by Cambridge University Press, New York

www.cambridge.org
Information on this title: www.cambridge.org/9780521584500

First published 2000
This digitally printed first paperback version 2005

A catalogue record for this publication is available from the British Library

Library of Congress Cataloguing in Publication data
Smith, Vernon L.
    Bargaining and market behavior : essays in experimental economics / Vernon L. Smith.
        p.   cm.
    Includes bibliographical references.
    ISBN 0-521-58450-7
    1. Economics – Methodology.   2. Economics – Simulation methods.   3. Economics
    – Psychological aspects.   I. Title.
    HB131.S59   2000
    330´.01 – dc21   99-15975
                                                                                              CIP

ISBN-13 978-0-521-58450-0 hardback
ISBN-10 0-521-58450-7 hardback

ISBN-13 978-0-521-02148-7 paperback
ISBN-10 0-521-02148-0 paperback

Jonathan Roberts Tyson Hughes

A Memorial

On this occasion
we are privileged to celebrate
the memory of a wonderful life;
one that spanned sixty-four years;
one that touched and altered
dozens, likely hundreds, of other lives.

In his life John taught us how to live
– with energy, splendor, joy, and hope.
In his death he taught us how to die
– with stubborn resistance, candor, optimism, and inspiration.

I am awash with delightful memories,
but I will remember best and miss most
his unflagging personal support;
no one else could get as genuinely excited
about your work
as about his own.

He believed in his friends,
as he would have them believe in themselves.
He never allowed me not to believe in myself,
nor other friends not to believe in themselves.
He awakened the hidden strength within you.

When he wrote of the history he had learned
it was as if he had experienced it,
much as he spoke and wrote of the history he had truly lived:
down the white water rapids of Idaho's Bruneau River;
playing jazz clarinet in Ely, Wells, Elko, and Fish Haven;
the Great Strike of 1951 at Nushagak Station.

I first read the *Vital Few*,
and its masterful essay on Brigham Young,
in manuscript,
then entitled *The Good Land*.
I was astonished for it read like he had been there, lived it all.
That's when I knew how good writing is born of personal
– even if vicarious – experience,
that draws the reader into the phenomena, as it lived.

I was disheartened that the title was changed
to the colorless,
though accurate, *Vital Few*,

thus eliminating John's ringing text from Exodus (3:8):
And I come down to deliver them
out of the hand of the Egyptians,
and to bring them up out of that land
unto a good land and a large (land),
unto a land flowing with milk and honey.

John loved the land, because he was of the land:
Idaho, Utah, Nevada, Washington, Indiana, Illinois, Vermont.
His heroes were most especially
of the Good Land
that flowed with the milk and honey
of nineteenth-century opportunity.

John catapulted himself into your life
– a fact that,
shall we say,
was not universally appreciated.
I welcomed and blossomed from this warm intrusion
for he was the brother I never had,
the confidant who nourished so very deeply, and meaningfully.

He came to Purdue for one reason:
he told me that he could no longer tolerate
his Federal Reserve Bank superior
blue-penciling all his work.
Such was his fierce Mormon independence.

After Purdue,
although there were sometimes long spaces
between our encounters,
somehow we managed always to pick up
where we had ended,
as if it had been but an hour, or a day.
With John there were no beginnings or endings;
just the flow of experience shared.

It was this continuity, this dependability, and reliability
in the face of unimportant interruption
that most significantly defined our relationship.
Others, I think, must have shared a similar experience,
because of who he was.
That continuity defined and gave sustenance
to an enduring thirty-six year bond between us.
I shall miss that bond dearly,
but without repining,
because of the strength he inspired.

His works,
his personal influence,

will of course live,
as resistant to extinction as was his spirit to the end.
This is assured by those of us here, on this day,
and elsewhere,
who were touched so intimately by him,
for with John there were no beginnings or endings.

Now it is for each of us,
the living,
privately,
as well as through this congregation,
to find whatever meaning for our lives,
that is contained in his death.

He came
as dust
delivered of the good land;
he chose to return
as dust, for renewal,
unto a land made sweeter by his coming.

Vernon Smith
Tucson, Arizona
Delivered at Northwestern University
Alice Millar Chapel
October 25, 1992

Contents

ix

Preface

The first volume of my *Papers in Experimental Economics* (New York: Cambridge University Press, 1991) included most of my research papers in experimentation up to 1990. This second volume includes papers published largely from 1990 to 1998 plus some earlier pieces that can be conveniently classified under the headings of bargaining or markets. Almost all the papers herein have been coauthored with others. Even more than is indicated in *Papers in Experimental Economics*, experimentation has become an effort requiring many bases to be covered, and the research is most efficaciously conducted by teams of coequal scholars who each bring special skills and expertise to the bench. Some of the themes in this collection are continuations of works included in the earlier volume, in particular market institutions and experimental methodology. This is because my coauthors and I have found them to be viable long-term research programs. Other themes, involving bargaining, psychology, and reciprocity sparked our interest in the mid- to late 1980s and began to appear in this decade in published papers.

I believe that experimental economics, as an important methodology of inquiry cutting across all fields in economics is here to stay, although there remain pockets of resistance to this development. Such resistance is welcome for it has helped to invigorate, challenge, and strengthen experimentation. For me, the methodology is of value in proportion to its capacity to help us understand human behavior broadly in economic societies. Hence, we see the importance of linking behavior in the laboratory to field data from the modern economy, as well as economic history, archeological, biological, and ethnographic data from prehistory. Understanding is advanced only a little by isolated studies unconnected with broader knowledge of human social and economic development.

It is a pleasure to acknowledge, and express my appreciation for, the crucial contributions of my several coauthors, some of whom have participated with me for many years in many projects. I also recognize the contributions and invaluable support from Patricia Kiser, my long-time administrative assistant, who has grown with us all, learning and taking

on increasing new responsibilities connected with managing the research
records and funding that have made this volume possible.

Vernon L. Smith
Tucson, Arizona
July 1999

PART I

Economics and Psychology

Introduction

Economic theorists and cognitive (decision behavior) psychologists agree on several core (maintained) hypotheses about human decision making: (1) rationality in social and economic contexts derives directly from the rationality of individual decision makers – if surveys of isolated individuals indicate irrational responses, ipso facto, markets and other group interaction decision systems will be irrational; (2) individual rationality is a self-aware cognitive process – if people get things right, it is through thinking about and understanding the processes in which they partake; and (3) the human mind is modeled as a general purpose problem-solving machine that governs reasoning, learning, memory, and decision making with "no features specialized for processing particular kinds of content" (Gigerenzer, 1996, p. 329). Thus, the economist's model of decision making is expected utility maximization in all decision making under uncertainty. Kahneman and Tversky's (1979) model is maximization of a weighted value function that modifies the objective probabilities (judgments) and utilities of expected utility theory to descriptively account for decision making under uncertainty.

The work of experimental economists has focused more explicitly on the behavior of markets and other interactive rule-governed institutional mechanisms in which individual decision making is not isolated from that of others. This perspective has generated methodological differences between experimental economics and cognitive psychology that have led to a divergence in the questions asked and the research procedures used.

The chapters in Part I address some of these issues in detail. One issue is whether the research results of cognitive psychologists are robust with respect to behavior in markets, to substantial monetary rewards, and to institutional context, although the last potentially overlaps the study of "framing" effects in psychology. Another is whether discrepancies between theory and observation can be resolved in a testable way by appropriate modifications of extant theory. Part I deals with cases testing whether this seems feasible, whereas the chapters in Part II, dealing with experimental results in two-person bargaining, suggest that a more

3

fundamental reorientation in theory, and particularly its interpretation, may be necessary, although I believe that most of the conceptual foundation for that reorientation is already contained within game theory. It is in this context that the perspective of evolutionary psychology is introduced in Part II. I and my coauthors believe that perspective may be promising and is worthy of serious attention from experimental economists as a means of generating alternative hypotheses to those based exclusively on noncooperative game theory and its elaboration.

Chapter 1 provides an overview of the economic and cognitive themes, as I see them, in the debate between the economic and the cognitive psychology views of decision, particularly from the perspective of experimental economics. One of the more significant discoveries in experimental market studies is that efficiency and convergence to competitive equilibria occur ubiquitously in experimental markets without subjects having the remotest awareness and understanding of the unconscious ends they have achieved. This issue is neither addressed nor recognized in either mainstream economics (Hayek and the Austrians are, of course, a long-standing exception) or mainstream behavioral cognitive psychology, although it is quite explicit in the evolutionary psychology program (see Chapter 9 in Part II).

The Endowment Effect

An important behavioral principle from prospect theory establishes that the marginal utility for losses is much greater than the marginal utility for a gain measured from the status quo state. Thaler has proposed that this fundamental principle implies that out-of-pocket costs receive a higher cognitive weight than forgone gains, a phenomenon he refers to as the endowment effect. This in turn implies a discontinuity in the individual's demand schedule at his existing asset position, which accounts for the well-known tendency for minimum willingness-to-accept to be much larger than maximum willingness-to-pay as measured in surveys. A corollary is undertrading. If you endow half of $2N$ people at random with a good (e.g., an emblem mug) and half with appropriate comparable amounts of money, an exchange market between the N buyers and N sellers should result in $N/2$ mugs being exchanged. In Chapter 2, using a market mechanism well known to yield very high efficiency and competitive outcomes, we find support for undertrading.

But one of the research problems in this test is that the revealed supply and demand schedules are very gently sloped so that small errors in the supply and demand have a multiplied effect on trading volume.

A Decision Cost Model, the Predictions of Rational Theory, and Extending the Model

Chapter 3 develops the idea that decision making is cognitively costly and that observed decision outcomes are the result of an individual unconsciously weighing this cost against the value of the outcome. The underlying hypothesis is that this is the way the brain works; in the absence of disorder in its circuitry, it responds more or less aggressively in reaching decisions, depending upon whether the quality of the decision has high or low value. Hence, the failure of "rational" models is in part a failure to take into account all costs (or value since the decision process may have excitement value, relieve boredom, etc.). Is it irrational to devote few cognitive resources to a difficult decision problem when the consequences have little value?

The resulting model predicts that either increasing the monetary stakes or decreasing the complexity of difficult tasks in experiments will tend to reduce the variance in outcomes and, where there is a discrepancy, move them closer to the equilibrium predicted by reward maximization. The latter prediction follows in spades if the equilibrium is on the boundary of the decision's constraint set. These predictions are in qualitative conformity with a wide range of experimental observations, although, as always, the data exhibit noise relative to this prediction. The model also predicts that if subject experience (learning) enables cognitive effort to be reduced, then outcomes will move closer to the reward-maximizing equilibrium. Again, Chapter 3 reports experimental evidence relevant to this prediction.

But there are sure to be contrary cases because anomalies are inevitable in the most accurate and plausible theories. For example, in one version of the ultimatum game, when the stakes are increased from $10 to $100 (see Chapter 7), proposals are reduced (but not significantly – either economically or statistically), but the rejection rate increases significantly.

This suggests that the decision cost model may need to account for strategic considerations explicitly to encompass contrary cases. In fact, a shortcoming of Chapter 3 is that it treats strategically interacting subjects as if each were in a game against nature, an assumption better suited for n-person markets than to two-person bargaining. This shortcoming has been corrected recently in Smith and Szidarovszky (1999) who show how the results of Chapter 3 can be extended to equilibrium bargaining between agents.

Fairness in Markets

Fairness – in the sense of interpersonal utility considerations, or perceptions of what constitutes a fair division – has been shown by Kahneman et al. (1986, 1987), using questionnaire data, to influence what people believe about the acceptability of price increases in retail markets in the short run. They do not claim that such fairness considerations will necessarily have an impact on market behavior in the long run but that it may account for sluggishness in a market's response to external conditions. This is an issue discussed briefly in Chapter 1, but examined more rigorously by explicit market experiments in Chapter 4. The particular experimental framework used to study this issue is adapted from studies by Kachelmier and co-workers (Kachelmier and Shehata, 1991; Kachelmier et al., 1991a, b). The bottom line in Chapter 4 is that such fairness considerations do limit short-run price increases compared with control experiments where such considerations do not apply, but over time market prices asymptotically approach equilibria predicted by the standard competitive equilibrium model of markets organized under posted offer retail pricing. This implies that "fairness" is a property of agent short-run expectations, rather than a property of agent utility functions: Buyers believe and expect that price increases, resulting from external market considerations, should not produce higher ("unearned") profits to sellers, whereas sellers temporarily accept this norm. This results in a temporary expectational equilibrium with no increase in price. But there is excess demand at this price, and seller competition for that excess demand causes price to rise gradually to the competitive equilibrium in successive market trading periods. Because economic theory provides no rationale for why markets impacted by external parameter changes do not leap to the new static equilibrium, psychology fills this gap with a testable explanatory hypothesis; of course, there may be others. Thus, behavior may become autonomic in a static equilibrium. A change in that equilibrium requires more cognitive resources to consciously reconsider old responses and to adjust, and this is time consuming.

CHAPTER 1

Rational Choice: The Contrast Between Economics and Psychology

Vernon L. Smith

Rational Choice (Hogarth and Reder, 1987) is about economics and psychology, or, as noted by Zeckhauser (1987, pp. 251–4), the rationalist versus behavioralist views of economics. One would have hoped that in this book, given the potential of psychologists and economists to learn from each other, the record would have shown more tangible evidence of this learning.

This chapter discusses the themes in this debate, a debate that is never quite joined: The psychologist's provocative claims are neither answered nor echoed by the economists. My comments will arise from the perspective of experimental economics, which reflects equally the rational and behavioral intellectual traditions. Generally, I want to address the reference to "a growing body of evidence – mainly of an experimental nature – that has documented systematic departures from the dictates of rational economic behavior" (Hogarth and Reder, 1987, p. vii). This suggests a contest between economic theory and the falsifying evidence from psychology. But there is a third view, that of experimental economics, which documents a growing body of evidence that is consistent with the implications of rational models, although there are many important exceptions. In the latter, often the data can be comprehended by modifying the original models. The result is to deepen the concept of rationality and simultaneously increase consistency between the observations and the models; better normative models more accurately predict the experimental results. Psychologists almost uniformly report results contrary to rational theory, which leads them to conclude that the "normative and descriptive analyses of choice should be viewed as separate enterprises" (Tversky and Kahneman, 1987, p. 91).

I.   Rationality as Conscious Cognition

"My first empirical proposition is that there is a complete lack of evidence that, in actual human choice situations of any complexity, these [rational] computations can be, or are in fact, performed . . . but we cannot, of course, rule out the

7

possibility that the unconscious is a better decision maker than the conscious" (Simon, 1955, p. 104).

Throughout much of *Rational Choice*, one sees the frictional tension between psychology and economics. But from the perspective of experimental economics, I believe that the basic problem stems not from the numerous areas of claimed disagreement expressed in *Rational Choice*, but from two unstated premises on which there is implicit agreement between psychology and mainstream theory: (1) rationality in the economy emanates and derives from the rationality of individual decision makers in the economy, and (2) individual rationality is a cognitively intensive, calculating process of maximization in the self-interest. A third shared tenant, which is a correlate of points 1 and 2, is that (3) an acceptable and fundamental way to test economic theory is to test directly the economic rationality of individuals isolated from interactive *experience* in social and economic institutions.[1] Economists do not usually challenge this tenet. They are merely skeptical of the way psychologists implement it: by asking subjects how they would choose among stated hypothetical alternatives. It is reasonable to conjecture from this that the methodology would be acceptable if the decision maker had a "stake" in the decision, in which case the issue could in principle be resolved empirically. But according to point 1, nothing is added or addable by the conjunction of individuals in, and with, markets that cannot be captured by giving the subject a verbal description of the particular market decision-making context. Market rationality is then the direct result of individual choice rationality in that described context.[2] But experimental economics

---

[1] Arrow, recognizing point 1 as an implicit assumption in traditional theory, is concerned with correcting this view: "I want to stress that rationality is not a property of the individual alone. ... It gathers not only its force but also its very meaning from the social context in which it is embedded" (1987, p. 201). But Arrow's point is about theory: His main theme is that the power of theory derives from the conjunction of rational individuals with the concepts of "equilibrium, competition, and completeness of markets" (p. 203). For example, theory assumes complete information and common knowledge as part of the rationality of individuals, making rationality a social phenomenon.

[2] Of course, psychologists are interested in studying cognitive processes in decision-making situations that appear to be remote from market processes. But such decisions may still have a social context, such as hospital and medical committees in the case of physician decisions. The study of isolated cognitive processes is of interest in its own right but also needs to be studied explicitly in other social contexts. It is desirable to know whether the strong effect of framing (survival versus mortality probabilities) on physicians' stated preferences is related to their actual decision to use one therapy rather than another. Presumably, "best practice" therapies evolve in a social context not from isolated individuals thinking about alternatives in terms of probabilities. Experiments that would attempt to capture these social processes would be analogous to the experimental economist's program of studying market decision making in particular institutional contexts.

research suggests that different results obtain when subjects' choices are interactively governed by an institution. Although the rediscovery of institutions in economic theory began about 1960 with the contributions by Shubik (1959), Coase (1960), Hurwicz (1960), and Vickrey (1961), the new thinking, hypothesizing that institutions matter, is still not well integrated with both theory and laboratory evidence.

That individual rationality is a consciously cognitive phenomena is fundamental in the rhetoric of microeconomic and game theory. The theorist, if called on, says that the model assumes complete information on payoffs (utilities) and more. "The common knowledge assumption underlies all of game theory and much of economic theory. Whatever be the model under discussion ... the model itself must be assumed common knowledge; otherwise the model is insufficiently specified, and the analysis incoherent" (Aumann, 1987, p. 473). Without such common knowledge people would fail to reason their way to the solution arrived at cognitively by the theorist. This is echoed by Arrow when he notes that a "monopolist, even ... where there is just one in the entire economy, has to understand all these [general equilibrium] repercussions ... has to have a full general equilibrium model of the economy" (Arrow, 1987, p. 207). Indeed, it has been hard for either the theorist or the psychologist to imagine optimal market outcomes being achieved by other than conscious cognition; it can't occur by "magic," so to speak.[3] The reason is that neither has traditionally modeled markets as a learning process, capable of converging to a rational equilibrium outcome. A noteworthy exception is to be found in Lucas (1987), in which some examples are used to motivate the hypothesis that myopic agents with adaptive expectations converge to steady states, which sometimes correspond to a Muthian rational expectations equilibrium.[4]

What has emerged from 30 years of experimental research is that the preceding premises 1–3 are false. Plott (1987) summarizes many examples. In these experiments (also Smith, 1962), all information on the

---

[3] Simon (1955) is open to the possibility that unconscious decisions may be better than the conscious. But Simon (1987, p. 39) says that "in situations that are complex and in which information is very incomplete (i.e., virtually all real-world situations), the behavioral theories deny that there is any magic for producing behavior even approximating an objective maximization of profits or utilities." Yet there are a great many, very complex, experimental markets, with very incomplete information, that converge to outcomes that precisely approximate those derived from maximizing objectives. We badly need the kind of cooperation between economics and psychology that would help us to better understand how, in Simon's (1987, pp. 26–8) well-known terminology, the procedural rationality of the individual allows substantively rational outcomes to be achieved over time in these markets.

[4] Other important contributions to the study of the market process are provided by Blume and Easley (1982) and Bray (1982); see also Kalai and Lerher (1993).

economic environment (values) is private; far from having perfect or common information, subjects know only their own "circumstances." All trading is carried out by an institution such as the decentralized "open outcry" rules of the continuous double auction in which every agent is both a price maker who announces bids to buy (offers to sell) and a price taker who accepts a standing offer to sell (bid to buy). What these and many hundreds of other experiments have shown is that (1) prices and allocations converge quickly to the neighborhood of the predicted rational expectations competitive equilibrium, and (2) these results generalize to a wide variety of posted-price, sealed-bid, and other institutions of exchange, although convergence rates tend to vary and can be influenced by extreme parameter conditions.

Postexperiment discussion with the subjects in the earliest experiments made it plain that (1) subjects are not aware that they are achieving maximum profits collectively and individually, in equilibrium, and, in fact, deny this when asked; and (2) before seeing the results, subjects describe the market situation as confused and disorderly ("How can you get anything out of these experiments?"). When asked what strategies they used, they are unable to convey insight to the experimenter: "I tried to buy low (sell high)" or "I waited until near the end to squeeze the other side." These and other bidding, auctioning, and price-posting experiments show the predictive power of noncooperative equilibrium concepts (competitive or Nash) without any requirement that knowledge be complete and common. In these cases, economic theory works, predictively, under weaker conditions than expected, and no support is provided for the interpretation that the equilibrating process is consciously cognitive. The verbal behavior of subjects strongly contradicts what their actual behavior achieves.

The fact that private-information experimental markets converge more quickly and reliably to certain rational predictions than complete-information markets do directly contradicts the conclusion of Tversky and Kahneman (1987, p. 88): "Perhaps the major finding of the present article is that the axioms of rational choice are generally satisfied in transparent situations and often violated in nontransparent ones."[5] This is correct in their context, but in experimental markets rational theory often performs best in the "nontransparent" (low information) environ-

[5] According to one of my referees, "Isn't it odd that one would find this quote [by Tversky and Kahneman] in a book in which Plott demonstrated the operation of a near continuum of markets (the signaling example)? Somehow the psychologists miss the point of examples even when the examples are placed directly in front of them. As I reflect on these papers I do not recall any psychological explanation of any of the papers that have used experimental economics techniques. It seems to me that the psychologists have not done their homework."

ment and worst in the "transparent" (high information) environment. The leap is so great when one goes from data on responses to individual choice problems to observed behavior in experimental markets that conclusions of this sort are reversed! This underscores the criticism by Coleman (1987) of the implicit premise of the conference that the greatest gains for theory will come from a more sophisticated model of action. "It is deficiencies in the apparatus for moving from the level of the individual actor to the behavior of the system that hold the greatest promise of gain" (p. 184). I think this is the most important implication of experimental economic research. What is imperfectly understood is the precise manner in which institutions serve as social tools that reinforce, even induce, individual rationality. Such economic concepts as noncooperative equilibrium and incentive compatibility are helpful, but they are inexorably static and do not come to grips with the interactive process between agents and institutions. One misses all of this in research limited to the individual expressing an opinion about described situations or alternatives.

It is natural to expect that the unconscious can be a good decision maker only when complexity is absent. The single-market experiments discussed earlier are simple in the sense that there is but one isolated market characterized by stationary supply and demand, but the observed results still follow in some institutions when demand is constantly shifted privately without public announcement of any kind (McCabe et al., 1993). Furthermore, there are many examples showing that in much more complicated multiple-market experiments, convergence to competitive equilibria is observed.[6]

II.   Verbal Behavior: Unreliable and Not Worth Studying?

The preceding discussion might lead some to infer, incorrectly, that nothing worth knowing can be learned by studying verbal behavior. Verbal behavior, when studied with the skills of the psychologist, tells one a lot about how people think about choice problems. Their choices

---

[6] See Smith (1986, p. 169) and Williams et al. (1986) for examples with three commodities and two markets; see Plott (1988) for an example with 19 connected markets. Another type of complexity occurs in experimental asset markets in which the asset dividend is not only uncertain but also dependent on a sample of likelihood information. It is well known that psychologists find judgment biases that contradict the Bayesian updating of subjective probabilities from sample information. One important study finds that "in eight experiments with inexperienced subjects, prices tend toward the Bayesian predictions, but there is some evidence of exact representativeness bias in prices and allocations. However, the degree of bias is small, and it is even smaller in experiments with experienced subjects. All other non-Bayesian theories can be rejected" (Camerer 1987, p. 995).

deviate from the predictions of rational choice theory, and, as noted earlier and in the studies summarized later, verbal behavior deviates from actual behavior in market experiments. The nature of these discrepancies is a legitimate object of investigation. But to be most informative for economics, such studies should be conducted in the context of experimental (or field) markets, where one observes both verbal intentions and actual choices. The paper by Kahneman et al. (1987) provides an example of what I mean. People, when asked, state that it is fairer to allocate surplus football tickets (above season subscriptions) by lottery or queue than by auctioning to the highest bidders. But what would be the effect on behavior and attitudes toward fairness if the auctioning of tickets makes it possible to lower the price of season tickets or build an addition to the stadium? Economic reality consists of both the unseen and the seen – both the indirect and direct consequences of decision. What economics brings to the analytical table is the broader perspective that choice decisions have repercussions, which actual decision makers experience but may not perceive. These effects are omitted from opinion surveys, but they may have an impact on attitudes as well as behavior. Opinion polls tend to reflect the psychologist's direct perception of reality and not the economist's view that "decisions have consequences." This is why secondary effects and equilibrium concepts are an integral part of the designs used by experimental economists.[7]

Another example of the insights to be gained by embedding fairness questions into a broader decision context has been provided by Hoffman and Spitzer (1985b). They study Coase (1960) bargaining between pairs of subjects, one of whom has been given a position of advantage assigned by a coin flip. All subjects bargain to an efficient solution, but none of the privileged bargainers receives the larger individually rational share afforded by the property right. To see what might be driving these results, Hoffman and Spitzer replicated their experiments with the following change: Instead of by a coin flip, the position of advantage is awarded to the winner of a game of Nim, and both subjects are told that the winner of this pregame will have "earned" the right to be the controller in the bargaining game. Now two-thirds of the controllers negotiate individually rational bargains. This finding suggests that assigning rights at random induces a very strong unintentional fairness ethic that largely disappears when the rights are earned. Because rights in the economy do not arise by random assignment but are acquired through some eco-

---

[7] I am not criticizing the idea put forward by Kahneman et al. (1987) that norms of fairness may be necessary to explain certain data. The point is that there are naïve and sophisticated notions of "fairness"; also, in experimental markets, self-interested behavior tends to overcome any fairness norms.

nomic or political process, the interpretation of fairness opinion research is ambiguous without a deeper examination of the circumstances.[8] Thus Kahneman et al. find that most people consider it fair for a firm to lower price if input costs decline; but if costs decline because of an invention by the firm, then it is fair to retain the resulting profit. (They earned it?) But do these opinions have anything to do with observed behavior in a market? There is abundant evidence that prices fall, over time, in experimental markets when the induced supply schedule is increased. Kahneman et al. could answer this question by first soliciting people's opinions, as discussed earlier, and then doing market experiments under two different announced explanations for the cost reduction: an input price decline and an innovation. I would bet on no significant difference, in equilibrium, although initially I think it is plausible that market prices will be higher in the second treatment. The point is that these are researchable questions, and we can ask how verbal behavior relates to motivated behavior in experiments. Fairness is likely to be most important in understanding the regulated firm: how regulation came to be and how it operates politically.

Some research that combines verbal and actual market behavior has been reported by experimental economists. I will summarize three studies: (1) verbal, or choice, versus actual marketlike behavior in the context of preference reversal phenomena; (2) the relation between opinion polls and a presidential stock market; and (3) laboratory stock markets in which verbal behavior does not contradict and helps to explain market behavior.

A.   *Preference Reversals and Markets*

The standard preference reversal problem is easily described. The subject chooses gamble A over B (or B over A) but then states that his or her minimum willingness-to-accept price for A is less (more) than the minimum willingness-to-accept price for B. Such choice-revealed preference reversals vary from 24 to 68% of subject samples, with monetary rewards making it in a subject's interest not to preference reverse (Chu

---

[8] There is also a problem with all the bargaining literature in which there is a first-mover advantage (see Kahneman et al., 1987, for references). This literature reports overwhelming evidence that a bargainer's utility functions include fairness norms, but as far as I have been able to determine, in all such cases, the first-mover advantage is awarded at random. The usual interpretation of the Hoffman-Spitzer result is that it shows how fairness is sensitive to framing. But what it shows is much more significant: that equal-split bargaining results may be due, generically, to an important treatment thought to be benign, namely, the standard use of random devices to allocate subjects to initial conditions.

and Chu, 1990, p. 906). These results have been replicated many times, with a great variety of gambles going back to the path-breaking work of Lichtenstein and Slovic (1971). Chu and Chu (1990) construct a marketlike con game for subjects in which each is asked to state a preference between two gambles, with the understanding that if later the subject were holding a gamble that was not a preferred one (inferior or no preference), then a "trader" (one of the experimenters) could exercise the right to exchange the other gamble for the one held. Because each subject's exchange price was also solicited, the experimenter was in a position to return to the earlier choice and arbitrage the subject's holding. Up to three arbitrage transactions were performed against preference-reversing subjects in a sequence of decisions and trades. The results dramatically reduced the frequency of preference reversals: "three transactions were all that was needed to wipe out preference reversals completely" (Chu and Chu, 1990, p. 909). Arbitrage makes rational choice transparent.

B.   The Iowa Presidential Stock Market

Comparative data on verbal versus market behavior are provided by the presidential stock market conducted by experimentalists at the University of Iowa (Forsythe et al., 1991). In return for an initial minimum expenditure of $35, subjects received ten $2.50 portfolios consisting of ten shares in each candidate (at the time, Bush, Michael Dukakis, Jesse Jackson, and the rest of field) plus a $10 deposit credit from which further net purchases in the market were deducted. All funds invested were paid to shareholders in the form of a single dividend payment accruing at 9:00 A.M., November 9, 1988, when the market closed. The dividend paid to each share held on that date was $2.50 times the proportion of the popular vote cast for each candidate.[9]

In the Iowa experiments, Bush's lead as predicted by the market (Bush price – Dukakis price)/$2.50, rose to 8 points by October 20 and varied from November 2–9 within the range 6.8–8. The final results showed Bush winning by a margin of 7.8%. During the same period, Bush's margin in the opinion polls varied from 4 to 14%. The market was both more accurate and less volatile than the polls' measurement of

---

[9] Because uncertainty in this experiment was not of the usual balls-in-urns variety, it relates directly to the critique by Einhorn and Hogarth (1987), who "believe that it is time to move beyond the tidy experiments and axiomatizations built on the explicit lottery" (p. 64). This view is discussed by Zeckhauser (1987, pp. 257–8). Of course, in all market experiments, subjects face uncertainty about the behavior of others, but subject values either are certain or are generated by lotteries. Forsythe et al. (1991) is an innovative exception.

verbal behavior based on standard representative sampling techniques. The subject sample was not, however, representative; it consisted of those who bought presidential portfolios (restricted to the University of Iowa community). Furthermore, opinion polls were not "news" to the market. The frequent publication of poll results had little if any discernible effect on market prices. Hence, the well-known inaccuracy of political opinion polls was appropriately discounted by the market. Five surveys of candidate preferences and beliefs among the stock market participants revealed judgment biases of the kind found by psychologists and political scientists in the study of opinion. But Forsythe et al. were unable to identify significant patterns of trading behavior due to presidential preferences. For example, male–female differences in preferences for Bush, as expressed in polls, are large but were not reflected in differences between male and female holdings of Bush; the greatest difference was 4.2%, which was not statistically significant.

C.   *Laboratory Stock Markets: Verbal Behavior Can Complement Actual Behavior*

I shall close this section with a discussion of laboratory stock market experiments, in which verbal behavior does not contradict, and complements, actual behavior by helping to provide an "explanation" of behavior in terms of subjects' perceptions of their experience. Dozens of laboratory stock market experiments have documented that price bubbles arise naturally from the home-grown capital gains expectations of subjects in environments in which probabilistic dividend value is common information in each trading period of the horizon (Smith et al., 1988; Schwarz and Ang, 1989). These bubbles are particularly pronounced with first-time subjects, show a reduced amplitude and trading volume when subjects return for a second market experiment, and essentially disappear in a third session in which prices deviate much less from fundamental dividend value and volume is very light. Shares ultimately trade near their rational expectations value, but it takes three 15-period trading sessions in a stable environment to yield this equilibrium. These results do not inspire confidence in rational expectations theory in asset markets where the determinants of share value are not common information.

The verbal behavior of subjects following a bubble experiment is revealing. Some are puzzled by the failure of shares to trade at fundamental dividend value and with the "panic buying" they observe. Many report amazement at the speed with which a market crash can occur; they had expected to sell out ahead of the others when the crash came.

After the market turns, some are hesitant to sell because they cannot bring themselves to take the capital loss or because they hope for a recovery. Many report a reluctance to sell before the crash because they were "too greedy." Somehow, the volatile behavior of the market was due to the other traders. Although they have no causal explanation of their experience (prices rise "without cause") and their consensus forecasts never predict the crashes, their comments are consistent with the market observations, with a self-reinforcing expectations view of the boom, and with the tendency of the market crash to dividend value to take two or three periods to occur.

Why is verbal behavior helpful to the researcher in this environment and so obviously misleading in the supply and demand experiments discussed previously? The primary difference, I think, resides in the complete common information characteristics of the first environment and the private information state of the second. Subjects understand the structure of the stock market experiments, but they have divergent expectations and are uncertain about the behavior of others (until they come to have common expectations). Consequently, they are all drawn into myopic behavior. They are aware of this and reveal it in their verbal responses. In the supply and demand experiments, they are not aware of a structure to understand beyond their private circumstances and therefore are unable to relate to what happens in the market, which is unfathomable. If this interpretation is correct, it suggests that the solicitation of verbal responses is more likely to be of interest and to provide insights to the researcher in games of complete rather than private information. This is unfortunate because the world is more likely to conform to the private- than to the complete-information environment (Shubik, 1959, p. 171).

III.   On the "Little" Evidence That Monetary Rewards Matter

Monetary incentives are commonly absent in the research of psychologists. This has made their work vulnerable to the criticism that the results are not meaningful; rational choice, it is argued, is a theory that assumes high stakes. This is a specious argument in that it is not offered as a formal part of the theory and is invoked informally only upon finding that the theory does poorly in the face of the experimentalist's data. But it is a legitimate question, and so long as psychologists avoid systematic (not casual) comparisons of the effect of payoffs on decision, they avoid joining this issue. Instead, what we see is the claim that there is "little" evidence of improvement when monetary rewards are introduced (Tversky and Kahneman, 1987, p. 90; Thaler, 1987, p. 96). It is unclear how seriously one should take this claim when it is converted immediately into a straw man with statements of the form, "the evidence that high stakes do not always improve decisions" (Tversky and Kahneman, 1987, p. 90) or "the assertion that systematic mistakes will always disappear if the stakes are large enough" (Thaler, 1987, p. 96). I know almost no one who would use the adverb *always* in these contexts. In support of the claim – Grether and Plott (1979) is the popular citation, but strangely missing, because it is said that there *is* a little evidence – are any of the many citations that could have been offered showing that monetary rewards matter. Plott (1987, p. 120) is more eclectic, and credible, in citing evidence on both sides because his work includes a case in which money didn't matter (individual choice) and a case where it did (committee decisions).

A considerable number of experimental studies have assessed the effect on decisions of rewards versus no rewards, and/or varying the level of rewards. Seventeen such studies showing increased support for rational models with increased rewards, and new data on auction behavior when rewards are varied from 0 to 20 times the level customarily used, are reported in Smith and Walker (1993a, b). These studies include a wide variety of institutions and environments: Bernoulli choice decision (see following discussion), bilateral bargaining, Cournot oligopoly, Bertrand oligopoly, casino betting, and double-auction trading. In almost all cases, one effect of increased payoffs is to reduce the standard error of the observations around the predicted or estimated optimal decision. These results are consistent with decision cost models that postulate a trade-off between the benefits of better decisions and the subjective cost of making them.

IV.   Is It Rational To Be "Rational"?

"To predict how economic man will behave we need to know not only that he is rational, but also how he perceives the world – what alternatives he sees and what consequences he attaches to them." (Simon, 1956, p. 271)

Siegel (1959, 1961) appears to be the first psychologist to respond to Simon's suggestion that rational behavior needs to be examined from the perspective of the individual's perception and experience of the decision situation. Simon's thinking was ultimately transformed into concepts of "satisficing" and "bounded rationality," which were secondary interpretations of the more fundamental characteristic of humankind quoted earlier. Anyone familiar with the rational choice paradigm who thinks along implementational lines will realize that the subjective cost of exploring options and figuring out what to do must be part of the problem of rational choice as experienced by the decision maker. Decision cost is the cost of concentration, attention, information acquisition, thinking, monitoring, checking, deciding, and acting – all the things you do to realize a decision. When the benefits are small, the decision cost may not be worth it, or the decision cost incurred may be, rationally, correspondingly small so that the pain fits the pleasure, marginally speaking, although the typical subject will not consciously think about it in such terms. Alternatively, in familiar or repetitive situations the decision process may be so automatic, programmed, and instinctive that decision cost is nothing. The decision cost model does not imply that introducing rewards will always improve normative performance, but merely that there is a bounded trade-off between the cost of decision and its value (Smith, 1976a). For example, increasing the monetary stakes may have little effect in a signal detection experiment where the subject's hearing capacity is already strained to its physiological limit. It is therefore somewhat surprising that some signal detection experiments report improved performance with increased reward (Swets and Sewell, 1963, pp. 123–4; Calfee, 1970, pp. 898–9); improvement is often not statistically significant because improvement is small relative to variability for each individual. But the number of such individuals dominates the sample.

Siegel (1961) reexamined the Bernoulli trials experiment. In this task, the subject is importuned to "do your best" to predict, on each trial, which of two events will occur. One event was programmed to occur with probability p, so that its complement would occur with probability $1 - p$. The subjects made repeated choices over a great many trials (up to 1,000; see, e.g., Edwards, 1961). The standard result was "probability matching"; that is, the mean prediction was approximately p for the frequent event. The standard conclusion was that people were not "rational" because one "should" choose the frequent event 100% of the time if one wants to maximize the expected number of correct predictions. Siegel wondered, since there was no monetary or other explicit reinforcement for getting it "right," whether perhaps the results were not the exception that proved the maximizing rule. Utility theory does not predict that people will maximize something when it is not in their interest to do so. He also pondered what the beleaguered subjects saw in this long string of repeat choices and conjectured that they must be incredibly bored. So he hypothesized in the form of a model that individuals diversified their predictions to relieve boredom. In the absence of monetary rewards, the model was consistent with probability matching; with monetary rewards, the model predicted a shift toward choosing the frequent event more often, and the greater the incentive the greater the shift. Siegel ran experiments with different reward levels, with conditions that afforded subjects the opportunity to relieve boredom without the necessity of diversifying choice, with adult subjects, and with children. In all cases the model qualitatively predicted the observed shifts in the data (Siegel, 1959, 1961; Siegel et al., 1964).

Others (Swensson, 1965; Tversky and Edwards, 1966) also report Bernoulli choice experiments comparing monetary rewards with "do your best" instructions, showing that mean responses shifted upward on the frequent event when rewards were used. In the light of the preceding discussion, the Tversky-Edwards case is noteworthy for the reason that the authors discounted the significance of the increased support for maximization under the reward condition. They conclude that, although the results were in the direction predicted by the normative model, they were "far indeed" from the predictions of that model (p. 682). In closing, they conjecture that a formal model of the results might introduce a "cost associated with making a decision" (p. 683), as indeed it might, and did, 7 years earlier! It seems that today psychologists who "argue that the deviations of actual behavior from the normative model are too widespread to be ignored, too systematic to be dismissed as random error, and too fundamental to be accommodated by relaxing the normative system" (Tversky and Kahneman, 1987, p. 68) are able to do so by ignoring contrary interpretations and evidence over extended periods of time.

If the experimenter is open to the possibility, subjects teach us something about rationality that is not part of standard theory. A good example concerns the matter of incentive compatibility in the (two-sided) sealed-bid-offer auction where each buyer and seller has multiple differing values for units in the aggregate market demand and supply schedules. It is well known that such auctions are not incentive-compatible: If all agents submit fully revealing bids and offers except the buyer with the marginal valuation, then that buyer can increase personal profit on intramarginal units by underrevealing the marginal unit and setting a lower price. Because of this incentive incompatibility, theory has supposed that outcomes cannot be efficient. In privacy experiments, no one knows who has the marginal units, but in repeat play in stationary environments, subjects soon discover that one or more of their units are near the realized "crossing" prices and that any person determining price can manipulate it to the advantage of his or her side of the market. What subjects learn in repeat play is to submit almost all their bids to buy and offers to sell at prices very near or equal to the estimated auction price, where the latter tends to converge to the competitive equilibrium. This causes the reported supply and demand schedules to be elastic but to cross in the neighborhood of the true crossing, with many tied bids. This unconscious group strategy has the property that each side is protected from manipulation by the other side; any seller whose offer is equal to the auction price and who (thinking that she is determining the price) offers at a higher price next period simply gets replaced by a tied alternative seller with no change in the auction price. This is best described as superrational: a better strategy than has been deduced from rational theory and one that clearly violates the behavioral implications of the standard impossibility theorems.

V.   Sunk Costs and Opportunity Costs

According to the usual interpretation of economic theory, the optimizing firm or individual should ignore sunk costs in weighing gains and losses at the margin and should treat out-of-pocket costs as equivalent to opportunity costs. These are strong predictions, based on extremely simple models of maximization, and there is no shortage of verbal measures of behavior showing that these predictions are not confirmed (Thaler, 1980; Kahneman et al., 1987). At the conscious level, the disutility of loss may stimulate unusual effort to recover sunk costs, whereas opportunity costs may require a sophistication in decision analysis that is not quickly attained without formal training. But, as we have already seen, it is common for experimental markets to approximate optimal results in the absence of participant understanding of the private or social conditions that define their market situation. Plott (1987, pp. 122–5) presents experiments in which buyers and suppliers representing the basic demand and supply environment are separated, with intermediary traders purchasing units from the suppliers at one location and then reselling them separately to the buyers at another. These results showed no evidence of market failure due to the sunk cost fallacy. The same is true of a much larger number of intertemporal competitive equilibrium experiments going back many years (Miller et al., 1977; Forsythe et al., 1982; Williams and Smith, 1984). In these experiments, traders who have acquired inventory to carry over for resale at a different place or time tend to take their lumps when they have paid more than they can recover in the resale market. This doesn't mean that there are never any individual cases of irrationality; it means only that such behavior is not important enough to vitiate the static competitive model in these experiments.

Experimental markets for two interdependent commodities (Smith, 1986, p. 169; Williams et al., 1986) do not support the implication that the opportunity cost fallacy upsets the empirical validity of the competitive model in this more complicated setting. In these experiments, the demand curve for each commodity is conditional upon the price (opportunity cost) of the other commodity. Yet these markets converge to the competitive equilibrium. The convergence is somewhat slower than in single markets, and many subjects do not reach the exact maximizing commodity two-tuple. But those who buy too much of one or the other of the two commodities tend to be offset by those who buy too little. In this case, individual errors are not rare, but they tend to be offsetting so that the market predictions of the model are very good. Economists sometimes suggest that irrationalities lead to random error and can be ignored, but psychologists are right in asserting that this is an empirical question requiring evidence.

The opportunity cost fallacy in the psychology literature often arises in the context of fairness and framing: "For example, most respondents believe that it is unfair for a store to mark up the jars of peanut butter in its stock when wholesale prices rise, apparently because they associate the cost to the individual jar" (Kahneman et al., 1987, p. 113). It is traditional retail practice to relabel shelf stock when the wholesale price rises. Does this mean that retail store managers must "understand" the opportunity cost principle? No, it means merely that this institutional tradition encodes the social learning that results when, historically, managers have tried policies other than what the economist calls the opportunity cost principle. A simple real scenario illustrates this process. Suppose the policy is not to change the price of shelf stock either when wholesale prices rise or when they fall or both. This policy doesn't work for price declines. Either the manager must wait until all the existing shelf stock is sold, in which case she has empty space unutilized, or she must have merchandise marked with two different prices. Price-conscious customers will note this and take the cheaper stock so that the manager will have trouble selling the older stock. It becomes outdated, and customers complain that the stock is not fresh. A customer who did not notice the different prices discovers in the checkout line that somebody else paid less and complains to the manager that this is not "fair." The policy also does not work for rapid price increases. I observed this in California in 1974. The price of sugar rose very rapidly (enough so that cafeterias, rationally, stopped putting sugar packets on the tables; one had to ask for sugar at the checkout counter, where it could be monitored; and managers did not have to think, "monitoring cost is now lower than the cost of pilfered sugar!"). The supermarkets had succumbed to consumer activist group pressure, and whenever wholesale prices rose, they followed the policy of not marking up the price of shelf stock. This created the temporary situation in which the retail sugar price was below the wholesale price. Bakers, candy makers, and other wholesale buyers discovered this, and cleaned out the retail shelves. This situation is hardly fair, but it is a predictable consequence when prices are not permitted to equilibrate. The point is that pricing rules evolve in response to experience, not logical analysis, and policies that are disequilibrating (causing the manager trouble) are altered; this process of alteration continues until we have a tradition. The current manager does not know about opportunity cost or even why the policy is what it is; only that she learned it from the last manager. She is an instrument of the "law" of one price in a market, which is not a law at all, but a tendency that gets encoded in markup relabeling policies. Because psychologists are not, by training, fully informed on these matters, they ask oversimplified questions. The appropriate question is whether it is "fair" to depart from the traditional policy of remarking shelf stock in response to price changes when such departures cause the kinds of problems enumerated here. One does not ask the appropriate question because no one understands all the ramifications. One cannot learn much of anything about economic process by limiting oneself to these kinds of verbal observations. One can, of course, understand something about people's perceptions, but a model of the system can't be built around such observations. What they do help us to see is how simple-minded and unworkable interventionist policies get on the political agenda.

VI.   Criticism of Experimental Economics

Psychologists since Siegel have not attempted to apply their perspective and questions to market experiments of the kind studied by experimental economists, although there are numerous examples of research by experimental economists who have examined questions studied by psychologists. Mutual understanding is therefore limited, as can be inferred from the two criticisms of experimental economics contained in Hogarth and Reder's introduction to their book. The first notes that schemes designed to provide incentive compatibility add complexity, and "it is not clear that subjects understand the full implications of such reward structures" (1987, p. 12). They fail here to understand why experimental economists use incentive-compatible rules. We want to see whether such rules make a difference in the observations when compared with procedures that do not use them (as in comparing uniform price and discriminative price institutions). There is no presumption in these comparisons that people "understand the full implications" of such rules. We do not expect such understanding to occur, certainly not in the sense that theorists can be said to understand incentive compatibility. But "understanding" need not have and often does not have anything to do with effectiveness, as we have observed in thousands of experiments. The question comes back to the conditions under which people achieve socioeconomic outcomes that are not part of their conscious intention; our data tell us that they do. Psychologists do not study this question because psychologists are avowedly, rightly, and appropriately concerned to study cognitive processes. Their experiments are designed for and limited to this worthy objective; our experiments have rather different objectives, and we would not claim that our subjects understand all or any of their situation.

The second criticism of experimental economics is that the introduction of constraints determined by the limit-price supply and demand constraints "places such severe restrictions on subjects' actions that psychologists may wonder whether the underlying economic theory is in fact being tested" (Hogarth and Reder, 1987, p. 12). This criticism reveals ignorance of the large literature in which limit-price constraints are not used – auctions, multiple markets, asset markets, and supply and demand markets with uncertain redemption values (Plott and Agha, 1983).

Experimental economics can benefit greatly from the criticisms of psychologists, but in order for this to occur, their knowledge and understanding of the literature and its motivation will have to move beyond the superficial levels of familiarity exhibited in *Rational Choice*.

VII.   Concluding Discussion

Why is it that human subjects in the laboratory frequently violate the canons of rational choice when tested as isolated individuals but, in the social context of exchange institutions, serve up decisions that are consistent (as if by magic) with predictive models based on individual rationality? Experimental economists have no good answers to this question, although adaptive learning models such as those of Lucas (1987) are suggestive. We need the help of psychologists, undeflected by battles with straw men. It seems evident that an important part of the answer resides in the properties of exchange institutions and how privately informed, but globally poorly informed, decision making is mediated by institutions. Although institutional rules, since Vickrey (1961), have attracted increasing interest among theorists, that development has been slow. In any case, we tend to analyze institutions as given in history not to address the question of why institutions have the structure and rules we observe. I want to suggest that perhaps the structures we observe have survived because of their merit in coaxing Pareto-efficient behavior out of agents who do not know what that means.

Language learning in children occurs in a social context (Brown, 1973). Without contact with people, children do not learn to speak. If they have such contact, they learn to speak in the total absence of formal instruction. But the same can be said of decision making: I could substitute "make market decisions" for "speak" in the last two sentences and they would apply to what we have learned in the laboratory about adults. On the basis of cognition alone, without the language of the market and ongoing social interaction with other agents, rational decision is frustratingly illusive.

CHAPTER 2

Experimental Tests of the Endowment Effect[1]

*Robert Franciosi, Praveen Kujal, Roland Michelitsch,
Vernon L. Smith, and Gang Deng*

Individual decision-making studies have shown that human subjects reveal an asymmetric response pattern toward losses (loss aversion) as contrasted with gains measured relative to any individual's initial status quo position (Kahneman and Tversky, 1979). Consequently, if one's initial wealth endowment is X_0, then the hypothesis is that the utility function, $u(\cdot)$, has the property that $u(X_0 - DX) > u(X_0 + DX)$ for all deviations DX from any initial X_0. Although Kahneman and Tversky (1979) were concerned with prospect theory as a modification of utility theory for risky decisions, in a fundamental extension Thaler argued that "any of the elements of prospect theory can be used in developing descriptive choice models in deterministic settings" (Thaler, 1980, p. 41). Thaler observed that the utility property, $u(X_0 - DX) > u(X_0 + DX)$ implies that out-of-pocket costs are more heavily weighted in utility assessments than opportunity costs (i.e., a forgone gain has lower utility value than the actual loss of the same amount). This cognitive under-weighting of opportunity costs by the individual was referred to as the *endowment effect* and was used to explain a number of questionnaire survey examples.

Subsequently, Kahneman et al. (1991; hereafter KKT) suggested that the discrepancy between willingness-to-pay (WTP) and willingness-to-accept (WTA), widely observed in hypothetical surveys and in motivated exchange experiments, were all manifestations of the endowment effect. (See KKT, Table 1 for a summary.) However, they argue (KKT, p. 1327) that the endowment effect does not apply when goods are purchased for resale rather than use. Thus there is no endowment effect for the retail firm, only for the consumer purchasing the firm's goods. Similarly, they note that it does not apply to the exchange of tokens (or rights) to which private redemption values, or induced values, have been assigned by the experimenter (Smith, 1976a). Empirically, they show

---

[1] We thank Jack Knetsch for providing us with copies of the collected data from the KKT Experiments 6 and 7.

this to be approximately the case in experiments establishing an endowment effect for Cornell and other coffee mugs but not for induced value tokens.

The results of nine experiments are reported by KKT. Some of these were exchange experiments, others were choice experiments using the Becker et al. (1964; hereafter BDM) procedure. In Section I, we discuss their choice experiments, introduce our modifications in their procedures, and present the new results. We replicate their procedures in pure choice experiments by removing all references to "buying" and "selling." The purpose is to remove all differential strategic motivation that might be suggested by these terms. In Section II, we discuss their exchange experiments and present the results of 10 new exchange experiments using the uniform-price double-auction mechanism which, because of its real-time information feedback features, achieves high efficiency in a single-period exchange.

I.   Choice Tests of the Endowment Effect

A.   The KKT Experiments

In their typical choice experiment, half of a group of subjects are randomly designated sellers and the others buyers. University coffee mugs costing about $6 in the local university bookstore, are then distributed to the sellers, and all buyers are given the opportunity to examine a mug. The forms shown below are then executed by all sellers (buyers) (see KKT, p. 178, for their instructions).

For example, on this form a seller might indicate a preference for keeping the mug for all prices at or below $5.00, selling it at all prices above $5.00. The subject's WTA would then be assessed at $5.25.

After the forms were executed, an equally likely price was drawn from

	I will sell (buy)	I will keep (not buy) the mug
If the price is $0	————	————
If the price is $0.50	————	————
...		
If the price is $9.50	————	————

Table 2.1. *Mean WTA and WTP for university emblem mugs*

Experiment	WTA sellers	WTP buyers	WTA choosers	WTA-S/ WTP-B	WTA-S/ WTA-C	Sample size, N
KKT 6[a] and 7[b]	$6.89	$1.91	$3.05	3.61	1.60	194
	WTA Group 1	WTP Group 2	WTA Group 3	WTA-1/ WTP-2	WTA-1/ WTA-3	
UofA[c]	$5.36	$2.19	$3.88	2.45	1.38	120

[a] Mugs and subjects from Simon Fraser University.
[b] Mugs and subjects from University of British Columbia. Price tags were left on the mugs.
[c] Mugs and subjects from University of Arizona. All subjects make choices. In Group 1, each is endowed with a mug; in Group 2, each is endowed only with the money earned in a preexperiment; in Group 3, each is endowed with the right to choose either a mug or additional money.

the list between $0 and $9.50, and exchanges based on this price were conducted by the experimenter.[2] The results of their experiment 5 were typical of those reported by KKT: The median selling price, $5.75, is more than double the median buying price, which is consistent with an endowment effect. But, as recognized by KKT, this interpretation is clouded by the fact that the experiment did not control for the income effect in standard preference theory.

To address this objection KKT (pp. 179–80) use three groups instead of two: sellers, buyers, and choosers. The sellers/buyers make the same sales/purchase decisions as before, whereas the choosers are asked to choose at each prospective price between the mug or cash. Thus sellers are given a mug, and choosers are given the right to either a mug or cash as they choose; any income effect on sellers as distinct from buyers, should also apply to choosers.

KKT report median prices for the three groups for each of two experiments (KKT, experiments 6 and 7, pp. 179–80). Mean prices for their data are shown in the first row of Table 2.1: Choosers behave much more like buyers than sellers, although choosers value mugs 60% more highly than buyers.

---

[2] In some experiments, the ordered individual WTPs and WTAs are crossed, and the exchange is directly between buyers and sellers at a common clearing price. But in these cases, it is no longer true "that your decision can have no effect on the price . . ." as stated in the KKT instructions (p. 178).

B.   *Choice Experiments Controlling for Differential*
       Instruction Effects

Because these last two experiments were critical to the hypothesized endowment effect, we conducted four experiments each with 24 subjects (8 in each group), having been motivated by the three-group design. However, we made several instructional changes, which, we conjectured, might be of substance.

Psychologically, buying, selling and choosing are distinct emotive terms. The first two are laden with strategic connotations – buyers are motivated to buy low and sellers to sell high – whereas choosing appears to be not so laden. To control for effects due only to differences in the KKT wording of the tasks for each of the three groups of subjects, we neutralized our instructions so that each group was presented with a choice task – not buying, selling, and choice tasks. Our instructions, common for all subjects, and the choice sheet for each of the three groups, now referred to with antiseptic evenness as Group 1, Group 2, and Group 3, are shown in an appendix supplied on request. Each member of Group 1 is an owner of an Arizona Wildcat mug and has the task of choosing, for each amount of money (not a price), between retaining the mug or accepting the additional amount of money. Each member of Group 2 is designated as having the right to choose between accepting a mug or retaining an amount of money out of their earnings in a previous experiment in the same session. Finally, each person in Group 3 is designated as having the right to choose between accepting a mug or accepting an additional amount of money. Thus, all subjects are symmetrically described as choosers, but under different initial conditions.

All our experiments were run at the end of two simultaneous posted-offer market experiments (6 buyers, 6 sellers in each), reported in Franciosi et al. (1994). The positions of Groups 1, 2, and 3 were assigned at random among the 24 subjects. All subjects were paid their earnings in cash at the end of the market experiments. Earnings ranged from $8.75 to $44.50, providing all Group 2 subjects with adequate funds to give up for a mug if they chose.

The mean monetary amounts (prices) for each of Groups 1, 2, and 3 are shown in the second data row of Table 2.1. The mugs were priced at $9.95 (price tags removed) in the campus bookstore.

From Table 2.1, our subjects reported a substantially lower Group 1 WTA, a somewhat higher WTP, and a higher Group 3 WTA than did the KKT subjects. Substituting a choice task for the buying and selling tasks appears to narrow substantially the WTA/WTP discrepancy. But from Table 2.2 row 1, the *t* test shows that all pairwise comparisons of our

Table 2.2. *Group distribution differences and comparisons with KKT results for buyers, sellers, and choosers using* t *tests*

Hypotheses	G1 = G2	G2 = G3	G3 = G1
Group 1–3	$t = 7.33$	$t = -4.01$	$t = -2.98$
	$\alpha = 0.000$	$\alpha = 0.000$	$\alpha = 0.004$
	G1 = S	G2 = B	G3 = C
KKT S, B, and C Groups	$t = -3.73$	$t = 1.10$	$t = 2.12$
	$\alpha = 0.00$	$\alpha = 0.27$	$\alpha = 0.04$

three groups come from different distributions. Row 2 compares the KKT results with ours and shows that the reduction in selling prices and the increase in buying prices are significant using the t test. Because these comparisons did not control for differences due to subjects and experimenters, we cannot attribute them only to the treatment differences.

We also asked if being in the role of buyer or seller in the prior market experiments affected the value revealed for a mug. The effect was insignificant using the Epps-Singleton test ($\alpha = 0.37$). Finally, we asked if the amount paid to subjects in the prior market experiments affected their revealed values in the mug experiment. A regression of the latter on the former yielded no significant relationship ($R^2 = 0.007$). This suggests that any "house money" income effect on mug valuation is nil (Thaler and Johnson, 1990).

II.   Exchange Tests of the Endowment Effect

A.   The KKT Exchange Experiments

In addition to their choice experiments, KKT report the results of several exchange experiments. The typical experiment proceeds as follows. Of $2N$ subjects, N are randomly designated buyers, and N, sellers. The latter are each endowed with a mug; the former use their own money. Buyers each submit a bid price to buy a mug, sellers each submit an offer price to sell their mug. Their "bids" or "offers" are solicited by asking each subject to choose between a price and a mug for a series of prices as in the choice procedure. The bids (WTPs) of the subjects are then ordered from highest to lowest, whereas the offers (WTAs) are similarly ordered from lowest to highest. The intersection of these reported supply-and-demand schedules determines the price and quantity exchanged. If there are no endowment or income effects, then due to the random allocation of subjects to the buy or sell category the supply schedule of those given the mugs should be the symmetric mirror image of the demand schedule for those not given the cups [i.e., Demand " $D(P^*) = S(P^*)$ " $N - D(P^*)$ and $D(P^*) = N/2$]. Consequently, the prediction is that $N/2$ mugs will trade. For example (KKT, pp. 170–3), with 44 subjects, and $N = 22$ buyers and 22 sellers, 11 mugs are predicted to trade. In fact, between one and four trade at prices between \$4.25 and \$4.75. Although there are several bid/offer trials, only one is chosen at random to be binding. Table 2.3 summarizes their results for induced value tokens, mugs, and pens for all trials in four experiments.

According to the endowment hypothesis, the predicted number of trades will be realized for induced value tokens because one is simply trading dollars for identical dollar claims. In fact, on average, there is undertrading (in Experiments 2, 3, and 4 but not 1). This is consistent with other studies showing a tendency to underreveal (token) demand and/or supply by subjects in uniform price, sealed bid institutions (Smith et al., 1982). But with consumer goods (mugs, pens) there is substantial undertrading – much less than half the predicted volume is observed to trade.[3] If there are income effects, then the demand by subjects not endowed with mugs is less than the demand by the endowed subjects, $d(P) < D(P)$. Hence $d(P^*) = N - D(P^*) < N - d(P^*)$ and $d(P^*) < N/2$. But our finding reported earlier, showing no income effect, suggests that this cannot account for the results in Table 2.3.[4]

We should add that the KKT procedure does produce an incentive to underreveal demand (supply). When subjects are asked to choose between an object and a price, they know that their crossover price is, in effect, a bid price for a buyer and an ask price for a seller. Then "the market price was the point at which the elicited supply and demand curves intersected" (KKT, footnote 2, p. 171). This procedure means that if the highest accepted ask is less than the lowest accepted bid, $A_H < B_L$, then there are many prices that clear the market. The typical (fair?) procedure is to set the clearing price at $P_C = (A_H + B_L)/2$. The mug price in trial 6 of experiment 1 is an example in which P_C is half way between

---

[3] Sometimes it has been suggested that subjects trade in induced value experiments because they think the experimenter expects it and brought them to the lab for this purpose. The KKT results are quite contrary to this interpretation.

[4] One could also use our WTP and WTA data from the choice experiments to determine a hypothetical exchange quantity based upon the BDM elicitation procedures. We performed this exercise by crossing the Group 1 WTA with the Group 2 WTP and found that of 20 predicted trades only 8 would occur. This undertrading is consistent with the findings of KKT. If we use the Group 3 data as a better estimate of "true WTA" and cross these with the Group 2 WTP, we still get only 12 of 20 predicted trade.

Table 2.3. *Predicted and observed trades for different objects*

Experiment	Total	Number subjects	Object	Price	Observed trades	Predicted trades
1	1	44	Tokens	$3.75	12	11
1	2	44	Tokens	$4.75	11	11
1	3	44	Tokens	$4.25	10	11
1	4	44	Mugs	$4.25	4	11
1	5	44	Mugs	$4.75	1	11
1	6	44	Mugs	$4.50	2	11
1	7	44	Mugs	$4.25	2	11
1	8	44	Pens	$1.25	4	11
1	9	44	Pens	$1.25	5	11
1	10	44	Pens	$1.25	4	11
1	11	44	Pens	$1.25	5	11
2	1	38	Tokens	$3.75	10	10
2	2	38	Tokens	$4.75	9	10
2	3	38	Tokens	$4.25	7	8
2	4	38	Mugs	$1.75	3	9.5
2	5	38	Mugs	$2.25	3	9.5
2	6	38	Mugs	$2.25	2	9.5
2	7	38	Mugs	$2.25	2	9.5
2	8	38	Binoculars	$1.25	4	9.5
2	9	38	Binoculars	$0.75	4	9.5
2	10	38	Binoculars	$0.75	3	9.5
2	11	38	Binoculars	$0.75	3	9.5
3	1	26	Tokens[a]	—	5	6.5
3	2	26	Pens[a]	—	2	6.5
3	3	26	Pens[a]	—	2	6.5
3	4	26	Pens[a]	—	2	6.5
3	5	26	Pens[a]	—	1	6.5
4	1	74	Tokens[a]	—	15	18.5
4	2	74	Tokens[a]	—	16	18.5
4	3	74	Mugs[a]	—	6	18.5
4	4	74	Mugs[a]	—	4	18.5
4	5	72	Mugs[a]	—	4	18
4	6	73	Mugs[a]	—	8	18
4	7	74	Mugs[a]	—	8	18.5

[a] Prices are not reported in experiments 3 and 4 in these experiments; "the subjects were asked for minimum selling or maximum buying prices rather than answer the series of yes or no questions used in Experiments 1 and 2" (KKT, p. 175).

Table 2.4. *Bid, offers and trades uniform-price double-auction experiment 7302, period 12*

ID No.	Bid	Rank	Offer	ID No.
2	400	1	220	19
6	325	2	290	24
9	310	3	300	22
4	310	4	300	21
11	301	5	300	17
12	300	6	300	27
10	311	7	329	25
7	300	8	330	26
1	300	9	347	18
8	280	10	362	23
5	270	11	380	20
3	200	12	—	—

the discrete values $4.25 and $4.75 on the subject's choice form. If subjects believe that $A_H < B_L$ is a possible outcome, it pays any seller (who may turn out to be the marginal seller) to ask more than her WTA (or marginal buyer to bid below his WTP). Because the distribution of the consumer good object values is highly uncertain and unknown to both the subjects and the experimenters, the incentive to underreveal may be more pronounced than with tokens.

B.   The Uniform-Price Double-Auction Mechanism

There exists a trading institution that results in a single block trade called the Uniform-Price Double Auction but that has the real-time feedback characteristics of the continuous double auction. It has been extensively studied in the laboratory (McCabe et al., 1993; Friedman, 1991). Bids and offers are displayed in real time and continuously crossed to yield a provisional clearing price and quantity while the market is open. When the trading period ends, all trades become binding at the price and quantity standing at the close. This institution is particularly well suited for examining the exchange predictions of the endowment effect because it has been shown to have excellent revelation properties for marginal units, resulting in fully efficient exchange. Table 2.4 and Figure 2.1 illustrate the state of all bid and offer realizations at the market close for a typical trading period in an experiment (period 12, experiment 7302).

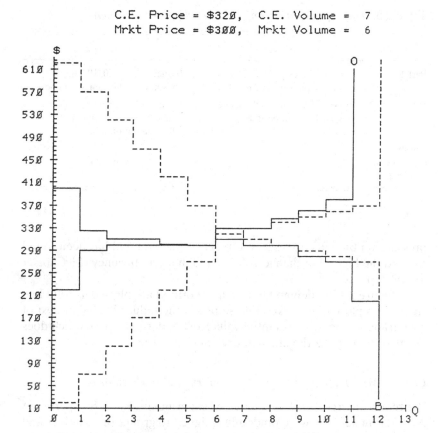

C.E. Price = $32Ø, C.E. Volume = 7
Mrkt Price = $3ØØ, Mrkt Volume = 6

FIGURE 2.1. Graph of induced supply and demand and of bid/offer realizations. UPDA experiment 7302, period 12.

The first column lists the identification number of each buyer, followed by that buyer's bid (column 2). The rank order (high to low of bids, low to high of offers) is shown in column 3. Column 4 displays each seller's offer followed by the seller's identification number in column 5. The horizontal line below the sixth ranked bid and offer separates the accepted bids and offers above from the rejected bids and offers below the line. The accepted bids and offers form contracts at a uniform price (300 cents in Table 2.4). Several alternative information feedback and price algorithm procedures for this mechanism have been studied. We use the procedure in which subjects see displayed in real time only the best rejected bid and offer (311 cents and 329 cents in Table 2.4). This places maximum

Table 2.5. *Description of treatments in exchange experiments*

	Series 1	Series 2
Part 1	Induced values [0, $9.99]; random equilibrium; 4-min periods	Induced values [0, $9.99]; constant equilibrium; 4-min periods
Part 2	Buyers: $9.99 each; sellers: one mug each; 4-min periods	Buyers: $9.99 each; sellers: one mug each; 4- and 6-min periods; $9.95 tag left on mug
Number of experiments (subjects)	4 (96)	6 (144)

pressure on the outside traders to reach agreement and has been found to yield the highest exchange volume and market efficiency (McCabe et al., 1993, p. 320).

In Figure 2.1 the demand bids (supply offers) are plotted as solid line steps. Also plotted as broken line steps are the induced value or cost of each trader. Note the substantial value/cost underrevelation, which does not thereby impede the efficient exchange of six units.

C.   *Mug Exchange Using the Uniform-Price Mechanism*

We report the results of two series of experiments. In each experiment 24 different subjects were randomly assigned to groups of 12 buyers and 12 sellers. Each series was divided into Parts 1 and 2 (see Table 2.5). In Part 1 of Series 1, each buyer was assigned a value and each seller a cost by a random draw with replacement from the uniform distribution on [$0, $9.99] at the beginning of each of 10 (or 12) trading periods. This baseline served as a training session. All periods lasted 4 minutes. In Part 2, Series 1 and 2, each buyer was endowed with a $9.99 cash balance, which was theirs to keep if no mug was purchased; each seller was endowed with a University of Arizona emblem mug priced at $9.95 in the university bookstore and theirs to keep if not sold. Each subject was paid in cash all of his or her earnings from the induced value training experiments in Part 1 of each of the sessions. In Series 2, Part 1 used the constant volume equilibrium environment shown in Figure 2.1, but in each period a random constant was added to each value, and the values were randomly assigned to individuals. Part 2 of Series 2 was like that of Series 1 except that the price tag ($9.95) was left on each mug, and this was pointed out to the subjects. This was a treatment to reduce uncertainty concerning the cash or market value of the mug in each group. Also in Series 2 we increased the trading time for the mug exchange from 4 to 6 minutes in four of the six experiments. This is because it appeared that the subjects were still adjusting their bids and offers when the period ended after 4 minutes. Table 2.5 summarizes the experimental design.

D.   Results of Exchange Experiments

Table 2.6 lists the predicted competitive equilibrium volume and the corresponding observed trading volume in periods 1–10 for the random equilibrium-induced value environment. The induced value results are those recorded for periods 1–10 in four experiments. The mug exchange volume is recorded in period 11 for each experiment, with the corresponding clearing price shown in parenthesies.

Table 2.7 lists the volume data for the experiments using a constant equilibrium volume environment for periods 1–12 in the training baseline. Period 13 records the volume in the subsequent mug exchange experiments, with the clearing price shown in parentheses.

In both Tables 2.6 and 2.7, as we move from induced value exchange to mug exchange, volume relative to the prediction is decreased. However, when we compare the mug exchange volume in Tables 2.6 and 2.7 with the various objects exchanged in Table 2.3, it is clear that our exchange mechanism results in much less undertrading than was observed by KKT. In 3 of our 11 experiments, half or more of the mugs traded as predicted by standard theory.

Because earnings in the induced value experiments vary from zero to $34, we can ask if there are any income effects on the submitted bids or offers of subjects in the mug experiments. Separate regressions of such bids (offers) on earnings for buyers and for sellers yield no significant effect of earnings on subject WTP or WTA for a mug (the regression coefficients yield t values of -0.28 for sellers and -0.20 for buyers). Again, there is no income, or house money effect.

Each mug exchange experiment provides a sample of bid and offer prices standing at the close of each experiment. Because the exchange mechanism provides full opportunity for each subject to adjust his or her bid or offer price to the level needed to produce a trade, if a trade is truly desired, the resulting distributions of bids and offers provide market incentive-based measures of WTA and WTP that are distinct from the BDM measures elicited in Groups 1 and 2 in Section 1. It is therefore of interest to compare the distribution of the Group 1 WTA prices with the distribution of closing exchange offers and the Group 2 WTP prices with

Table 2.6. *Volume traded in exchange experiments series 1, random equilibrium*[a]

UPDA experiment[b]	5282 Volume		6012 Volume		7162 Volume		7232 Volume	
Trading period	Predicted	Observed	Predicted	Observed	Predicted	Observed	Predicted	Observed
1	8	8	7	6	6	5	5	5
2	7	8	6	5	5	5	6	7
3	6	6	4	4	6	6	6	5
4	8	7	5	5	7	6	7	6
5	4	5	7	6	7	6	7	7
6	6	6	7	6	6	6	5	4
7	7	6	6	5	6	5	5	4
8	6	5	8	7	6	5	6	5
9	5	5	7	7	5	5	5	5
10	7	6	5	4	6	5	6	6
11[c]	6	6 (189¢)	6	3 (300¢)	6	3 (100¢)	6	4 (101¢)

[a] In each period, 1–10 values were drawn with replacement from the uniform distribution on [0, $9.99].
[b] Experiment numbers refer to date experiment was conducted (e.g., 5282; May 28, 1992).
[c] Volume for number of mugs traded in period 11. Price in cents is shown in parenthesis.

Table 2.7. *Volume traded in exchange experiments series 2, constant equilibrium[a] 4- and 6-minute mug trading periods*

UPDA experiment[a]	7302[b]		1062[b]		10152[b]		01263[c]		01283[c]		02193[c]		02243[c]	
	Volume		Volume		Volume		Volume		Volume		Volume		Volume	
Trading period	Predicted	Observed	Predicted	Observed	Predicted	Observed	Predicted	Observed	Predicted	Observed	Predicted	Observed	Predicted	Observed
1	6-7	6	6-7	8	6-7	8	6-7	6	6-7	7	6-7	7	6-7	6
2	6-7	6	6-7	7	6-7	7	6-7	6	6-7	6	6-7	6	6-7	6
3	6-7	6	6-7	8	6-7	6	6-7	7	6-7	7	6-7	6	6-7	6
4	6-7	7	6-7	7	6-7	6	6-7	6	6-7	7	6-7	5	6-7	6
5	6-7	6	6-7	7	6-7	7	6-7	6	6-7	7	6-7	7	6-7	6
6	6-7	6	6-7	6	6-7	6	6-7	6	6-7	6	6-7	6	6-7	6
7	6-7	6	6-7	6	6-7	5	6-7	7	6-7	7	6-7	6	6-7	6
8	6-7	6	6-7	6	6-7	7	6-7	6	6-7	7	6-7	6	6-7	6
9	6-7	6	6-7	6	6-7	7	6-7	7	6-7	6	6-7	6	6-7	7
10	6-7	6	6-7	6	6-7	7	6-7	7	6-7	6	6-7	6	6-7	7
11	6-7	7	6-7	7	6-7	6	6-7	6	6-7	6	6-7	6	6-7	6
12	6-7	6	6-7	6	6-7	6	6-7	6	6-7	6	6-7	6	6-7	6
13[d]	6	2 (223¢)	6	7 (143¢)	6	3 (250¢)	6	6 (350¢)	6	5 (85¢)	6	3 (452¢)	6	3 (215¢)

[a] One set of values is drawn with replacement from the uniform distribution on [0, $9.99]. A random constant was added to all values in each period 1–12, and the individual assignments randomized.

[b] Each period was 4 minutes duration.

[c] Periods 1–12 were 4 minutes duration; period 13 was 6 minutes duration to allow more time for mug trading.

[d] Volume for number of mugs traded in period 13. Price in cents is shown in parentheses. The price tag, showing $9.95, was left on each mug, and this was pointed out to the subjects.

Table 2.8. *Comparison of UPDA bids, offers, and exchange prices with choice valuations*

		Bids	Offers	Prices
Group 1 WTAs	t statistic prob. level	—	-8.68 (0.00)	-4.14 (0.00)
Group 2 WTPs	t statistic prob. level	-9.043 (0.00)	—	0.14 (0.89)

closing exchange bids. We report these t test comparisons in Table 2.8. In these comparisons, we use only the bid–offer data for the exchange experiments in which the mug prices were unknown because this was the treatment condition in the choice data for Groups 1 and 2. Both the offer and the bid distributions are significantly below the corresponding Group 1 WTA and Group 2 WTP distributions. The choice procedure does not yield valuations that are good predictors of the actual bids and offers submitted in the iterative market setting.

Also in Table 2.8 we report comparisons of the Group 1 and 2 valuations with the sample of all mug prices from the exchange experiments. These comparisons show that prices are significantly below the Group 1 WTAs but not the Group 2 WTPs. Thus the WTPs based on choice data are a better indicator of the level of exchange prices than are the WTAs. Coursey et al. (1987) report similar findings in their study of the disparity between WTA and WTP.

In a new study using repeated second price auctions to measure WTP and WTA for goods with close substitutes (candy bars and mugs), Shogren et al. (1994) found no significant difference between the *average* of WTA and WTP (or price) for these goods. These carefully conducted new experiments cast doubt upon the WTA/WTP discrepancy for goods with close substitutes, and they rejected the KKT hypothesis of an endowment effect. Thus, for mugs Shogren et al. (1994, p. 265) reported WTA/WTP ratios of only 1.08 and 1.05 in two treatments on the final three trials 8–10.

We have no disagreement with their results or conclusions. Their results are not inconsistent with our market results because we directly examine trading volume *not* the WTA/WTP discrepancy. It is very important to realize that mean differences between WTA and WTP in two situations can be indistinguishable statistically, yet trading volume can differ substantially. To see this look at Fig. 2.1. On average, a slight decrease (increase) in the last four accepted bids (offers) would have no discernible effect on the difference between WTA and WTP; however, volume would decrease from 6 to 2 units. Similarly, variation in the WTA/WTP ratio of 1.08 to 1.05 could, in our setting (and that of KKT), yield considerable differences in trading volume. The ratio of mean WTA to mean WTP in Table 2.4 is only 1.05, but the market trades fully (except for the equal marginal units that add nothing to efficiency).

III.   Conclusions and Discussion

This chapter has reexamined the KKT experimental procedures for identifying an endowment effect for consumer goods; it is based on a series of individual choice experiments and an independent series of market exchange experiments.

In our choice experiments, we removed all reference to *buying, selling,* and *prices* and reformulated the task uniformly across KKT's three treatment groups as a choice problem. Because each experiment in the choice series was an addendum to a prior unrelated market experiment in which the subjects earned substantial, but highly variable amounts of money, we were able to obtain a measure of any effect on choices due to differential incomes earned or to the buyer/seller role in the previous experiment. We found no income (house money) or role effects.

Comparing the KKT results with those of our pure choice experiments, we find that the KKT use of different instructional descriptions – buyers, sellers, choosers – seems to exaggerate sellers' WTA, but their hypothesis of an endowment (possession) effect is supported by our choice data. Consequently, although we observe smaller WTA/WTP discrepancies, their qualitative choice results are robust under the replication procedures we used.

The results of our mug exchange experiments parallel those of the choice experiments, although the methodology is quite different. The training experiments using induced valuation, generated a wide disparity in the earnings of both buyers and sellers. Because the buyers (sellers) subsequently submit bids (offers) for a mug, we could ask whether the reported WTP (WTA) was affected by prior income earnings: for neither buyers nor sellers was there a significant income or house money effect. The theory predicts that, in the absence of an income effect, half of the 12 sellers' mugs should trade. We observed this in 2 of 11 experiments. In 7 experiments 2–4 mugs traded, in one 5 mugs traded, and in one 7 traded. This discrepancy is larger (relative to prediction) than observed in the token (induced value) exchange experiments but not nearly as large as reported by KKT. Our exchange procedures narrow the discrepancy reported by KKT but do not eliminate it. We concur with KKT that there does, indeed, appear to be *undertrading* due to an endowment effect. But, as noted later, our interpretation is different.

A comparison of the bid (offer) distribution in the mug exchange experiments with the WTP (WTA) distribution in the choice experiments shows that both the bid and the offer distributions in exchange are below those in the choice experiments: Buyers bid less and sellers offer less in actual exchange than is revealed by the choice procedure. A similar comparison with the exchange mug prices reveals that the WTP distribution in the choice experiment is a better indicator of market value than the WTA distribution.

We accept the Shogren et al. (1994) finding of no *statistically* significant difference between WTA and WTP (for mugs, candy bars) using second price auction measures. They show that the difference does indeed become trivial *relative* to sampling variability over time. But we observe undertrading relative to predictions, which is entirely consistent with persistent small statistical differences between WTA and WTP. Consequently, we are unable to reject the KKT undertrading hypothesis. Statistical insignificance in the WTA–WTP space is associated with economically significant reductions in trade. This can be explained by the fact that in our experiments and in KKT, the reported supply and demand schedules are very flat. Thus, very small discrepancies between WTA and WTP have large effects on undertrading.

As we interpret the evidence, the key hypothesis in KKT that withstands market scrutiny is not the disparity between WTA and WTP but undertrading. The latter, however, appears to be primarily an artifact of the gently sloped reported supply and demand.

Is the endowment effect an important characteristic of behavior that should concern us? As an observation contrary to standard preference theory, it cannot be lightly dismissed. As a matter of practical importance in markets, it is perhaps of little concern. Trade is almost entirely between specialist firms selling to other firms or consumers, not consumers selling to consumers. Garage sales are an exception to the latter where it appears that the propensity to truck barter and exchange is alive and well, even if there is undertrading. Finally, if Shogren et al. (1994) are right – the WTA/WTP discrepancy becomes trivial over time – then significant undertrading may be an artifact of flat supply and demand schedules.

CHAPTER 3

Monetary Rewards and Decision Cost in Experimental Economics

Vernon L. Smith and James M. Walker

This chapter provides a theoretical framework and some evidence about how the size of payoffs affects outcomes in laboratory experiments. We examine theoretical issues related to the question of how payoffs can matter and what the trade-offs with nonmonetary arguments might be in individual utility functions. Essentially, we accomplish this with an effort theory of subject behavior.

Experimentalists frequently argue that experimental subjects may have other motivations besides monetary gain that impinge upon the subject's decision making and that experimental results should be interpreted with this caveat in mind.[1] The literature on adaptive and behavioral economic modeling often cites decision-making cost as part of the implicit justification for such models.[2] Conlisk (1988) provides some examples of how optimizing cost (we will use the term *decision cost*) can be explicitly integrated into modeling problems and suggests a generalization for the class of quadratic loss functions. Our approach is to formulate the decision cost problem as one of balancing the benefit against the effort cost of reducing "error," the latter defined as the difference between optimal decision in the absence of decision cost and the agent's actual decision. This normalization has the advantage that the implications of the model can be directly tested from data on the error properties of a wide range of reported experiments. Our approach also attempts to encompass and formalize the argument that decision makers may fail to optimize because of the problem of flat maxima, as in von Winterfeldt and Edwards (1986), or because of low opportunity cost for deviations from the optimal as in Harrison (1989). Because standard theory predicts that decision makers will make optimal decisions, despite how gently rounded the payoff function is, the theory is misspecified and needs modification. When the theory is properly specified, there should be nothing left to say about opportunity cost or flat maxima (i.e., when the benefit margin is weighed against decision cost, there should be

---

[1] As in Siegel (1959), Smith (1976a, 1980, 1982), and Wilcox (1989, 1992).
[2] Some who do so are Day and Groves (1975), Nelson and Winter (1982), and Heiner (1986).

nothing left to forgo). This is consistent with the arguments of Harrison and von Winterfeldt and Edwards.

The theoretical approach we examine is based on a perspective originally suggested by Simon (1956), and operationalized by Siegel (1959): Rational choice theory is a correct first approximation to the analysis of decision behavior, but it is incomplete, and making it more complete requires the guidance of data from experimental designs motivated by this objective. Simon's original thesis was that "To predict how economic man will behave we need to know not only that he is rational, but also how he perceives the world – what alternatives he sees and what consequences he attaches to them" (1956, p. 271). Thus there is no denial of human rationality; the issue is in what sense are individuals rational and how far can we go with abstract objective principles of how "rational" people "should" act?

But if a study of payoff effects is in need of a theoretical foundation, it also requires evidence. If traditional economic models assume that *only* monetary reward matters, psychologists tend to assume that such rewards *do not* matter.[3] The facts reviewed here support the more common-sense view that rewards matter, and that neither of the polar views – only reward matters, or reward does not matter – are sustainable across the range of experimental economics. There will always be discrepancy between precise theory and observation, and thus room for theory improvement. Because rational theory postulates motivated decision makers, it follows that varying reward levels is one of the many important tools needed to explore this discrepancy. Our fundamental view is that the experimentalist has as much to learn from experimental subjects about subjective rationality as human decision makers have to learn from the models that we call rational.

I.   Motivation Theory in the Presence of Decision Cost

In this section, we develop a simple theoretical framework to help (i) improve understanding of the circumstances that might yield predicted

---

[3] See, for example, Siegel (1959) and von Winterfeldt and Edwards (1986), also Kroll et al. (1988) who are among the important exceptions. In fact, rewards are not of exclusionary importance, and one of our concerns in the model to be presented is to account for the fact that one does not observe arbitrary and random behavior when there are no salient rewards. But because rewards do matter, they cannot be ignored in testing the models proposed by economic and game theorists. We think psychologists have focused on experiments without rewards because they are primarily interested in cognitive processes as in Smith (1991). Their research suggests that monetary rewards are not crucial in studying such processes, but this is controversial.

optimal decisions or deviations therefrom and (ii) provide guidance in experimental design and in interpreting observations.

We begin with a statement of rational theory, as derived from the perspective of the theorist/experimentalist. Letting X, W, Θ, and Z be convex sets, the variables we want to identify are defined next.

1. $x \varepsilon X$, the subject's message decision variable such as price, quantity, bid, or forecast. This variable is defined by the experimenter's interpretation of a theory in the context of a particular experimental design and institution.

2. $w \varepsilon W$, an environmental variable controlled as a "treatment" by the experimenter such as commodity value(s), asset endowment, or production cost.

3. $\theta \varepsilon \Theta$, a random variable with distribution function $F(\theta)$ defined on Θ. F, chosen by the experimenter, generates the appropriate probabilities in games against nature or the appropriate uncertainty about other player types when modeling the subject's choice in a Harsanyi game of incomplete information. Thus, in a private value auction, v is the uncertain value for each of the $N - 1$ competitors of a given bidder.

4. $\pi(x,w,\theta)$, the outcome function, controlled by the experimenter, denominated in experimental money (tokens, francs, etc.), and based on the motivation assumptions in the theoretical model. The function π is assumed to be strictly concave in x, so that given w and $F(\theta)$, the experimenter predicts that x^* will be the unique optimal x chosen by the subject.

5. λ, the scalar payoff transformation rate, controlled by the experimenter, that converts experimental money into the reward medium. We assume that this marginal conversion rate is constant, although there are experiments in which it is not [i.e., the conversion rate is some nonlinear increasing function $\lambda(\pi)$ of outcome].

The standard expected utility function, in terms of the above variables, is written

$$U(x,w,\lambda,\pi,F) = \int_{\Theta} u[\lambda\pi(x,w,\theta]dF(\theta) \tag{1}$$

The first-order condition for $x^* = \arg \max U$ is

$$\lambda\varphi_1 = 0, \qquad \text{where } \varphi_1 = \int_{\Theta} u_1\pi_1 dF(\theta) \tag{2}$$

where a subscript j denotes differentiation with respect to argument j. If utility is increasing in reward ($\lambda > 0$) then (2) implies $\Omega_1 = 0$, with solution $x^* = x(w,F)$. The function $x(w,F)$ is the source of testable experimental hypotheses concerning the subject's predicted choice x^*. Note that if u is linear, or a power function of π, then x^* is independent of $\lambda > 0$, and is optimal however small the opportunity cost, $\pi_{11}(x^*)$ is.

We now examine the same problem from the perspective of the decision maker (subject). To achieve this, we augment the preceding list of five variables with the following:

6. $y \; \varepsilon \; X$, the value of the decision variable chosen by the subject, given his or her perception, evaluation, analysis, and understanding of the instructions (augmented by experience where there is replication) and the task that he or she is to perform. Outcome is now written $\pi(y,w,\upsilon)$.

7. $z \; \varepsilon \; Z$, an unobserved decision process variable controlled consciously, or unconsciously, by the subject in executing the task that results in y. Think of z as the decision cost or effort (concentration, attention, thinking, monitoring, reporting, acting) that the subject applies to the task presented by the experimenter. As with quarks in particle physics, we may have no direct measures of z, but we look for traces of its effects on the choice of y. If z is recognized as lurking within every subjective model of decision, then we are primed to expect to find its traces, and where z is thought to be of substantial importance (as in Siegel's model, discussed later, and in the general model we propose), we seek to establish this proposition by manipulation of the experimental procedures that affect z and thus y.

8. Now consider the equation

$$y = x^* + \varepsilon(z,s) \tag{3}$$

[e.g., $\varepsilon(z,s) = s\xi(z)$, $\xi'(z) < 0, \xi''(z) > 0$], where $\varepsilon(z,s)$ is a function, normalized with respect to x^*, specifying the effect of z on subject choice of y. Think of $\varphi(z)$ as the subject's production transformation function of effort z into decision y. An unobserved random variable s, describing the "state" of the person at the time of decision, induces randomness on ε conditional on z. Observations on the effects of s are obtained by repeated play of the task. More effort is postulated to narrow the distance between predicted optimal (x^*) and actual (y) choices and thereby increases payoff. ε is naturally interpreted as prediction decision error and is random across repeated play choices of y for given z.[4] Some hypothe-

---

[4] Note, however, that ε is not "error" from the point of view of the subject weighing (albeit unconsciously) benefit against decision cost. It is the experimentalist who interprets ε as a prediction error of the theory, whose randomness derives from the unobserved random

sized properties of the error function are suggested in the following discussion.

9. $\mu > 0$ is a scalar characteristic of the subject that measures the monetary equivalent of the subjective value of outcome π on the assumption that there is self-satisfaction, weak or strong, in achieving any outcome π. This parameter is assumed to be additive with the reward scalar, $\lambda \geq 0$, and allows the model to account for nonrandom behavior when the salient exogenous reward is $\lambda = 0$.

It will be evident to the reader that any of the variables x, y, z, w might be represented by vectors in place of scalars, but the latter are sufficient for examining the principles we want to address. Also, we omit the subscript i on the appropriate variables and functions, it being understood that the perspective is always that of some particular person i, such as yourself.

We can now write the subjective expected utility function using the new variables,

$$\psi(y,z,w;\lambda,\mu,\pi,F] = \int_{\Theta} u[(\mu+\lambda)\pi(y,w,\theta),z]dF(\theta) \qquad (4)$$

where $u_2 < 0$ is the marginal decision cost (disutility) of effort z. Substituting from Equation (3), the first-order condition for $z^* = \arg \max \psi$ is

$$\varphi_1 \geq \varphi_2 / (\mu+\lambda)\varepsilon_1$$

where $\varphi_1 = \int_{\Theta} u_1 \pi_1 dF(\theta)$ and

$$\varphi_2 = \int u_2 dF(\theta) \qquad (5)$$

We will examine three cases, each representing a possible solution to Eq. (5).

A.   Bounded Rationality Case

When $>$ holds in Equation (5), we have a constrained solution with z^* on the boundary of the set Z, (e.g., if $Z = [0, \bar{z}]$, we have $z^* = \bar{z}$). This bounded rationality case can be important. There are physiological and intellectual limitations on human decision making ability; when these limits are binding the agent's constrained optimal decision is $y^* = x^* + \varepsilon(\bar{z}, s)$ *independent of the reward* λ. One should think of λ as operating

---

variable s. For other theoretical treatments of the effect of errors specific to particular decision problems, see Hey and Di Cagno (1990) and Berg and Dickhaut (1990). In none of these approaches need the subjects be aware that they are making "mistakes" in choice or be aware of the effects of effort on decision. Our motivation is to model the decline in errors that is often associated with increased payoffs.

on motivation not physiological and mental capacity. This case provides one formalization of Simon's concept of bounded rationality in decision making.

Now consider interior solutions where the equality condition holds in (5). First, note that in contrast with Equations (1) and (2), we have in (4) and (5) a well-defined maximum problem when $\lambda = 0$. This is essential in explaining why subject decisions are not just random responses in the absence of salient rewards.

B.   Pure Decision Error Case

Consider the degenerate case in which marginal decision cost and $\varphi_2 \equiv 0$ and $\varepsilon(z,s) \equiv \varepsilon(s)$ in Equations (3) and (4). Under these conditions, effort does not enter the criterion function (4), the costless direct decision variable is y, and instead of (5) we get the condition $\varphi_1 = 0$, which determines $y^* = y(w)$, where $y^* = x^* + \varepsilon(s)$. This formulation is the same as in (1) and (2) except that it implements the decision-making hypothesis with an econometric specification of a decision error term [as in McElroy (1987) for an examination of error models in production, cost, and derived demand equation systems]. This is usually recognized, ex post, in the form of the assumption that decision error, $y^* - x^* = \varepsilon$ is randomly distributed with mean zero and variance σ^2 (i.e., ε is not biased). Hypothesis testing normally proceeds on this maintained assumption. As we will see in the following survey, the data often do not contradict the condition $E(\varepsilon) = 0$ – subject choices y^* are distributed around a mean (or median) that is "close" to x^*. But there are exceptions, and at least some of these exceptions occur when the Euclidean distance between x^* and the *boundary* of the set X is at or near zero. In that case, the data suggest that $E(\varepsilon) \neq 0$. If decision error is random, then $E(\varepsilon) = 0$ is incompatible with boundary maxima. So the idea is this: Part of the reason why data may be consistent with predictions is that x^* is far enough into the interior of X that random *unbiased* decision errors cause no difficulty. Of course, they may be biased, but for sure errors are biased at boundary optima, where the distribution of ε is asymmetrically truncated.

C.   Dominance Case

Now consider the more general interior maximum defined by (5). In particular (5) informs us that *if equilibrium marginal decision cost* $-\varphi_2/(\mu + \lambda)\varepsilon_1$ *goes to zero as* $\lambda \to \lambda \leq \infty$ *then we have dominance* at the reward level λ and higher (i.e., rewards are sufficiently salient to swamp decision cost effort).[5] Whether this property holds in any particular case, and what level of $\bar{\lambda}$, if any, is sufficient for dominance is *entirely* an *empirical* question. We have already seen why this property might not hold: the solution value z^* from (5) may be on the boundary of Z. Additional physical, mental, or sensory effort may not be possible. Thus in a signal detection experiment, once a subject approaches the boundary of his or her auditory capability, little if any additional auditory improvement may be forthcoming by escalating reward payments. Similar considerations may apply for some subjects in almost any task.

The methodological implications of the preceding analysis are clear. In a new experimental situation, if the experimenter finds that decision error ε is biased enough to contradict the theory, then the first thing to question is the experimental instructions and procedures. Can they be simplified? If not (the task is inherently difficult), does experience help? These are techniques that, a fortiori, may help to reduce decision cost. The second thing to question is the payoff level. Try a double, triple, or n-fold increase in λ. We do it frequently, and reported in Smith and Walker (1993a) the effects of 5-, 10-, and 20-fold increases in auction experiments. This is not done for realism because there are both low stakes and high stakes economic decisions in life, and all are of interest. You manipulate payoff to increase understanding of possible trade-offs between the benefits and costs of optimal decision and to explore the depths and limits of objective optimality.

Where our model of the technology of errors is applied to the Nash equilibrium analysis of behavior, we assume that subjects are "boundedly rational" in the sense that they do not behave as if their equilibrium choice behavior takes into account the error properties of their rivals' choices (or is a best response to other subjects' actual error-prone choices). That such errors may affect the calculation of Nash "trembling-hand" equilibria has been demonstrated in the path-breaking theoretical work of Selten (1975), provided that the error structure of decision making is common knowledge: ". . . all the players have the same notions about how their fellow players slip . . ." (Kreps, 1990b, p. 439). But experimental studies in bargaining, oligopoly, and auction markets going back to Fouraker and Siegel (1963) have found that Nash models of single play behavior that assume common (payoff) knowledge actually perform best in repeated games under *private* (incomplete) information and depart from such models under *common* information. Consequently, such models truly exhibit equilibrium behavior in that subjects tend to gravitate to, and remain near, such an equilibrium but with error. In the

---

[5]　C.f., Harrison (1989) and Smith (1976a).

examples in Section III, we have not found a need to suppose that, from
their point of view, subjects are solving for a trembling-hand equilibria.
Subjects are getting it right on average in the interior optimum cases.
Thus, the simpler Nash models account for the central tendencies of the
data, but not for the error.[6]

II.   Some Comparative Treatment Predictions with Additive Separability

In this section, we consider the implications of the case in which Ψ in (4)
can be written in the additively separable form:

$$\psi = \varphi(x^* + \varepsilon) - C(z, \gamma) \tag{6}$$

where

$$\varphi(x^* + \varepsilon) = \int_\Theta u[(\mu + \lambda)\pi(x^* + \varepsilon(z, s), w, \theta)] dF(\theta)$$

The function $C(z, \gamma)$ expresses the subjective cost of effort z, with shift
parameter γ. In addition to the conditions on $\varepsilon(z, s) = s\xi(z)$ in (3), we
assume $\varphi_1 > 0$, $\varphi_{11} < 0$, $C_1 > 0$, $C_{11} > 0$, $C_{12} > 0$. Also, let $s \in S$ have the distribution function $H(s)$. In Smith and Walker (1993a), we applied these
assumptions and tested their implications, for first-price auction theory.

Now approximate φ in (6) with the first three terms of its Taylor's
expansion at the point x^*. Then, since $\varphi_1(x^*) = 0$, the linear term involving ε vanishes, and we are left with

$$\varphi(x^* + \varepsilon) \cong \varphi(x^*) + \varphi_{11}(x^*)\varepsilon^2 / 2 \tag{7}$$

Next, substitute from (6) and (7) and define

$$\psi(z) = \int_s \psi(s) dH(s) = \varphi(x^*) + \varphi_{11}(x^*) \frac{\mathrm{var}(s)\zeta^2(z)}{2} - C(z, \gamma) \tag{8}$$

From the subject's perspective, the problem is to choose $z^* = \arg \max$
$\psi(z)$, which is determined by[7]

---

[6] But there are clearly games in which one can account for the predictive failure of the
complete information model by reformulation as an incomplete information game in
which each player responds strategically to the error in the play of other(s). For an excellent example, see McKelvey and Palfrey (1990) where the standard model fails to predict
outcomes in the centipede game, but a reformulation as a game of incomplete information, in which the players make action errors and hold beliefs subject to error, is able to
account for the experimental data. As they suggest, the model could probably be
improved by making error rates depend upon decision utility differences.

[7] See Theil (1971, p. 192) for a derivation showing that the variance of error in a behavioral equation is inversely proportional to the second derivative of the criterion function
at its optimum. Theil's interpretation, however, is the reverse of ours in that the actual
decision (y, in our notation) is treated as nonstochastic and the optimal decision (our x^*)
as stochastic as in Theil (1971, p. 193); nor does Theil interpret the error as an economic
variable subject to control by the decision effort of the agent.

$$\zeta(z^*)\zeta'(z^*) = \frac{C_1(z^*,\gamma)}{\varphi_{11}(x^*)\mathrm{var}(s)} \tag{9}$$

By differentiating the equilibrium condition (9), it is straightforward to sign the following derivatives:

$$\frac{dz^*}{d\lambda} > 0; \qquad \frac{dz^*}{d\lambda} < 0; \qquad \frac{d\,\mathrm{var}\,\varepsilon}{d\lambda} < 0; \qquad \frac{d\,\mathrm{var}\,\varepsilon}{d\gamma}$$

Increases in payoffs and/or decreases in decision cost are associated with increased decision effort, the *observed* consequence of which is a reduced variance of decision error. One "treatment" for lowering decision costs is experience: With increased experience, decisions become easier and more routine, and we predict a reduction in decision error variance for given payoff levels.

III. Effect of Incentive Rewards and Opportunity Cost on Performance in Experimental Economics

There is a long experimental literature, going back at least to Siegel (1961) and Siegel and Fouraker (1960), in which monetary payments affecting subject opportunity cost are varied as a treatment variable, and their controlled effects on performance are measured. There is also a large experimental literature on choice among risky alternatives by cognitive psychologists. Most of the psychology literature reports the results of experiments conducted without monetary reinforcement, but in which the "subject is instructed to do his best" as in Siegel (1961, p. 767). Psychologists defend such hypothetical choice procedures on the grounds that money either does not matter or matters insignificantly, so that monetary rewards are unnecessary. For example, Dawes (1988, pp. 122, 124, 131, 259) cites several examples of decision-making experiments in which the use of monetary rewards yields results "the same" or "nearly" the same as when choices were hypothetical: Slovic et al. (1982), Grether and Plott (1979), Tversky and Kahneman (1983), and Tversky and Edwards (1966). But some contrary citations in the psychology literature showing that monetary incentives do matter are as follows: Goodman et al. concluded that "These data, though far from conclusive, should not enhance the confidence of those who use elicitation methods based on obtaining certainty equivalents of imaginary bets" (1979, p. 398); Siegel et al. stated, "we have little confidence in experiments in which the 'payoffs' are points, credits[8] or tokens" (1964, p. 148); and Messick and Brayfield

---

[8] It is now well documented that grade credits compare well with monetary rewards when the payments are salient as in Isaac et al. (1991) and Kormendi and Plott (1982).

(1964), passim, and Kroll et al. (1988) agreed. Even in the psychology literature, there is evidence of cases where rewards matter.

In the economics literature, there is the important study of 240 farmers in India by Binswanger (1980, 1981) comparing hypothetical choice among gambles with choices whose real payoffs ranged to levels exceeding the subjects' monthly incomes; the hypothetical results were not consistent with the motivated measures of risk aversion; with payoffs varied across three levels, subjects tended to show increased risk aversion at higher payoffs. Similarly, Wolf and Pohlman (1983) compared hypothetical with actual bids of a Treasury bill dealer and found that the dealer's measure of constant relative risk aversion using actual bid data is four times larger than under hypothetical assessment. In a recent study of risk preferences under high monetary incentives in China, Kachelmeier, et al. (1991) reported a significant difference between subject responses under low and very high monetary payoffs and no difference between hypothetical and low monetary payments, but the usual anomalies long documented in tests of expected utility theory remain.

Several other studies report data in which monetary rewards make a difference in results. Plott and Smith (1978, p. 142) reported results in which marginal trades occur far more frequently with commission incentives than without; Fiorina and Plott (1978) reported committee decisions in which both mean deviations from theoretical predictions and standard errors are reduced by escalating reward levels; Grether (1981) reported individual decision-making experiments in which the incidence of "confused" behavior is reduced with monetary rewards, but subjects who appear not to be confused behave about the same with or without monetary rewards.

A dramatic example of how payoff levels can matter is found in Kroll et al. (1988), who provided experimental tests of the separation theorem and the capital asset pricing model in a computer controlled portfolio selection task. Two experiments are reported: experiment 1 (30 subjects) and experiment 2 (12 subjects). The payoffs in experiment 2 were ten times greater than the payoffs in experiment 1, averaging $165 per subject, or about $44 per hour (30 times the prevailing student hourly wage in Israel). The authors found that performance is significantly improved, relative to the capital asset pricing model, by the tenfold increase in stakes, and suggested that "This finding casts some doubt on the validity of the results of many experiments on decision making which involve trivial amounts of money or no money at all" Kroll et al. (1988, p. 514).

Forsythe et al. (1994) found that results in the dictator game are affected significantly by monetary incentives and that under no-pay conditions the results in ultimatum games are inconclusive because they fail to be replicable. Doubling payoffs does not affect behavior. With monetary incentives the authors strongly reject the fairness hypothesis.

Finally, an important study by McClelland et al. (1991) directly manipulated forgone expected profit in incentive decision mechanisms with treatments making the payoff optimum more or less peaked. They find that where the mechanism is "transparently" simple (low decision cost) flat maxima do as well as peaked maxima, but where the mechanism is "opaque," requiring search, the absolute deviation of subjects bids from the optimal was significantly reduced when the payoff function was more peaked.

A.   Decision Making and Decision Cost Under Uncertainty

The study by Tversky and Edwards (1966) is of particular interest because they found that paying (charging) 5 cents (as compared with no salient reward) when a subject makes a correct (incorrect) prediction is sufficient to yield outcomes closer to "the optimal" outcome. The task is the standard binary choice prediction experiment: Two lights illuminate by an "independent trials" Bernoulli process with fixed probabilities p and $1 - p$, but these probabilities are unknown to the subjects. The standard result, replicated dozens of times without subject monetary reinforcement, but with the exhortation that subjects do their best, is for the average subject to reach a stable asymptote characterized by probability *matching*. That is, the pooled proportion of times the more frequent event is predicted is $\hat{x} \cong p$. Because the expected number of correct predictions is $xp + (1 - x)(1 - p)$, when the more frequent event is chosen with frequency x, "the optimal" response is to set $x^* = 1$ $(p > 1/2)$. Tversky and Edwards report higher (than matching) pooled total frequencies for 1,000 trials: $\hat{x} = 0.705$ when $p = .60$ and $\hat{x} = 0.76$ when $p = .70$; the asymptotic levels (not reported) can be presumed to be somewhat higher. But they conclude that "Though most differences between the treatment groups were in the direction predicted by a normative model, Ss were far indeed from what one would expect on the basis of such a model" (1966, p. 682). In passing, they conjecture that "A formal model for the obtained data might incorporate a notion such as cost associated with making a decision" (p. 683).

In fact such a formal model attempting to do this had been published and tested somewhat earlier by Siegel (1959), Siegel and Goldstein (1959), Siegel (1961), Siegel and Andrews (1962), and Siegel et al. (1964). Instead of accepting the standard conclusion that people did not behave rationally and rejecting the utility theory of choice, Siegel elected to explore the possibility that the theory was essentially correct but incomplete. In particular, citing Simon (1956), he argued that one should keep in mind the distinction between objective rationality, as viewed by the experimenter, and subjective rationality as viewed by the subject, given his perceptual and evaluational premises. In effect, Siegel placed himself in the position of a subject faced with hundreds of trials in the binary choice experiment. He postulated that (i) in the absence of monetary reinforcement the only reward would be the satisfaction (dissatisfaction) of a correct (incorrect) prediction and (ii) the task is incredibly boring, since it involves both cognitive and kinesthetic monotony, and in this context there was a utility from varying one's prediction. A general two-state form of Siegel's model is to write the expected utility function (2) in the form

$$U = u(a_{11})px + u(a_{12})x(1-p) + u(a_{21})p(1-x)$$
$$+ u(a_{22})(1-x)(1-p) + bx(1-x) \qquad (10)$$

Again, p is the probability of event E_1, $(1-p)$ is the probability of event E_2, and x is the proportion of trials (the probability for one trial) in which the subject chooses E_1. The term $u(a_{ij})$ is the utility of outcome a_{ij}, where i refers to the prediction (choice) of E_1, and j refers to the subsequent occurrence of event E_j. Hence a_{11} is the outcome when the subject correctly predicts E_1, and a_{12} is the outcome when E_1 is incorrectly predicted. Now suppose we assume that $u(a_{ij}) = u_{ij}^o + u_m\,(a_{ij})$, where $u_m(0) = 0$, u_{ij}^o is the utility of the *outcome* (i,j) in the absence of monetary reward, a_{ij} is the monetary payment (or charge) when (i,j) obtains, and u_m is the utility of money.

It is seen that (10) is simply a special form of (4); one in which the control variable is $F \equiv p \in [0,1]$, v is 1 if E_1 occurs and 0 if E_2 obtains, "effort" is assumed to be measured directly by $z \equiv x \equiv y \in [0,1]$, and the utility of outcome is additively separable from the term $bx(1-x)$, which Siegel calls the utility of response variability (or the subjective value of relieving monotony). Response variability is measured by $x(1-x)$, a function with the desirable property that it is maximized at $x = 1/2$, when diversification is largest. The constant b is then the marginal utility of variability. Siegel's particular test model is the special case in which (i) $u_{ij}^o = u_o$, $a_{ij} = a$, if $i = j$, namely that the reward a is paid when the subject's prediction is correct on either event, and the outcome utility u^o for a correct prediction is the same for either event; (ii) $a_{ij} = a'$, $u_{ij}^o = 0$, if $i \neq j$, where a' is the reward (cost if $a' < 0$) when the prediction is wrong on either event, and outcome utility is zero any time the prediction is incorrect. Then (10) becomes

$$U = (u^0 + u_m(a))[px + (1-x)(1-p)] + u_m(a')$$
$$[x(1-p) + p(1-x)] + bx(1-x) \qquad (10')$$

where $u^0 + u_m(a)$ is the marginal utility of a correct prediction, and $u_m(a')$ the marginal utility of an incorrect prediction. Because U is everywhere strictly concave on [0,1], for an interior maximum of (10'), we want to satisfy

$$U_x = (2p-1)[u^0 + u_m(a) - u_m(a')] + b(1-2x) = 0 \qquad (11)$$

There are three cases for which Siegel reported data.

Case 1. $a = a' = 0$, the no payoff treatment. Then (11) yields

$$x_0^* = \frac{1}{2}\left[\frac{(2p-1)u^0}{b} + 1\right] \qquad (11.1)$$

This case is particularly interesting because it explains probability matching behavior. If the marginal rate of substitution of variability for a correct prediction is unity, $(u^0/b) = 1$, then from (7), $x_0^* = p$.

Case 2. $a > 0$, $a' = 0$, the payoff treatment (i.e., you get paid when you are right, pay nothing when you are wrong). Then from (11),

$$x_1^* = \frac{1}{2}\left[\frac{(2p-1)(u^0 + u_m(a))}{b} + 1\right] \qquad (11.2)$$

Case 3. $a = -a' > 0$, the payoff–loss treatment; you receive a cents when you are right and lose a cents when you are wrong. Then

$$x_1^* = \frac{1}{2}\left[\frac{(2p-1)(u_o + u_m(a) - u_m(-a))}{b} + 1\right] \qquad (11.3)$$

Because $b = u_o < u_o + u_m(a) < u_o + u_m(a) - u_m(-a')$, *by construction we get the testable implication that* $p = x_0^* < x_1^* < x_2^*$.

Based on data in Siegel et al. (1964), Figure 3.1 provides histograms of the distribution of subjects' choice frequencies $\hat{x}$ in the final (stable-state) block of 20 trials (100 total trials) under each of the reward conditions: no payoff, payoff, payoff–loss. In the payoff condition, $a = 5$ cents, and in payoff–loss, $a = -a' = 5$ cents. As predicted by the Siegel model, there is an observed increase in the pooled mean choice proportion, $p = .70 = M(\hat{x}_0) < M(x_1) < M(x_2)$. with increasing payoff motivation. We also compute from Siegel et al. (1964) the root mean square (decision) error S in Figure 3.1, and note that it declines monotonically with increasing motivation. Not only do subject predictions shift toward the objective

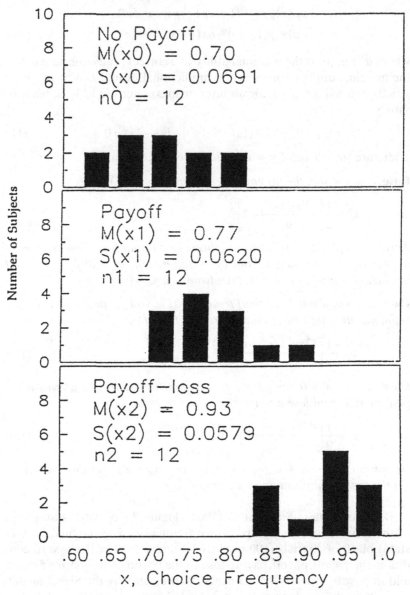

FIGURE 3.1. Histogram of frequency choices in binary prediction under alternative payoff conditions.

optimal choice, $x^* = 1$, with increasing rewards, but the variability of choices also decreases, and under the highest motivation, payoff–loss for one in four subjects are at this boundary maximum.[9]

Siegel's model proposed a resolution of the paradox of "irrational" behavior in binary choice and provided new testable implications that were consistent with the results of new experiments. He showed that the previous psychology literature, which had concluded that people were not expected utility maximizers, was the exception that proved the rule: Subjects had no monetary incentive to maximize expected utility.

How far one can go in using decision cost concepts to resolve anomalies in standard individual decision theory remains open. A test case may be provided by the interesting work of Herrnstein et al. (1991). They studied a much more complicated environment for the subject than the Bernoulli binary choice problem in which the reward from playing right or left depends upon the fraction of right-key choices in the previous N trials, where N is a treatment variable controlled by the experimenter. In the steady state, if R is the number of right-key choices in the last N trials, then payoff is

$$\pi(R / N) = (R / N)f(R / N) + [(N - R) / N]g(R / N), \qquad 0 \le R \le N$$

where $f(\cdot)$ and $g(\cdot)$ are the current payoffs on right and left, respectively. If N is large, the effect of the current choice on future behavior is small and myopically difficult to perceive. Maximization for interior solutions is determined by the condition that

$$f(R / N) + (R / N)f'(R / N) = g(R / N) - [(N - r) / N]g'(R / N)$$

Matching behavior in this case (Herrnstein called it melioration) leads to the condition that $f(R/N) = g(R/N)$. Herrnstein et al. (1991) reported results with varying degrees of support for the two hypotheses. For example, better information and rewards (coin values) improved maximization marginally. But the payoff functions (Herrnstein et al., 1991, Figures 2, 4, 6, 7, 8) are all characterized by flat maxima, thus making the decision problem sensitive to decision costs and other factors affecting net subjective value.

[9] There are two technical problems concerning this literature. It appears that in all cases the research design constrained the event realizations so that in fact the process was *not* Bernoullian. Siegel et al. (1964) followed the earlier literature in randomizing by blocks of 20 trials. This means that for $p = .75$ in every sequence of 20 trials, the realizations were constrained to yield 15 "left" and 5 "right" (i.e., sampling occurred without replacement). A second shortcoming of this literature is that in its day no econometric procedures were available to estimate individual asymptotic probabilities using all the data (e.g., logit), and the analysis did not focus on individual behavior, which is what Siegel's model is about.

B.   Bilateral Bargaining and Cournot Oligopoly

In their first work on bilateral bargaining, Siegel and Fouraker (1960) studied a simple two-person – one buyer, one seller – form of what later became known as the double auction. The buyer is given a profit schedule based on a concave redemption function $R(Q)$ for differing quantities Q of the commodity he might purchase from the seller, and the latter is given a profit schedule derived from a convex cost function $C(Q)$ for different quantities she might sell to the buyer. The message space for each is the two-tuple (P,Q), a price and a quantity bid or offered. Thus the buyer (seller) might begin with (P_1,Q_1). The seller either accepts or makes an offer (P_2,Q_2). The buyer responds with an acceptance, or a new bid (P_3,Q_3), and so on until an agreement is reached or the time limit expires. In one experiment, consisting of 11 bargaining pairs, the Pareto optimal solution had the property that a one-unit deviation in quantity from the optimum led to total profit deviations of 10 and 16 cents. Referring to column 1 in Table 3.1, we call this the low payoff condition. The author's expressed concern that this relatively "flat maximum" might contribute to the variability of outcomes across the bargaining pairs. Consequently, they altered the payoff tables so that the joint profit declined symmetrically by 60 cents with a one-unit deviation in quantity from the optimum and conducted two replications of the original experiment (22 bargaining pairs). This is referred to as the high payoff condition in Table 3.1. Note that the mean error declined from \$0.545 to \$0.091, and, as reported by the authors, this treatment has no statistically significant effect on the strong tendency for bargainers to approach the predicted Pareto optimal outcome. However, the mean square error declined substantially from the low to high payoff condition so that increasing the opportunity cost of missing the optimum induced a tighter clustering of the data in the neighborhood of the optimum.

This concern for the relevance of payoff levels and the opportunity cost of deviations from the theoretical predictions carried over in their subsequent studies of bargaining and oligopoly. In Fouraker and Siegel (1963), their two-person bargaining experiments were extended to the first-mover case in which the seller begins by announcing a price, followed by the buyer choosing a quantity. In the repeated game, this process is replicated for a total of 19 regular transactions, followed by an announced "final" 20th transaction, followed by a special 21st transaction in which all payoffs were tripled. In Table 3.1 we summarize three experiments, columns 2, 3, and 4, in which the results of the 20th low payoff transactions are compared with the 21st high payoff transactions. Upon comparing the mean, M_L and M_H, in these columns, for both buyers

Table 3.1. *Outcome mean and mean square errors by experiment*

	(1) Bilateral bargaining[a] Seller: price-quantity Buyer: price-quantity	(2) Bilateral bargaining[b] Seller: price Buyer: quantity		(3) Bilateral bargaining[b] Seller: price Buyer: quantity		(4) Bilateral bargaining[b] Seller: price Buyer: quantity		(5) Cournot duopoly[c] Sellers quantities	(6) Cournot triopoly[c] Sellers quantities
Institution									
Messages, x_i									
Information	Incomplete	Incomplete		Complete		Complete		Incomplete	Incomplete
No. exps. high payoff	22	9		10		12		16	11
No. exps. low payoff	11	9		10		12		9	8
Outcomes for	Buyers & sellers	Sellers	Buyers	Sellers	Buyers	Sellers	Buyers	Sellers	Sellers
$M_{\mathrm{L}}(x_i - x_i^*)$	0.545	-0.222	0.222	-1.6	2.0	1.0	1.083	0.719	0.576
$M_{\mathrm{H}}(x_i - x_i^*)$	0.091	-0.555	0.555	-0.9	1.6	1.167	-2.833	0.778	0.667
$S_{\mathrm{L}}^2(x_i - x_i^*)$	5	10.25	10.25	8.667	20.222	6.182	6.636	7.194	10.844
$S_{\mathrm{H}}^2(x_i - x_i^*)$	0.19	2.375	2.375	2.111	11.778	5.091	28.727[d]	5.529	11.826[d]
$S_{\mathrm{L}}^2/S_{\mathrm{H}}^2$	26.9	4.32	4.32	4.11	1.72	1.21	0.23	1.30	0.917

[a] In the high payoff group, there was a 60-cent profit differential between the (Pareto) optimal quantity and next adjacent quantities; in the low group, these differentials were 10 and 16 cents. Based on data from Siegel and Fouraker (1960; Chapter 3; experiments 1, 4, and 5).

[b] In the high payoff groups, all profit table entries were tripled relative to those in the low payoff groups. Fouraker and Siegel (1963; experiments 3–5, pp. 227, 233, 239).

[c] In the high payoff groups, the top three profit makers received bonuses of $8, $5 and $2; no such bonuses were paid in the low groups. Fouraker and Siegel (1963; experiment 17, pp. 164–5, 304–6).

[d] A single outlier observation accounts for the higher mean square error.

M_{L}, M_{H}; mean error, $\frac{1}{N}\sum_i (\hat{x}_i - x_i^*)$, in low and high payoff conditions, respectively.

S_{L}^2, S_{H}^2; mean square error, $\frac{1}{N-1}\sum_i (\hat{x}_i - x_i^*)^2$, in low and high payoff conditions, respectively.

and sellers in the bargaining pairs, generally we observe comparably small mean error deviations under the two payoff conditions. But the mean square error S_L^2 tends to be higher for the low payoff (and low opportunity cost) condition than the mean square error S_H^2 for high payoffs. An exception occurs in column 4 for the buyers. In this case, one buyer among the 12 high payoff bargaining pairs responded with a punishing quantity of zero. This outlier depressed the mean error and greatly increased the mean square error. In columns 5 and 6, we report the results from Siegel and Fouraker in which payoffs were manipulated in their Cournot oligopoly experiments. Here the authors departed from their use of a final triple-payoff round with the same subjects. Instead, they ran one group of duopolists and one of triopolists with *bonus* rewards in addition to the profit table rewards used in the regular groups. The bonuses were $8, $5, and $2 paid to the first, second, and third highest profit makers. As recorded in columns 5 and 6, this caused no important change in mean error between the low and high payoff groups. The mean square error declined for duopolies and increased slightly for triopolies (the latter occasioned by one outlying observation).

From the foregoing summary, it is apparent that, although Siegel and Fouraker undertook no thoroughly systematic investigation of the effect of payoff opportunity costs on market outcomes, they nevertheless demonstrated sensitivity to the possibility that such effects might be important. In particular, their data suggest that the most likely effect of increasing the opportunity cost of nonoptimal decision is to reduce the mean square error deviation from optimality.

Recently, Drago and Heywood (1989, p. 993) reported data for tournament and piece rate experiments as in Bull et al. (1987), showing a very large reduction in the variance of observations when the payoff function was transformed so that it was more sharply peaked. Support for the predicted optimal behavior was observed, however, in all reported payoff environments. The tournament is a strategic game; the piece rate is a game against nature. In both environments, the optimum is an interior point in a nonnegative real interval.

C.   Double-Auction Markets

In the "swastika" supply and demand market underlying the results in Table 3.2, each of 11 buyers was assigned an induced value of $4.20, and each of 16 sellers was assigned a cost of $3.10 as in Smith (1965, 1976a). Thus excess supply is $e = 5$ units at all prices in the interval [3.10, 4.20]. A commission of $0.05 is paid to provide a minimum inducement to trade marginal units. Under low payoffs, 4 of 27 subjects were chosen

Table 3.2. *Mean and mean square errors for low and high payoffs double auction, swastika design (11 buyers, 16 sellers; one unit each)*

Mean and mean square error, low and high payoffs[a]	Trading period			
	1	2	3	4
$M_L(x_i - x_i^*)$	49.5	33.6	21.36	13.64
$M_H(x_i - x_i^*)$	47.3	17.0	5.32	1.90
$S_L^2(x_i - x_i^*)$	2,962.5	1,275.	547.5	240.0
$S_H^2(x_i - x_i^*)$	2,650.	436.9	61.9	15.
S_L^2/S_H^2	1.12	2.92	8.84	16.0

[a] In the high payoff condition, each subject is paid his or her realized surplus plus a 5-cent trading commission, whereas under low payoffs, 4 of 27 subjects are selected at random at the end of each trading period to receive these payoffs. Based on data for two experiments with high and one with low payoffs (Smith, 1965).

randomly to be paid. Under high payoffs, all were paid. The competitive equilibrium is $3.10 in the sense that price will tend to decrease at any price above $3.10, although there is excess supply at $3.10. In this case, the equilibrium is at a boundary optimum with all surplus obtained by the buyers. In Table 3.2, we list the mean and mean square errors by low and high payoff condition for each trading period. The somewhat slower convergence for these markets than is the rule for more symmetric markets is particularly pronounced under the low payoff treatment. Note that experience across periods lowers error variance for both low and high payoff treatments. In this design, all price error (deviations from equilibrium) are necessarily positive for individually rational agents. Hence, decision error is biased, and insofar as low motivation increases such error the effect must necessarily reduce support for theoretical predictions.

Jamal and Sunder (1991) undertook the first systematic examination of the effects of (salient) monetary rewards in oral double-auction trading using symmetric supply and demand designs. Their preliminary results support the conclusion that, in the absence of prior experience and salient rewards (i.e., using fixed payments, independent of performance), markets do not converge reliably to the competitive equilibrium prediction but do converge in the presence of such rewards. However, once subjects are experienced using salient rewards, subjects converge in the usual double-auction manner, even though they receive only fixed nonsalient rewards. Our interpretation is that, in effect, they become detached professionals, whose actions require little thought or attention, once sufficiently motivated to have mastered the process of double-auction trading in simple environments.

IV.   Summary and Conclusions

A survey of experimental papers, which report data on the comparative effects of subject monetary rewards (including no rewards), shows a tendency for the error variance of the observations around the predicted optimal level to decline with increased monetary reward. Some studies report observations that fail to support the predictions of rational models, but as reward level is increased, the data shift toward these predictions. Many of these latter studies have the common characteristic that the predictions of rational theory represent a solution on the boundary of the constraint set. For example, in the binary choice task, the optimal response is to predict the more frequent event 100% of the time. Any decision error in these contexts necessarily yields a central tendency that deviates from the rational prediction. Before such cases can be judged to have falsified the theory, it is necessary to establish that increased payoffs fail to move the observations closer to the predicted boundary maxima.

Many of these results are consistent with an effort or labor theory of decision making. According to this theory, better decisions – decisions closer to the optimum, as computed from the point of view of the experimenter/theorist – require increased cognitive and response effort, which is disutilitarian. From the point of view of the decision maker, the problem is to achieve a balance between the benefits of better decision and the effort cost of decision. The experimenter/theorist predicts an optimal decision, which is a special case of the decision that is optimal from the perspective of the subject. Because increasing the reward level causes an increase in effort, the new model predicts that subject decisions will move closer to the theorist's optimum and result in a reduction in the variance of decision error. But this predicted shift toward optimality is qualified if effort is already constrained by the maximum that can be supplied, which would be the case for very complex decision problems. An example of the latter may be in the task studied by Herrnstein et al. (1991).

CHAPTER 4

Fairness: Effect on Temporary and Equilibrium Prices in Posted-Offer Markets

Robert Franciosi, Praveen Kujal, Roland Michelitsch, Vernon L. Smith, and Gang Deng

I.   The Problem

A.   Background

Survey studies of attitudes toward pricing in retail markets (Kahneman et al., 1986, hereafter KKT; 1987) have reported that respondents do not consider it fair for a firm to increase prices and profits when there is a short-run change in the economic environment that is not justified by a cost increase. For example, the following hypothetical circumstances are posed (KKT, p. 201): "Question 1. A hardware store has been selling snow shovels for $15. The morning after a large snowstorm the store raises the price to $20. Please rate this action as: Completely Fair ——— Acceptable ——— Unfair ——— Very Unfair ———." Eighty-two percent of respondents rate this action as unfair or very unfair. What is fairness? This question is not addressed by KKT. In the light of our data, and related literature, we return to the issue of interpreting fairness in Section V.

Okun (1981, p. 170) had earlier argued that fairness considerations explain why firms operate with backlogs in periods of shortages (e.g., automobiles) and why sports tickets are often not priced to clear the market. Okun and others have argued that such instances of fair behavior by firms constitute actions which are in their long-run profit-maximizing interest: the social rules of fairness define the terms of an implicit contract that is enforced by virtue of punishment of unfair price behavior.[1] But KKT (p. 201) argue that in many situations people report

---

[1] Our investigation of the pricing of basketball tickets at the University of Arizona is consistent with a rational implicit contract interpretation. Historical holders of season tickets who renew each year have an entitlement to continue renewal. They pay $262 per ticket plus a required "contribution" (tax deductible) of $100 to the Wildcat Club. New tickets (not many become available each year through release; a recent auction of entitlements for two tickets brought $13,500 in a bankruptcy settlement) are priced under several options designed to clear that market. Two of them are: (1) buy each year a loge season ticket for football for $1,400–$1,800 and get the right to a basketball ticket for $362 (including the contribution) and (2) buy an entitlement with a $5,000 contribution to the

61

that they would follow fair policies in the absence of enforcement through punishment. Thus people report that they would leave restaurant tips (about 15%) even in cities they did not expect to visit again.[2] Respondents also report that they expect automobile repairmen to treat tourists and regular customers alike in spite of the differing possibilities for long-term punishment strategies (KKT, pp. 212–13).

These considerations lead to the proposition that markets in which a firm makes pricing decisions that affect customers (e.g., posted prices in retail markets) will fail to clear if excess demand is not justified by increases in supplier costs (KKT, p. 213). This is because of the principle of dual entitlements, under which customers have a right to the terms of a reference transaction, while the firm has a right to its reference profit (Zajac, 1985, pp. 139–41). Recent posted prices can serve to define the reference transaction (KKT, pp. 201–12). But people do adapt: "Psychological studies of adaption suggest that any stable state of affairs tends to become accepted eventually, at least in the sense that alternatives to it no longer come to mind. Terms of exchange that are initially seen as unfair may in time acquire the status of a reference transaction . . . they adapt their views of fairness to the norms of actual behavior" (KKT, p. 203). These considerations imply that the short-run price response to excess demand will be sluggish in markets in which a price increase is not justified by an increase in unit supply cost; if the excess demand persists, only new higher prices are sustainable, and people will adapt by redefining the reference transaction. The equilibrium may still be that which is predicted from economic theory. In this chapter we assume that

---

Wildcat Club. Why is the $100 contribution not included in the official price of the ticket? Very simply, it gives the athletic department more budget flexibility under state spending rules. The athletic department does not price all tickets to clear the market to avoid a feared firestorm of protest from the legislature, the alumni and the community who bought their tickets years earlier in loyal support of a less popular basketball program. Many of these individuals may feel that they have earned their implicit entitlement contract, and many contribute additional money to university programs.

[2] Although tipping in such situations has been described by KKT as due to a fairness ethic, it is important to realize that it is based on a widely accepted expectation that tipping is an exchange – a payment for service. The IRS considers tips an exchange and taxes the employer's estimate as income. The powerful expectations that drive tipping are clear in the following incident involving one of us (Smith): Ten people go to a Mexican restaurant at the end of a conference day. No one leaves a tip in the belief that with groups of six or more an automatic 15% gratuity is included. The waiter follows the payer into the parking lot and demands to know what was wrong with the service? It was fine. But you left no tip. Wasn't a tip included in the bill? No. Forthwith he is given $20. Upon reporting this experience in various seminar presentations, other such incidents of outraged waiters (blocking the exit door) and taxi drivers (hurling coins at a fleeing customer) are brought forward. Clearly, there is a strong mutual expectation that service requires a reward, which is recognized and taxed by the state. This is so whether or not an exchange will be repeated.

the hypothesized short-run failure of markets to clear depends upon buyers knowing that increased profits would result from the higher prices. In the absence of such information, buyers do not have a common reason for resisting the actions.

B.   Question 1 Responses: Market Effects

In order to better understand the responses to KKT's Question 1, we conducted two variations on it. First, we noticed two features of their question that seemed unusual. It used the words *fair* and *acceptable* within the same instrument, precluding the possibility that a situation might be judged unfair but nonetheless acceptable. Also, questionnaires normally allow respondents to register "No Opinion." Consequently, in our first variation of Question 1, everything was the same as in KKT except that we removed the word *fair*, asking our respondents to please rate the store's action as: Completely Acceptable (29.7%) Acceptable (32.4%) No Opinion (5.4%) Unacceptable (27.0%) Completely Unacceptable (5.4%). For $N = 37$, our results are shown in the parentheses. We get 32.4% who rate the action as Unacceptable or Completely Unacceptable. We use these results as a subject control for introducing a treatment change. Using a different sample of respondents from the same pool of undergraduates, our second variation of Question 1 posed the same situation, but added the sentence: "The store does this to prevent a stockout for its regular customers since another store has raised its price to $20." Changes in the economic environment have implied consequences in the behavior of markets; our purpose was to express the sort of market consequence that might reasonably follow such a change.[3] The issue here is whether the store's response to market competition could serve to justify its action (in addition to KKT's postulate that people will accept a price increase, relative to a reference transaction, if it arises from an excess demand that is cost-justified). Our results for $N = 41$ are: Completely Acceptable (34.1%) Acceptable (39.0%) No Opinion (7.3%) Unacceptable (19.5%) Completely Unacceptable (0%).

---

[3] When markets fail to clear at below-equilibrium prices, both buyers and sellers are hurt by the resulting stock-out approach to rationing. Some buyers, who would be submarginal at the equilibrium, can profitably buy at the disequilibrium price; this displaces intramarginal buyers for whom purchase is more profitable, with consequent losses of buyer profit (surplus). In particular, if we postulate KKT's local stores, one unfair consequence of not raising price is that some units are sold to crossover buyers who thereby displace sales to neighborhood customers. If the store refuses to sell to strangers (besides being actionable in court), it is vulnerable to the charge that this is unfair to all who drive out of their way to buy at the lowest cost. Given a change from the reference baseline, all alternative policies are unfair to some subset of buyers.

With a market justification the percentage in the last two categories falls from 32.4 to 19.5%.

These data suggest the need for reward-motivated experiments, in a posted-offer market setting, to further explore the KKT hypothesis that subjects might trade off self-interested behavior against concerns of fairness.

C.   *Previous Experiments*

Kachelmeier et al. (1991a; hereafter KLS) report laboratory experiments designed to measure the effect of the foregoing fairness considerations on actual price responses and convergence behavior in experimental markets using *buyer* posted bid pricing. In their environment, five buyers and five sellers trade for ten periods under stationary value/cost conditions. Buyers independently post bid prices, and sellers respond with individual sales by accepting bids. Then a change is introduced for a new ten-period sequence. In the first sequence, sellers are subject to a 50% profit tax such that, at the competitive equilibrium price and volume, the sellers' share of total surplus is exactly 50%. But in the second sequence of ten trading periods, the sellers' 50% profit tax is replaced by a 20% sales tax on each seller's revenue. The effect of this sales tax is to raise the previous marginal cost supply schedule, $MC(q)$, to $1.25 \, MC(q)$. This increases the competitive equilibrium price, lowers the volume, and increases the sellers' share of total profit. Each of three different information treatment conditions is replicated three times with different subjects (90 subjects total): (1) seller marginal cost information is disclosed to all subjects; (2) the sellers' share of aggregate profit (surplus) is disclosed to all subjects; (3) no marginal cost or profit information is disclosed. With profit disclosure, buyers are fully informed that, compared with the previous ten reference transactions periods, the change to a sales tax regime has shifted net surplus from buyers to sellers. With marginal cost disclosure, buyers are informed that prices must increase to cover the new seller costs. Consequently, profit disclosure focuses on the KKT principle that sellers are only entitled to their previous reference profit (it is unfair for sellers to profit from the tax), whereas marginal cost disclosure reinforces the principle that any price increase is justified by a unit cost increase. The treatment with no marginal cost or profit disclosure provides experimental control. The prediction hypotheses, based on KKT, are as follows (KLS, p. 697).

H1:   The initial price response to a change from an income to a sales tax will be greater under marginal cost disclosure than under profit disclosure.

Convergence over time relative to the baseline control experiments will be

H2: faster under marginal cost disclosure;
H3: slower under profit disclosure.

KLS report statistical support for all three hypotheses.[4] Our results for posted-offer pricing are completely consistent with those of KLS, except for some minor deviations in the efficiency results, which we discuss in Section III.

D.   Extension: Posted Bid Versus Posted Offer

The institution used by KLS is posted-bid pricing. "The trading rule allowed only buyers to propose prices" (KLS, p. 700). This was defended on the grounds of "intentional experimental artificiality." That is, since fairness directly concerns the perceptions and response of buyers, this device enables direct measurement of that response in terms of posted buying prices.

On this note, we propose to examine the robustness of the KLS results using the familiar retail institution in which sellers post prices to buyers. This institution is quite clearly the one that KKT have in mind in their consumer market examples (although they do discuss labor markets in which wage bids are made by firms). To wit: "For example, 68 percent of respondents said they would switch their patronage to a drugstore five minutes further away if the one closer to them raised its prices when a competitor was temporarily forced to close. . . . Retailers will have a sub-stantial incentive to behave fairly if a large number of customers are pre-pared . . . to avoid doing business with an unfair firm" (KKT, p. 212). Thus, customers will withhold demand from an unfair firm, and, antici-pating this, the firm will have an incentive to price fairly. In the follow-ing experiments in which sellers independently post prices to the buyers, we can study not only buyer demand withholding behavior but also the sellers' indirect attitudes toward fairness as expressed in the prices they post to buyers. Of course, if sellers post lower prices under profit disclo-sure, we cannot know whether it is because they are being fair or because they are simply responding rationally to avoid expected punishment by buyers.

We employ the Novanet (Plato) posted-offer mechanism described by Ketcham et al. (1984), with the modification that, in the following

---

[4] In a related study, Kachelmeier et al. (1991b) examine fairness using the oral double-auction trading rules with a different experimental design and perspective. The basic result, however, a tendency for the fairness effect to dissipate over time, is the same. In this chapter, we use the design reported in KLS (1991a).

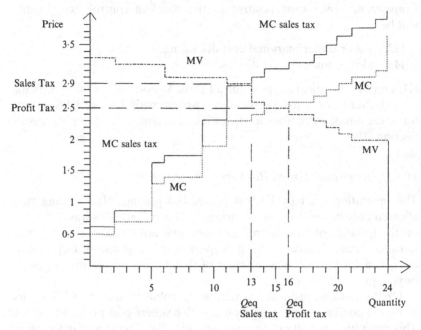

FIGURE 4.1. Supply and demand environment. ——, MC sales tax; ......, MC profit tax; –·–·–, marginal values.

experiments, sellers could *not* see each other's prices after independently posting them in each period. This has the effect of reducing the ability of sellers to undercut each other's prices (i.e., by this procedure one expects to observe a purer and perhaps more persistent individual fairness response, thereby giving the KKT theory its best shot in the experimental market context). This is not to deny that markets may be more competitive when sellers observe each other's prices. Rather, our point is that the reported experiments control for this, and, if the effect of fairness disappears, then under this interpretation we have a stronger result. The effect of publicizing price information can always be studied using the experiments herein as a comparison control.

II.   Experimental Design

Essentially, we used the same experimental design as in KLS. The information disclosure treatments are identical to those described in Section I. Our supply and demand environment, also identical with that of KLS, is shown in Figure 4.1 for both the profit tax regime in part one of the experiment, and the sales tax regime in part two. Our design and procedures differed from KLS only in the following respects.

1. We used six buyers and six sellers, rather than five each. (This was to accommodate a second independent follow-on experiment that required 12 subjects.)

2. Each of the three treatment conditions, parts one and two, were replicated four times instead of three times (144 subjects total).

3. Two control experiments were run for 12 price/purchase periods in part one; the others were run for 10 periods. Two profit disclosure experiments were run for 20 periods in part two; the others were run for 10 periods. The two longer profit disclosure experiments allowed us to determine if any equilibrating tendencies continued after the first 10 periods.

4. Between parts one and two of their experiments, KLS scheduled a break allowing buyers and sellers to be separated (ostensibly to pay them privately) and given the required separate instructions for the part two, sales tax (no disclosure), regime. We did not do this but rather elected to simply pass out different instruction forms to buyers and to sellers in the control experiment; since everyone received paper, this disguised the different treatment of sellers. The instructions to buyers simply informed them that their redemption values in part two were the same as in part one, whereas sellers were told that starting in the next period they would pay a sales tax rather than a profits tax. Table 4.1 contains a summary of all handouts for the different information treatments which can be compared with the KLS procedures (pp. 691–703, 715–16).[5] Subjects earned nontrivial amounts of money. Payoffs for the experiments, which lasted usually between 2 and $2^{1}/_{2}$ hours, ranged from $8.75 to $62.50, averaging about $26 ($3,700 total). These payoffs substantially exceeded our subjects' usual opportunity costs. For a survey of papers that have evaluated the importance of monetary rewards, see Smith and Walker (1993b).

III. Hypotheses and Experimental Results

H1. In period 1, part two, the first period of trading under the sales tax regime, the KKT fairness argument will yield prices ordered as follows:

---

[5] All forms and supplemental instructional handouts are available by writing to the authors (Smith).

Table 4.1. *Handouts for fairness experiments*

	Control experiment		Marginal cost disclosure[a]		Profit disclosure	
	B	S	B	S	B	S
First part of experiment						
How a buyer calculates profit	A1	A1	A1	A1	A1	A1
How a seller calculates profit	A2	A2	A2	A2	A2	A2
Explanation and graph of profit tax					A3	A3
Form: expected price, actual price, sellers' share of profits					4	4
Second part of experiment						
Notice: nothing changed[b]	B1					
Notice: new instructions		B2				
MC disclosure			B3	B3		
Explanation and graph of sales tax					B4	B4
Form: expected price, actual price, sellers' share of profits					4	4

B, buyers; S, sellers.
[a] Same as control experiment (no disclosure) in first part of experiment.
[b] Buyers were informed that their values are the same as in part one.

> Prices (marginal cost disclosure) > Prices (no disclosure) > Prices (profit disclosure)

H2.   By period 10, part two, the prices under the various treatment conditions will be indistinguishable.

H3.   Under the profit disclosure treatment, the two experiments that continue for 20 periods in part two will show convergence to the competitive equilibrium.

The weighted mean contract price (each posted price is weighted by volume) for the four experiments in each information condition is shown plotted across all periods in both parts of the experiments in Figure 4.2. In part two, there is initially (period one) a clear separation of mean observed prices in accordance with H1. Under marginal cost, disclosure prices jump immediately to the new equilibrium, whereas under profit disclosure they do not change from their previous "reference transaction" level. By period 10, the mean price under all three information conditions has converged to near the new competitive equilibrium price ($2.90). Finally, the two experiments that were extended for 20 periods

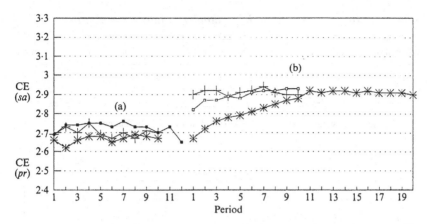

FIGURE 4.2. Mean contract prices: profit tax and sales tax. (a) ■, PRC; +, PRM; *, PRP; (b) □, SAC; +, SAM; *, SAP. The experiments have two stages. With (i) profit tax (*pr*); (ii) sales tax (*sa*). (*c*), control; (*m*), MC; (*p*), profit disclosure.

in part two stabilize at slightly above the competitive equilibrium price in periods 11–20.

We test H1 and H2 using the nonparametric Jonckeere test that the samples (mean contract prices), of size $m_i(= 4)$, are from an a priori ordering of $n(= 3)$ distributions against the null alternative that the samples come from the same distribution. The Jonckeere test is a generalization of the one-tailed Wilcoxon test. For H1, we reject the null hypothesis with a test statistic $J_1(3, 4) = 2.34$ ($p = .01$). For H2, we are unable to reject the null hypothesis, $J_2(3, 4) = -0.439$ ($p = .33$).

In the profit tax regime (part one, periods 1–12, Figure 4.2), although prices in all treatment conditions hover above the competitive equilibrium, prices are lowest under profit disclosure. The three series come together, however, by period ten. Consequently, even in the baseline series, with no reference transaction, initially we observe lower prices under profit disclosure. Profit disclosure blunts the profit-seeking behavior of sellers relative to the other experiments. But the effect of profit disclosure is even more striking under the sales tax regime, given the previous reference transactions in the baseline. The tendency of the "profit disclosure" price path to be below that of the "marginal cost" and "no disclosure" treatments is evident, but the control and marginal cost disclosure price paths are indistinguishable after the first three periods in part two.

In Table 4.2, we report the frequency with which demand is withheld

Table 4.2. *Buyer withholding by treatment in fairness experiments*

Withholding	Control	MC disclosure	Profit disclosure	Sum
Profit tax	—	1	4	5
Sales tax	2	2	23[a]	27

[a] 22 of these cases were in experiment SA4P and involved three buyers.

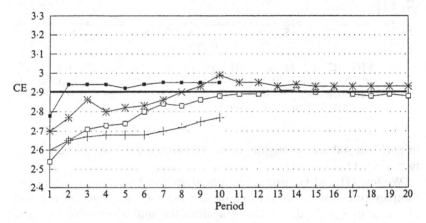

FIGURE 4.3. Mean posted prices: sales tax, profit disclosure. ■, SA1P; +, SA2P; *, SA3P; □, SA4P.

(underrevealed) by buyers. This frequency is determined by counting the number of instances in which each buyer fails to buy at a price equal to or below his/her redemption value. Although the incidence of withholding, in the profit disclosure treatment, is far greater in the sales tax regime (23) than in the profit tax regime (4), we saw 22 cases in one experiment! Furthermore, that experiment yielded mean prices below that of two other experiments. This observed withholding was an uncontrolled "treatment" variable. It is important to note that the mean posted prices in that experiment were *not higher* than in the other experiments with sales tax. On the contrary, in all periods they were *lower* than in two other experiments, and in the first period after the tax change they were the lowest of all. For the detailed price path, see Figure 4.3; the experiment in which the withholding occurred is SA4P. It would appear that the tendency of sellers to post lower prices earlier but not later in the sequence of trading periods was the result of either seller fairness behavior or anticipation of strategic buyer withholding, not a response to buyer withholding.

Withholding did not significantly affect efficiencies, mainly because often (though not always) only marginal units were withheld. However, there is one efficiency difference between our experiments and KLS. One of their hypotheses was that "Profit information will lead to lower volume and lower market efficiency than in either the cost-disclosure or no-disclosure markets" (KLS, p. 698), and they reported support for this hypothesis. Our data did not support this hypothesis. In only two periods (6 and 10) was the average efficiency and the trading volume in the profit disclosure experiments the lowest of all treatments. Similarly, we observed lower efficiency and trading volume in the marginal cost disclosure treatment than did KLS. Minor differences are to be expected because the microstructure of the institutions (rules) of trade are different. But overall the results reported by KLS are robust with respect to the change to posted-offer pricing.

IV. Discussion

Economists and econometricians have long allowed that nonmonetary and noneconomic factors influence behavior, although the standard rational model has always been more prominent. The exceptions are implicit in concepts of external economies in consumption. Recent work (e.g., KKT) has shown how survey evidence can be used to study systematically, and categorize, a wide variety of behaviors that may deviate from the narrow interpretation of rational self-interested models of equilibrium behavior.

In this chapter, we studied the effect of alternative information disclosures on the prices posted by sellers subsequent to an exogenous increase in seller marginal costs (a sales tax). If, as argued by KKT, buyers are more receptive to price increases that appear to be cost justified than to price increases that increase profits above reference transaction levels, then, recognizing this, sellers will post lower prices under profit disclosure than under marginal cost disclosure. Over time, however, this discrepancy need not persist because, as KKT argue, actual (equilibrium) behavior may allow the establishment of a new reference transaction that does not violate social norms of fair behavior. Our results support this argument. Consequently, the prediction that equilibrium outcomes will reflect the rational behavior of standard economic models is supported, although the transition path to the new equilibrium is affected by such fairness considerations. This result is particularly strengthened by the fact that sellers could not see each other's prices. Hence, convergence was not helped by a seller seeing that others were raising prices. Our results also support the value of survey data in uncovering potential anomalies, which can then be tested in the context of motivated decisions to see if the findings survive in actual behavior.

According to the *New York Times* (Lohr, 1992), Hurricane Andrew, striking South Florida on August 24, 1992, provided a fine example of how the KKT fairness considerations are needed to modify economic theory. "What happened in the plywood market here after the storm is a classic example of fairness constraints at work. . . . The big companies (Home Depot, Georgia Pacific and Louisiana-Pacific) performed far differently (increasing the price only about half as much as the 'market') than the price-gougers selling ice, water and lumber from the back of pickup trucks at wildly inflated prices in the first week after the hurricane hit. Classic economic theory, of course, defends these . . ." (Lohr, 1992, p. C2). Actually what classical theory does is to explain, not defend, the competitive market operated out of the back of pickup trucks. In a competitive market, those who would attempt to charge low prices would stock out more quickly, and thus are under pressure to raise prices, given the limited supplies; otherwise, arbitrage profits will be collected by third parties. Modern economics, in the form of reputation theory, also explains the actions of the large firms who have much greater control over their market. Their national sources of supply enable them, through transfers, to replenish stocks more quickly, price less aggressively, and build a long-term reputation for not "price gouging" (with free advertising, courtesy of the *New York Times* article) but simultaneously reap supra normal profits (they did raise prices, if only half as much as the competitive fringe). But one does not need a utilitarian fairness ethic to explain the repeated game (versus one-shot) nature of the long-run outlook of large suppliers. Similarly, optimization theory predicts that if buyers believe that they can conserve their resources by complaining about price gouging being unfair, then they will do it. The long-term result (hidden from the average consumer) may actually build the market power of the large firms, reduce competition, and decrease welfare; all in the good name of fairness. Would a rose by another name smell so sweet?

V.   What Is Fairness?

We think that the answer to the question What is fairness? is likely to depend on the particular context in which *fairness* is used. In the context that we study here, the results are not consistent with the idea that fairness considerations belong in the utility function, as an externality in consumption that alters in a sustainable way the equilibrium behavior predicted by the standards own utility maximizing model.[6]

We suggest that fairness in our context is best characterized as affecting agent expectations, not their utility functions. Thus, buyers expecting (feeling that they have a right to) fair treatment believe that price increases resulting from external cost increases should not produce higher profits for sellers. Sellers, accepting this norm of fair treatment, or fearing retaliation, do not attempt initially to "extract" higher profit. These expectations yield no change in prices, initially, but such prices are unsustainable as an equilibrium (i.e., there is excess demand). In the absence of a utility being fair, sellers gradually do what comes naturally: They raise prices and find rewards in higher profits. If sellers received utilitarian value from fairness, they would be satisfied with lower profit by accepting the profit-fairness trade-off. If buyers received utilitarian value from fairness, their final equilibrium demand levels would not be predicted from the model that maximizes their monetary reward. By this interpretation, the expectations of both buyers and sellers as to what is acceptable or fair changes over time. This also explains why fairness dominates the questionnaire responses of subjects. Their answers are based upon their expectations, not on the unanticipated and unanticipatable adjustments that can occur in the dynamics of actual market or experimental market behavior. This is because no one (except the experimenter in a market experiment) can anticipate the new equilibrium and its possible effect on transient expectations of what is fair.[7]

---

[6] To illustrate, suppose that there are two commodities, X and Z, and that the utility function for each buyer has the form, $u(x, z\backslash\pi / \pi_0) = z + ax - (b/2)x^2 - \alpha x[(\pi / \pi_0) - 1]$ with income constraint, $I = z + px$, where p is the price of X in units of Z. Note that, with the parameter $\alpha > 0$, an externality (π/π_0) appears in the utility function, where π_0 is the profit of each seller in a reference (initial) situation, and π is the corresponding profit in a new situation. If buyers each maximize u subject to their income constraint, this leads to the demand equation: $p = a - bx - \alpha[(\pi/\pi_0) - 1]$. If each seller has quadratic increasing total costs, the profit function (y = output) can be written, $\pi = py - (1/2\beta)y^2$, which at a maximum yields the supply function, $y = \beta p$. Initially, let $a = a_0$ and $\pi = \pi_0$. Then $x_0 = y_0$ (demand equals supply) implies $p = p_0 = a_0 - b\beta p_0$ and $p_0 = a_0/(1+ b\beta)$; $\pi_0 = (\beta/2)p_0^2$. Now let demand increase with $a = a_1 > a_0$. Then $x_1 = y_1$ implies the new equilibrium, $p = p_1 = a_1 - b\beta p_1 - a[(\pi_1/\pi_0) - 1]$, with $(\pi_1/\pi_0) = pp_1^2/p_0^2$. Clearly, if $\alpha > 0$, the externality equilibrium, $x_1 = y_1$, is distinct from that which would prevail, where $x_1^* = y_1^*$, based on the absence of the externality ($\alpha = 0$). The price and quantity levels to which our experimental data converge over time correspond to the situation in this example in which ($\alpha = 0$) (i.e., the results in part two of the experiment are predicted from the standard own-maximizing model of utility).

[7] Our expectations interpretation of fairness is consistent with the results of Hoffman et al. (1994) in their ultimatum and dictator game experiments, although here the results are stronger because there are six (not one) bargainers on each side of the market. Also

Also, questionnaire data summarize average, not marginal, opinion, and we know from hundreds of controlled laboratory experiments that competitive outcomes and efficiency are driven by marginal analysis (sometimes called the marginal trader hypothesis). Thus, in markets like the one in Figure 4.1, average MV and average MC are irrelevant to determining the equilibrium, where $MV(Q_e) \geq MC(Q_e)$. The marginal trader hypothesis explains why the Iowa Presidential stock market is a much more accurate predictor of the popular vote than opinion polls, although the participants prove to have, on average, all the standard opinion biases established by political science and sociological studies (Forsythe et al., 1992).

Fehr et al. (1993) provided a different context in which the word *fairness* is associated with deviations from self-interested behavior. First movers (buyers) compete by announcing buying prices (anonymously by telephone through an experimenter) to sellers who can accept but not make counter offers. Sellers then choose a "quality" or effort level for the good they produce; given any accepted price, it is in the sellers' interest to choose low effort but in the buyer–seller joint interest to choose high. Buyers do best individually with a low price, if sellers choose high effort, but the dominant strategy of sellers is to choose low. Cooperative play requires buyers to buy at a high price and to trust sellers to reciprocate with a high effort. In this two-stage market game, the gains from exchange are maximized by cooperative (fair) behavior not by competitive action in the self interest. The market study reported here is the opposite: the gains from exchange are maximized by competition, and reduced by fair behavior (unless their is utilitarian compensation from fairness).

The Fehr et al. (1993) experimental data across pairs and periods shows a statistically and economically significant positive relationship between price and quality. The results are especially interesting since the pairings by the market are not constant through time so that reciprocity is diffuse.

It is not clear, however, in what sense these results are explained by

see Binmore et al. (1992) who reported Nash bargaining experiments in which the median subject optimizes in the long run in accordance with the theory using trial-and-error adjustment processes. "However, the subjects seem to see no contradiction between such optimizing and 'fair' behavior, since the median subject reports as fair pretty much what actually happens towards the end of the games he or she played. These results are consistent with a view that regards behavior as being shaped by social norms in the minds of the subjects, but which sees the social norms themselves being determined by evolutionary considerations of which the subjects are only dimly aware" (Binmore et al., 1992, p. 34). This is consistent with KKT, with the adaptive results in the psychology literature, and with the results reported in this chapter.

a (utilitarian?) fairness ethic as opposed to a mutual expectation/recognition by all parties that individual rewards will deteriorate across time if there is not reciprocity (e.g., better quality for better prices). Parallel results have been reported by Berg et al. (1995) in the single play of a two-stage dictator game run under double blind conditions (see Hoffman et al., 1994: subjects pairings are anonymous with respect to each other and the experimenter who cannot know who made what decision). In Stage I, subjects in room A choose how much of their $10 endowment to send to an anonymous counterpart in room B. Each dollar sent will be tripled (common knowledge) before it reaches the counterpart, who, in Stage II, chooses how much of this tripled amount to pay back to the person in room B. The dominant strategy for subjects in room A is to keep all the money because it is a dominant strategy for any money received in room A to be retained. The average amount sent is $5.16 with an average payback of $4.66. In a second "social norm" treatment, all subjects are given a common history: the outcomes from all plays in the first treatment. The average sent is now $5.36 with a payback of $6.46.

Berg et al. (1995) do not suggest that their results are due to fairness. As they describe it, they are studying trust and reciprocity. Subjects in room A can substantially leverage their endowments by "investment" in amounts sent to room B. But this requires trust and an expectation of reciprocity. They are studying mechanisms of social exchange and how the social norms that support such exchange can emerge from historical experience. These mechanisms allow gains from exchange to be captured in situations where traditional economic analysis would suggest market failure. Such mechanisms are metarational, and materially extend the rational choice paradigm to include the evolution of institutions that promote gains from exchange in situations that are not incentive compatible.

We think the results of our chapter and those of Fehr et al. (1993) and of Berg et al. (1995) contribute to a unified understanding of anomalous behavior usually attributed to fairness. The contexts differ in the three studies, but the anomalous results are not explained satisfactorily by a utilitarian fairness ethic, by expectations that are not sustainable (in our study), or by trust coupled with expectations of reciprocity (in the other two studies). The common outcome across the three studies is for subjects to approach the efficient maximization of the social monetary gains from exchange.

PART II

Bargaining Theory, Behavior, and Evolutionary Psychology

Introduction

Ultimatum and dictator game experiments have exposed major and fundamental weaknesses in the traditional assumptions underlying game theory (Guth et al., 1982). But I and my coauthors believe that these, and other important experiments, have also brought new understanding of human behavior, which may turn out to reflect favorably on game theory through a reinterpretation of key game-theoretic concepts in the light of these new experimental findings. This is potentially significant in setting the research agenda for both game theory and experiments to explore the scope and validity of this perspective. It is still too soon to say anything definitive about its validity. The chapters in this section represent the unfolding of this perspective in our research thinking. That thinking has changed dramatically in the course of our research program, particularly while conducting the research reported in Chapter 5, and in revising that chapter through several drafts, as we continued to do experiments to clarify our understanding of the phenomena. Subsequent papers, reprinted here as Chapters 6–9, reflect the further development of this research program. In this introduction, I will attempt to provide an integrative and summary statement based on this evolving point of departure from traditional game theory and the consequent alternative interpretations of the experimental results.

The primary objective of our ultimatum and dictator game research was to examine the sensitivity of the results to treatments designed to introduce explicit social conditions or contexts, which a priori we predicted would alter subject expectations and hence decisions. The purpose was to see how far we could progress with nonutilitarian interpretations of what had previously been attributed to *fairness* – a term used loosely to label but not actually explain "anomalous" outcomes. The problem with attributing anomalous outcomes to utilitarian causes is that this stops the research conversation because utility is alleged to be a first cause. If utility is indeed the cause, then one needs to ask how to test it, why people have these utilities and not the ones we classically assumed, what function they serve in furthering a person's well-being, and where they come from. But early in our research program, we realized that subjects could be considered to be conditioned or programmed from life experiences for decision making in repeat interactions composed of sequences of different games. Consequently, subjects are hypothesized to fall into reputational types, some of whom develop reputations for being cooperative and/or using punishment strategies to discipline those who are seen as noncooperative. From this perspective, cooperative behavior in "one-shot games," which appears to be contrary to their self interest, takes on a meaning consistent with game theoretic conjectures (i.e., the Folk theorem). Thus, subjects need not perceive a laboratory game as a single-trial decision, a hard core maintained hypothesis by the game theoretic motivated experimenter. From the perspective of repeated game theory, and the concept of reputational types, the observation of cooperative-like behavior does not seem strange. Rather what is needed, perhaps, is to reevaluate the experimenter/theorist's premise that subjects will view such experimental situations as a single-trial game, without a history or a future connected with the subject's reputational self image. Under this interpretation, there could be a divergence between the perspective of the subject and that of the experimenter/ theorist as to what constitutes a single-play game without a history or a future, and what is merely an instance in an ongoing sequence of life's experiences. What may be wrong is the very idea that instances of human decision interaction can be construed as without a history or a future. Also, the core maintained hypothesis that reputation is a phenomenon formed entirely within the confines of the move sequence in a particular repeated game, as distinct from a longer-term development of the individual across games which is then imported into specific games to determine, at minimum, one's initial responses, may be wrong.

The Ultimatum Game

The ultimatum game is a particularly transparent and simple illustration of the implications of the standard assumptions of game theory in which it is postulated that each agent is self-interested and attributes self-interested motives to others with whom they interact strategically. In our version, person A, anonymously matched with person B, makes an offer of X one-dollar bills out of a total of $M \geq X$ one-dollar bills. If person B accepts, he or she receives X, and A receives $(M - X)$; if B rejects the offer, each gets zero. If B is self interested, the minimum positive offer of $1 will be strictly preferred to zero and will be accepted. Person A, being self interested and assuming that B is also, is predicted to offer $1, which is predicted to be accepted by B. As first established by Guth et al. (1982), subject agents A offer substantially more than the minimum unit of account, and, for self-interested reasons, if they do not, agents B may well reject the offer. The research problem has been to determine why this pattern has been observed, what are its limits, and what is the motivation of B in leaving money on the table. Given the expectation of B's behavior, A's behavior is rationalizable.

Results

In the projects of Chapter 5, we began by seeing if we could replicate the ultimatum game results of Forsythe et al. (1994). We did so, but with some variations on their procedures that enabled us to introduce some hypothesized treatment variations for comparison purposes. We thus established that their results were robust with respect to the "minor variations" we introduced to facilitate the treatment comparisons we had in mind. It is now well established in the experimental community that if you want to determine the effect of variations on the treatment used by other experimenters, you cannot credibly do this unless you first show that you can replicate their results before introducing your own treatment changes for comparison. By replicating the previous researchers' results, you eliminate the possibility that the results from your comparison treatment were due to the use of a different experimenter using different subjects. Without completing this step, you *cannot* attribute differences in the observed results to differences in the treatments applied. This methodology is particularly important in game environments that are sensitive to small variations in the procedures.

Having replicated the ultimatum game results of Forsythe et al. (1994), we explored the effect of three treatment changes: (1) formulating the ultimatum game interaction between each subject pair as an *exchange* between a seller who moves first by quoting a price and a buyer who responds by electing to buy or not to buy; (2) awarding the property right of being in the first mover position to subjects who score highest on a general knowledge test, and who thereby "earn" the right to the advantageous first mover position; and (3) combining (1) and (2). Following earlier precedents, in Forsythe et al. (1994) and our replication of their results, subject role entitlements were awarded at random, not earned, but since lotteries are a common means of fair division in our society, this can be interpreted as defining the task as one of being fair. Also, subjects were told that "you and your anonymous counterpart have been provisionally allocated $10"; therefore, the property right to the money was ambiguous. Finally, they were told that their task was to "divide" the $10, a term that can suggest sharing, and not merely allocating. [Thus, among Webster's definitions of *divide* are included (a) to deal out in parts, apportion, share; (b) to share something with others; (c) in math, to separate into equal parts by the process of division.]

Our hypothesis was that these treatment alterations would yield less generous offers by first movers than we observed in the baseline replication of Forsythe et al. (1994), and the hypothesis was confirmed by the data. Furthermore, although first movers offered less, second movers did not increase their frequency of rejecting these offers. Hence, first movers expected to be able to retain more of the pie, and second movers behaved as if they found this to be acceptable. As we saw it at the time, subjects come to the experimental laboratory from a social context, a world of repeat interaction in which single transactions are not isolated but are part of an ongoing sequence. This social context allows expectations that determine decision behavior to form. Thus, in an exchange in which sellers post prices and buyers decide whether or not to buy, the cultural right of the seller to post prices is not questioned. Similarly, explicit earned rights are considered legitimate, as a form of investment, and it is fitting for the rights to be exercised to the advantage of the rights holder. We interpreted treatments (1)–(3) as triggering responses appropriate to the implied social contexts to which subjects have become well adapted. As we see from the results, those responses are more self interested than when the *same underlying game* is imbedded in an abstract interaction in which subjects are randomly assigned to the position of first or second mover, have an ambiguous right to the money, and are asked to "divide" it. Our interpretation was that the treatments legitimatized self-interested behavior. In the absence of explicit socially recognized roles, subjects revert to the reputational types they play out in day-to-day polite, unconscious, personal interactions with other like persons. In such interactions, a common type is one who, without information to the contrary, is prepared to initiate cooperation, expects cooperation, and may incur costs to punish perceived noncooperative acts (see the following discussion entitled "Cooperation in Extensive Form Bargaining").

Experiments reported by Roth et al. (1991) provide insightful evidence for the hypothesis that subjects see "repeat single play" interaction as part of a repeated game. In these experiments, subjects are matched repeatedly, but with distinct pairing so that each subject never encounters the same counterpart twice. Consequently, the second mover results show a substantial increase in rejections relative to single play, yet the condition of repeat play with distinct partners is assumed in game theory to yield single-play conditions, while allowing subjects to obtain experience. The reported rejection rates, which are in the range 10–44%

(even 10% is high in a single-play game), are consistent with subject concern for disciplining noncooperative behavior – punishing cheaters – and to reputation-maintenance across repeat interactions. The theorist/experimenter has traditionally assumed, qua *hypothesized*, without evidence, that subjects will perceive the interactions as independent.

In the projects of Chapter 7, we replicated the random entitlement and exchange/earned-entitlement treatments in ultimatum games with a tenfold increase in stakes. Essentially, under both entitlement treatments, there is no significant reduction in offers when the stakes are increased. There is, however, a discernible (if statistically insignificant) reduction in offers under the exchange/earned-entitlement condition, and this significantly increases the rejection rate. This is the first treatment condition we have encountered that creates a significant divergence in expectations between first and second movers (i.e., the subjects fail to read each other well).

The Dictator Game

The ultimatum game becomes a dictator game by removing the second mover's right to reject the offer, and thus eliminates the strategic feature of the ultimatum game. Forsythe et al. (1994) used this game to see if the ultimatum game results could be explained entirely in terms of fairness in the sense of other-regarding utility. They found that dictator offers were significantly (both statistically and economically) smaller than ultimatum offers, although dictators were more generous than suggested by game theory.

Results

We found (Chapter 5) that dictator offers could be reduced still more by combining the exchange and contest entitlement treatments, as mentioned earlier. We also ran dictator games double blind using a transparent procedure guaranteeing that the experimenter and others could not know individual subject decisions. By thus removing the task from all social context – a possible history and a future – we observed, as hypothesized, by far the least generous dictator offers, with over two-thirds of the subjects giving nothing. Subsequently, Eckel and Grossman (1996b) replicated our double blind procedure and results; then they did a treatment variation in which the recipient was the American Red Cross in place of another like individual. Dictator offers now increased significantly, showing that the characteristics of the recipient are important even after double blind controls for others knowing the decisions. Burnham (private communication) has also replicated our double blind procedures and results.

Our procedures removed as many elements as we could think of that might connect subjects unconsciously with the social world of repeat interactions, leading to a large effect on dictator offers. We next asked if we could accomplish a step-by-step shift in the data back to normal levels by removing these elements one at a time. The resulting ordered sample distributions are reported in Chapter 6, on social distance and other-regarding behavior.

Our interpretation of these data rested on a model in which subjects are conjectured to have been conditioned culturally to expect interpersonal decisions to have reputationally future consequences in the form of reciprocity. The model [see Chapter 6, Equations (1) and (2) and footnote 6] postulated a self-interested utility to the dictator which depends not only on the monetary reward, $M - X$, but a hypothesized subjective future value, Y_1, supported by the first mover's social reputation as a cooperative other-regarding person. Instructional treatments that vary social distance are then assumed to have an impact on the dictators' expectations, $F(Y_1|X,M,I)$, of future value Y_1, given X, M, and the instructions, I.

Cooperation in Extensive Form Bargaining

The extensive form games studied in Chapter 8 allow one player to choose between two alternative branches of a decision tree – one containing a symmetric subgame perfect equilibrium outcome and the other containing a symmetric joint maximum outcome – but from which the other player can defect to his advantage provided the player signaling cooperation does not, at a cost to herself, punish the defection. Although in a single play of the game self-interested bargainers are predicted to go to the subgame perfect outcome, 43% play the cooperative side of the tree. This cooperative tendency increases when repeated with distinct partners, and is little changed in a pure-trust, single-play version of the game in which defection cannot be punished. These results are consistent with the hypothesis that there exists a sizable cohort of people who are programmed by their past experience and biological endowments to follow strategies in which cooperation is supported by reciprocity. Although failures to reciprocate are sometimes punished if that option is available, when it is not, trust and trustworthiness alone are effective in achieving high rates of cooperation among anonymously paired like individuals.

Specialized Versus General Logic-Driven Models of Mind

A referee of the paper reprinted here as Chapter 6 called our attention to the fact that our implicit assumption, that the socialization conditions of the model were culturally derived, was subject to another interpretation by evolutionary psychologists (Cosmides and Tooby, 1992). This lead-in to the evolutionary psychology literature has had the effect of substantially broadening our working hypothesis as to the origins of reciprocity. This new dimension to our thinking is reflected in Chapters 8 and 9. Chapter 9 surveys some of the work of evolutionary psychologists, introducing the concept of specialized mental models, and develops its relation to reciprocity explanations of experimental decision behavior.

The standard mental model of decision that has characterized mainstream thinking in economics and other social sciences is the hypothesis that the mind is a culturally developed general purpose, content independent, information processing organ that solves decision problems by the application of logical principles and algorithms to the data of such problems. Human decision making is thus a consciously cognitive, calculating, logical process. The evolutionary psychology hypothesis is that human decision relies on specialized domain-specific mental modules and algorithms "designed" by biological selection to solve discrete adaptive problems. Examples would be (1) "cheater detection" mechanisms identifying, for punishment, individuals who violate implicit social exchange contracts (Cosmides, 1985), and (2) algorithms for language inflection rules, such as adding -ed to form the past tense of regular verbs, or adding -s to form the plural of regular nouns in English. The idea is that humans are born not with such specific capabilities but with blueprints or circuitry awaiting to be initialized for such capabilities – circuits whose switches are set by developmental experiences. So there is plenty of room for nurture, given the genetic endowment of nature. Nature versus nurture is an inappropriate dichotomy. The decisions that result from these mental modules may be strongly nonconscious, so that individuals are not explicitly aware of how or why they "know" to decide as they do. Almost all of your natural (spoken) language ability you learned without explicit instruction as a preschooler, and without remembering how or when you learned it.

The standard economic (and social science) model of the mind is parsimonious – all problems with the same underlying logical structure have the same technical–methodological formulation and solution. Three inadequacies of this model remain unaddressed: (1) The standard model does not explain why economics is so hard to teach, apply, and understand – even experts backslide into error; (2) it does not explain where culture – the source of the standard model – comes from; and (3) it is difficult for it to account for nonconscious and intuitive decision. The evolutionary psychology model of mind is a natural development paralleling the accelerating trend of recent biological research in which many human characteristics, once thought to be exclusively of cultural origin, have been found to be phenotypes of genetic transmission. But the model is too new to have been subjected to many tests like those performed by Cosmides (1985) and Cosmides and Tooby (1991). Some have argued that these latter results can be explained by other "simpler" or less "speculative" principles (Kahneman and Tversky, 1996). But, of course, we know that there are always multiple alternative explanations of anything. This is because theories imply observations, but never the reverse; also what is seen as "speculative" by one person simply fits into an expected pattern as seen by another.

Much of the case for the working hypothesis that decision making derives from specialized mental modules is based on the success that this model of mind has had in understanding vision (Marr, 1982) and language (Pinker, 1994) development. Brain damage in the form of Broca's aphasia, and inherited disorders of the mind such as Williams' Syndrome (Pinker, 1994, pp. 46–53) provide numerous cases in which people are language impaired but have normal intelligence or vice versa. Similarly, damage to the amygdala has been shown to impair the ability to interpret facial expressions and detect eye direction – a crucial element in social interaction (Adolphs et al., 1994). Autism, whose incidence in families and twins suggests an inherited component, impairs a person's awareness of mental phenomena in others (Baron-Cohen, 1995). Thus an autistic person has a problem inferring from experience that another person can hold a false belief. Obviously, the human ability to read minds is essential to the sort of strategic interaction that is at the core of game theory. The evidence suggests that this ability is the result of discrete modules in the brain that may be independent of other abilities. Thus, autistic people may well register high intelligence as measured by IQ.

If specific mental modules are at work in interactive decision making as in the situations defined by experimental games, what are these modules and what are their function? Here are some conjectured examples that might help inform hypothesis formulation.

A Friend-or-Foe Detector

If friend-or-foe (FOF) detection is an identifiable mental mechanism, it is surely one of our highest priority screens. Noncooperative game theory is about foes who identify each other as foes in which each assumes that the other will maximize own interest at the expense of the other. But when people are matched anonymously, whether single or double blind, they generally know that they are matched with another like person. When they are not, as in the Eckel and Grossman (1996b) experiments where the recipient is the American Red Cross, it makes a difference. One of the many characteristics of this organization surely must be that it is perceived positively as a helping friend. Sensitivity to in-group versus out-group effects – long documented by social psychologists and also studied by economists (see particularly Ball and Eckel, 1995, and Ball et al., 1996) – is why careful bargaining experiment instructions normally refer to the bargainers neutrally as "counterparts" (or some such designation) rather than "partners" or "opponents" because the latter terms run the risk of triggering postures appropriate for friends or for foes.

Of course, depending upon the purpose of the experiments, one might *want* to trigger these modes by introducing them as treatments. Burnham et al. (1998) reported experiments in which the trust game (game 2) discussed in Chapter 8 uses instructions in which the bargainers are referred to as "partners" in one treatment and "opponents" in the comparison treatment. The results supported the prediction that the use of "partners" will increase trust (offers to cooperate) and trustworthiness (nondefection) relative to the use of "opponents."

A Cheater Detection and Punishment Mechanism

There is now an extensive literature, beginning with Cosmides (1985) showing that people have difficulty selecting among alternatives that falsify "if P, then Q" statements, unless it is in the context of detecting cheating on social contracts, or exchanges. On these, they do very much better.

Trust and Trustworthy Detection

Friend-or-foe detection may provide only gross screening: "I am matched with another undergraduate, but is he or she trustworthy? I will try a test signal to get an indication." If the counterpart is identified, say its the American Red Cross, then I know the recipient is trustworthy. The FOF detection is a prescreen for more in-depth evaluation, which, in extreme cases, forces the mammal into a fight-or-flight mode.

Mind Reading

Baron-Cohen (1995) has offered a description of the specific mechanisms, or mental modules (not necessarily exhaustive), which together produce a mind-reading capability. One is an Intentionality Detector, which is activated by inputs that identify something as an agent with a goal. For example, the agent wants to eat. The second is an Eye Direction Detector, which is aware of the presence of other eyes, computes whether the eyes are directed toward or away from the entity, and infers that the other organism sees what the eyes are directed toward. For example, the agent sees me, or is looking at the tree. The third is a Shared Attention Mechanism, which is concerned with triadic representations rather than dyadic relations, which is the focus of the first two. For example, Mary and I both see the on-rushing car. Finally, there is a Theory of Mind Mechanism, which is a system for inferring mental states from an organism's behavior or expressions. This is the mechanism that allows you to grasp naturally and intuitively the notion that another person can entertain a false belief because you experience it in your own mind.

Can a person, in the spirit of mind modularity, have some of these mechanisms but not all? Apparently, the answer is yes. Autistic children are well aware of others having wants (ice cream) or desires (to go swimming). They can also tell whether a person in a photograph is looking at them or away from them, whereas people with damaged amygdalas cannot do this. Most (but not all) autistic children appear to have no active Shared-Attention Mechanism, and only a minority demonstrate from experiments that they have a Theory of Mind Mechanism.

Clearly, mind reading is an essential part of strategic interaction in human social interaction in life and in games. An effective decision maker must be able to use information about other people's types to infer their behavior and condition one's own behavior accordingly.

These considerations, for example, imply that an autistic person's behavior in an ultimatum or other such interactive game would not be influenced by information about his counterpart's type. Treatments intended to manipulate subject expectations of others would not be effective. There is the further implication, however, that autistic people can learn through experience what to expect of others and, based on their acquired memory of this experience, increase their performance, but only in specific circumstances. They fail to develop the intuitions, based on unconscious awareness of mental phenomenon in others, that enable them to readily size up unfamiliar situations.

Autism, of course, is a polar case of an incapacity to effectively mind-read from actions, expressions, or situations. In normal humans, we would expect there to be a frequency distribution of such intuitive mind-reading capacities, which may help to explain the bifurcation of subject samples between noncooperative and cooperative reciprocation. This proposition has testable implications.

One implication is that if payoff information is private in a two-person extensive form game, this controls for mind reading by making it impossible for each player to infer what might be the intentions of the other. Each player must necessarily focus only on his or her own payoff. In the extensive form games discussed in Chapter 8, the prediction is greater support for the subgame perfect noncooperative equilibrium under private rather than complete payoff information. The comparison experiments reported in McCabe, Rassenti, and Smith (1998) strongly support this prediction.

Another testable implication is that there should be more cooperation in these extensive form games (Chapters 8 and 9) than when they are played in their corresponding "equivalent" normal (strategic) form. This prediction is also supported by the comparisons reported in McCabe, Smith, and LePore (1998).

CHAPTER 5

Preferences, Property Rights, and Anonymity in Bargaining Games

Elizabeth Hoffman, Kevin A. McCabe,
Keith Shachat, and Vernon L. Smith

The ethnologist, Diamond Jenness, who was asked by the Canadian government in 1913 to join Stefansson's Arctic expedition to study Eskimos for three years, records the following in his diary:

> Not all the cabins that stood empty had been vacated until the next winter . . . and from two poles dangled a score or more fox skins. It was the latter that particularly caught my attention. Here were what amounted to a year's earnings exposed wide open to the heavens, where the first passerby could appropriate them at his leisure. In reality, of course, they were as safe as in Brower's storeroom, for with a population so small, everyone always knew who was living where, and a pilferer had little or no chance of escaping detection. . . . honesty comes much more easily in a tiny community than it does in a great city, where misconduct always hopes that the multitude of alien tracks will cover up its own footprints. (Jenness, 1957, pp. 128–9)

Noncooperative, nonrepeated game theory is about strangers with no shared history, like the residents of Jenness' "great city." They meet, interact strategically in their individual self interests according to well-specified rules and payoffs, and never meet again. These stark conditions are necessary to ensure that the noncooperative, nonrepeated game theoretic prediction for the interaction is not part of a sequence with a past and a future. Thus, repeated games are analyzed differently because now strangers can potentially cooperate by developing their own history and future. Moreover, the outcomes in two-person bargaining games are thought to be particularly sensitive to procedures affecting subject anonymity and the context of bargaining, since it is easy to identify individual actions when there are only two players. Thus, experimental studies of two-person bargaining games regularly take elaborate precautions to guarantee between-subject anonymity. In spite of these precautions, the results of bargaining experiments are generally not consistent with the game theoretic predictions, and they do not always replicate across subject populations, particularly in the absence of monetary rewards (Forsythe et al., 1994).

For example, recent experimental research on ultimatum games has found that first movers in such games tend to offer more to their counterparts than noncooperative game theory would predict. In fact, the modal offer is half the surplus to be divided, although noncooperative game theory would suggest an offer by the first mover of the minimum positive amount feasible. In this chapter, we report the results of nonrepeated ultimatum and dictator game experiments designed to explore the underlying reasons for this apparent taste for "fairness." We found that if the right to be the first mover is earned by scoring high on a general knowledge quiz, and that right is reinforced by the instructions as being earned, then first movers behave in a significantly more self-regarding manner. Because our instructional procedures followed those in the literature and provided for intersubject anonymity as a partial control for the effect of social influences, on choice, we conducted double blind dictator experiments, in which individual subject decisions could not be known by the experimenter or by anyone else except the decision maker. The results yielded by far our largest observed proportion of self-regarding offers – significantly more than obtained in any of our other treatments or in any previously reported in the literature. Our interpretation is that offers in ultimatum and dictator games appear to be determined predominantly by strategic and expectations considerations. Other-regarding behavior is primarily an expectations phenomenon – what evolutionary biologists call "reciprocal altruism" or simply reciprocity (Trivers, 1971; Hawkes, 1992) – rather than the result of an autonomous private preference for equity.

I.   Ultimatum and Dictator Games

In an ultimatum game, an amount of money M is to be divided between two subjects. One subject, designated the proposer, announces a split of $M - X$ to the proposer and X to the proposer's counterpart. After the proposal is made, the counterpart either accepts or rejects it. If the counterpart accepts, then the proposal is carried out; but, if the counterpart rejects, then both the proposer and counterpart get zero. If the counterpart is rational and nonsatiated in money, then he or she should accept $X = \varepsilon > 0$, where e is the minimum unit of account. Thus the subgame perfect equilibrium prediction is for the proposer to offer $X = \varepsilon$ and for the counterpart to accept. Experiments on nonrepeated ultimatum games by Guth et al. (1982; hereafter GSS), Kahneman et al. (1986), Forsythe et al. (1994; hereafter, FHSS), Roth et al. (1991), and others show that first-mover proposers in such bargaining games offer more to their counterparts than noncooperative game theory leads one to expect. This tendency toward equal split has been described as due to fairness considerations or to "social norms" of distributive justice. Such terms simply name the observed tendency toward equal outcomes observed in these experiments; they fail to explain the phenomenon in terms of more fundamental considerations that are testable. Bolton (1991, p. 429) offers a formal model in which distributional considerations are incorporated into the bargainers' utility functions, an approach suggested earlier by Ochs and Roth (1989).

These experimental results are in contrast to those of a game with ultimatum strategic structure reported by Fouraker and Siegel (1963, pp. 34–6, 218–21; hereafter FS). They found strong support for the subgame perfect (Bowley) equilibrium bargaining prediction in the context of a single transaction. The equal-split payoff solution was distinct from the equilibrium point, but none of the 11 bargainers chose equal split. The procedure used was what today we call a posted offer: the seller begins the process by choosing a price; this price is communicated to the buyer, who then chooses quantity, thus ending the game. Consequently, the seller makes an ultimatum (take-it-or-leave-it) price offer to the buyer. The FS procedures and design differed from the preceding ultimatum experiments in three ways: (1) all bargaining was described as a buyer–seller transaction; (2) the Nash equilibrium yielded more than an ε payoff to the buyer – in the asymmetric design the Nash equilibrium buyer's payoff was \$2.44 and the seller's was \$6.44; (3) both sellers and buyers have multiple price–quantity (and payoff) choices available so that the all-or-none feature of the ultimatum game was not present, but the buyer is free to reject the price offer by choosing a zero quantity. These early FS findings, which helped to motivate the first ultimatum game experiments by GSS, suggest that the results of recent ultimatum games may be due to (1) the different context or procedures used or (2) the fact that the second mover is expected to accept a minuscule reward (ε) at the Nash equilibrium. Thus, the ultimatum game may be a boundary experiment that asks if the Nash prediction still holds when the second mover is required to accept a much smaller payoff than the first mover (GSS, p. 369).

FHSS also ran an important baseline control for strategic behavior in the ultimatum game – the dictator game. In the dictator game, the proposer decides on a split of money, M, which is final. The counterpart cannot reject the offer. In the ultimatum game, the proposer must form expectations on the reservation value of the counterpart (i.e., the amount X which the counterpart will reject). Thus, concerns for fairness are confounded by the proposer's strategic expectations over reservation values. Because the proposer's split is final in the dictator game, expectations about the counterpart's reservation values are not assumed to enter into the proposer's decision. Theory predicts that a self-interested, nonsatiated dictator will take M, leaving nothing for the counterpart. FHSS find that proposers in the dictator game take significantly more (where M is either \$5 or \$10) than proposers in the ultimatum game. However, a substantial number, about 20%, do still split 50–50. They concluded "that the distribution of proposals in the ultimatum game cannot be fully explained by a taste for fairness among proposers" (FHSS, p. 23). But how do we reconcile the ultimatum data with the dictator data?

A reasonable rational model of the data in both games can be stated in terms of subjects' expectations. In such simple experiments, particularly the dictator game, subjects may ask themselves (unconsciously) What is the experimenter's objective? (1) They may think that their actions in this game will affect the experimenter's decision to have them participate in future experiments. (2) They may think they *will* be chosen to participate in future experiments; but they may be concerned that their current decisions will affect *which* later experiments they are selected for. (3) They may be concerned about appearing greedy and being judged so by the experimenter. Under this latter interpretation, "fairness" is not "own" preference, but a derivative of judgment by others. Note that none of these "explanations" requires a personal fairness ethic or utility-of-sharing considerations.

In the ultimatum game, the proposer must form expectations about his or her counterpart's reservation value. Thus, a risk averse proposer may give his or her counterpart more than is predicted by noncooperative theory in order to ensure acceptance of the proposal. Rational behavior is to choose $X^* = \arg \max u(M - X)F(X)$, where $F(X)$ is the first mover's subjective probability that offer X will be accepted, and capture the expectations of the proposer. But even a subject dictator may still be influenced by expectations about the experimenter's judgment, or future (subject recruiting) behavior, and thus may still give the counterpart a positive amount of money.

Experimenter knowledge of subject expectations is null, and control over them is limited to instructions and pregame treatments. Moreover, certain controls may be inadvertent. For example, in past experiments, subjects were randomly assigned a type. Usually, randomization would be justified; when we cannot control for a variable, we randomize its effect. But, in the ultimatum experiments, randomization may not be neutral, since it can be interpreted by subjects as an attempt by the experimenter to treat them fairly. Lotteries are often used for the fair award of rights such as hunting permits and basketball seats. Thus experimenters may unwittingly induce a "fair response." Subjects may feel that, because the experimenter is being fair to them, they should be fair to each other.

II.   Property Rights

A property right is a guarantee allowing action within guidelines defined by the right. The guarantee is against reprisal, in that a property right places restrictions on punishment strategies that might otherwise be used to ensure cooperative behavior. Property rights can be viewed as a means by which society legitimizes – makes fair (acceptable) – the action of a rights holder. Such rights are taken for granted in private ownership economies, but is this so for the subjects in bargaining experiments?

In bargaining experiments, subjects' expectations may be more compatible, and the first mover may be less influenced by the possibility of punishment strategies by a counterpart, if the former has earned the right to make use of the advantaged position and the process of right acquisition is common information. Hoffman and Spitzer (1982, 1985b; hereafter HS) present experimental data that support this view.[1] In the HS (1982) experiments, two persons bargained face to face over the split of $14. Before bargaining began, one subject was chosen at random to be the controller. If subjects could not agree on a split, the controller would receive $12; the controller's choice was final. In these experiments, 12 out of 12 pairs agreed to split the $14 evenly even though this gave less to the controller than he or she could obtain by not agreeing. In the HS (1985b) experiments, when the controller earned the right in a contest, and this right was reinforced as common knowledge in the instructions, only 4 of 22 bargaining pairs split equally, and on average, proposers took $12.52. Similarly, Guth and Tietz (1986) show that if first- and second-mover rights in the ultimatum game are auctioned independently to subjects, offers to second movers are much reduced.

Our contest assignment is meant to extend the HS (1985) assignment treatment to ultimatum games.[2] This contest is a current events quiz

---

[1] Also see Burrows and Loomes (1989) who investigated further the hypothesis that people behave in a more self-interested manner when they have earned the right to do so. They report support for the hypothesis, but their results also show that people continue to place a value on fair outcomes, which is consistent with Hoffman and Spitzer (1985b).

[2] Other experimental treatments might also result in similar changes in the expectations of first movers in ultimatum games. For example, Harrison and McKee (1985) and

where subjects are ranked from highest to lowest using correct answers. This assignment technique had been used previously by Binger et al. (1991), Cech (1988), and Wellford (1990).[3] If there are ties, subjects' total time answering questions is used as a tiebreaker (i.e., shortest time first). In HS (1985b), a game of Nim was played by two players to see who would be the controller, but partners were randomly paired. In the contest reported in this chapter, both the choice of proposer and the pairings of proposers and counterparts are determined by subjects' ranking in the contest.

Except for two control experiments (and two double blind experiments) in which we use the FHSS instructions and the subjects' task is to divide $10, all our experiments are formulated as an exchange between a buyer and a seller as in FS. This allows us to test for the effect of Exchange versus Divide $10. Usually, bargaining is treated as an exchange. This context may itself confer legitimacy and common expectations on a more self-regarding offer by the first mover.[4]

III.   Experimental Design

In each experimental session, 12 subjects participate simultaneously. Each subject is paid $3 for arriving on time for the experiment. When all subjects have arrived, they first read and then have read to them (by Hoffman) a set of instructions that describe the buy–sell task. In the random assignment treatment, subjects are then randomly assigned the positions of buyer and seller and randomly (and anonymously) paired with one another.[5] In the contest assignment treatment, subjects answer

---

Burrows and Loomes (1989) essentially replicate the Hoffman and Spitzer (1985b) experimental results using different mechanisms for inducing a sense of justification for being the first mover.

[3] Contest software for use on IBM networked personal computers is available on disk by writing author Smith.

[4] Typically, experimenters want to infer some conclusion about markets when discussing their experimental results. For example Kahneman et al. (1986, pp. 105–6) report experiments in which subjects are asked to reallocate $10, provisionally allocated to each pair, using simultaneous move rules (i.e., the second mover marks those first-mover offers that are acceptable and those that are not before knowing the first mover's decision). They report a strong tendency toward equal split with a substantial portion of second movers willing to reject positive offers. The authors suggest that such resistance to unfairness "is of the type that might deter a profit-maximizing agent or firm seeking to exploit some profit opportunities" (p. 106). In order to better justify the extension of such results to firms, we hypothesize that it may be important to describe the setting as an exchange between a buyer and a selling firm, and not as one of reallocating $10 provisionally allocated to each pair.

[5] We do not, however, use the word *random* in the instructions to the subjects. We tell them they have been paired anonymously. See the instructions labeled "random" in the appendix.

Seller Chooses

PRICE

		$0	$1	$2	$3	$4	$5	$6	$7	$8	$9	$10	
	BUY	$0	$1	$2	$3	$4	$5	$6	$7	$8	$9	$10	Seller profit
Buyer Chooses to		$10	$9	$8	$7	$6	$5	$4	$3	$2	$1	$0	Buyer profit
	NOT BUY	$0	$0	$0	$0	$0	$0	$0	$0	$0	$0	$0	Seller profit
		$0	$0	$0	$0	$0	$0	$0	$0	$0	$0	$0	Buyer profit

FIGURE 5.1. Payoff chart given to subjects.

ten current events questions. The subject ranked No. 1 is the seller, paired with the subject ranked No. 7 as the buyer. The subject ranked No. 2 is paired with the subject ranked No. 8, and so on. No subject is informed of the identity of his or her counterpart and each experimental session involves only one pairing and one decision. Participants earn $0.25 for each correct answer, in addition to their earnings in the subsequent experiment.

After the buyer and seller assignments have been made, each seller chooses a price given the payoff chart shown in Figure 5.1. This payoff chart shows that the game is essentially an ultimatum game embedded in an exchange. There is $10 to divide between the seller and the buyer. If the seller states a price of $9 and the buyer agrees to buy, the seller gets $9, and the buyer gets $1. Similarly, if the seller states a price of $8 and the buyer agrees to buy, the seller gets $8, and the buyer gets $2. As in other ultimatum games, and in FS, if the buyer decides not to buy, both buyer and seller receive $0.

While the sellers are choosing prices, the buyers are answering a questionnaire (labeled Buyer Questionnaire in the appendix). The questionnaire serves two purposes. First, it allows us to give a piece of paper to each participant, thus obscuring the identification of the buyers and sellers. Second, the questionnaire asks the buyer to tell us both what price he or she would have chosen and what price he or she expects the seller to choose. These data allow us to test whether expectations are affected by the assignment of the property right.

Table 5.1. *Number of bargaining pairs for ultimatum and dictator experiments*

	Ultimatum		Dictator	
	Divide $10	Exchange	Divide $10	Exchange
FHSS results	24		24	
Random entitlement, FHSS instructions	24			
Contest entitlement, FHSS instructions	24			
Random entitlement		24		24
Contest entitlement		24		24
Double blind 1			36	
Double blind 2			41	

After the sellers have chosen prices, we circle the appropriate seller's price choice on each buyer's choice form and ask the buyers to circle BUY or NOT BUY. While the buyers are making their choices, we ask the sellers to answer a questionnaire about their expectations of buyer behavior. Simultaneously passing out the questionnaire also serves the additional purpose of continuing to obscure the identification of buyers and sellers. Once the buyers have made their decisions, we determine each individual subject's earnings, including payment for correct answers in the current events quiz, and pay them individually and privately.

These procedures are also applied to the dictator game, except that the buyer has no decision to make. In the exchange context, this means that the buyer has a prior commitment to make the purchase whatever the price chosen by the seller.

Table 5.1 lists the number of bargaining pairs that participated in all the experiments that we report here. For example, we ran 24 subject pairs in Ultimatum Exchange and in Dictator Exchange, as indicated by the column headings, and with Random Entitlement, as indicated in the row heading. In row 1, for comparison, we list those experiments reported by FHSS that we describe here as the Divide $10 experiments to distinguish them from our Exchange experiments. Thus, in the FHSS instructions, subjects are told that "A sum of $5 ($10) has been provisionally allocated to each pair . . ." (FHSS, p. 27; also see Kahneman et al., 1986, p. 105).

Note particularly that this instruction suggests that neither bargainer has a clear property right to the money; literally it provisionally belongs to both of them. FHSS paid their subjects a $3 participation fee in addition to the proceeds of the division of $10. In all but one of the experiments reported here, we also paid our customary $3 participation fee in addition to each bargainer's split of the $10.

As a means of comparing our subjects and procedures with those of FHSS, we conducted one random entitlement and one contest entitlement experiment using the FHSS Divide $10 instructions. Note, however, that we did not follow FHSS in assigning buyers and sellers to separate rooms because our contest treatment required the same-room (common knowledge) condition, and we wanted to maintain comparability with our other experiments. These are not intended as pure replications of FHSS. Rather we ask if their results are robust with respect to the experimenters, subjects, and same-room condition.

As indicated previously, we also have been concerned that subjects in bargaining experiments may be influenced by either (1) imagined use by the experimenter of their decisions to decide whether to recruit or how to use subjects in a later experiment or (2) judgments of the subject's decision by the experimenter, or others who see the data in spite of guarantees of anonymity. The point is that in all the "anonymous" bargaining experiments known to us, the subject knows that the experimenter is fully informed as to who made what decision. Anonymity means that neither bargainer in a pair knows the identity of the other subject and that subjects across bargaining pairs do not know one another's identities or decisions, but the experimenter still knows everything.

This particular kind of between-subject anonymity has been standard in private bargaining studies going back to Siegel and Fouraker (1960). This protocol was continued in FS and in all recent private bargaining studies. The procedure has been justified on the grounds that the absence of anonymity, as in face-to-face interactions, brings into potential play all the social experience with which people are endowed, causing the experimenter to risk losing control over preferences (also see Roth, 1990).

We agree with this assessment, but propose that it also applies to the experimenter as a potential socializing factor. To eliminate observation by the experimenter, we designed a new set of Divide $10 experiments in which subject are guaranteed anonymity with respect to everyone: other subjects, the experimenter, and anyone who might view their decisions. Because subject decisions and payoffs are anonymous with respect to both the experimenters and the subjects, we call this treatment double blind.[6]

In the Double Blind 1 reported in this chapter, 15 people were recruited to room A and 14 to room B. The same instructions were read by each subject and then read orally by an experimenter in each room (A, McCabe; B, Smith). All subjects were paid a $5 show-up fee (now standard in our lab, this experiment being one of the first). One of the subjects in room A is voluntarily selected to be the monitor in the experiment. The monitor is paid $10. The instructions state that 14 plain white unmarked opaque envelopes contain the following: 2 of the envelopes contain 20 blank slips of paper each, and 12 contain 10 blank slips and 10 one-dollar bills each. Each subject is given an envelope by the monitor, proceeds to the back of the room, and opens the envelope inside a large cardboard box, which maintains his or her strict privacy. The subject keeps 0 to 10 of the one-dollar bills and 10 to 0 of the blank slips of paper, so that the number of bills plus slips of paper add up to 10. For the envelopes with 20 blank slips, 10 are returned to the envelope. (In this way all returned envelopes feel equally thick. Moreover, each person in room A knows that if his or her counterpart in room B receives an envelope with 10 slips of blank paper, it could be because there was no money in the envelope originally. Thus, it is really true that "no one can know.")

After everyone is finished in room A, the monitor goes to room B, sits outside the room and calls each person out one at a time. The person selects an envelope, opens it, and keeps its contents, which are recorded by the monitor on a blank sheet of paper containing no names. The experimenter accompanies the monitor to answer any questions that arise but does not participate in this process. These procedures are intended to make it transparent that room A subjects are on their own in deciding how much to leave their counterparts in room B, and that no one can possibly know how much the others left their counterparts. The use of a monitor minimizes experimenter involvement and guarantees that someone from room A besides the experimenter can verify that there is actually a room B with 14 subjects, as stated in the instructions.

The preceding procedures represent a substantial departure from

---

[6] The conventional use of *double blind* in medical experiments means that neither the subject nor the experimenters know which subject is receiving which treatment. This use of the term is not appropriate in economics experiments because the subject must necessarily know the treatment (instructions and situation) in order to perform the task. We propose a more appropriate use for the term *double blind* in economics. Moreover, our use of the term has already been adopted by others, and it is not the first use of the term to denote anonymity from two points of view (Blank, 1991).

those used in our other experiments. This was deliberate; we wanted to do a step-out experiment that would include everything we thought might be important in protecting the subjects' total anonymity. The results, as we discuss later, were dramatic in reducing the distribution of offers. Which of these procedures are most important? The use of a monitor who is paid $10 may help to suggest that the subjects in room A should take all the money. Contrary to this, the examples used in the instructions (giving $2 and $9; see appendix) suggest that something should be given. Again, having two envelopes with only blank slips may suggest that giving nothing is in order. Using envelopes actually containing the money is itself a departure from having subjects choose numbers, then paying them afterwards. Any or all of these features could be important.

As a first step among many variations that we intend to study, we conducted a series of Double Blind 2 experiments (41 pairs). In these experiments, we eliminated the paid subject monitor; that function was performed by the room A experimenter. Second, we eliminated the use of the envelopes with 20 blank slips of paper and did three replications, each using 14 envelopes containing 10 one-dollar bills and 10 blank sheets of paper each. (In one session we had only 13 subjects in each of the rooms.)

IV.   Ultimatum Game First-Mover Results

FHSS evaluated the power of five nonparametric tests to distinguish between different sample distributions: the Cramer-Von Mises, Anderson Darling (AD), Kolmorogov-Smirnov, Wilcoxon rank-sum, and Epps-Singleton (ES) tests. They found that the AD and ES tests have the most statistical power in the context of ultimatum games. They also note that the ES test has the added advantage of not requiring the distributions being tested to be continuous. Epps and Singleton (1986) also investigated the power of the ES test versus the Anderson-Darling, Cramer-Von Mises and Kolmorogov-Smirnov tests. Epps and Singleton found that the power of the ES test was superior to the other tests in distinguishing between different continuous distributions. Furthermore, the difference is even more pronounced when the distributions being compared are discrete.

The ES test is based upon characteristic functions. It compares the difference between the characteristic functions of two samples to test the null hypothesis that the characteristic functions, hence the distributions, are equal. In Table 5.2 we report the results of pairwise comparisons

Table 5.2. *Pairwise Epps-Singleton tests for ultimatum and cictator experiments*

χ^2 statistic (probability significance level)	FHSS results, Divide $10, dictator	Random entitlement, Divide $10, FHSS Instructions, ultimatum	Contest entitlement, Divide $10, FHSS Instructions, ultimatum	random entitlement, ultimatum exchange	Random entitlement, dictator exchange	Contest entitlement, ultimatum exchange	Contest entitlement, dictator exchange	Double blind 1, divide $10, dictator
FHSS results, divide $10, ultimatum	30.0 (0.00)	5.2 (0.27)	30.5 (0.00)	22.4 (0.00)		35.5 (0.00)		238.4 (0.00)
FHSS results, divide $10, dictator					7.3 (0.12)		5.7 (0.22)	23.6 (0.00)
Random entitlement, divide $10, FHSS instructions, ultimatum			10.4 (0.03)	10.4 (0.03)		19.3 (0.00)		304.6 (0.00)
Contest entitlement, FHSS instructions, ultimatum				2.7 (0.60)		6.1 (0.19)		283.7 (0.00)
Random entitlement, ultimatum exchange						4.9 (0.29)		144.4 (0.00)
Random entitlement, dictator exchange					6.4 (0.17)		13.2 (0.01)	44.9 (0.00)
Contest entitlement, ultimatum exchange								114.4 (0.00)
Contest entitlement, dictator exchange								11.8 (0.02)
Double blind 2, divide $10, dictator								3.0 (0.56)

using the ES test with the small sample correction.[7] Because comparisons using the ES test are not based only on the first moment of the distribution, we include charts that show how our data shifted with the treatments and Table 5.3, which reports results from the Wilcoxon rank-sum test (also called Mann-Whitney; the test was discovered at least five times going back to 1914; see Kruskal, 1957). All comparisons in Tables 5.2 and 5.3 that are significantly different in the ES test are also significant for only the rank-sum measure of a shift in the distribution. However, the "good" results (lower significance levels) in many of the comparisons for the Wilcoxon test are qualified because of this test's poor power characteristics.

Figure 5.2 charts the data from FHSS for their $10 ultimatum experiments and their $10 dictator experiments. Because the FHSS paper and data provided one of the three major motivations for the present study (the second being HS, 1985; the third being FS, 1963), Figure 5.2 sets the stage for reporting our results. In the comparison of Figure 5.2,

---

[7] The tests are conducted in the following manner. The first step is to form a vector representing the real and imaginary parts of the characteristic function for each sample (treatment)

$$g(X_{km}) = \left(\cos \hat{t}_1 X_{km}, \ \sin \hat{t}_1 X_{km}, \ \cos \hat{t}_2 X_{km}, \ \sin \hat{t}_2 X_{km}\right)$$

where $\hat{t} = t/\hat{\sigma}$ and t is a real number,

$$g_k = n_{k-1} \sum_m g(X_{km})$$

m is an index on the observation within a specific sample, and k is an index on samples. Epps and Singleton (1986; hereafter ES) provide calculations to determine the power maximizing values for t_1 and t_2. $\hat{\sigma}$ is a scaling measure for t and is calculated;

$$\hat{\sigma} = 0.5\left[\frac{(Y_U + Y_{U-1})}{2} + \frac{(Y_L + Y_{L+1})}{2}\right]$$

where $\{Y_i\}$ is samples 1 and 2 combined and then placed in ascending order; L is the greatest integer in $(n_1 + n_2)/4$; and U is $n_1 + n_2 - L$. The test statistic is W_1 given by

$$2W_1 \equiv N(g_1 - g_2)' \Omega^{-1}(g_1 - g_2)$$

where

$$\hat{\Omega} = \left(\hat{S}_1 + \hat{S}_2\right) N[(n_1^{-1} + n_2^{-1})]/2$$

and

$$\hat{S}_k = n^{-1}{}_k \sum_{m-1}^{n_k} g(X_{km}) g(X_{km})' - g_k g_k'$$

If the null hypothesis that the characteristic functions are the same is true, then the test statistic is distributed as a chi square with 4 degrees of freedom.

ES also derive a small sample correction that improves the power of the test in small samples.

The small sample correction is given as

$$\hat{C}(n_1 n) = \left[1 + (n_1 + n_2)^{-0.45} + 10.1(n_1^{-1.7} - n_2^{-1.7})\right]^{-1}$$

$$W_2 = W_1 \cdot \hat{C}$$

The results reported in Table 5.1 include the small sample correction.

Table 5.3. *Pairwise Wilcoxon rank-sum tests for ultimatum and dictator experiments*

Wilcoxon W (probability significance level)	FHSS results, Divide $10, dictator	Random entitlement, Divide $10, FHSS instructions, ultimatum	Contest entitlement, Divide $10, FHSS instructions, ultimatum	Random entitlement, ultimatum exchange	Random entitlement, dictator exchange	Contest entitlement, ultimatum exchange	Contest entitlement, dictator exchange	Double blind 1, Divide $10, dictator
FHSS results, divide $10, ultimatum	-4.61 (0.00)	-1.74 (0.08)	-4.33 (0.00)	-3.63 (0.00)		-4.83 (0.00)		-6.04 (0.00)
FHSS results, divide $10, dictator					-0.822 (0.41)		-2.20 (0.03)	-3.52 (0.00)
Random entitlement, divide $10, FHSS instructions, ultimatum			-3.09 (0.00)	-2.69 (0.00)		-4.09 (0.00)		-5.88 (0.00)
Contest entitlement, FHSS instructions, ultimatum						-1.92 (0.02)		-5.58 (0.00)
Random entitlement, ultimatum exchange					-2.06 (0.04)	-1.66 (0.09)		-5.86 (0.00)
Random entitlement, dictator exchange							-3.08 (0.00)	-3.86 (0.00)
Contest entitlement, ultimatum exchange							-4.28 (0.00)	-5.25 (0.00)
Contest entitlement, dictator exchange								-1.71 (0.09)
Double blind 2, divide $10, dictator								-0.52 (0.61)

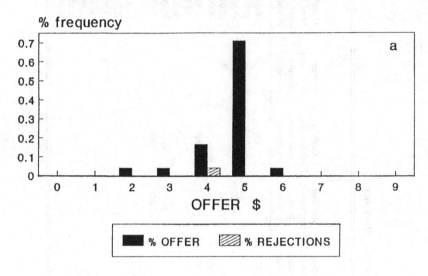

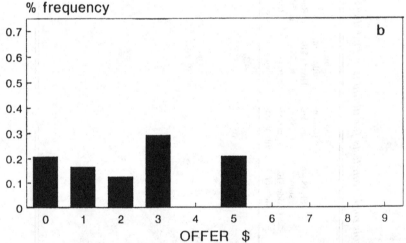

FIGURE 5.2. Results from the FHSS experiments: (a) Ultimatum, Divide $10 experiment, $N = 24$; (b) Dictator, Divide $10 experiment, $N = 24$.

FHSS reported that the dictator results are significantly different (more self-regarding) from the ultimatum data (also see Tables 5.2 and 5.3).

Figure 5.3 provides a four-way comparison among our Divide $10, Random, and Contest experiments using FHSS instructions, and the par-

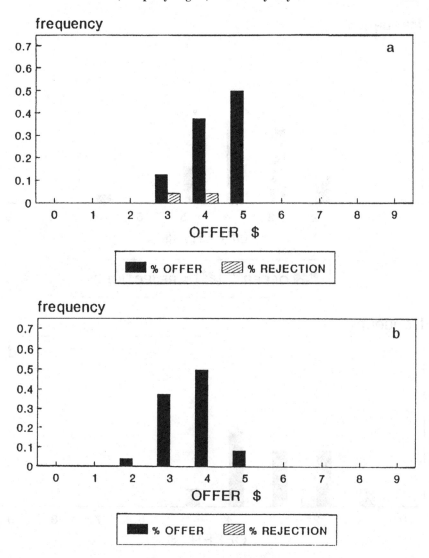

FIGURE 5.3. Comparison of results obtained from Divide $10 experiments presented using the FHSS instructions and those obtained from experiments presented as a buyer–seller exchange. $N = 24$ in all cases. (a) Ultimatum, Random entitlement, FHSS instructions, Divide $10; (b) Ultimatum, Contest entitlement, FHSS instructions, Divide $10; (c) Ultimatum, Random entitlement, Exchange; (d) Ultimatum, Contest entitlement, Exchange.

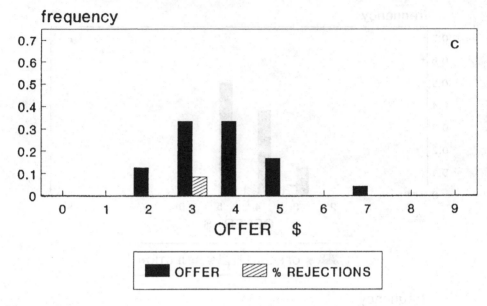

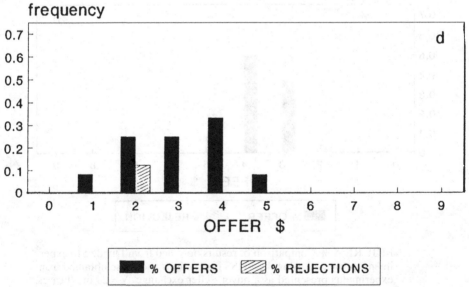

FIGURE 5.3. *Continued.*

allel experiments presented as a buyer–seller exchange. Note first that our Divide $10 ultimatum experiments [Figure 5.3(a)] replicate those of FHSS [Figure 5.2(a)]; that is, different subjects, different experimenters, and "same room" conditions yield results that are not significantly different from the FHSS results (p is .27 in Table 5.2 and .08 in Table 5.3). Comparing Random versus Contest when presented as Divide $10 [Figures 5.3(a, b)], we observe a statistically significant (p = .03 in Table 5.2) shift toward lower offers in the contest treatment. In the experiments presenting the task as a buyer–seller exchange, the contest entitlement also shifts the offers to a lower level as compared with the random entitlement [Figures 5.3(c, d)]; the difference is not significant by ES (p = .22 in Table 5.2), but is significant by Wilcoxon. Comparing Divide $10 versus Exchange under Random entitlement [Figures 5.3(a, c)], Exchange shifts the offers to a significantly lower level (p = 0.03 in Table 5.2). With contest entitlements [Figures 5.3(b, d)], however, the lowering of offers as a result of the exchange treatment is not significant (p = .22 in Table 5.2). Comparing the combined effect of exchange and contest [Figure 5.3(d) with Figure 5.3(a)], we observe a highly significant (p = .00, Tables 5.2 and 5.3) shift toward self-regarding offers.[8] Much of this shift, however, is due to the effect of *exchange alone*, which helps to account for the strong results reported by FS.

The results of our seller questionnaire, providing data on seller expectations of buyer (or second-mover) acceptance behavior, were as follows. Using the FHSS (Divide $10) instructions, every first mover expected his or her offer to be accepted under both the Random and Contest entitlements; also, all sellers stated that they would have accepted if they had been buyers. Under the Random/Exchange treatment, one seller stated that he/she did not expect the buyer, who in fact did buy, to buy; all would have bought if they had been buyers. Under the Contest/Exchange treatment, all sellers expected their buyers to accept; however, one would not have accepted his/her own offer of $2 if he/she had been the buyer. It was accepted anyway. Overwhelmingly, across all treatments, first movers expected their offers to be accepted. This is consistent with the high observed acceptance rate discussed in the next

---

[8] By "self-regarding offers" we mean simply lower offers. One reader interpreted it as meaning that realized expected utility, $U(M - X^*)F(X^*)$, increases with the exchange and contest treatments and stated that this was *not* the case. This is incorrect. Because our first-mover results show that X^* decreases significantly, whereas our second-mover results (Section V) show that the net rejection (and acceptance) rates, $F(X^*)$, do not alter significantly, it follows that $U(M - X^*)F(X^*)$ increases with our treatments. First movers are made subjectively better off, on balance, with the exchange and contest treatments and can therefore be said, in the expected utility sense, to have made more self-regarding offers.

section. It is also consistent with self-regarding offer motivation tempered by expectations (the risk of rejection), as indicated previously by the analysis of Section II.

V.   Ultimatum Game Second-Mover Results

The hatched bars in Figures 5.3(a–d) provide frequency data on the second-mover rejection rates for each of our treatments. These rates are very low: 2/24 (8.3%) in Random/Divide $10; 0/24 in Contest/Divide $10; 2/24 (8.3%) in Random/Exchange; and 3/24 (12.5%) in Contest/Exchange. None of these rates is significantly different from any other, nor from those of FHSS [Figure 5.2(a)]. The buyer (second-mover) questionnaires for all treatments yielded only one buyer (in the Contest/Exchange treatment) who thought the seller expected his/her offer to be rejected. That buyer, in fact, accepted the offer.

The importance of these results is indicated by the fact that most ultimatum game experimenters (see following discussion) have emphasized that a substantial proportion of positive offers are rejected and that this is taken into account by first movers. Because all our procedures (and those of FHSS that used a $10 pie) resulted in little or no, and in any case no significant, differences in rejection rates, we concluded that our treatments were highly successful in inducing common expectations on the bargaining pairs. In particular, our Contest and Exchange treatments not only produced significantly lower offers relative to Random/Divide $10, but this was also accomplished without any detectable increase in the rejection rates. Thus, *first movers accurately gauged the willingness of second movers to accept lower offers as we shift to treatments eliciting lower offers*. It is therefore appropriate to say that in these treatments the self interest of first movers was served not only in offering less but also in their expectations that their risk of rejection would not rise accordingly. Statistically, the risk of rejection of the lower offers remained unchanged.

VI.   Dictator Game Results

Figures 5.4(a, b) chart the frequency distributions of the data for our dictator games under the Random and Contest entitlements, respectively. The contest treatment lowers the offer distribution and the difference is significant ($p = .01$ in Table 5.2). In Figure 5.4(c), we chart the distribution of our Double Blind 1 dictator data. From the latter, it is clear that

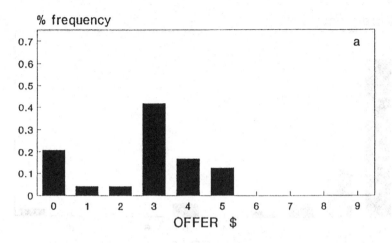

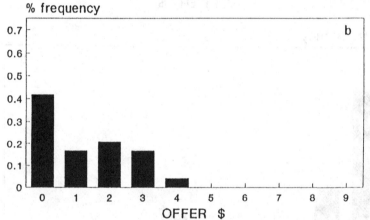

FIGURE 5.4. Results for Dictator experiments. (a) Dictator, Random entitlement, Exchange, $N = 24$; (b) Dictator, Contest entitlement, Exchange, $N = 24$; (c) Dictator, Random entitlement, Divide \$10, Double Blind 1, $N = 36$; (d) Dictator, Random entitlement, Divide \$10, Double Blind 2, $N = 41$.

the double blind treatment is by far our most potent. When no one can know what the first mover offers his/her counterpart, the offer distribution is dramatically lowered relative to all dictator and ultimatum treatments. With one exception (Double Blind 2), the Double Blind 1 dictator

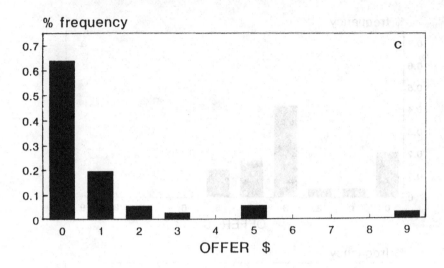

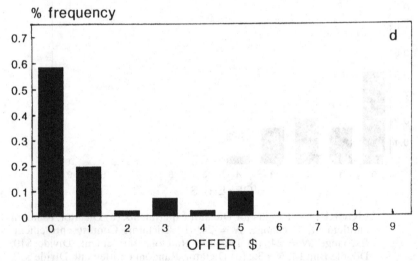

FIGURE 5.4. *Continued.*

results are significantly different (lower offers) as compared to all our other treatments and the FHSS treatments.

If we look just at the proportion of dictators giving $0 to their counterparts, the differences become quite clear. In the FHSS and

Random/Exchange treatment, only about 20% offer $0; a similar proportion still offers $5. In the Contest/Exchange treatment about 40% offer $0; another 40% offer $1 or $2. In the Double Blind 1 dictator treatment, over two-thirds of the first movers now offer $0, and 84% offer $0 or $1; only 2 of 36 subjects offer $5.

In Figure 5.4(d), we chart the Double Blind 2 data. Comparing Figures 5.4(c, d) shows the robustness of Double Blind with respect to the use of a paid monitor, and the use of two padded, no money, envelopes. Although the offers are slightly higher, the statistical comparisons in Tables 5.2 and 5.3 show that the double blind results are robust to the indicated procedural factors ($p = .56$ and $.61$). Clearly, Double Blind 1 and 2 are both powerful treatments relative to all our other experiments. The results also further reinforce our general conclusion that the class of games we are considering is sensitive to the procedural, contractual, and instructional setting of the experiment.[9]

VII.   Relation of Results to the Theoretical and Experimental Literature

Bolton (1991) has proposed a formal extension of standard bargaining theory in which a bargainer's welfare depends upon her own monetary payoff and upon a comparison of her own earnings with that of her counterpart with whom the pie is shared. Potential counterparts prefer more equal splits, including the possibility of $(0, 0)$, to proposals that offer them substantially less than the proposer. First movers must take this fact strategically into account in deciding how much to offer. Bolton's model is thus a mixture of fairness considerations in the sense of tastes, and strategic considerations in the sense of a subgame perfect equilibrium as in the standard ultimatum game. The difference is that payoff and relative payoff are substitutes in bargainer utility functions. It is important to emphasize that the model is directly motivated by data from previous ultimatum game experiments but has new testable implications that hold up well in the new experiments reported.

We like Bolton's methodological approach, which is (1) to modify the conventional model, rather than abandon it prematurely, retaining the

---

[9] The use of an experimenter to monitor the Double Blind 2 experiments allowed an impressionistic "observation" to be made: Some subjects in room A did not seal their envelopes as instructed, and we could not help but observe that such subjects tended predominantly to be the ones who left positive amounts in their envelopes. It would appear that people are ambivalent about completely anonymous giving. As we were unprepared for this, we did not record any observations. What would have been the effect on giving if we had insisted that all envelopes be sealed before the subjects left the privacy of their boxes?

assumptions of maximizing, perfect equilibrium, behavior, and (2) to test it. The model is not, however, consistent with either the FHSS or our results for the dictator game. This is because Bolton's bargainers desire fair treatment only for *themselves*, and first movers must take this into account in deciding their ultimatum offers. In the dictator game, Bolton's decision makers should ignore the concerns of their counterparts and take the entire pie. Most subjects do not do this except in our double blind dictator games. Consequently, the latter approaches consistency with the Bolton model.[10]

Guth and Tietz (1986) determine the bargaining positions in the ultimatum game by independent auctions of the right to be the first or second mover. For example (Guth and Tietz, 1986, Table 2), a subject paid DM 25 for the right to move first in an ultimatum game for splitting DM 55. The subject was matched with another subject who paid DM 5 for the right to move second. Finally, the first mover offered DM 20 to the second, who accepted it. The first mover's net payoff was DM 10, and the second DM 15. Although data for only 12 subjects are reported (each participating in 3 rounds of ultimatum games), the results are consistent with the outcomes of our Contest/Exchange treatment. Guth and Tietz (1986, Table 12) report that in only 2 of 36 rounds do first movers offer as much as half of their pie. In our Contest/Exchange treatment only 2 in 24 subjects offer this much. Auctions tend to increase the incidence of self-regarding offers for two reasons: (1) They serve to legitimize the right to exploit the first mover advantage, but (2) what constitutes an equal outcome is redefined as the original pie net of auction prices.

Thus, in the preceding example, the first mover demanded DM 35, asking for a profit of only DM 10 over his/her auction price of DM 25. The offer of DM 20 was two-thirds of the pie net of auction price (DM 30). We like the auction approach to allocating first-mover rights, but our Contest/Exchange treatment is designed to examine legitimacy ("earning" rights) *without altering* the net pie to be divided. First movers in the Guth and Tietz (1986) experiments offer very liberal percentages of the pie net of auction price, whereas our subjects offered comparatively low percentages of the pie under Contest/Exchange.[11]

---

[10] A taste for fairness is not necessary to comprehend that the ultimatum results have been demonstrated using a model of *rivalrous* bargainers and incomplete information on the part of the first mover (Burnell et al., 1992).

[11] Since the auction winners in Guth and Tietz (1986) did not know the prices paid by their counterparts, they faced considerable additional uncertainty, above that in the known-pie ultimatum experiments, as to how much their counterparts would find acceptable. Our Contest/Exchange treatment creates a common-knowledge property right in a certain amount of money. Our results could be compared with those of an auction procedure that allows both bargainers knowledge of the net pie to be divided.

Roth et al. (1991) have conducted the most extensive and ambitious study of ultimatum bargaining behavior yet attempted: an international comparison of behavior in ultimatum bilateral and multilateral (market) bargaining. In their market experiments, nine buyers with value M each state a buying price (offer of a split of the pie). The seller, with zero cost, can accept or reject the highest of these offers. If the seller accepts a buyer's offer, the pie is divided between the seller and that buyer according to the terms of the offer and all the other buyers get zero. If the seller rejects all offers, all get zero. Each player learns whether a transaction occurred and the price. The process is repeated for ten periods with a changing population of buyers. Viewed as a market, the supply is inelastic at 1 unit with willingness-to-accept of zero. The maximum willingness-to-pay demand is constant at M per unit, the amount of the pie to be divided, up to nine units. The excess supply is constant at 8 units for all prices from zero up to the equilibrium price of $M - e$ (actually any price from $M - e$ to M is an equilibrium). This environment is known in the experimental literature as a swastika supply and demand design and has been studied extensively, under both complete and private information (see, for example, Smith, 1965, 1976a, b, 1980; Smith and Williams, 1990; Cason and Williams, 1990). This is known to be an extremely competitive environment [unless selling and buying capacities are equal (Smith and Williams, 1990) or nearly equal (in Smith, 1965, the case with only two excess sellers is among those examined)]; such markets converge easily in less than ten periods. Roth et al. (1991, pp. 1075–82), nicely replicate these results in the context of what is customarily called the (buyers) posted price trading institution. They then compare the market results to the results of the ultimatum bargaining experiments, which show consistently lower first-mover prices.

We agree with their interpretation that first movers both in the market and in bilateral bargaining environments are making offers that are directed to maximizing expected return. This is true in the markets because those buyers posting prices less than the equilibrium get rejected; it is true in bilateral bargaining because the first mover believes (correctly) that less than equilibrium prices are accepted with high enough probability to yield an acceptable risk–reward trade-off.[12]

---

[12] However, Roth et al. suggest that the "competitive pressures" (behavior away from equilibrium) in the market need not be due to income-maximization, and they give an example (p. 1093) based on fairness preferences in which a buyer punishes other buyers by bidding above them. This contradicts earlier studies showing (Smith, 1976a, b, 1980) that convergence to equilibrium is *more* rapid under private than complete information: under private information fairness preferences cannot enter the explanation; only

Turning to the bargaining data in Roth et al. (1991), the overwhelming difference in their results vis-á-vis ours is the very large rejection rates by their second movers. They report rejection rates that vary from 10% to a remarkable high of 44%, with averages (across rounds) varying from 22 to 29%. These high rejection rates indicate a substantial divergence of expectations between bargainers. The standard game theoretic assumption of common expectations ("knowledge") is clearly not satisfied.

Why do our results yield such low rejection rates, when the Roth et al. results yield such high rejections rates? We offer three reasons. First, in the light of our Exchange treatment results, and the buyer–seller results of FS, the choice of the buyer instead of the seller to be the first mover in Roth et al. is problematic.[13] Culturally, almost everywhere, it is the seller who is thought to be justified in naming a price, not the buyer. Casting the buyer in this role creates the likelihood of a considerable role-reversal conflict in both subjects' behavior. Second, the use of rounds introduces the possibility that punishment strategies will be invoked because subjects treat them as socially relevant, not appreciating the game theoretic assumption that punishment is not supposed to be viable when you never get matched twice with the same partner. McCabe et al. (1996) report a surprising incidence of strategies clearly intended to punish noncooperative behavior, although the bargaining pairs are rerandomized after each play. To control for this, play should not be repeated in ultimatum games. Third, subjects were actually paid on only one of the ten rounds, the round being chosen at random. This makes expected payoffs quite low and greatly reduces the lost profit consequence to rejecting the first mover's offer. The FHSS ultimatum data show that rejection rates decrease as rewards increase: With no reward, rejections are 8/48 (16.6%); with $5 pies, rejections are 3/43 (6.98%); with $10 pies, rejections fall to 1/24 (4.17%). All our experiments used a pie of $10. In Roth et al. (1991), expected payoffs in a round are (1/10) $10 = $1 and (1/10) $30 = $3.00 for the U.S. data.

---

income maximization and competitive considerations can apply. Consequently, based on all the data, the interpretation is as follows: Under complete information, income maximization overwhelms any preference for equity, but the presence of the latter *could* be a factor (it could also be due to strategic behavior) in retarding the convergence rate relative to that under private information. Thus equity consideration cannot explain convergence in the Roth et al. market experiments, although they might possibly tell us why convergence was not still faster than that observed.

[13] Note that in the published version of their paper, the bargaining/ultimatum game is discussed as divide-the-prize. In their working paper, which included instructions, it is clear that they use an Exchange context. This indicates the importance of having instructions when trying to understand specific experimental results.

VIII.   Conclusion and Discussion

Here is a brief summary and interpretation of our primary findings.

1. In ultimatum games first mover offers are sensitive to the instructional (property right and contractual) setting of the experiment. In particular, offers are smaller if the context is that of an exchange between a seller and a buyer instead of a Divide $10 task, or if the first mover earns the (instructionally reinforced) right to his/her role instead of having it assigned in a random manner. When an earned entitlement is combined with exchange, less than 45% of the first movers offer $4 or more. When we combine Random Entitlement with Divide $10, more than 85% offer $4 or more, in line with previously reported ultimatum game outcomes. But the strategic/expectational character of ultimatum games makes it impossible to conclude from offer data alone whether offers in excess of $1 are due to other-regarding preferences or to the first mover's concern that his/her offer might be rejected unless it is deemed satisfactory by the second mover. The dictator game proposed by FHSS controls for strategic considerations in the ultimatum game.

2. In dictator games reported by FHSS, where the task is to divide $10 (Random Entitlement), only about 20% of the first movers offer $4 or more. Our replication of FHSS reinforces their results, although our subjects are in the same room.

3. We find that dictator games are also sensitive to the instructional (property right and contractual) settings of the experiment. When exchange is combined with the contest entitlement, only 4% of first movers offer $4, none offer $5. But, over 20% give $3 or $4; so these results also show that some incidence of other-regarding behavior cannot be ignored entirely as an element in either dictator games or ultimatum games under the usual anonymity conditions.

4. What is the nature of this other-regarding behavior? We only begin to answer this question with the double blind dictator experimental results summarized in this chapter. In this design, subjects are guaranteed anonymity not only with respect to other subjects but also with respect to the experimenters and everyone else – only the first mover can possibly know his/her offer. In our Double Blind 1 experimental results only 4 in 36 subjects, or 11%, give $3 or more to their counterparts. This may

approach the appropriate indicator of fairness as a pure prefer-ence phenomenon. The full data are not significantly altered in our Double Blind 2 experiments, which eliminate the paid mon-itors, and the use of 2 in 14 envelopes padded with blank white paper and including no money. But other aspects of the double blind procedures require experimental examination to identify what is driving the outcome; an envelope containing the cash might be an important factor.

5. These double blind dictator results (which, so far, are robust) imply that the outcomes in both dictator and ultimatum games should be modeled not primarily in terms of other-regarding preferences (or fairness) but primarily in terms of expectations – either explicit strategic expectations as in ulti-matum games or implicit concern for what the experimenter (or others) might think or do in dictator games. These double blind experimental results are inconsistent with any notion that the key to understanding experimental bargaining outcomes is to be found in subjects' autonomous, private, other-regarding prefer-ences. At the very minimum, these results suggest that other-regarding preferences may have an overwhelming social, what-do-others-know component and, therefore, should be *derived* formally from more elementary expectational consider-ations. These results also suggest that the argument for the use of anonymity in bargaining experiments as a means of con-trolling for social influences on preferences has not gone far enough. The presence of the experimenter, as one who knows subjects' bargaining outcomes, can be one of the most significant of all treatments for reducing the incidence of self-regarding behavior.

The results of these double blind experiments also appear to raise fun-damental questions regarding the nature and origins of other-regarding behavior in our society. The results suggest that such behavior may be due not to a taste for fairness (other-regarding preferences) but rather to a social concern for what others may think and for being held in high regard by others. If this view is correct, other-regarding behavior can be interpreted as a form of social exchange, in which I share some of my resource claims with others, in return for their esteem and good offices (and thus in return for shares of their resource claims, as is frequently observed in aboriginal tribes).[14] This interpretation accords with our

---

[14] This interpretation predicts that truly anonymous gift giving, where the contribution is not even known to family members or close friends, would be rare. For example, it is customary at church services to pass collection plates in public, during the service.

opening quotation from Jenness wherein the Eskimo were found to be oblivious to possible theft.[15] Jenness did not say this was *due* to "honesty," which was just a word for the phenomenon, not an explanation; instead he attributes it to the close community ties that allow monitoring and community discovery of theft. The contemporary ethnology literature, which is much focused on understanding sharing traditions in aboriginal societies, uses the term *reciprocity* (Hawkes, 1992, and Trivers, 1971, call it "reciprocal altruism") for the phenomenon in which individuals incur short-term costs for their sharing in exchange for delayed benefits from others' sharing. Consequently, repayment from reciprocators provides a net benefit in the self interest. Participants in this exchange process discriminate against those who do not return favors. Social traits like honesty and sharing are best, rational, policies. Such actions are possible in close-knit communities because each individual can "keep score" and punish free-riders with sanctions. Such relations break down where sociability is pushed to the edge of credibility, as in our double blind experiments.[16] But this simply shows how very strong is the game theoretic assumption that bargainers have no social relationship before or beyond the single instance in which they interact in their self-interest. That theory, together with this experimental testing, has, however, served an important function in explicating these diehard social issues.

Appendix: INSTRUCTIONS FOR EXPERIMENTS

FHSS Replication, Random Entitlements

Instructions

You have been asked to participate in an economics experiment. In addition to the $3 you already received for participation, you may earn an

---

[15] It is further illustrated by Hughes's (1982) account of the closing of the seasonal Alaskan salmon cannery where he worked as an accountant in the summer of 1951. The half-Eskimo watchman was removing locks and chains from various items of equipment; when asked why, he stated the locks and chains are not needed now that the Christians are gone.

[16] It is also well known that they break down under conditions of catastrophic destruction: riots, floods, earthquakes, and war devastation. Such conditions produce mini-doomsdays in which, temporarily, there is no tomorrow like yesterday, and one observes looting by normally law-abiding citizens. Reciprocity must be reestablished in the aftermath of the event. In the interim, the police are often reinforced with troops such as the national guard.

additional amount of money, which will be paid to you at the end of the experiment.

In this experiment each of you will be paired with a different person in this room. You will not be told who that person is either during or after the experiment, and he or she will not be told who you are either during or after the experiment.

The experiment is conducted as follows: a sum of $10 has been provisionally allocated to each pair, and person A in each pair can propose how much of this each person is to receive. To do this, person A will fill out a "Proposal Form." The proposal consists of an amount that person B is to receive and the amount that person A is to receive. The amount that person A is to receive is simply the amount to be divided, $10, minus the amount that person B is to receive.

When each person A has made a proposal, the proposal forms will be distributed to the appropriate Bs and each person B will be given a chance to accept or reject the proposal made by his or her counterpart person A. If person B accepts the proposal, then the amount of money will be divided as specified in the proposal. If person B wishes to accept the proposal, he or she should check "accept" on the proposal form. If person B does not wish to accept the proposal, he or she should check "reject" on the proposal form. If person B rejects the proposal, both A and B will be paid nothing.

After all the Bs have accepted or rejected the proposal made by the As each person will be paid according to the terms of the proposal.

Are there any questions?

FHSS Replication, Contest Entitlements

Instruction Changes

[The first two paragraphs and the first sentence of the third paragraph are identical to the random instructions.]

[Paragraph three continues . . .] The positions of persons A and B in each pairing will be determined by your scores on a general knowledge quiz. The quiz will be given concurrently to 12 participants. Each of you will be asked to answer the same set of 10 questions, selected from a large data bank of questions. Your quiz score will be the number of questions you answer correctly. Quiz scores will be ranked from highest to lowest, and ties will be decided by giving a higher ranking to the person who finishes the quiz in the shortest amount of time. Note #1 is the highest rank while 12 is the lowest. Once the complete ranking of participants is determined, those ranked 1–6 will have *earned* the right to be As. Notice that being an A and making the proposal is a definite advantage in this experiment. The other six participants will be Bs. The A with the highest rank (A1) will be paired with the highest ranking B (B7), the A with the second-highest rank (A2) will be paired with the second-highest ranking B (B8), and so on. Your total score will not be publicized under your name.

Once person A has *earned* the right to be an A, he or she will fill out a "Proposal Form." The proposal consists of an amount that person B is to receive and the amount that person A is to receive. The amount that person A is to receive is simply the amount to be divided, $10, minus the amount that person B is to receive. [The rest of the instructions are identical to the random instructions.]

FHSS Replication

Proposal Form

(1) Identification Number   ___A___
(2) Paired With   ___B___
(3) Amount to divide   _____
(4) Person B receives   _____
(5) Person A receives (3) – (4) _____
(6) Accept ——— Reject ———

Ultimatum, Buy–Sell, Random Entitlements

Instructions

In this experiment you have been paired anonymously with another person. One of you will be the seller, the other the buyer. The seller chooses the selling PRICE. *Then* the seller's choice is presented to the buyer who chooses to BUY or NOT BUY. In the following table, each cell shows the possible profit, in dollars, in the upper right corner for the seller, and in the lower left corner for the buyer. For example, if the seller chooses PRICE = $8, and then the buyer chooses BUY, the seller will be paid $8 and the buyer will be paid $2. If the seller chooses PRICE = $1, and then the buyer chooses BUY, the seller makes $1, and the buyer $9. If the buyer chooses NOT BUY, each of you will be paid nothing, whatever might have been the seller's choice of PRICE. The seller will be given a choice form. After he/she has circled a PRICE choice, the exper-

imenter will circle this PRICE on the buyer's choice form, and the buyer
will choose BUY or NOT BUY.

Ultimatum, Buy–Sell, Contest Entitlements

Instruction Changes

In this experiment, you will be paired with another person. One of you
will be the seller, the other the buyer. The positions of buyer and
seller in each pairing will be determined by your scores on a general
knowledge quiz. The quiz will be given concurrently to 12 participants.
Each of you will be asked to answer the same set of 10 questions, selected
from a large data bank of questions. Your quiz score will be the number
of questions you answer correctly. Quiz scores will be ranked from
highest to lowest, and ties will be decided by giving a higher ranking
to the person who finishes the quiz in the shortest amount of time.
Note #1 is the highest rank, while 12 is the lowest. Once the complete
ranking of participants is determined, those ranked 1–6 will have *earned*
the right to be sellers. Notice that being a seller and choosing price is
a definite advantage in this experiment. The other six participants will
be buyers. The seller with the highest rank (seller 1) will be paired with
the highest ranking buyer (buyer 7), the seller with the second highest
rank (seller 2) will be paired with the second-highest ranking buyer
(buyer 8), and so on. Your total score will not be publicized under your
name.

Once the seller has *earned* the right to be the seller, he/she chooses
the selling PRICE. [The rest follows from sentence two of the random
instructions.]

Ultimatum, Buy–Sell, Random Entitlements

Seller Choice

You are the seller. Please circle your choice of PRICE in the top row of
the following profit table.

Ultimatum, Buy–Sell, Context Entitlements

Seller Choice (Changes)

You have *earned* the right to be the seller. [Sentence two of random seller
choice follows.]

Ultimatum, Buy–Sell, Random Entitlements

Buyer Questionnaire

1. If you had been the seller in this experiment, what PRICE would you have chosen? ——— (write in the PRICE).
2. What PRICE do you *expect* the seller to choose? ——— (write in the PRICE).
3. What choice do you think the seller expected you to make? BUY ——— NOT BUY ——— (check your answer).

Ultimatum, Buy–Sell, Contest Entitlements

Buyer Questionnaire (Changes)

1. If you had *earned* the right to be a seller in this experiment, what PRICE would you have chosen? ——— (write in the PRICE).

[Questions 2 and 3 are the same as for the random entitlements.]

Ultimatum, Buy–Sell, Random Entitlements

Buyer Choice

You are the buyer. The price chosen by the seller is shown circled in the top row of the table below.

Please circle your choice of BUY or NOT Buy in the left column of the following profit table.

Ultimatum, Buy–Sell, Contest Entitlements

Buyer Choice (Changes)

[Add the following sentence at the end of the first paragraph]: Recall that the seller *earned* the right to be a seller.

[The rest is the same as for the random entitlements.]

Ultimatum, Buy–Sell, Random and Contest Entitlements

Seller Questionnaire

1. If you had been the buyer in this experiment would you have chosen to BUY ———, or NOT BUY ———? (check your answer).

2. What did you *expect* the buyer to choose? BUY ———, or NOT BUY ——— (check your answer)
3. What PRICE do you think the buyer expected you to choose? ——— (write in the PRICE)

Ultimatum, Buy–Sell, Random and Contest Entitlements

Choice Form

Seller Chooses PRICE

	$0	$1	$2	$3	$4	$5	$6	$7	$8	$9	$10	
Buyer chooses to												
BUY	$0	$1	$2	$3	$4	$5	$6	$7	$8	$9	$10	Seller profit
	$10	$9	$8	$7	$6	$5	$4	$3	$2	$1	$0	Buyer profit
NOT BUY	$0	$0	$0	$0	$0	$0	$0	$0	$0	$0	$0	Seller profit
	$0	$0	$0	$0	$0	$0	$0	$0	$0	$0	$0	Buyer profit

Dictator, Buy–Sell, Random Entitlements

Instructions

In this experiment you have been paired anonymously with another person. One of you will be the seller, the other the buyer. The seller chooses the selling PRICE, and the buyer must buy at that price. This determines the profits of both the seller and the buyer. In the following table, each cell shows the possible profit, in dollars, in the upper right corner for the seller, and in the lower left corner for the buyer. For example, if the seller chooses PRICE = $8, the seller will be paid $8 and the buyer will be paid $2. If the seller chooses PRICE = $1, the seller makes $1, and the buyer $9. The seller will be given a choice form. After he/she has circled a PRICE choice, the experimenter will collect the forms.

Dictator, Buy–Sell, Contest Entitlements

Instruction Changes

In this experiment you will be paired with another person. One of you will be the seller, the other the buyer. The positions of buyer and seller in each pairing will be determined by your scores on a general knowledge quiz. The quiz will be given concurrently to 12 participants. Each of you will be asked to answer the same set of 10 questions, selected from a large data bank of questions. Your quiz score will be the number of questions you answer correctly. Quiz scores will be ranked from highest to lowest and ties will be decided by giving a higher ranking to the person who finishes the quiz in the shortest amount of time. Note #1 is the highest rank while 12 is the lowest. Once the complete ranking of participants is determined, those ranked 1–6 will have *earned* the right to be sellers. Notice that being a seller and choosing price is a definite advantage in this experiment. The other six participants will be buyers. The seller with the highest rank (seller 1) will be paired with the highest ranking buyer (buyer 7), the seller with the second-highest rank (seller 2) will be paired with the second-highest ranking buyer (buyer 8), and so on. Your total score will not be publicized under your name.

Once the seller has *earned* the right to be the seller, he/she chooses the selling PRICE, and the buyer must buy at that price. This determines the profits of both the seller and the buyer. [The rest follows from sentence 3 of the random instructions.]

Dictator, Buy–Sell, Random Entitlements

Seller Choice

You are the seller. Please circle your choice of PRICE in the top row of the following profit table.

Dictator, Buy–Sell, Contest Entitlements

Seller Choice (Changes)

You have *earned* the right to be the seller. [The second sentence is the same.]

Dictator, Buy–Sell, Random Entitlements

Buyer Questionnaire

1. If you had been the seller in this experiment what PRICE would you have chosen? ——— (write in the PRICE).
2. What PRICE do you *expect* the seller to choose? ——— (write in the PRICE).

Dictator, Buy–Sell, Contest Entitlements

Buyer Questionnaire (Changes)

1. If you had *earned* the right to be a seller in this experiment what PRICE would you have chosen? ——— (write in the PRICE).

[Same question 2.]

Dictator, Buy–Sell, Random and Contest Entitlements

Buyer Form

You are the buyer. The price chosen by the seller is shown circled in the top row of the table below.

Dictator, Buy–Sell, Random and Contest Entitlements

Choice Form

Seller Chooses PRICE

$0	$1	$2	$3	$4	$5	$6	$7	$8	$9	$10	
$0	$1	$2	$3	$4	$5	$6	$7	$8	$9	$10	Seller profit
$10	$9	$8	$7	$6	$5	$4	$3	$2	$1	$0	Buyer profit

Dictator, Divide $10, Double Blind 1 Instructions[17]

You have been asked to participate in an economics experiment. For your participation today we have paid you $5 in cash. You may earn an additional amount of money, which will also be paid to you in cash at the end of the experiment.

In this experiment each of you will be paired with a different person who is in another room. You will not be told who these people are either during or after the experiment, and they will not be told who you are either during or after the experiment. This is room A.

You will notice that there are other people in the same room with you who are also participating in the experiment. You will not be paired with any of these people.

One of the persons in room A will be chosen to be the monitor for today's experiment. The monitor will be paid $10 in addition to the $5 already paid. The monitor will be in charge of the envelopes as explained below. In addition the monitor will verify that the instructions have been followed as they appear here.

The experiment is conducted as follows: Fourteen unmarked envelopes have been placed in a box. Twelve of these envelopes contain 10 one-dollar bills and 10 blank slips of paper. The remaining 2 envelopes contain 20 blank slips of paper. The monitor will be given a list of names of people in the room. He or she will call one person at a time to the back of the room, and hand each person an envelope from the box. The person who was called will then go to one of the seats, with a large box on top, in the back of the room.[18] The envelope will then be opened privately inside the box. Only the person who was given the envelope will know what the envelope contains.

Each person in room A must decide how many dollar bills (if any) and how many slips of paper to put in the envelope. The number of dollar bills plus the number of slips of paper must add up to 10. The person then pockets the remaining dollar bills and slips of paper. Examples: (1) Put $2 and 8 slips in the envelope, pocket $8 and 2 slips. (2) Put $9 and 1 slips in the envelope, pocket $1 and 9 slips. These are examples only the actual decision is up to each person. If the envelope has 20 blank slips, put 10 blank slips in the envelope and pocket the other 10. This is done in private, and we ask that you tell no one of your decision. Notice

---

[17] The instructor emphasized orally that the subjects were to remain quiet and ask only procedural questions. This is important to keep subjects from communicating editorial comments about the experiment.

[18] The experimenter maintained a substantial distance between himself and the subjects using the boxes. Also, two boxes, well separated, were used to speed up the process.

that each envelope returned will look exactly the same. Also note that no one else, including the experimenter, will know the personal decisions of people in room A.

Once you have made your decision you will seal your envelope and place it in the box marked return envelopes.[19] You may then leave the room.

After all fourteen envelopes have been returned, the monitor will take the box to room B. There are 14 people in room B. Each of these persons has been paid $5 to participate. The monitor will be given a list of names of people in room B. The monitor will then call up the people in room B. The monitor will choose an envelope from the box, open the envelope, record its contents, and give the contents of the envelope to the person called up. He or she is then free to leave. The monitor will continue until all the envelopes have been handed out and everyone else has left the room. The experiment is then over.

Dictator, Divide $10, Double Blind 2

Instruction Changes

[These instructions are the same as Double Blind 1, except all references to a student monitor and to envelopes containing 20 blank slips of paper are removed.]

---

[19] Not all subjects sealed their envelopes. The experimenter should reinforce this instruction with a reminder as the envelopes are passed out.

CHAPTER 6

Social Distance and Other-Regarding Behavior in Dictator Games

Elizabeth Hoffman, Kevin A. McCabe, and Vernon L. Smith

In this chapter, we ask if instructional and procedural manipulation can be used in a systematic way to understand the social norms that have been said to be the cause of deviations from game theoretic predictions in dictator and other games.[1] We find that such manipulations, intended to affect subjects' degree of social distance from the experimenter and assumed to affect expectations of reciprocity, play a key role in determining and understanding behavior.

Dictator games with and without monetary rewards have been compared by Forsythe et al. (1994; hereafter FHSS). In this game, a subject and his or her anonymous counterpart in another room "has been provisionally allocated" $10. The subject's task is to decide how to "divide" the $10; the counterpart has no recourse but must accept the allocation. These phrases appearing in quotation marks constitute the exact language that appears in the instructions to the subjects. As we shall see, this language is not entirely benign. It was first used by Kahneman et al. (1986, pp. 105–6; hereafter KKT); and FHSS desired to stay close to this originating study to examine its replicability and the effect of reward variations in this version of the game.

Dictator games are an interesting vehicle for studying the meaning and interpretation of fairness. The dictator game controls for strategic behavior in the ultimatum game where the fairness interpretation first emerged prominently. In the ultimatum game, player 1 offers any amount of the $10 to player 2. If player 2 accepts, the $10 is divided according to the terms of the offer; if player 2 rejects, each player gets 0. The subgame

---

[1] Coleman (1990, pp. 243–6) defines a norm to be a condition where the right to control a specific action is not held by the actor but by others. Norms can affect self-interested behavior by making individuals aware of potential acts of reciprocity in response to an action. See also Brewer and Crano's (1994) textbook statement of the definition of social norms as ". . . widely held rules of conduct. . . . Norms generally do not entail legal sanctions, but we feel considerable pressure to abide by them nonetheless" (p. 240). One of the norms of social exchange identified by Brewer and Crano is reciprocity, a key element in our interpretation.

perfect Nash equilibrium is to offer $1 (or 0), if there are 10 one-dollar bills, and for player 2 to accept. In experimental ultimatum games, however, the modal offer is observed to be half the pie to be divided. This has been attributed to a fairness norm. (See KKT and the references therein.) FHSS showed that offers are lower in the dictator game than in the ultimatum game, and argued that this indicated that fairness alone does not account for the generous offers by player 1 in the ultimatum game; strategic concerns also play an important role.

In this chapter, we explore further our interest, initiated in Hoffman et al. (1994; hereafter HMSS), in the conditions that affect outcomes in the dictator game. In HMSS, we found that when a double blind procedure, intended to guarantee the complete social isolation of the individual's decision (no one including the experimenter or any subsequent observer of the data could possibly know any subject's decision), was used, 64% of the offers were $0 with only 8% offering $4 or more.[2] On the other hand, our replication of FHSS (FHSS-R) using the language quoted earlier, results in only 18% offers of $0, with 32% offering $4 or more. Compare the cumulative distributions for Double Blind 1 and FHSS-R in Figure 6.1. The difference between these two distributions is highly significant with a Wilcoxon statistic $W = 4.02$ ($p < .0001$). We also note that there was no significant difference between the results reported by FHSS and FHSS-R.

We explore in detail the large observed discrepancy between these two very disparate versions of the dictator game. Our working hypothesis is that the difference is due to the concept of social distance or sense of coupling between the dictator and his or her counterpart, or others who know the dictator's decision.[3] We systematically vary this distance by changing elements of the language and procedures that a priori bear on the degree of the dictator's anonymity, and social isolation, in each of these two polar treatments. The significance of social isolation is in the removal of all suggestion of the quid pro quo of reciprocity. We believe that this experimental exercise is fundamental to understanding the received evidence for other-regarding behavior that is frequently manifest in bargaining game experiments, but in which strategic reciprocity and utilitarian elements are confounded in interpreting observed outcomes.

[2] Our double blind procedure does not guarantee ignorance of the identity of who received which treatment, as with a medicine or a placebo in medical treatments. We use the term to refer to ignorance over subject-message identity (as in Blank, 1991, dealing with author–referee identity in the reviewing process for journals).

[3] Social distance can be defined as the degree of reciprocity that subjects believe exists within a social interaction. By design, economic or material action is unidirectional in the dictator game viewed as an isolated interaction.

Percent

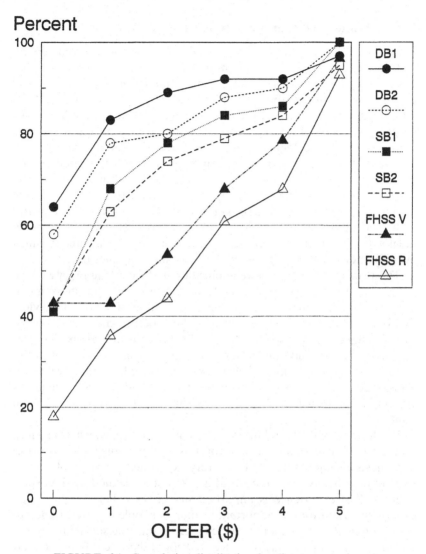

FIGURE 6.1. Cumulative distribution for dictator experiments.

I.   Culture and Sharing, or "Cooperative," Behavior

For perhaps a century or more, ethnologists have studied, and compared, cultures in which they have identified an immense range of sharing customs in close-knit tribal and extended family associations. A good example is in the study by Kaplan and Hill (1985a) of the Ache hunter–gathers in Paraguay. The products of gathering are stable low risk sources of food and are not commonly shared beyond the immediate family, whereas the high risk meat products of hunting, with a 40% chance that a given hunter will return empty handed, are widely shared throughout the band. Consequently, Ache "culture" has adapted the reach of its cooperative traditions to fit the fine structure of external resource costs. Other-regarding behavior is not a universal but varies with context depending upon opportunity costs. The wide sharing of meat within the band is supported as a repeat interaction game in which every hunter benefits on some days, contributes on other days.[4]

This principle finds extensive application in the contemporary anthropology literature (in particular see Hawkes, 1992, 1993, for an examination of competing hypotheses for the explanation of sharing behaviors that builds upon game theoretic and public good principles). This literature highlights cases in which reciprocal altruism is offered as an explanation of sharing traditions in terms of private (direct or opportunity) costs that reinforce reciprocal actions by deterring free-riding behavior. Thus, reciprocal altruists discriminate against, and punish, individuals who do not return favors such as the sharing of meat obtained from hunting.

But how does all this relate to the dictator game, in which, ostensibly, reprisal by the dictator's counterpart is not possible? Our a priori hypothesis is simply stated. In laboratory experiments, we cannot assume that subjects behave as if the world is completely defined by the experimenter. Past experience is important insofar as beliefs are based on experience. The future is important insofar as people are accustomed to operating in an environment in which there is ongoing social interaction and insofar as subjects may be concerned about the extent to which their decisions have postexperimental consequences or that others may judge

---

[4] There is something of a problem, however, with the most superior hunters. If they are not treated asymmetrically, they might leave the band and join another (interband mobility is high among the Ache). Kaplan and Hill (1985b) address hypotheses dealing with this issue and find that the better hunters have higher reproductive success than the less skilled hunters. This is due to both increased survival of their children and increased access to extramarital affairs that yield illegitimate offspring. Consequently, there is a private good modification of the public good sharing tradition when applied to the superior hunters.

them by their decisions. In short, subjects bring their repeated game baggage and reputations from the world into the laboratory, and the instructional language, especially in single-play sensitive experiments like the dictator game, can subtly suggest more or less isolation from that interactive experience. It is well documented in the experimental literature that the framing of a decision can influence expectations by associating a subject's decision with past experience.[5] But the nature and interpretation of such framing is not well understood; it needs further exploration in dictator games.

Thus, dictator instructions stating that the subject and his or her counterpart "have been provisionally allocated $10" and suggesting that the task is to "divide" the $10, may imply that the objective is to share the money with someone, who, though anonymous, is socially relatively near to the decision maker. At the other pole, defining the greatest social distance, is our double blind procedure, which goes to some pains to guarantee the decision maker absolute privacy and isolation from any social consequence or association with the person's decision.[6]

Based on this reasoning we relaxed a few elements at a time in the instructional language in each of the two extreme treatments. We predicted a priori that these treatments will both narrow the perceived social distance between the dictator and others and increase offers. We thus manipulated instructional language with the objective of showing how it can influence decision making by associating the subject's task with his or her prelaboratory reciprocity experience in ordinary day-to-day social intercourse. The less remote the conditions of the experiment from that experience, the more other-regarding the decision.

II.   Instructions and Procedures: Defining Variations on Perceived Social Distance

Double Blind 1 (DB1). In our original double blind dictator experiments, 15 subjects are recruited to room A and 14 subjects are recruited

---

[5] For example, HMSS reported that the distribution of offers in the ultimatum game is shifted to a significantly lower level when the game is formulated as an exchange between a buyer and a seller, and the right to be the first-mover seller, whose offer is a selling price, is earned by scoring highest in a pregame general knowledge quiz.

[6] Our manipulations to vary social distance are similar to those used by social psychologists to vary group pressure in studying individual conformity to a group opinion. See Allen (1965, pp. 133–75) for a review of this literature. Of particular interest is the use of envelopes by Argyle (cited and discussed in Allen, 1965, p. 146) to guarantee privacy, similar to our double blind treatment. Allen reports that increases in privacy reduce conformity.

to room B. Subjects are met by an experimenter, paid a $5 show-up fee, given a set of instructions, and asked to sit at assigned seats that are positioned to keep subjects as separate as possible. Subjects are also reminded that there should be no talking or other attempts to communicate during the experiment. The instructions are reproduced in the appendix of HMSS (Chapter 5) under "Dictator, Divide $10, Double Blind 1."

In the following description, sentences labeled (i)–(iv) represent conditions that are altered in subsequent instructional treatments. (i) One subject from room A is chosen to be the monitor and will be paid $10. The experimenter then reads aloud the instructions. By listening to the instructions read aloud, the subjects can verify that they all have the same instructions. After the instructions are read, the decision making part of the experiment begins. (ii) The instructions inform the subjects that there are 14 envelopes. Twelve envelopes contain 10 one-dollar bills and 10 blank slips of paper, and 2 envelopes contain 20 blanks slips of paper. Subjects in room A are called one at a time and are asked to bring personal belongings with them. This ensures a clean exit. Once called, a subject is handed an unmarked opaque envelope chosen at random from the box of 14 envelopes. The subject takes the envelope to the back of the room and sits behind a large cardboard box, which maintains his or her privacy. (iii) The subject opens the envelope and decides how many one-dollar bills to keep and how many bills to leave for a person in room B; all bills are replaced by blank sheets of paper, so that the envelopes are all the same thickness. (iv) After a subject has made a decision, he or she is asked to seal the envelope and return it to a box near the exit door. The subject then leaves the experiment. This is repeated until all subjects have left room A. The experimenter next takes the box of envelopes to room B.

Upon arriving at room B, the monitor (and experimenter) sit outside the room, and the subjects are called one at a time. In the subject's presence, an envelope is chosen and opened, and the envelope's contents are recorded by the monitor on plain paper containing no names. The subject is then given the envelope's contents, and he or she leaves the experiment. This is repeated until all subjects have left room B. At this point the monitor is paid and the experiment is over.

In our DB1 experiments, we guaranteed complete anonymity by including the 2 envelopes containing 20 blank slips (ii). Without this precaution, if everyone in room A took all $10, then each person's decision was clearly known by the experimenter, and perhaps others. However, with the existence of two dummy envelopes, the experimenter and the receivers in Room B could not know whether any one person in room

A has left no money or merely received a dummy envelope. The blank envelopes (ii) were expected to magnify the dictator's sense of isolation, and the existence of a monitor (i) removed the experimenter as an executor of the procedure (although as noted in HMSS, paying the monitor $10 may help the subjects to justify keeping the money).

Double Blind 2 (DB2). We examined these hypotheses in a second treatment that omitted (i) the paid monitor and (ii) the 2 blank envelopes (DB2). Complete anonymity was now no longer guaranteed but is highly likely as long as someone leaves money. Offers in DB2 are expected to increase because we have weakened the sense of social isolation. It was in conducting DB2 that we first observed aspects of subject behavior that sensitized us to the subtle features of anonymity and social distance (HMSS, footnote 9). Not all the subjects in room A sealed their envelopes as instructed, and both experimenters (in this case McCabe and Smith) noted that, most revealingly, there was a pronounced tendency for those leaving no money to seal their envelopes and for those leaving positive amounts of money to not seal their envelopes. We had not had the opportunity to observe this in DB1 because of the use of a subject monitor. This experience brought home to us the features of detectability made possible by the presence of an experimenter, but which, from the perspective of the subject, reduces privacy.

Single Blind 1 (SB1). In our next treatment, SB1, everything was the same as in DB2, except that we modified (iv) so that the experimenter now learned each decision maker's decision. The appendix (available upon request from the authors) contains the instructions for SB1. This was done by (a) having the subject return to the experimenter after deciding what to leave in the envelope and (b) having his or her unsealed envelope opened behind a large cardboard box at the experimenter's desk. This ensured isolation with respect to other subjects but not the experimenter. (c) The amount he or she had offered was then recorded, (d) the envelope was then sealed, and (e) the subject dropped it in the return box and left. We predicted that allowing the experimenter to know the subjects' decisions would reduce their social isolation, and increase offers; except for the use of envelopes containing the money, we moved closer to the procedures used by FHSS and others.

Single Blind 2 (SB2). Our last condition, SB2, is identical to SB1 except that we modified (iii). The envelope now contained a decision form for making the decision, instead of money, and we used the following procedure. (a) A subject filled out the form in the back of the room behind a cardboard box. (b) The subject returned to the experimenter at the front of the room, where (c) his or her envelope was opened behind a cardboard box, and (d) the subject was paid the amount he or she decided to keep. This was recorded opposite the person's name on a data sheet. (e) If the decision gave money to a subject in room B, the money was placed in the envelope, and the envelope was sealed; then (f) the subject dropped it in the return box as he or she left the room. The actual instructions are in the appendix (available on request). This treatment corresponds to the standard way that subjects are paid in experiments, but the use of an intermediate form further socializes the transaction. We asked whether it makes a difference if the envelope contains a credit (or IOU), to be exchanged for money with the experimenter, instead of money to be directly divided. Because SB2 created a direct transaction between the subject and the experimenter (in order to get paid), social distance was narrowed, and we predicted that offers would increase relative to SB1.

A.   FHSS Replication and Variation (FHSS-R and FHSS-V)

Having relaxed in three steps (DB2, SB1, SB2) components of DB1 that had an impact on the dictator's hypothesized degree of social isolation or distance from others (subjects and experimenter), we turned next to the other treatment pole – our replication of FHSS – and weakened the dictator's sense of community with his or her counterpart. We did this with only one change: We dropped the phrases suggesting that the dictator and his or her anonymous counterpart "have been provisionally allocated" $10 and that the task is to "divide" the $10. The appendix (available on request) contains the full instructions that we used for FHSS-R, and for the indicated variation (FHSS-V). We predict that this change in the KKT/FHSS instructions will cause a reduction in offers.

Finally, we note that there remain several differences between our SB2 instructions and FHSS-V.[7] The most important we suggest is that in SB2 (in common with SB1, DB1, and DB2) all subjects in room A act out, and observe others acting out, the privacy conditions articulated in the instructions (e.g., the decision form is in an envelope, the subject

[7] For example, we used illustrations and the privacy of a box. We also shortened the instructional description. In HMSS our original DB1 treatment constituted a large step-out experiment from FHSS, designed to include everything we thought might be important in creating the greatest social isolation for subject dictators. In order that the resulting instructions would not become too lengthy, we shortened or eliminated elements of the FHSS instructions which we thought were unessential to our objectives. We carried these allegedly "minor" difference through to SB2. Despite these changes, our FHSS-R experiments *do* replicate the results of FHSS.

Table 6.1. *Dictator experiment design*

	Experiment	Number of observations	Anonymity condition	Decision type
1	DB1	36	Double blind and blanks[a]	Dollars
2	DB2	41	Double blind	Dollars
3	SB1	37	Single blind	Dollars
4	SB2	43	Single blind	Form
5	FHSS-V	28	Single blind	No sharing language
6	FHSS-R	28	Single	Sharing language

[a] Includes two envelopes with 20 blank slips and monitor paid $10.

chooses an envelope and carries it to the privacy at a large box, and returns it to the experimenter). Consequently, we expect offers to be less generous in SB2 than in FHSS V.

III.   Experimental Design and Research Hypothesis

Our experimental design is summarized in Table 6.1. If we let $F(\cdot)$ be the population distribution of offers for each of the six treatments (DB1, DB2, SB1, SB2, FHSS-V, and FHSS-R), our research hypothesis is

$$H_R: F(\text{DB1}) > F(\text{DB2}) > F(\text{SB1}) > F(\text{SB2}) > F(\text{FHSS} - \text{V}) > F(\text{FHSS} - \text{R})$$

which will be tested against the null hypothesis that the distributions are identical.

IV.   Results

A descriptive summary of the data for all six treatments is displayed in the cumulative distributions of offers shown in Figure 6.1. As we weaken the anonymity or social isolation conditions (from treatment DB1 to FHSS-R), we observe that the offer distributions increase as predicted. With the Jonckeere nonparametric order test statistic equal to 3.77 ($p < .0001$), we reject the null hypothesis that the distributions of offers are the same across treatments in favor of our predicted ordered alternative. The individual pairwise treatments are not generally significantly different, but this was not our claim. Rather our prior prediction was that the nested series of treatments would be ordered as indicated.

V.   Discussion and Conclusions

Anomalous results in ultimatum games have been interpreted as due to a fairness utilitarian ethic. In FHSS this interpretation was tested by comparison with the dictator game, which controls for the first mover's expectations of rejection by the second mover. The resulting decrease in offers showed that fairness alone could not account for the anomalous behavior in ultimatum games; nevertheless 62% of the dictators still gave $2 or more to their counterparts. We hypothesized that the latter arises from subject expectations of reciprocity – a social norm emerging from experience with repeat interaction outside the laboratory. We explore this hypothesis using the dictator game, by varying the distance between dictator and experimenter, and, presumably, the degree of potential reciprocity in the dictator/experimenter relationship. Our data supported the hypothesis that as social isolation increases, there is a further shift toward lower offers.

We interpreted the data as generally supportive of the economic assumption of self-interested behavior, but we placed three caveats on this assumption. First, in DB1 a few subjects still sent their corresponding player 2s a considerable amount of money. This may reflect true utilitarian other-regarding preferences. Alternatively, these subjects may have been suspicious of our procedures to guarantee anonymity. Second, our experiments were conducted among relative peers, that is, college undergraduates, with relatively low stakes involved. Third, our double blind procedure may not result in more self-interested offer distributions in ultimatum games. This would occur if the first players' expectations that the offer will be rejected, dominate any and all affects caused by complete anonymity.

Independent replication by other researchers provides additional evidence for the importance of social distance. Eckel and Grossman (1996b) replicated our Double Blind 1 procedures with their subjects. They then compared the results with parallel experiments in which the dictator makes an offer not to another person like himself or herself but to a charity – the American Red Cross. They showed a significant increase in the distribution of offers using the charity treatment. The American Red Cross has a long history of providing benefits, thus inviting reciprocity. The Eckel-Grossman results suggest that history matters, and we think their results help to corroborate our reciprocity interpretation.

Our experiments raise important questions about the nature of expectations in the occurrence of other-regarding outcomes. Similar questions are involved when economists ask: Why is fiat (paper) money valuable? In answering this question, economists do not conclude that people accept money out of a desire to be fair to the holder of paper money. Instead, the value of money is better understood as derived from the more basic desire to consume goods and resources through the normal process of reciprocity in ongoing exchange. People accept paper money, which is intrinsically valueless, because other people are expected to accept it for goods and services; as a by-product, this results in socially more efficient trade. For example, McCabe (1989) reports fiat money experiments in which, as the end-game approaches, people refuse to accept ultimately worthless paper money in exchange for goods. As the cycle is repeated, this refusal occurs earlier and earlier. In the limit, no one accepts fiat money because no one expects others to accept it. In this process, we think of people bringing their repeated game exchange experience into the laboratory with them. They begin by accepting fiat money in trade but learn over successive cycles that the conditions of the experiment do not support their unconscious expectation that the money will be accepted by others. Over time, their expectations adapt to the unfamiliar conditions in the laboratory experiment.

Similarly, we can ask, what is it that is being consumed when someone rejects an offer in an ultimatum game, or when someone gives money away in either the ultimatum or the dictator experiments. From the perspective of this experiment, the answer, which we will call reputation (or image), is largely explained as self-regarding, that is, people act as if they are other-regarding because they are better off with the resulting reputation. Only under conditions of social isolation are these reputational concerns of little force. As with fiat money, it seems unreasonable to believe that people directly consume their reputations in isolation but instead value their reputations because of the long-term personal benefits that result. In addition, people value social interactions with others, and a good reputation increases the chance of continued social interaction.[8]

Evidence consistent with this interpretation also comes from evolutionary psychology. This approach to social cognition has been succinctly conveyed by Cosmides and Tooby (1992): ". . . the mind should contain organized systems of inference that are specialized for solving various families of problems, such as social exchange, threat, coalitional relations and mate choice. Advocates of evolutionary views do not deny that humans learn, reason, develop, or acquire a culture; however, they do argue that these functions are accomplished at least in part through the operation of cognitive mechanisms that are content-specialized . . ." (p. 166). Continuing, this contrasts with the standard model of economics and other social sciences in which ". . . the faculty of reasoning consists of a small number of processes that are designed to solve the most inclusive and general class of reasoning problems possible . . ." Cosmides and

---

[8] Thus, individuals who value social interaction and recognize that they will be ostracized for loss of reputation might commit suicide rather than reveal information that would cost them their reputations.

Tooby then summarize a research program they interpret as showing that the cognitive processes that involve reasoning about social exchange contain design features that you would expect if they are adaptations shaped by evolutionary selection pressures (pp. 179–221).

As we interpret this literature in relation to our "social distance" manipulation in the dictator game, people have unconscious, preprogrammed rules of social exchange behavior that suit them well in the repeated game of life's interaction with other people. These patterns are imported into the laboratory. There, when they encounter a dictator game for the "division" of $10 "provisionally allocated" to them and an anonymous counterpart, not many act in their strict self-interest because the situation seems similar to the day-to-day sharing characterizing repeat play interaction. As these cues are modified by lengthening the distance between the individual and others, and finally imposing "complete isolation" in the double blind treatment, we trigger increasingly fewer automatic responses and allow decision processes that recognize more prominently strictly self-interested actions. Future research will explore the link between reciprocity in the laboratory and work by evolutionary psychologists. See Chapter 9, this volume, for a more extended discussion of these issues.

CHAPTER 7

On Expectations and the Monetary Stakes in Ultimatum Games

Elizabeth Hoffman, Kevin A. McCabe, and Vernon L. Smith

In an ultimatum game, player 1 makes an offer of X from a total of M to player 2. If player 2 accepts the offer, then player 1 is paid $(M - X)$ and player 2 receives X; if player 2 rejects the offer, each gets zero. In the ultimatum game experiments reported in the literature, M is typically not more than \$10 (see Forsythe et al., 1994, hereafter FHSS; Hoffman et al., 1994, hereafter HMSS, and the literature cited therein). We report new results for 50 bargaining pairs in which $M = \$100$ and compare them with previous outcomes from 48 pairs with $M = \$10$. The need for an examination of the effect of increased stakes on ultimatum bargaining is suggested by a literature survey of the effect of varying the stakes in a wide variety of decision-making and market experiments over the last 33 years (Smith and Walker, 1993b). Many cases were found in which the predictions of theory were improved when the monetary rewards were increased. There were also cases in which the level of monetary rewards had no effect on the results. Consequently, it is necessary to examine the stakes question on a case-by-case basis. The previously reported effect of instructional changes, which define different institutional contexts, on ultimatum game outcomes, and the effect of stakes reported here, suggest a game formulation that explains changes in the behavior of both players as a result of changes in the instructional treatments. We formulated such a model and indicate how it might be further tested.

I.   Theory and Previous Results

Suppose the payoffs and individual rationality of the players are common knowledge. Then the unique strict subgame perfect equilibrium of the ultimatum game is $X^* = \$1$, if \$1 is the minimum unit of account (i.e., if M consists of ten one-dollar bills to be allocated between the two players). The universal and highly replicable result reported in the experimental literature is for the mean (or median) offer, X, to be substantially in excess of \$1. The distribution of reported offers, however, is also influenced by the conditions that describe or define the bargaining

139

task. For example, FHSS reported results in which 24 pairs of subjects, 24 in one room and 24 in another, are paired anonymously and each is told that $10 "has been provisionally allocated to each pair" and M is described as "the total amount to be divided."[1] In this ambiguous property right formulation, the modal player 1 offer is $5. HMSS replicated these results, using the same instructional clauses, although the anonymously paired subjects resided in the same room, and consisted of six pairs in each of four sessions. The resulting distribution of offers is shown in Figure 7.1(a).

This result is altered if two changes are made in the conditions of bargaining: (1) 12 subjects first engage in a pregame general knowledge quiz with the instructional emphasis that the six highest scoring subjects will "earn" the right to the position of first mover, each paired respectively with the subjects who ranked 7–12 in the quiz scores; (2) player 1s are described as sellers who choose a price that is communicated to the buyer with whom they are paired who then chooses to either "buy" or "not buy" at the offered price. The set of possible profit outcomes is identical to those in the ultimatum game, the difference being that the outcomes are intended to be perceived as arising from the gains due to exchange instead of from the "division of $10." The conditions (1) and (2) are intended as treatments for legitimatizing the property right implied by player 1s' assignment to the advantageous position of first mover. Such assignment conditions are predicted to reduce the distribution of offers relative to the ambiguous entitlement treatment. In fact, this prediction is supported quite strongly. See Figure 7.1(b) and compare it with Figure 7.1(a).

II.   The High Stakes Argument

In seminar presentations and informal discussions of the failure of the perfect equilibrium model to predict ultimatum game behavior, it is often argued that the strongly falsifying results are an artifact of the low stakes ($M = $10). The argument, as we have encountered it, is stated as follows: Although subjects, as observed, may reject sums of $1 or $2, who, rationally, would reject $10 or $20? According to this line of reasoning, if the

---

[1] This particular instructional language used by FHSS followed that used by Kahneman et al. (1986, p. 105). The fact that a sum M is described as having been "provisionally allocated to each pair" suggests an uncertain and ambiguous private right to the money. Describing the task as one of "dividing M" suggests that the two individuals are solving a sharing problem, not a strategic interaction problem. It is as if you and I are walking along the street, and we see an envelope on the sidewalk. I pick it up. It contains 10 one-dollar bills. I hand five to you and keep five.

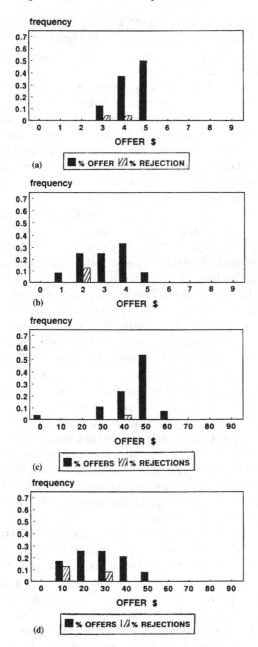

FIGURE 7.1. Effect of $10 versus $100 stakes in Divide Ultimatum (a and c) and in Contest/Exchange treatment (b and d).

stakes are increased tenfold, say to $M = \$100$, keeping the unit of account proportionally constant (that is M consists of ten \$10 bills), then the first mover offers will be proportionally decreased, and second movers will readily accept all positive offers.

Telser (1993) offers a carefully reasoned argument along the following lines. Think of fairness as a commodity such that consumption is maximized when the split is equal. It is reasonable to assume that fairness varies inversely with its price. Therefore, if we raise the stakes, the price of fairness increases (i.e., offers of some small percentage of the total get larger, and it is not implausible that such amounts will be accepted for large M). Telser's argument is consistent with the decision cost model proposed in Smith and Walker (1993b), except that decision cost has its sign changed to reflect the commodity value of fair behavior. His argument receives direct support in the "price of fairness" bargaining results reported by Eckel and Grossman (1996a). They report that although the demand for fairness by males is highly inelastic with respect to the price of fairness, the demand by females is relatively elastic. Females exhibit predominantly fair behavior when the opportunity cost of fair behavior is \$1 but shift to unfair behavior when the opportunity cost is \$2.

Although Telser's example involves raising the stakes to millions of dollars, we propose (consistent with our budget limitations) experiments in which the stakes are raised from \$10 to \$100. The sum of \$100, for an experiment that lasts about 20 minutes, is very generous for volunteer undergraduates whose opportunity cost is a small fraction of \$100. Our subjects eagerly revolunteer for additional experiments after having earned \$10–20 in other types of experiments. Also, as reported by Eckel and Grossman (1996a), the price of fairness as they measure it is low. Hence the predictive hypotheses for $M = \$100$ are (1) first-mover offers will decrease significantly and (2) the rejection rate will decrease. Because the rejection rates are so low in Figures 7.1(a) (2 in 24) and 7.1(b) (3 in 24), we do not expect a (statistically significant) reduction in the rejection rates with increased stakes.

How might the stakes argument fail in the ultimatum game? The first thing to note is that player 1s' potential loss as well as gain from a non-equal split of M increases with M. Player 1 might be so concerned about the "unthinkable" – a rejection by player 2 – that player 1 becomes all the more committed to guaranteeing acceptance by offering $X = \$50$. Thus the silent, anonymous, veto power of player 2 may loom even larger in the mind of player 1 when the stakes are \$100 than when they are \$10. Second, a more formal consideration is the prospect that, in terms of utility theory for risky choices, player 1 exhibits constant relative risk aversion *in the dollars earned in the experiment*. This means that increasing the stakes by any factor does not change the proportional risk encountered, which in turn does not change the percentage of M that is offered to player 2. Empirical evidence favoring the constant relative risk-averse model of decision making has been reported in auction experiments, in which the stakes have been varied by factors as high as 20 (Smith and Walker, 1993a); and in the revealed behavior of a Treasury bond dealer (Wolf and Pohlman, 1983) where the stakes range in the millions of dollars.

III.   Subject Recruitment Procedures

Subjects were recruited according to the usual recruitment procedures used at the University of Arizona Economic Science Laboratory. During any typical week, several experiments are running throughout the week, and subjects are recruited both from classes and by telephone to participate in "an experiment." A sum of $3 ($5) is promised to each subject who signs up in advance and arrives on time. Each subject is called and reminded the night before. They are also told that they will be paid more money, in cash, at the end of the experiment, depending on their decisions. Every subject who participates in any particular experiment is logged into a database, allowing the experimenter to check for previous participation in that experiment.

Because of the unusual nature of the $100 experiments, the $100 Contest/Exchange and Random entitlement experiments were run in two short periods separated by several months. Other experiments, involving the usual $10–40 payoffs, were running at different times on the same days. Thus, subjects could not know that they would be participating in a $100 experiment, even if word got around that such experiments existed. Moreover, recruiters are always told not to give prospective subjects any information about a particular experiment. There was no evidence during the runs of the $100 experiments that subjects arrived expecting to make $100.

IV.   Description of Experimental Design

In each of eight experimental sessions, 12 subjects participate simultaneously in one,[2] and only one, ultimatum game. Each subject is paid for

[2] Under the Contest/Exchange entitlement treatment, we had a no-show in one of the sessions, and therefore only 5 pairs so that $N = 23$. Under the Random entitlement treatment we had a few experienced subjects, who had been in a previous ultimatum game, slip through our screen. These data were not used. We are very strict in excluding experienced subjects because it is well established in work reported by Roth et al. (1991) and

arriving on time and signing in for the experiment.[3] When all the subjects arrived, they were assigned to separate cubicles in the same room; then they read and had read to them a set of instructions that described the task. In the Random entitlement treatment, subjects were randomly assigned the positions of person A and person B and randomly and anonymously paired with one another. Each person A was asked to divide $100, in $10 units, between himself or herself and the corresponding person B. Once person A proposed a division, person B indicated whether he or she accepted or did not accept. Once each person B made a decision, subjects were paid individually and privately and left the experiment one at a time.

In the Contest/Exchange treatment, subjects answered 10 current events questions. The subject ranked ←1 was the seller, paired with the subject ranked ←7 as the buyer. The subject ranked ←2 was paired with the subject ranked ←8, and so on. No subject was informed of the identity of his or her counterpart, and each experimental session involved only one pairing and one decision.[4]

After the buyer and seller assignments had been made, each seller chose a price, given the payoff chart for the Contest/Exchange treatment. (See the appendix in Chapter 5, this volume, but with $M = \$100$.) This payoff chart showed that the game is an ultimatum game embedded in an exchange. There was $100 to divide between the buyer and the seller. If the seller stated a price of $90 and the buyer agreed to buy, the seller

others that ultimatum game behavior is markedly affected by repeat-play conditions even when subjects are always paired with a different person, and this is common information. (See Chapter 5, this volume, for a discussion.) Also, under the Random entitlement, an observation was excluded because, undetected by the experimenters until it was too late, a player 1 who offered $30 wrote the following note on his decision form to player 2: "Don't be a maryter [sic]; it is still the easiest $35 you've ever made." (The "$35" refers to the $30 offer plus the $5 show-up fee.) Player 2 not only rejected the $30 offer but responded with the following explanatory note to the experimenters: "*Greed* is driving this country to hell. Become a part of it and pay."

[3] Subjects in the $10 experiments were paid $3, the standard show-up fee at the time those experiments were run. Subjects in the $100 experiments were paid $5, the current standard payment.

[4] Typically experimenters want to infer some conclusion about markets when discussing their experimental results. For example Kahneman et al. (1986, pp. 105–6) reported experiments in which subjects were asked to reallocate $10, provisionally allocated to each pair, using simultaneous move rules (i.e., the second mover marks those first-mover offers that are acceptable and those that are not before knowing the first mover's decision). They reported a strong tendency toward equal splits with a substantial portion of second movers willing to reject positive offers. The authors suggested that such resistance to unfairness "is of the type that might deter a profit-maximizing agent or firm seeking to exploit some profit opportunities" (p. 106). In order to better justify the extension of such results to firms we hypothesize that it may be important to describe the setting as an exchange between a buyer and a selling firm, and not as one of reallocating $10 provisionally allocated to each pair.

Table 7.1. *Property rights and stakes in the design for Ultimatum games*

Number of bargaining pairs (observations) by treatment	Monetary stakes	
Property right condition	$M = \$10$	$M = \$100$
Divide M; Random entitlement	24	27
Exchange; Contest entitlement	24	23

got \$90 and the buyer got \$10. Similarly, if the seller stated a price of \$80 and the buyer agreed to buy, the seller got \$80 and the buyer got \$20. As in other ultimatum games, and in Fouraker and Siegel (1963), if the buyer decided to NOT BUY, both buyer and seller received \$0.

Once the sellers chose prices, we circled the appropriate seller's price choice on each buyer's choice form and asked the buyers to circle BUY or NOT BUY. Once the buyers made their decisions, subjects were paid individually and privately, and they left the experiment separately.

Table 7.1 provides the 2 × 2 experimental design listing the number of observations (bargaining pairs) in the previous control, and in the new treatment, conditions. All hypothesis tests refer to the difference between Random/Divide and Contest/Exchange, and between \$10 and \$100. Instructions for the \$10 experiments are printed in the appendix to Chapter 5 in this volume.

V. Empirical Results

Histograms for the relative frequency distribution of first-mover offers are charted as solid black bars in Figures 7.1(c, d) for each property right treatment, and $M = \$100$. The striped bars charted for some offers indicate the percentage of the total observations that were rejected for each offer amount.

Table 7.2 lists the pairwise Wilcoxon and Epps-Singleton test statistics and corresponding significance levels for each of the four treatments: the two property right treatments and the two stake levels. Notice that we cannot reject the null hypothesis that the offers are identical with \$10 stakes and with \$100 stakes, with and without the Contest/Exchange

Table 7.2. *Ultimatum test of comparisons[a] when property rights and stakes are varied*

Wilcoxon (W) statistic[b] (prob) Epps-Singleton (ES) statistic (prob)	Random entitlement, FHSS instructions, Divide $10	Contest entitlement, Exchange $100
Contest entitlement, Exchange $10	W = −4.09 (0.00) ES = 24.46 (0.00)	W = 0.91 (0.36) ES = 1.37 (0.85)
Random entitlement, FHSS instruction, Divide $100	W = 0.79 (0.79) ES = 2.79 (0.59)	W = 4.93 (0.00) ES = 36.82 (0.00)

[a] Test statistics are based on the null hypothesis that the compared samples were drawn from the same population.
[b] Sign is based on row minus column comparison.

treatment. Moreover, we can reject the hypothesis that the results are the same for the FHSS instructional clauses, and the Contest/Exchange instructions, for both high and low stakes. These results provide strong evidence that multiplying the stakes by 10 (from $10 to $100) does not affect the first movers' perceptions of acceptable outcomes under the two treatments. Subjects continue to offer nearly half the stakes under ambiguous property rights and to make significantly smaller offers under the Contest and Exchange treatment.

Comparing Figures 7.1(b, d) for stakes of $10 and $100, respectively, under Contest/Exchange, there appears to be a slight reduction in offers as the stakes are increased: There are fewer offers of 40% of M and more offers of 10% of M. Thus some player 1s appear to reason that player 2s will not reject $10 offers. There is also an increase in the rejection rates. With $10 stakes there are 3 rejections in 23, whereas 5 in 27 are rejected when the stakes are increased to $100 (but this difference is not statistically significant); 3 of the 4 offers of $10 are rejected, and 2 of the 5 offers of $30 are rejected. (Actually it was 3 of 6; see footnote 2.) Comparing the random entitlement with Contest/Exchange, when the stakes are $100, the rejection rate increases from 1 in 27 to 5 in 23, a significant increase ($p < .001$). Several subjects in the $100 experiments routinely reject offers equal to and greater than the entire stakes in the $10 experiments. This means that the change in shared expectations associated with the Contest/Exchange treatment with $10 stakes does not carry to the $100 experiments. A few first movers assume that they can now offer less, but more second movers do not consider the change to be legitimate.[5] Generally, however, the first-mover results, for both the random and the Contest/Exchange entitlement treatments, are consistent with an expected utility formulation of the game, as developed below, in which first movers are constantly relatively risk averse.

FHSS reported ultimatum games with Random entitlements results in which the stakes are varied from no pay to $5 to $10. They report no significant difference in offers between pay and no pay and none between $5 and $10. But the FHSS results do show a pronounced decline in rejection rates as the stakes are increased. Pooling the HMSS data with those of FHSS for $10, and adding our results from this chapter for $100, we record a monotone decrease in rejection rates as the stakes are increased. The difference between no pay and $5 is very large and serves to illustrate the importance of using monetary rewards (Smith and Walker, 1993b). These data are plotted in Figure 7.2.

VI.   An Expected Utility Model of the Ultimatum Game Results

We interpret the preceding experiments as implying that subjects' expectations have an important effect on the observance of fair outcomes (i.e., the latter is neither fundamentally nor exclusively due to other-regarding utility preferences). Thus the utility of the monetary reward retained, and, arguably, of that given, is not judged to have changed because the game context has been altered from "divide M" to an exchange in which the buyer/seller surplus is M. Rather, expectations are assumed to change primarily because describing the first mover as a seller and requiring that the role of the first mover be earned confers legitimacy and common expectations on a more self-regarding offer by the first mover. It cannot be assumed that subjects abandon their naturally occurring norms of reference and standards for legitimacy when they enter the laboratory to participate in allegedly "one-shot" decision experiments. When the first mover is cast as a buyer, an unfamiliar position of power (Roth et al., 1991), rejection rates are much higher, suggesting common expectations are not attained.

Subjects also may be concerned about appearing greedy and being judged so by the experimenter, or by others who review the decisions. A general reputation for greediness may invite retaliation, poor social

---

[5] Our results provide a clear example of a point often made by McCloskey (1985), and others, that statistical significance is not equivalent to behavioral economic significance. We observe a statistically insignificant shift toward lower offers, but the rejection rates rise to levels larger than observed in any of our previous experiments. Hence, for the first time in our research program, we find a treatment ($100 combined with Contest and Exchange) that causes first- and second-mover expectations not to shift in concert.

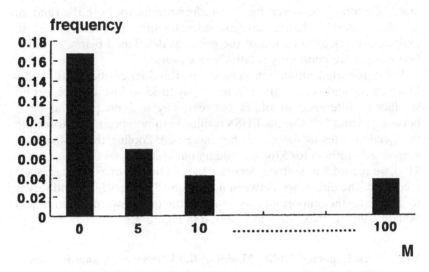

FIGURE 7.2. Rejection frequency versus stakes, M, in Ultimatum games; Random entitlements.

acceptance, and an inability to participate profitably in informal social exchange mechanisms – conditions that characterize the ordinary repeated games in social interaction. The habits that produce a good reputation require opportunistic short-run benefits to be given up for longer-run reciprocal benefits in future social exchange. This requires a readiness both to moderate one's own greedy behavior and to punish excessive greed in others, when the occasion arises (again, see footnote 2).

In the ultimatum game, beginning with player 2, we assume that these considerations imply subjective expectations over an external value to player 2, Y_2, which is realized after play of the ultimatum game. Y_2 is conditional on the current decision, A_2 ($= 1$, if accept; 0 otherwise); on player 1's offer, X; the stakes, M; and the instructions I, which trigger contexts for the various considerations discussed earlier. That is $G(Y_2|X, M, A_2, I)$ is player 2's subjective probability that $Y_2 \varepsilon S_2 = [0, Y_2^{\max}]$ will occur given (X, M, A_2, I). Both M and X must enter into the expectations function in order to explain the sizable increase in the rejection rate across subjects when $M = \$100$ under the Exchange treatment. Player 2, with a utility of monetary payment function, $V(A_2, X, Y_2)$, is then modeled as determining

$$A_2^* = \arg\max_{S_2} \int V(A_2, X, Y_2) dG(Y_2 | X, M, A_2, I) \qquad (1)$$

For any offer X, there is a large enough probability weight on external return, Y_2, such that the value of A_2^* will depend upon $G(\cdot)$. If $A_2^* = 0$ and $X > 0$, then in effect player 2 gives up immediate cash benefits in return for perceived future value by punishing miserly offers. To do otherwise is to jeopardize reputation and lasting benefits.

Player 1 is assumed to have subjective expectations $F(Y_1|X, M, A_2^*$, $I)$ over a future value, $Y_1 \varepsilon S_1 = [0, Y_1^{\max}]$ 2 and a subjective probability that $A_2^* = 1$ given by $p(X, M, I)$. Player 1 with utility of reward, $U(M - X, Y_1)$, determines

$$X^* = \arg\max\left\{p(X,M,I)\int_{S_1} U(M-X,Y_1)dF(Y_1|X,M,A_2^*=1,I)\right.$$
$$\left.+\left[1-p(X,M,I)\right]\int_{S_1} U(0,Y)dF(Y_1|X,M,A_2^*=0,I)\right\}_1 \qquad (2)$$

Since the value of X^* is observed to be proportional to the value of the stakes, M, we conclude that in (2), X^* is homogeneous of degree one in M.[6] Of course, our $M = \$100$ data do show a *small* shift downward in X^*, but we cannot reject the hypothesis that this is due to sampling variation from a distribution of offers that is independent of M.

VII. Interpreting Subject Effect Differences

The ultimatum game model (1) and (2) is consistent with results showing that economics and business students make smaller player 1 offers than students in psychology and other disciplines (Kahneman et al., 1986; Carter and Irons, 1991). Either by training or by self-selection, economics and business students may be more in tune with the short-run incentive implications of decision making in the ultimatum game than students in other fields. Consequently, they may be more likely to shed the baggage of repeated game reciprocity incentives when confronted with the one-shot ultimatum game and to perceive it as an end-play situation. Of course professional economists also are trained to be aware of incentive incompatibilities in public policy prescriptions that can cause policy failures. Even so, economics and business students make offers far in excess of the subgame perfect equilibrium prediction.

---

[6] In the dictator game, the second mover must accept the first mover's offer. Thus in (2), $p(X, M, T) \equiv 1$, and dictators, depending on the expectations function F, may offer some positive amounts of money, as is observed in experimental dictator games. But, as shown in Hoffman et al. (1996d) dictators can be induced to offer less and less under instructional treatments that progressively increase the dictators' social isolation or distance from others. Thus (2) in its degenerate form, with $p = 1$, explains our dictator data.

VIII.   Additional Tests of the Expected Utility Model

A more direct test of the model could be made with a pre-experiment survey instrument designed to screen subjects on a measure of how well they are integrated into networks that involve reciprocal relations with others. A high social connectedness score should be positively related to offers in the ultimatum game. Psychological survey instruments for measuring risk aversion have been found to be significantly correlated with risk aversion as measured by bidding in first-price sealed-bid auctions and as measured by choices between risky prospects (Harlow and Brown, 1990). In the current context, the instruments would be used to make a prior prediction as to the relative ability of individual subjects to adapt their accustomed behavior to the narrow-end play conditions of the ultimatum game. For a survey of existing instruments for measuring social psychological attitudes, see Robinson et al. (1991), especially Chapters 5 and 8.

IX.   Discussion and Conclusions

Previous ultimatum game results reported by FHSS found no significant difference in the offer distributions when the stakes were varied from $0 to $5 and from $5 to $10. Using the FHSS Random entitlement procedures, we also found no significant difference in the offer distributions when $10 stakes are compared with $100 stakes. Both the $10 and the $100 offer distributions, however, were significantly decreased when we went from an ambiguous property right (divide M) treatment to one in which the bargaining was formulated as a buyer–seller exchange, and the seller's first-mover (price announcement) position was earned by scoring high in a general knowledge quiz. Thus, subjects offered substantially less to their counterparts when they felt that their role as first mover was justified and legitimate, and this was independent of whether M was $10 or $100. This legitimacy was accepted by the second mover when the stakes were $10, as indicated by the observation that the rejection rate does not increase significantly with the lower distribution of offers. But with stakes of $100, the rejection rate increased significantly when we moved from the Random to the Contest/Exchange entitlement. Consequently, if the stakes are $100, second-mover expectations do not change coincidentally with those of the first mover when the entitlement condition is altered. But as the stakes are varied across amounts of $0, $5, $10, and $100, there is an associated steady decline in the frequency of rejections under the Random entitlement. Therefore, the knowledge that small offers are made is not per se sufficient to infer a high probability of rejection independent of the payoff treatment. Rejection behavior is of key importance in understanding the ultimatum game, since the second mover may show "resistance to unfairness" (KKT, p. 106), and this potential must be anticipated, rationally, by the first mover.

Our explanation of behavior in the ultimatum game, and also of the dictator game results reported in Hoffman et al. (1996d), is that people unconsciously import into the laboratory the repeated game expectations that characterize their daily life. They do not adjust their behavior immediately and spontaneously to the one-shot conditions of the laboratory experiment. This is particularly clear if one looks not only at ultimatum/dictator game results but also at other experiments that examine behavior in repeated games. Thus McCabe (1989) reports the results of finite horizon fiat money experiments. The extensive form of the game is such that no one has an incentive to accept the intrinsically worthless money on the sixth and last round. By backward induction, no one should accept it in the fifth round, and so on to the first round. Hence, the Nash equilibrium is no trade in any round. The six-round game is repeated 10, 15, or 20 times with the same group of subjects, with end time uncertain. Initially, there are many trades across a six-round play, but trades decrease as the game is repeated; refusals to trade at the end move toward the beginning of each successive six-round game. Initially, subjects, accustomed to accepting money in the world, do so in the experiment but learn over time that their habitual behavior in the world does not serve them well under the conditions of the experiment, and their expectations adapt to these conditions.

CHAPTER 8

Game Theory and Reciprocity in Some Extensive Form Experimental Games

Kevin A. McCabe, Stephen J. Rassenti,
and Vernon L. Smith

We use variations on a relatively transparent, two-person extensive form bargaining game to examine principles of self-evident play (Kreps, 1990a) using experimental analysis. Our game is transparent if players can be expected to understand the relationship between the possible sequences of plays with their counterparts and the resulting payoffs that can be achieved. However, how to develop strategy for a relatively transparent game may not be self-evident because it requires players to be confident about their counterparts' actions and reactions. So, when are players likely to be mutually confident?

Evolutionary psychology provides one approach to answering this question. Hoffman et al. (1996b) and the references therein give a more extended discussion of the role of evolutionary psychology in explaining many economics experiments that exhibit anomalous behavior relative to standard theory. Even though economic theory assumes that individuals employ general purpose consciously cognitive algorithms to optimize gains in any situation, evolutionary psychology assumes that individuals deploy domain-specific cognitive algorithms, with different algorithms being used for different situations, often in nonconscious ways. Economic theory disciplines our thinking by requiring behaviors that maximize individual utility, whereas evolutionary psychology disciplines our thinking by requiring blueprints for behavioral activity that can be adapted under natural selection. Of course the relative value of these blueprints from nature depends on their subsequent development by cultural interaction (nurture) and a continuing evaluation of behavioral success through experience.

In this chapter, we address the following question: Can we use principles from game theory, experimental economics, and evolutionary psychology to better understand what is self-evident to players playing our extensive form games?

152

I.   Principles of Behavior

The fundamental principles which underpin the propositions we examine experimentally can be stated as follows:

(i)   Nonsatiation. Players prefer more money to less.

(ii)   "Dominance. If a player has a choice between two moves one of which yields a payoff that dominates the payoff of the other, the dominate payoff will be chosen."

(iii) Backwards induction. In a sequential-move game tree (as in Figure 8.1) each player will analyze the game by applying the dominance principle to the last potential subgame, then the penultimate subgame, and so on back through the full game. (Note that, in games played with perfect information, such as those in Figure 8.1, every decision node begins a subgame.) This principle allows subjects to interpret the credibility of implied threats and promises.

Single-play game theory is about anonymous strangers, who meet once, interact strategically by applying the principles of dominance and backward induction, and never meet again (Hoffman et al. 1994, 1996d). These strong conditions are necessary to control for the effect of a history, and a future, external to the game in question but relevant to the current outcome. Without these controls on information, it would be extremely difficult to analyze a game with any confidence that the analysis can be restricted to that game.

(iv)   The Folk theorem (reputations). Repeated play makes endogenous a history and a future that can be used to enforce threats, keep promises, and maintain credibility. Currently, game theory cannot predict repeated play outcomes because a multiplicity of outcomes can be supported by some particular admissible trigger threat, or punishment, strategy. Neither can it predict which reputational equilibrium will occur. We will illustrate this later using game 1 in Figure 8.1.

Repeated play, where players have incomplete information about the characteristics of their counterparts, enables players to build reputations as individuals with particular sets of characteristics (or types) who will punish or reward in order to achieve cooperation.

(v)   Reciprocity. Contrary to the preceding principles, we can hypothesize that subjects exhibit a "habit of reciprocity": a specialized mental algorithm (Cosmides, 1985; Cosmides and Tobby, 1992) in which long-term self-interest is best served by

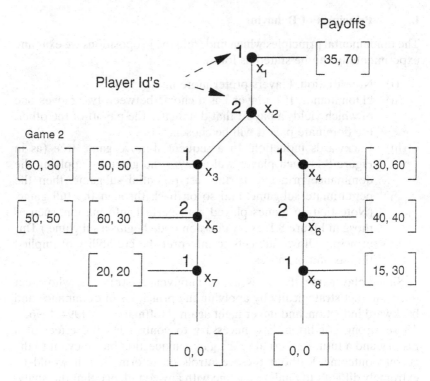

FIGURE 8.1. Game 1 in extensive form with initial vertex x_1. Players 1 and 2 take turns moving until a payoff box is reached. Player 1 receives the first amount; player 2 receives the second. Game 2 is identical to game 1 except the payoff boxes (60, 30) and (50, 50) are reversed.

promoting an image both to others and yourself that cheating on cooperative social exchanges (either explicit or implicit) is punished (negative reciprocity), and initiation of cooperative social exchanges is rewarded (positive reciprocity). Although some players may be sensitive to the difference between single and repeated game incentives in applying the reciprocity principle, other players will expect trust (cooperation without the option of punishing defection) to be rewarded by trustworthy responses even in single-play games. Still more players will initiate cooperation when defection can be punished, provided their own cost of punishment is not too high. Evolutionary psychology cannot currently predict the initial relative strength of the reciprocity algorithm within a player population or the short-run stability of this behavior within a particular set of repeated interactions.

II.   Experimental Design

In our experiments, we control for certain factors which either theory or empirical research suggests are likely to affect game-playing behavior. These factors are the presence or absence of the direct ability to punish noncooperative behavior, and the protocol used to match players during repeat interactions. By varying these factors, we expect to learn under what conditions dominance or reciprocity is the mutually self-evident principle of play. There are many experiments where players fail to play dominating strategies; instead, they seem to be using the principle of reciprocity. But these experiments typically do not offer players the choice between subgames where dominance alone is the principle of choice and subgames where reciprocity competes with dominance as the principle of choice. For example, in standard ultimatum (Hoffman et al., 1994) and investment (Berg et al., 1995) games, dominance clearly competes with reciprocity as the principle of choice because there is no alternative for first movers except to make decisions that must be conditioned by the reciprocity of second movers. In our design, the second mover, who must make the decision whether to trust his counterpart (in some treatments) or to punish his counterpart (in other treatments), now has the option to choose instead a subgame where the dominance principle is self-evident.

A.   *The Constituent Games: Analysis and Payoff Issues*

The constituent games studied in this chapter are shown in Figure 8.1. A play of the game begins with player 1 moving at decision node x_1. Players alternate making moves down the game tree until a payoff box is reached. The player identification at the upper left of each decision node indicates which player moves at that node. The left number in each payoff box is player 1's payoff, whereas the right number is player 2's payoff. In the text, we denote payoffs as ordered pairs with player 1's payoff first and player 2's payoff second. For example, if player 1 moves right at x_1, the game ends at the outcome with the maximum joint payoff, giving 35 to player 1, and 70 to player 2, denoted [35, 70].

In game 1, cooperation can lead to the largest symmetric outcome resulting in the payoffs [50, 50]. In order to reach [50, 50], player 2 must move left at x_2. But if player 2 moves left, player 1 can defect by moving down at x_3 making [60, 30] player 2's best choice. Alternatively, player 2 could make a costly choice and directly punish player 1 by choosing to move down in the subgame at x_5. But this direct punishment strategy is subgame dominated by the strategy of choosing left at x_5. This allows us to ask if subjects play subgame-dominated strategies. When the constituent game is repeated, players 2 can avoid playing dominated punishing strategies and follow an indirect, individually rational trigger strategy: If player 1 defects in repetition t, then player 2 moves left at x_5, but right at x_2 in repetition $t + 1$, punishing player 1 with at least the subgame perfect outcome [40, 40], then in repetition $t + 2$ returns to playing left at x_2. By using this strategy, every time player 1 defects, player 2 avoids the more costly direct punishment outcome [20, 20]. But for player 1 to be made strictly worse off, player 2 must punish, or credibly threaten to punish, right at x_2 more than once for each defection, since a single punishment gives player 1 $(60 + 40)/2 = 50$.

Game 2 is identical to game 1 except that we have interchanged the payoffs [60, 30] and [50, 50] thus removing the threat of direct punishment. This allows us to ask if trust, unsupported by a direct punishment option, affects the frequency of cooperation. In either game 1 or 2, the anticipated failure of cooperation may result in player 2 moving right at x_2. Once player 2 moves right, player 1 should reason that it is in both their interests to reach [40, 40]. We will call this outcome SP because it is the subgame perfect outcome (8). In both games, the cooperative outcome [50, 50] and SP outcome (40, 40) are symmetric, thus controlling for any payoff equity motivations in subject choice.

The preceding discussion, and the questions we pose for experimental investigation, make it clear why we selected the particular three payoffs on the left, and the three on the right, in constituent games 1 and 2. But why do we choose the play-stopping outcome [35, 70] at the top?

First, it provides an outside option that minimizes the multiple-move cost of transacting. Second, for player 1, it provides an outcome only 5 units inferior to the SP outcome. Therefore, it may be a subjectively rational outcome. If players 1 in the population want to avoid tedious multiple moves, avoid risk, avoid puzzling about what their player 2 counterparts will do, and incur a "sure thing" opportunity cost of only 5 units, then we will observe lots of right moves at x_1. The relative payoffs available at top right allow one to examine the background conditions under which game theoretic analysis becomes relevant. Third, when any of the constituent games are repeated, top right is a Nash equilibrium under a strategy in which player 2 always moves right at x_2 and down at x_6. This gives player 1 the individually rational payoff 15, and the self-interested option to subsequently move right at x_1.

This leaves the outcomes [0, 0] at nodes x_7 and x_8 to be explained under repeat play. Because [20, 20] at x_7 and [15, 30] at x_8 constitute punishing payoffs, why do we add the vindictive outcome [0, 0] at both nodes? We interpret choosing down at x_7 or x_8 by player 1 as a form of escalation: "If you are going to choose a punishing strategy, I will simply counterpunish." On the left, this is irrational escalation. If by moving down at x_7, player 1 is telling 2 not to punish, player 2 is not rationally going to learn to move left at x_2, and then accept defection at x_3. Rather, player 2 seems more likely to conclude that player 1 is not educable; the rational lesson is to simply move right at x_2 on subsequent plays and avoid such escalation on the left side of the tree. At x_8 moving down may be a form of rational escalation in which player 1, seeing that 2 is attempting to force a right move at x_1, signals that she is prepared to use deterrence tactics to neutralize 2's use of this strategy. Such counter-punishment is unlikely because we think it unlikely that players 2 will use strategies designed to achieve [35, 70] in the first place.

B.   Matching Protocols

When Selten and Stocker (1986) randomly paired anonymous players in ten repeated plays of a prisoner's dilemma game they found that cooperation begins to unravel. This suggests that in the dominant strategy Prisoners Dilemma, experience causes players to update their beliefs by giving less weight to the existence of types who would cooperate. If they believe that it is more likely that their opponent is only pretending to be a cooperative type, then subjects defect sooner in anticipation of a defection by their counterparts. A similar slow convergence to the Nash equilibrium was found by McCabe (1989) in a 6-period fiat money game, and by Smith, Suchanek, and Williams (1988) in a 15-period laboratory stock market. Thus, for finitely repeated games, there is a body of experimental literature which shows that the backward induction Nash equilibrium predicted by game theory does occur when players gain sufficient experience, and cooperation is strategically difficult or costly to attain. In this chapter we investigate players' ability to cooperate in two-person extensive form games, under single play or repeated play where the length of the supergame is unknown.

We examine four matching protocols for pairing players when play is repeated. (Refer to Table 8.1.) The protocol itself is always common information to all players. In Single, subjects play a randomly chosen counterpart once and then the experiment is over. The single-play design allows us to ask if cooperation is possible without repeat interaction. Game theory predicts no; players should end at SP. But reciprocity

Table 8.1. *Game tree experimental design: Treatments and number of pairs*

Designation	Constituent game	Matching protocol	No. pairs (observations)
Single 1	1	Single-play	50 (30)
Single 2	2	Single-play	26 (26)
Repeat Single 1	1	Repeat single play[a]	24 (360)[b]
Single 1 exp	1	Single-play	17 (17)
Same 1	1	Repeat same pairs	22 (440)
Same 2	2	Repeat same pairs	23 (460)
Random 1	1	Repeat random pairs and roles	24 (480)[b]
Random 2	2	Repeat random pairs and roles	24 (480)[b]

[a] Each player plays each counterpart exactly once with role alternating between player 1 and 2.
[b] Sessions consist of 16 players, 8 pairs matched repeatedly. Others consist of at least 8 players, usually 12.

theory implies that some players may be programmed by culture (or the biology of their minds) to attempt cooperation in single play as a habitual long-term strategy that increases the individual's long-term payoff. In Repeat Single, subjects play each counterpart in the population exactly once, with their own role alternating between player 1 and player 2. This protocol allows some learning about the sample while controlling, in theory, for repeated game effects. Again game theory predicts SP. In Single 1 Exp, experienced subjects from Repeat Single 1 return to the laboratory on a different day for a single-play session. Do increased experience, and single-play conditions, increase support for the game theoretic SP outcome?

In Random matching, each time the constituent game is played, subjects are randomly assigned a role, player 1 or player 2, and are randomly paired. "For a given sample size, this protocol maximizes the chance that on each play an individual is assigned a different role or paired with a different person, making it difficult for anyone to implement repeated game strategies with the same partner." In both Repeat Single and Random matching, subjects remain anonymous and are not given their counterparts' histories.

In Same pairings, subjects keep the same counterparts and roles throughout play. This design maximizes the opportunity for coupling: learning about one's counterpart and implementing repeated game strategies.

By considering behavior across the four protocols (Single, Repeat Single, Random, and Same) using a between-players design, we can ask if cooperation improves as you increase the probability of playing the same counterpart as conjectured by the Folk theorem.

C.   Treatments and Procedure

Our treatments are summarized in Table 8.1. For convenience, we adopted the convention of naming a cell by the matching treatment and the number of the game. Thus, Same 1 designates experiments where players keep the same counterpart and play game 1 repeatedly.

Players in repeated play experiments are recruited for 2 hours, even though the experiment lasts only slightly over 1 hour. Players are not told how long the experiment will last; this makes credible the expectation of a long series of repeated plays. Players are paid $5 as a nonsalient show-up fee and, at the end of the experiment, their accumulated earnings. The payoffs shown in the boxes are in cents for the constituent games that are repeated 20 times. In the single-play games, the payoffs are all multiplied by 20 to maintain payoff comparability with the repeated game experiments.

In the instructions, we were careful to avoid using terms like *game*, *play*, *opponent*, *partner*, or other potentially suggestive, value-laden terminology. In particular, players are informed that they will participate in a two-person decision-making problem involving themselves and a counterpart who will be designated DM1 or DM2, respectively. Subjects are given computer-programmed practice in making moves and are able to observe the recording of moves and payoffs in a game unrelated to the game they are to play in the experiment. They are allowed to ask questions privately at any time during the instructions.

Subjects' decisions are executed via touch or mouse-sensitive arrows, appearing in sequence, in the game tree on their screen displays. This procedure is intended to help concentrate their attention on their screens.

III.   Extending Bayesian Bernoulli Trials Theory

The data evaluations to follow will be based on conditional probabilities applied to a Bernoulli process [e.g., in Figure 8.1, each player 2 in the sample can move right or left at node x_2, with prior uncertainty – to the experimenter – as to the probability p, right, and $(1 - p)$, left]. This requires us to first extend the parameter space of standard Bernoulli trials theory to allow probability assessment of an extreme research hypothesis. Thus the strict game theoretic prediction is $p = 1$ for right play at node x_2 (also x_6). But the standard Bernoulli process generates the occurrence of r right outcomes in n independent trials, given p, defined on the *open* interval $0 < p < 1$. The situation is analogous to the possibility that a coin can be biased toward "heads" to any degree, including being two-headed (or two-tailed). If someone observes 5 heads in 5 trials, the coin cannot be two-tailed, but can be two-headed, biased or even fair, since five straight heads rules out only the state of being two-tailed. With standard Bernoulli trials theory, we cannot conclude that this coin is two-headed, only that it is more or less biased toward heads. In the following data, we observe many cases in which $n = r > 0$ and $n > r = 0$ and will want to assess the probability that $p = 1$ or 0.

We denote by $D'(p)$ anyone's (the experimenter's, the reader's) prior uncertainty about p, before experimentation. We let $D'(p)$ be a beta density on $(0 < p < 1)$, with parameters (r', n'), $P_0 > 0$ be the prior probability that $p = 0$, and $P_1 > 0$ be the prior probability that $p = 1$. Clearly, in Figure 8.1, a game theorist would associate some prior probability mass, P_1, with $p = 1$, the conditional probability that all players 2 will play right at x_2 in Single 1. Likewise in the repeated game, Same 1, the theorist would find it credible with some positive probability $P_0 > 0$ that all players 2 will move left at x_2. The prior mixed density/mass function is then

$$D'(p) = \begin{cases} P_1, & \text{if } p = 1 \\ kp^{r'-1}(1-p)^{n'-r'-1}, & \text{if } 0 < p < 1, \text{where } n' > r' > 0 \\ P_0, & \text{if } p = 0 \end{cases} \quad (1)$$

where $P_0 + P_1 < 1$. Because $D'(p)$ must have unit measure over the set, we must have

$$k = \frac{(1 - P_0 - P_1)(n'-1)!}{(r'-1)!(n'-r'-1)!} \quad (2)$$

Note that if $n' = 2$ and $r' = 1$, then the beta density is rectangular, and $k = 1 - P_0 - P_1$, the constant density on $(0 < p < 1)$.

The likelihood of observing that r of n subjects move right, conditional on p, is then

$$L(r; n|p) = \begin{cases} 0, & n > r \geq 0 & \text{if } p = 1 \\ 1, & n = r > 0 & \text{if } p = 1 \\ \dfrac{n!}{r!(n-r)!}p^r(1-p)^{n-r}, & n \geq r \geq 0, & \text{if } 0 < p < 1 \\ 1, & n > r = 0 & \text{if } p = 0 \\ 1, & n \geq r > 0 & \text{if } p = 0 \end{cases} \quad (3)$$

(3)

Equation (3) states that if $p = 1$ (all players 2 would elect right at x_2 or x_6), then there is zero likelihood of observing $r < n$ moves right, a certainty of observing $n = r$ moves right, the binomial probabilities (r, n) for $0 < p < 1$, and so on.

We next state the posterior distribution of p, $D''(p|r, n)$, given the sample observation (r, n), which is proportional to the product of the kernels (the parts that are functions of p) of Equations (1) and (3). The factor of proportionality, which depends on (r, n), gives D'' the property of the unit measure over $(0 \le p \le 1)$. Using node x_2 for illustration, there are three cases depending upon whether we observe both right and left moves, all right moves, or all left moves. In each case, we will compute D'', assuming that $D'(p) = 1 - P_0 - P_1$, with $n' = 2$ and $r' = 1$ in Equation (1). If $n > r > 0$

$$D''(p|r,n) = \begin{cases} 0 & p = 1 \\ \dfrac{(n+1)!}{r!(n-r)!} p^r (1-p)^{n-r}, & 0 < p < 1, \text{ if } 0 < n > r > 0 \\ 0 & p = 0 \end{cases} \quad (4)$$

Because both right and left are observed, none of the prior mass, P_0 or P_1, on the end points can affect the posterior. The result devolves to the standard Bernoulli process defined on $0 < p < 1$. For $n = r$,

$$D''(p|r,n,) = \begin{cases} \dfrac{(n+1)P_1}{1+nP_1} & p = 1 \\ \left(\dfrac{n+1}{1+nP_1}\right)(1-P_1)p^n & 0 < p < 1 \\ 0 & p = 0 \end{cases} \quad (5)$$

Hence, as $n = r$ gets large, we become increasingly sure that $p = 1$. For $r = 0$,

$$D''(p|r,n,) = \begin{cases} 0 & p = 1 \\ \left(\dfrac{n+1}{1+nP_0}\right)(1-P_0)(1-p)^n & 0 < p > 1 \\ \dfrac{(n+1)P_0}{1+nP_0} & p = 0 \end{cases} \quad (6)$$

As n gets large, we become increasingly confident that $p = 0$.

IV.   Results: Posterior Expected Probabilities

Using the posterior probability functions Equations (4)–(6), we calculated the expected probabilities of observing (r, n) if the prior probability function Equation (3) is rectangular, giving

$$E''(p \,|\, n > r > 0) = \frac{r+1}{n+2} \tag{7}$$

$$E''(p \,|\, n = r > 0) = \left(\frac{n+1}{n+2}\right)\left[\frac{1+(n+1)P_1}{1+nP_1}\right] \tag{8}$$

$$E''(p \,|\, n > r = 0) = \frac{(n+1)(1-P_0)}{1+nP_0} \int_0^1 p(1-p)^n \, dp \tag{9}$$

The results applied to the outcome (r, n) in each game treatment are shown in Tables 8.2 and 8.3 for four hypotheses: (i) right versus left move at node x_2; (ii) right move at node x_6 (SP) versus all other outcomes in the right branch of game 1; (iii) down move in game 1, or left move in game 2, at node x_3 (defection from signal to cooperate) versus no defection; (iv) down move in game 1 at node x_5 (punish defection) versus no punishment. In each case, we assume that $P_0 = P_1 = 1/4$, so that half the prior mass is divided equally between $p = 0$ and $p = 1$, whereas the other half is smeared over the interval $0 < p < 1$. The reader is free to express his or her own prior beliefs, before examining Tables 8.2 and 8.3, then make the calculations from Equations (1)–(3).

A.   Single-Play Experiments

Table 8.2 lists $E''(p|r, n)$ for each of the nodal choice hypotheses i–iv corresponding to each single treatment.

Result 1. *Right moves at* x_2 *(noncooperation) in game 1 are far less prevalent than implied by standard game theoretic analysis. The expected posterior probability of a right move at* x_2 *is 0.563 in game 1.*

Result 2. *Repetition of game 1 with distinct counterparts (Repeat Single 1) lowers the final-trial probability of right moves at* x_2 *to 0.423. Thus, experience and learning favor cooperation. When 17 of the latter 24 subjects return for a single-play session (Single 1 Exp), right move probability declines further to 0.263. Essentially, they return for a single trial with a 20-fold increase in stakes and play it more like another round in the repeated game than a situation calling for noncooperative play.*

Result 3. *Trust accounts for almost all the offers to cooperate by players 2 because removing the option to punish defection causes only a slight change in the frequency of right moves at* x_2. *This is indicated by the observation that the posterior probability of right moves at* x_2 *in game 2 is 0.536 compared with 0.563 in game 1.*

Result 4. *Consistent with the prediction of game theory, there is a high probability of achieving the SP outcome contingent on play being on the*

Table 8.2. *Frequency of outcomes and conditional expected posterior probabilities: Single experiments*

Treatment	Node x_2, right (noncooperation)			Node x_6, right (SP)			Node x_3, down game 1 or left game 2 (defection)			Node x_5, down game 1 (punish)		
	n	r	$E''(p|r,n)$	n	r	$E''(p|r,n)$	n	r	$E''(p|r,n)$	n	r	$E''(p|r,n)$
Single 1	30	17	0.563	17	16	0.895	13	2	0.20	2	1	0.50
Single 2[a]	26	14	0.536	14	14	0.990	12	6	0.50		na	
Repeat Single 1[b]	24	10	0.423	10	10	0.982	14	5	0.375	5	3	0.571
Single 1 exp[c]	17	4	0.263	4	4	0.938	13	5	0.40	5	2	0.429

na, not applicable.

[a] Note that in game 2, the move order of the outcomes [60, 30] and [50, 50] are reversed relative to game 1.

[b] Data for last trial only for comparability with other single experiments.

[c] From Repeat Single 1, 17 of the 24 pairs returned for a single play of game 1 with a 20-fold increase in payoffs.

Table 8.3. *Frequency of outcomes and conditional expected posterior probabilities: Repeated-play experiments*

Treatment	Node x_2, right (noncooperation)			Node x_6, right (SP)			Node x_3, down game 1 or left game 2 (defection)			Node x_5, down game 1 (punish)		
	n	R	$E''(p \vert r,n)$	n	r	$E''(p \vert r,n)$	n	r	$E''(p \vert r,n)$	n	R	$E''(p \vert r,n)$
Same 1	433	80	0.186	80	68	0.841	353	41	0.118	41	27	0.651
Same 2[a]	423	162	0.384	162	114	0.701	261	41	0.160		na	na
Random 1	471	154	0.328	154	149	0.962	317	102	0.223	102	69	0.673
Random 2[a]	453	293	0.646	293	278	0.946	160	70	0.438		na	na
Repeat Single 1	352	148	0.421	148	138	0.927	204	71	0.375	71	36	0.507

na, not applicable.

[a] Note that in game 2, the move order of the outcomes [60, 30] and [50, 50] is reversed relative to game 1.

164

right branch of the tree in both games 1 and 2. Thus, the probability of SP varies from 0.894 (Single 1) to 0.990 (Single 2). (See Table 8.3 showing that this result is generally supported in the repeated play treatments with differing matched pairs.)

Result 5. *Contrary to the game theoretic prediction based on dominance, in all treatments, the conditional probabilities of defection (player 1 moves down at x_3) from offers to cooperate (player 2 moves left at x_2) in game 1 are 0.4 or less.*

The observation that dominance characterizes moves in the right tree (Result 4), but not in the left tree is clear evidence in favor of the reciprocity hypothesis, since only moves within the left tree can reflect reciprocity responses.

Result 6. *In game 2, where defection (player 1 moves left at x_3) can occur without punishment, the defection probability rises from that in game 1, but only to 0.5 and is thus surprisingly low. This result, together with Result 3, implies that trust and trustworthiness occur with about equal probability: the probability that a player 2 will offer to cooperate is 0.464 (Result 3), whereas the probability of a positive reciprocal response by a player 1 is 0.5. (See Table 8.3 showing that the higher defection rate in game 2 relative to game 1 applies also to the repeated play treatments; Same 2 versus Same 1; Random 2 versus Random 1.)*

Result 7. *In game 1 the expected probability of punishment (player 2 moves down at x_5) is at least 0.429 across the three treatment conditions. This is contrary to the game theoretic prediction based on dominance but is consistent with the reciprocity hypothesis. Players 2, having offered to cooperate by left play at x_2, appear to feel some obligation in spite of the cost to themselves, to punish players 1 who defect. (See Table 8.3 showing that the conditional probability of punishment is at least 0.507 across all trials in the repeated play treatments: Same 1, Random 1, and Repeat Single 1.)*

B.   Repeat Play Experiments

Table 8.3 lists $E''(p|n, r)$ for choice hypotheses i–iv corresponding to each repeated play treatment.

Result 8. *The Folk theorem that repeat play favors cooperation is supported; when the same pairs interact repeatedly (Same 1) the probability of a right move at x_2 is 0.186, the lowest across all treatments. Similarly, comparing Single 2 in Table 8.2 with Same 2 in Table 8.3, repeated play* *increases cooperation in game 2 where the direct punishment option is not available.*

Result 9. *In game 1, as the probability of being matched with the same counterpart decreases from 1 to 0, across the three treatments (Same 1, Random 1 and Repeat Single 1), the probability of noncooperation (a right move at x_2) increases (0.186, 0.328, 0.421, respectively). Similarly in game 2, comparing Same 2 with Random 2, the probability of noncooperation increases from 0.384 to 0.646. This is qualitatively consistent with Folk theorem expectations.*

V.   Optimality and Efficiency of Player Choices

In Table 8.4 for all treatments we report calculations of the expected payoff to a player 2 of a left move at x_2, denoted $E(\pi_2|\text{Left})$. The calculations are based on the subsequent conditional likelihood probabilities of actual game play. Because the SP return to a player 2 from moving right at x_2 is 40, values of $E(\pi_2|\text{Left})$ greater than 40 imply that left at x_2 increases the expected payoff to player 2. Conditional on a left move at x_2, we also calculate the expected payoff to a player 1, $E(\pi_1|\text{Down})$, of defecting (moving down at x_3) in game 1. If $E(\pi_1|\text{Down})$ is greater than 50 (the return if player 1 does not defect), then defection is a best choice. Efficiency, appearing in the last column for each treatment, is the expected payoff, to a pair of subjects based upon observed conditional likelihoods from game play (beyond node x_2) divided by the cooperative joint payoff (50 + 50 = 100). Thus an efficiency of 80% implies that the individual pairs receive an average return equal to the SP joint payoff (40 + 40 = 80).

Result 10. *From the first column of data in Table 8.4, it is clear that players 2 who move left at x_2 earn a higher return than those moving right for the SP outcome. This is the case for all the treatments whether single or repeat play. Even Single 2 achieves an expected payoff of 40 on the left, equal to the SP payoff. The message is that those players who move left at x_2 are, on average, reading their counterparts correctly. It pays to initiate acts that invite positive reciprocity (trust) because such acts tend to be rewarded by positive reciprocation (trustworthiness), whether or not the invitation is reinforced by the option of punishing defection.*

Result 11. *Referring to the second column of entries in Table 8.4 for $E(\pi_1|\text{Down})$, it is seen that defection never pays. The defector, player 1, in all treatments receives a return less than 50. The claim by Cosmides (1985)*

Table 8.4. *Expected profits from a left move at* x_2 *and from defection*

Treatment	$E(\pi_2|\text{Left})^b$	$E(\pi_1|\text{Down})^c$	Efficiency, %^{d}
Single 1	46.2	30.0	83.8
Single 2^a	40.0	na	86.9
Single 1 exp^b	40.7	44.0	86.4
Same 1	46.6	31.3	90.6
Same 2^a	46.9	na	90.3
Random 1	40.7	30.8	82.6
Repeat Single 1	41.5	42.0	85.1
Random 2^a	41.2	na	84.7

na, not applicable.

^{a} Note that in game 2, the move order of the outcomes [60, 30] and [50, 50] is reversed relative to game 1.

^{b} Expected payoff to player 2 from moving left at x_2, given the relative frequencies of subsequent play by player 1s and 2s.

^{c} Expected payoff to player 1 from defecting at node x_3, game 1.

^{d} Efficiency is the percentage of the cooperative [50, 50] total payoff that is realized by all pairs.

that people's mental modules are programmed to punish cheaters is alive and well in our experiments. Defection is not always punished, but often enough to keep defection from being profitable. This implies a free-rider problem: Each individual wants to see defection punished but would prefer to see others incur the cost of punishment.

Result 12. *In all treatments, players jointly achieve more efficient outcomes – they collect more money from the experimenter – than is predicted by noncooperative game theory.*

VI. Evolution of Game Play over Repetitions

Tables 8.5–8.10 report conditional likelihood probabilities, aggregated over blocks of five repetitions each, for each payoff outcome corresponding to the repeated play experiments.

Result 13. *In Repeat Single 1 (Table 8.5) there is no obvious and important trend in any of the outcomes, although in the last repetition block the*

Table 8.5. *Conditional outcome probabilities[a] by repetition block Repeat Single 1*

Repetitions	Left branch[b]	50 50	60 30	20[c] 20	Right branch[b]	30 60	40 40	15[c] 30	$E(\pi_2|\text{Left})$	$E(\pi_1|\text{Down})$
1–5	68/116 = .586	43/68 = .632	12/25 = .48	13/13 = 1	48/116 = .414	7/48 = .146	41/41 = 1	0	40.7	39.2
6–10	71/117 = .607	46/71 = .648	15/25 = .60	10/10 = 1	46/117 = .393	2/46 = .043	43/44 = .977	0/1 = 0	41.6	44.0
11–15	65/119 = .546	44/65 = .677	8/21 = .381	13/13 = 1	54/119 = .454	0/54 = 0	54/54 = 1	0	41.4	35.2

[a] The conditional probabilities are likelihoods, based on (r/n) = (realizations/no. of observations).

[b] Moves right at x_1 ending with payoff [35, 70] can be inferred from the left and right branch denominators shown in these entries (e.g., 116 of 120 moved right or left in repetition block 1–5 implying that four pairs ended at [35, 70]).

[c] Moves ending with payoffs [0, 0] at these nodes can be inferred from these entries (e.g., if 0 of 1 end at [15, 30], then 1 of 1 ended at [0, 0]).

Table 8.6. *Conditional outcome probabilities[a] by repetition block Same 1*

Repetitions	Left branch[b]	50 50	60 30	20[c] 20	Right branch[b]	30 60	40 40	15[c] 30	$E(\pi_2|\text{Left})$	$E(\pi_1|\text{Down})$
1-5	78/109 = .716	64/78 = .821	6/14 = .429	8/8 = 1	31/109 = .284	2/31 = .065	28/29 = .966	0/1 = 0	45.4	37.2
6-10	88/108 = .815	76/88 = .864	1/12 = .083	7/11 = .636	20/108 = .185	0/20 = 0	19/20 = .95	0/1 = 0	45.1	16.6
11-15	94/106 = .887	87/94 = .926	4/7 = .571	3/3 = 1	12/106 = .113	0/12 = 0	12/12 = 1	0	48.2	42.8
16-20	93/110 = .845	85/93 = .914	3/8 = .375	4/5 = .8	17/110 = .155	1/17 = .059	9/16 = .563	4/7 = .571	47.5	32.5

[a]The conditional probabilities are likelihoods, based on (r/n) = (realizations/no. of observations).
[b]Moves right at x_1 ending with payoff [35, 70] can be inferred from the left and right branch denominators shown in these entries (e.g., 116 of 120 moved right or left in repetition block 1–5 implying that four pairs ended at [35, 70]).
[c]Moves ending with payoffs [0, 0] at these nodes can be inferred from these entries (e.g., if 0 of 1 end at [15, 30], then 1 of 1 ended at [0, 0]).

Table 8.7. Conditional outcome probabilities[a] by repetition block Same 2

Repetitions	Left branch[b]	60 / 30	50 / 50	20[c] / 20	Right branch[c]	30 / 60	40 / 40	15[c] / 30	$E(\pi_2|\text{Left})$
1–5	45/100 = .450	16/45 = .356	29/29 = 1	0	55/100 = .550	7/55 = .127	42/48 = .875	6/6 = 1	42.9
6–10	65/110 = .591	10/65 = .154	55/55 = 1	0	45/110 = .409	11/45 = .244	26/34 = .765	8/8 = 1	46.9
11–15	73/108 = .676	8/73 = .110	65/65 = 1	0	35/108 = .324	6/35 = .171	23/29 = .793	6/6 = 1	47.8
16–20	78/105 = .743	7/78 = .090	71/71 = 1	0	27/105 = .257	3/27 = .111	23/24 = .952	1/1 = 1	48.2

[a] The conditional probabilities are likelihoods, based on (r/n) = (realizations/no. of observations).

[b] Moves right at x_1 ending with payoff [35, 70] can be inferred from the left and right branch denominators shown in these entries (e.g., 116 of 120 moved right or left in repetition block 1–5 implying that four pairs ended at [35, 70]).

[c] Moves ending with payoffs [0, 0] at these nodes can be inferred from these entries (e.g., if 0 of 1 end at [15, 30], then 1 of 1 ended at [0, 0]).

170

Table 8.8. *Conditional outcome probabilities[a] by repetition block Random 1*

Repetitions	Left branch[b]	50 50	60 30	20[c] 20	Right branch[b]	30 60	40 40	15[c] 30	$E(\pi_2|\text{Left})$	$E(\pi_1|\text{Down})$
1–5	73/117 = .624	47/73 = .644	15/26 = .577	10/11 = .909	44/117 = .376	0/44 = 0	44/44 = 1	0	41.1	42.3
6–10	78/117 = .667	50/78 = .641	8/28 = .286	17/20 = .85	39/117 = .333	0/39 = 0	37/39 = .949	1/2 = .5	39.5	29.3
11–15	78/119 = .655	51/78 = .654	6/27 = .222	17/21 = .810	41/119 = .345	1/41 = .024	38/40 = .95	2/2 = 1	39.4	25.9
16–20	88/118 = .746	67/88 = .761	4/21 = .190	14/17 = .824	30/118 = .254	0/30 = 0	30/30 = 1	0	42.6	24.7

[a] The conditional probabilities are likelihoods, based on $(r/n) = $ (realizations/no. of observations).

[b] Moves right at x_1 ending with payoff [35, 70] can be inferred from the left and right branch denominators shown in these entries (e.g., 116 of 120 moved right or left in repetition block 1–5 implying that four pairs ended at [35, 70]).

[c] Moves ending with payoffs [0, 0] at these nodes can be inferred from these entries (e.g., if 0 of 1 end at [15, 30], then 1 of 1 ended at [0, 0]).

Table 8.9. *Conditional outcome probabilities[a] by repetition block Random 2*

Repetitions	Left branch[b]	60 30	50 50	20[c] 20	Right branch[b]	30 60	40 40	15[c] 30	$E(\pi_2 \mid \text{Left})$
1–5	32/110 = .291	9/32 = .281	23/23 = 1	0	78/110 = .709	4/78 = .051	73/74 = .986	0/1 = 0	44.4
6–10	43/112 = .384	17/34 = .395	26/26 = 1	0	62/112 = .616	0/69 = 0	66/69 = .957	2/3 = .667	42.1
11–15	47/116 = .405	26/47 = .553	21/21 = 1	0	69/116 = .595	1/69 = .014	66/68 = .971	2/2 = 1	38.9
16–20	38/115 = .330	18/38 = .474	20/20 = 1	0	77/115 = .670	2/77 = .026	73/75 = .973	0/2 = 0	40.5

[a] The conditional probabilities are likelihoods, based on (r/n) = (realizations/no. of observations).

[b] Moves right at x_1 ending with payoff [35, 70] can be inferred from the left and right branch denominators shown in these entries (e.g., 116 of 120 moved right or left in repetition block 1–5 implying that four pairs ended at [35, 70]).

[c] Moves ending with payoffs [0, 0] at these nodes can be inferred from these entries (e.g., if 0 of 1 end at [15, 30], then 1 of 1 ended at [0, 0]).

172

Table 8.10. *Joint relative frequency of cooperation (trust) and reciprocation (trustworthy): Repeat Single 1*

Relative frequency, reciprocation $(1 - P_D)$	Relative frequency, cooperation $(1 - P_N)$			
	0–0.33	0.34–0.66	0.67–1.0	Total
0.67–1.0	6/47 = 0.128	5/47 = 0.106	14/47 = 0.298	25/47 = 0.532
0.34–0.66	1/47 = 0.021	6/47 = 0.128	4/47 = 0.085	11/47 = 0.234
0–0.33	10/47 = 0.212	0/47 = 0	1/47 = 0.021	11/47 = 0.234
Total	17/47 = 0.362	11/47 = 0.234	19/47 = 0.404	47/47 = 1

P_N, frequency of noncooperation (right move) at x_2; P_D, frequency of defection (down move) at x_5.

probability of punishment increases, and the return from defection declines. It is not possible to say that players are "learning to play SP" over time. Neither are they learning to cooperate, although in every block the average return to a left move at x_2 is higher than 40.

Result 14. *In Same 1 (Table 8.6), left moves at x_2 followed by cooperation starts high and trends upward across repetitions, whereas support for right moves to SP declines. Defection declines only slightly across repetitions blocks. More interesting is that punishment begins at a modest 57% (8 in 14) in the first five repetitions and then increases to over 91% (11 in 12) in the next five repetitions and goes through a similar cycle in the last two blocks. It appears that defection is at first tolerated – players 2 are forgiving – then punishment is strongly invoked, and the effect is to reduce total defection from 14 to only 5 in the last block as defectors find that it does not pay.*

Result 15. *In Same 2 (Table 8.7), the proportion of left moves at x_2 starts at only 0.45, much lower than in Same 1 (0.716) and rises steadily to 0.743 in the last five repetitions; defection declines correspondingly. Hence, we see the substantial role of trust in achieving cooperation through reciprocity when the same pairs meet repeatedly. The expected profit from moving left at x_2 rises steadily from 42.9 to 48.2 across all blocks.*

Result 16. *The proportion of left moves at x_2 in Random 1 (Table 8.8) begins at 0.624 and rises to 0.746, uniformly below the corresponding results in Same 1 (Table 8.6), and demonstrating the game-theoretic folk principle that the same counterparts can better coordinate cooperation.*

Defections are higher in Random 1 than in Same 1, but in Random 1 players 2 tend to persist in left moves at x_2 and then increase their punishment rates: Without the same role and pairs, players 2 encounter many more defecting counterparts but proceed to incur the personal cost of punishing them. This strengthens the results in Cosmides (1985), where cheaters are identified, but costly punishment is not an issue.

Result 17. *Random 2 yields lower likelihoods of left play (Table 8.9) than Same 2 (Table 8.7) in every repetition block, and the modest growth in left play to 0.405 drops to 0.330 in the final block. Initially, the expected profit from left play is high then declines. This correlates with a modest increase in left game play in repetitions 6–10 and 11–15, but defections increase in these blocks, and the expected return from left play falls, leading to a decline in left game play in repetitions 16–20.*

VII.   Other Results

Generally, players 1 move down at x_1. Thus in Repeat Single 1, of 360 constituent game plays (see Table 8.4), 352 show right or left moves at x_2 implying that only eight moves by players 1 were right at x_1.

We also observe that moving down at x_6 is quite rare; it is most frequent in Same 2 where 21 (not shown) out of a total of 460 plays of game 2 involve moving down at x_6. These appear to have been intended to induce a right move at x_1 on the subsequent play, since total moves right at x_1 were 37.

VIII.   Do Trusting People Tend to Be Trustworthy?

In Repeat Single 1, subjects alternate between the roles of player 1 and player 2. Consequently, we have data on each subject in both positions, matched repeatedly against distinct persons. It is natural to hypothesize that, since subjects are matched anonymously from a particular population of like individuals (undergraduates), they can all consider themselves as a sample of size 1 from the characteristics of that population. If a person is a cooperative type and assumes that he or she is matched with a cooperative type, then offers to cooperate are expected to be reciprocated by cooperative responses. This assumes that trusting persons are also trustworthy (see discussion in Result 6). Do our data confirm this? That is, if a person in the player 2 role moves left, is that person, when in the player 1 role, less likely to be a defector in the left tree? Similarly, is a person who moves right as a player 2, likely to be a defector as player 1 in the left tree?

The results from Repeat Single 1 are compiled in Table 8.10. There were 48 subjects (24 pairs). One subject never recorded an outcome in the left tree branch as player 1. The remaining 47 recorded left branch outcomes in each role at least once, and the joint relative frequencies for the choices (cooperate as player 2, reciprocate as player 1) corresponding to moves left at x_2 and left at x_3 are shown in Table 8.10 aggregated by one-thirds. Thus 21.2% of the subjects exhibit the lowest frequency, 0–0.33, of cooperation and reciprocation. In the upper right corner, the modal outcome 29.8% falls into the highest frequency range of cooperation/reciprocation. As expected, if trust goes with trustworthiness, and vice versa, most of the probability mass is on the diagonal (63.8%).

IX.   Discussion and Conclusions

This chapter explores conditions that reinforce subjects' propensity to reciprocate or not. In our design, we allowed subjects to choose between a subgame where backward induction is self-evident and a subgame where reciprocity could be used as a means of achieving a cooperative outcome. We found substantial support for cooperation under complete information even in various single-play treatments. This support increased when play of the constituent game was repeated whether or not there was an opportunity to directly punish defection. This was consistent with the Folk theorem argument that repetition promotes cooperation. Game principles also explained the qualitative result that, in repeat interaction as the probability of being matched with the same person increases from 0 to 1, cooperation increases. Also strongly consistent with the predictions of game theory was the observation that under all treatments, conditional upon right game play, almost all players end up at the subgame perfect equilibrium. The considerable cooperation we observed in single-play and repeat single-play games was consistent with reciprocity being an innate characteristic of many people who are prone to cooperative behavior because they treat single-play games as part of a repeated series of different games across which they seek to establish "lifetime" reputations. To the extent that this is the case, then the standard game theoretic distinction between single and repeat play games may not be as strongly meaningful as customarily assumed.

It is important, however, in interpreting these results that subjects, although matched anonymously, be matched with like individuals. An important characteristic of the human mind may be a friend-or-foe detector, with a cooperative posture reserved for those who are at least not perceived as foes. There should be no presumption that our results would carry over when individuals are matched with those in an out-group who are seen as opponents ready to exploit any opportunity for gain.

CHAPTER 9

Behavioral Foundations of Reciprocity: Experimental Economics and Evolutionary Psychology

Elizabeth Hoffman, Kevin A. McCabe, and Vernon L. Smith

Theorists have long studied the fundamental problem that cooperative, socially efficient outcomes generally cannot be supported as equilibria in finite games. The puzzle is the occurrence of cooperative behavior in the absence of immediate incentives to engage in such behavior. For example, in two-person bargaining experiments, where noncooperative behavior does not support efficient outcomes, we observe more cooperative behavior and greater efficiency than such environments are expected to produce. Similarly, in public good experiments with group size varying from 4 to 100, people tend to achieve much higher payoff levels than predicted by noncooperative theory. Moreover, examples of the achievement of cooperative behavior by decentralized means have a long history in the human experience. Anthropological and archeological evidence suggests that sharing behavior is ubiquitous in tribal cultures that lack markets, monetary systems, or other means of storing and redistributing wealth (see, e.g., Cosmides and Tooby, 1987, 1989; Isaac, 1978; Kaplan and Hill, 1985b; Tooby and De Vore, 1987; Trivers, 1971).

In this paper we draw together theoretical and experimental evidence from game theory, evolutionary psychology, and experimental economics that provides the basis for developing a reciprocity framework for understanding the persistence of cooperative outcomes in the face of contrary individual incentives. Repeated game theory with discounting or infinite time horizons allows for cooperative solutions but does not yield conditions for predicting them (Fudenberg and Tirole, 1993). Recent research in evolutionary psychology (Cosmides and Tooby, 1987, 1989, 1992) suggests that humans may be evolutionarily predisposed to engage in social exchange using mental algorithms that identify and punish cheaters. Finally, a considerable body of research in experimental economics now identifies a number of environmental and institutional factors that promote cooperation even in the face of contrary individual incentives (Davis and Holt, 1993; Isaac and Walker, 1988a, b, 1991; Isaac

177

et al., 1984, 1991). Moreover, these experimental results indicate a much greater role for trust and trustworthiness than the evolutionary psychologists' punish-cheaters model would suggest. We hypothesize that humans' abilities to read one anothers' minds (Baron-Cohen, 1995) in social situations facilitate reciprocity.

I.   Repeated Games

Repeated game theory offers two explanations of cooperation based on self-interest: self-enforcing equilibria and reputations. Self-enforcing equilibria are based on the idea that players can credibly punish noncooperative defections. The nagging problem with self-enforcing cooperative equilibria is that there are many equilibria in such games with cooperation being only one possibility.

Experiments demonstrating that subjects cooperate in relative short finite horizons of repeated play (Selten and Stoecker, 1986; Rapoport, 1987) have reinforced the role of reputations in games with incomplete information (Kreps et al., 1982). The idea is that if players are uncertain about other players' types, then the possibility emerges that players will mimic (develop a reputation as) a type different from their own. In circumstances where cooperation is mutually beneficial, players have an incentive to mimic cooperative behavior.

In the Kreps et al. (1982) examples, players rationally compute strategies based on (utility or payoff) type uncertainty and cooperate from the beginning until near the end of the game and then defect. This is not, however, the observed pattern over time in experiments where it is common for cooperation to develop out of repeat interaction; also, defection near the end is often not observed.

The strength of the theory is that it is based on individual (but longer-run) self-interest and is parsimonious. The weakness is that it admits many possible equilibria without suggesting why cooperation is the most likely outcome. Moreover, for reputation-based equilibria, people must entertain beliefs about certain types.

But where do these beliefs come from? We introduce the hypothesis that types emerge from the evolutionary fitness of certain cognitive abilities that predispose many people toward reciprocity. Actual circumstances and experiences may lead to reciprocal behavior by many persons. Not everyone has to be a particular type; variability is the stuff from which selection occurs, and which allows nature to adapt to change. But the type must exist in sufficient numbers for people to believe that reciprocity pays. And if reciprocity pays, culture and norms develop to specify the forms that reciprocity will take.

II.   Mental Algorithms for Social Exchange: Strategies in Human Cognition That Support Cooperation

The complex organization of the human mind is thought to be the product of at least a few million years of evolutionary adaptation to solve the problems of hunting and gathering.[1] Evolutionary psychologists hypothesize that these problems were solved not only by neurobiological adaptations but also by adaptations in human social cognition (see Cosmides and Tooby, 1992, hereafter CT, and the references therein). The idea is that humans have special and highly developed cognitive mechanisms for dealing with social exchange problems, that mental modules for solving social problems are as much a part of the adapted mind as our vision and hearing-balance faculties.[2]

Examples of mental "computational" modules that solve specialized design problems include vision, language, and "mind reading." The mechanism that constitutes vision involves neural circuits whose design solves the problem of scene analysis (Marr, 1982). The solution to this problem employs specialized computational machinery for detecting shape, edges, motion, bugs (in frogs), hawks (in rabbits), faces, and the like. Just as we learn by exposure to see and interpret scenes without being taught, we learn to speak without formal training of any kind.

Although culture is known to operate on our mental circuitry for language learning, the deep structure of language is common across cultures (Pinker, 1994). Normal English-speaking preschoolers can apply mental algorithms to root words to form regular noun plurals by adding -s (Pinker, 1994, pp. 42–3) and the past tense of regular verbs by adding -ed. The preschooler even "knows" that you can say that a house is mice-infested but never that it is rats-infested, that there can be teethmarks but never clawsmarks – the mental algorithm here allows compound words to be formed out of irregular plurals but never out of regular

---

[1] But see Rice (1996) for an experiment in which female fruit flies are prevented from coevolving with males. After only 41 generations, male adaptation leads to a reduction in female survivorship in the genetic battle of the sexes.

[2] Research by neuroscientists on the amygdala, an almond-sized structure deep in the temporal lobe of the brain, has shown that it is directly involved in the perception of social signals. That the amygdala participates in the social cognition and behavior of animals has been known for many years, but recent studies have shown that these findings extend to humans (Allman and Brothers, 1994; Adolphs et al., 1994). Thus, subjects with damaged amygdalas are unable to recognize/distinguish expressions such as fear, surprise, and anger on faces in photographs of people. In one study, the subject had great difficulty determining whether individuals were looking at her or away from her. The amygdala operates preconsciously: "the evidence . . . clearly indicates that the amygdala is involved in the evaluation of complex stimuli long before they are completely analyzed cognitively, and probably long before they enter awareness" (Halgren, 1992, p. 194).

plurals. This is because of the way the unconscious brain works: regular plurals are not stem words stored in the mental inventory, but words derived algorithmically by the inflectional rule to add -s. Preschoolers in all languages automatically make these kinds of distinctions (Pinker, 1994, pp. 146–7), without being taught by their mothers or teachers.

That the mind contains blueprints for grammatical rules is further indicated by a language disorder in families, which appears to be inherited like a pedigree with a dominant gene. English speakers afflicted with this disorder are unable to inflect root words to form derivatives such as the -s rule for obtaining plurals.

"Mind reading" – the process of inferring the mental states of others from their words and actions – facilitates "social understanding, behavioral predictions, social interaction, and communication" (Baron-Cohen, 1995, p. 30). Autism in children makes them mind blind – they are not automatically aware of mental phenomena in others and cannot mind read (Baron-Cohen, 1995).[3] A genetic basis is suggested by its greater risk in identical twins and biologically related siblings. Baron-Cohen (1995, pp. 88–95) implicates the amygdala and related areas of the brain as jointly controlling the ability to detect eye direction in others and to interpret mental states (have a theory of mind) in others. Other detector mechanisms appear to include friend-or-foe – cooperation is not automatic for foes – and the fight-or-flight response to sudden danger.

The hypothesis that our minds are also predisposed to learn behavioral responses that promote cooperative outcomes does not mean that we are born with such behavioral responses. We only need to be born with the capacity to learn such responses developmentally from social exposure, much as we are born with the capacity to learn any language but not with the ability to speak any particular one. A capacity for the natural learning of strategies that induce cooperation in social exchange has fitness value. But the implementational form of what is learned varies widely, depending upon the environment, accidents of nature, and how parental, familial, and societal units organize exchange processes. Consequently, culture is endlessly variable, but, functionally, reciprocity is universal.

Naturally selected fitness strategies are hypothesized to be embodied in the designs that modulate reasoning about social exchange. An analysis of these strategies allows one to deduce the behavioral characteristics of the associated mental algorithms. This analysis also allows predictions about human responses in reasoning experiments of the kind

---

[3] Pinker (1994, p. 227), for example, provides the following exchange: Woman: "I'm leaving you." Man: "Who is he?" If you are not autistic you know what this conversation means.

that we summarize later. These psychology experiments are of particular interest to experimental economists because they complement subject behavior in many games of strategic interaction.

Consider the standard two-person Prisoner's Dilemma (PD) game, but think of the entries corresponding to C (cooperate) or D (defect) for the row and column players as net benefits and net costs measured in units that increase (or decrease) the individual's inclusive fitness. C might represent the strategy "trade," whereas D might represent "steal." As discussed earlier, game theory predicts that mutual cooperation will not emerge in a single-move game – people are all self-interested "foes."

Imagine a tournament that matches pairs from a large population of organisms so that the same two individuals are never matched a second time. Each member is matched, reproduces itself, and dies. The offspring inherits the strategy choice propensity of the parent, and the number of offspring is proportional to the payoff gains of the parent in its matched plays of the game. Each generation repeats this process.

Repeated game principles can be used to analyze equilibrium outcomes in such a game. Repeat interaction is a prominent characteristic of social exchange. Needs are rarely simultaneous. But, long before human societies invented a generally accepted medium of exchange, various cultural mechanisms provided social adaptations that allowed delayed mutual benefits to be gained: I share my meat with you when I am lucky at the hunt, and you share yours with me when you are lucky. Although this is commonly referred to as reciprocal altruism, we prefer to call it reciprocity. I am not altruistic if my action is based on my expectation of your reciprocation.

Reciprocity leads naturally to *property rights*. If I grow corn and you grow pigs, and we exchange our surpluses, then we each have an interest in the other's property right in what is grown. If either of us plays steal, that ends the trading relationship. Hence, mutual recognition and defense of informal property right systems needn't require the preexistence of a Leviathan.

But how might such mutual cooperation emerge in a repeated PD game? We know from the work of Axelrod and Hamilton (1981) that strategy C cannot be selected for in repeated play, but that the contingent cooperative strategy T (tit-for-tat) can be selected for. In general any strategy, including T, can successfully invade a population of defectors if (and only if) it cooperates with cooperators and punishes defectors (Axelrod, 1984). As noted by CT (1992, pp. 176–7), it is an empirical issue to determine which strategy, out of this admissible set, is actually embodied in human cognitive programs.

The need to solve the PD problem to achieve cooperation provides an abstract schema for organizing our thoughts about cooperation beyond immediate kin. However, simply referring to the motivating example of the PD will not carry us to a full understanding of human social exchange. In particular, it will not help us understand cooperative behavior toward anonymous strangers when there is no prospect for punishment. This is an anomaly in the CT evolutionary paradigm.

An important question for the evolutionary paradigm is whether the mental algorithms for social exchange consist of a few content-free generalized rules of reasoning, or whether they consist of designs specialized for solving social exchange problems. Economic/game theory is driven by the principle that humans naturally use content-free generalized rules of reasoning in solving decision problems. If this is so, why is economics so hard to teach? If these rules come only from culture, where does culture come from?

CT (1992) argue that the evolutionary perspective favors the specialized over the generalized rules. General rules, applicable to any subject matter, ". . . will not allow one to detect cheaters . . . because what counts as cheating does not map onto the definition of violation imposed by the propositional calculus. Suppose that we agree to the following exchange: 'If you give me your watch then I'll give you $20.' You would have violated our agreement – you would have cheated me – if you had taken my $20 but not given me your watch. But according to the rules of inference of the propositional calculus, the only way this rule can be violated is by your giving me your watch but my not giving you $20" (CT, 1992, pp. 179–80). That is, the way you falsify "if P, then Q," statements is to look for "P, not Q" evidence. In this example, giving me your watch is the P statement; my not giving you $20 is the not-Q statement. If such rules were the only ones contained in our minds, we would have no special ability to detect cheating.[4]

One theme in the CT research program is to design experiments that will test these kinds of propositions (CT, 1992, pp. 181–206]). The selection task that CT employ was developed by Wason (1966), whose motivation was to inquire as to whether the ordinary learning experiences of

---

[4] Unlike deductive logic, a cheater detection mechanism must account for intentionality. In the CT experiments, exchange is sequential: first, I give you the watch, then only later do you pay the $20. Here the clear interpretation is that the second mover has cheated if he or she does not pay the $20. This rules out the use of the biconditional statement, "You give me your watch," if and only if, "I give you $20," as a substitute for the conditional. Because the biconditional has an ambiguous intertemporal interpretation, it is less clear that a contract is implied. Suppose I give you $20, but you don't give me your watch. The biconditional is clearly false even if I haven't cheated you; when, for example, I give you the $20 altruistically. Note we can write the more complicated logical statement, if (we agree to P iff Q), then (P iff Q), to give the biconditional the correct intertemporal interpretation without committing to the order of trade.

people reflected the Popperian hypothesis testing logic outlined earlier. The procedure uses four cards, each carrying one of the labels P, not-P, Q, not-Q on the side facing up, and another of the same four labels on the side facing down. Each card corresponds to some situation with one of the labeled properties. The rule is violated only by a card that has a P on one side and a not-Q on the reverse side.

Subjects are asked to indicate only the card(s) that definitely need to be turned over in order to see if any cases violate the rule. The correct answer is to indicate the cards showing P (to see if there is a not-Q on the other side) and not-Q (to see if there is a P on the other side). In one example, a secretary's task is to check student documents to see if they satisfy the rule: If a person has a D rating, then his document must be marked code 3. Four cards show D, F, 3, and 7, and subjects should indicate the cards showing the letter D and the numeral 7. Less than 25% of college students choose both of these cards correctly.

Now consider a law, which states, "If a person is drinking beer, then he must be over 20 years old." Out of four cards, which also include "not drinking beer" and "25 years old," the correct response is to choose the cards labeled "drinking beer" and "16 years old." In this experiment about 75% of college students get it right. Why the difference from the previous example?

Although people do better in more familiar examples such as "If a person goes to Boston, then he takes the subway," less than half get it right. A survey of this literature (Cosmides, 1985) suggests that "Robust and replicable content effects were found only for rules that related terms that are recognizable as benefits and cost/requirements in the format of a standard social contract..." (CT, 1992, p. 183). Out of 16 experiments using social contracts, 16 showed large content effects. Out of 19 experiments that did not use contract rules, 14 produced no content effect, 2 produced a weak effect, and 3 produced a substantial effect.

These findings launched a number of studies designed to separate the social contract hypothesis from confounding interpretations, such as familiarity, or that the social context merely facilitates Popperian reasoning. CT report that the alternative hypotheses have not survived experiments designed to separate them from the cheater detection hypothesis.[5]

---

[5] Other experiments have examined violations of social contracts when they do not involve cheating (Gigerenzer and Hug, cited in CT, 1992, p. 195). Only 44% correctly solved the no cheating version, whereas 83% got the cheating version correct. Cosmides and Tooby (cited in CT, 1992, p. 198) examined social contract problems that distinguish violations due to cheating from violations due to innocent mistakes. The cheating version was correctly solved by 68% of the subjects, but the mistake version was only solved by 27% of

III.   Observability, Communication, and Intentionality Signaling

If humans are preprogrammed to learn to achieve cooperative outcomes in social exchange, then factors that facilitate the operation of these natural mechanisms should increase cooperation even in the presence of contrary individual incentives. For example, cooperation should increase if individuals can observe and monitor one anothers' behaviors, even if there are no direct mechanisms for enforcing specific behaviors. In Baron-Cohen's (1995) model of mind reading, the eye direction, shared attention, and intentionality detectors are used to identify and ratify the volitional states of others. Observation and monitoring activate one or more of these detectors. Moreover, if it is possible for agents to directly punish cheating by other agents, cooperation should increase even further.

Similarly, if agents can communicate with one another, they can frame a group decision as a social exchange problem and ratify one anothers' volitional states, thus activating natural inclinations to cooperate for increased individual gain. Thus, communication can increase cooperation even if there are no effective mechanisms for monitoring and punishing cheaters.

A.   *Voluntary Contribution Experiments*

The standard environment for studying the free-rider problem in the allocation of public goods is the voluntary contribution mechanism (VCM), extensively studied by Isaac and Walker and their coauthors (Isaac et al., 1981, 1984, 1985, 1989; Isaac and Walker, 1988a, b). In a VCM experiment, each subject is given a set of tokens at the beginning of each period. The subject may invest tokens in an individual exchange, with a fixed monetary return per token, and/or a group exchange, which returns money to the subject as a function of the total contributions of all the subjects in the experiment.

Typically, the individual incentives are designed to make strong free riding, or $0 contributions to the group exchange, the dominant strategy for each subject. On the other hand, the highest joint payoff for all subjects is achieved when all subjects contribute 100% of their tokens to the group exchange.

the subjects. Other social contract reasoning tasks asked subjects to detect altruists instead of cheaters. People are not good at detecting altruists. In fact, where the rule was a social law (public good) more people detected cheaters than altruists (CT, 1992, pp. 193–5 and footnote 17).

Isaac and Walker and their coauthors, as cited earlier, find that contributions to the group exchange are sensitive to differences in the rules of message exchange that relate to our previous discussion of cognitive mechanisms for social exchange. With subject groups of 4 or 10 subjects, if subjects make contributions in private, if there is no identified target level of contributions, and if they do not communicate with one another at any time during the experiment, then contributions to the group exchange decline from about 40% of tokens in period 1 to about 10% of tokens in period 10 (Isaac and Walker, 1988a; Isaac et al., 1984). These results extend to large groups of 40 or 100 people, but per capita contributions actually increase relative to groups of size 4 or 10 in some treatments.

In the same experimental environment, however, if subjects can talk with one another for a short period before *each* decision, contributions to the group exchange quickly rise to almost 100% of tokens, even if actual investment decisions are made in private (Isaac and Walker, 1988b). These results illustrate the importance of "cheap talk" communication in creating an environment in which agents expect one another to behave cooperatively and they abide by the reinforced norm even when all decisions are made in private and no individual's defection can be detected by others.

The results can also be interpreted in a signaling context. During the communication phase, individuals verbally signal that they will behave cooperatively and that they expect others to reciprocate. During the decision-making phase, individuals generally abide by the norm reinforced by the signal, and a cooperative outcome is achieved. Even though no direct punishment can be inflicted by other subjects in the event of defection, other subjects can exact general punishment by defection against other subjects in future rounds.

In other experiments (Isaac et al., 1989), the experimenter establishes a minimum provision-point contribution to the group investment. When comparing results with and without a provision point, and allowing no communication, contributions to the group account increase with the provision point. When the provision point is 100% of tokens, contributions rise even further, although many groups fail to attain it.

From a signaling perspective, the provision point signals an expected joint level of contribution to the group account and helps to induce common expectations of substantial contributions to the group account. With equal endowments, the implied signal is that each subject should contribute $(1/n)$-th of the announced provision point.

B.   *Ultimatum and Dictator Experiments*

Ultimatum and dictator experiments illustrate the importance of observability, shared expectations of social norms, punishment, and signaling in enforcing reciprocity behavior. In an ultimatum game, player 1 makes an offer to player 2 of X from a total of M. If player 2 accepts the offer, then player 1 is paid $(M + X)$ and player 2 receives X; if player 2 rejects the offer, each gets $0. In the dictator game, player 2 must accept player 1's offer.

Under the usual rationality assumptions, the noncooperative equilibrium of the ultimatum game is for player 1 to offer player 2 the smallest dollar unit of account, and for player 2 to accept the offer. In the dictator game player 1 offers $0 to player 2. In the ultimatum game, however, player 2 *can* punish player 1 for "cheating" on an implied social norm of reciprocal sharing across time, in social exchange, by rejecting player 1's offer. That response is a dominated strategy, if viewed in isolation, because both players would be financially better off even with a vanishingly small offer. But, in the absence of common knowledge of self-interested behavior, the possibility of punishment may change player 1's equilibrium strategy.

In Kahneman et al. (1986; hereinafter KKT), players 1 and 2 in an ultimatum game are "provisionally allocated" $10, and player 1 is asked to make an initial offer to "divide" the $10 between the two players. Player 2 may veto the division, in which case they both get $0. KKT found that most player 1s offer $5 to player 2s; offers less than $5 are sometimes rejected. Although there are some differences, the general features of these results have been replicated in cross cultural comparisons suggesting that the results are not strongly culture-specific (Roth et al., 1991). This suggests that the explanation may transcend culture.

Forsythe et al. (1994; hereinafter FHSS) replicated KKT's results from the ultimatum game and also studied the dictator game. They found that about 20% of dictator player 1s offer $0 to their player 2 counterparts, as noncooperative game theory would predict; however, more player 1s offer $5 than offer $0, and offers of $1, $2, $3, and $4 are approximately evenly distributed. Thus, removing the threat of punishment reduces sharing behavior but not by as much as game theory predicts.

Recognizing that the prospect of punishment might create expectations that change player 1's behavior, Hoffman et al. (1994; hereinafter HMSS) considered experimental treatments explicitly designed to affect subject expectations about operating norms of social exchange. The experimental instructions that describe the different treatments might be viewed as signals to the subjects of the expected social norm operating in each experiment.

Brewer and Crano (1994), in their social psychology textbook, list three norms of social exchange that may apply in ultimatum games. From our perspective, norms are the product of culture interacting with mental modules in order to solve specific problems of social exchange. Such norms can then inform a theory of mind mechanism as to another's volitional state. *Equality* implies that gains should be shared equally in the absence of any objective differences between individuals suggesting another sharing rule. *Equity* implies that individuals who contribute more to a social exchange should gain a larger share of the returns. *Reciprocity* implies that if one individual offers a share to another individual, the second individual is expected to reciprocate within a reasonable time. We distinguish negative reciprocity – the use of punishment strategies to retaliate against behavior that is deemed inappropriate – and positive reciprocity – the use of strategies that initiate or reward appropriate behavior.

The design of KKT and FHSS invokes the equality norm. No distinction was made between the two individuals "provisionally allocated" $10 and they are told to "divide" the money. Hence, deviations from equal division are more likely to be punished as cheating on the social exchange. Using the same task description, HMSS replicate the FHSS results in a Random/Divide $10 treatment.

To invoke equity, HMSS explored two variations on their Random/Divide $10 treatment in a 2 × 2 experimental design. First, HMSS described the Exchange treatment, without changing the reduced form of the game, as a market in which the seller (player 1) chose a price (division of $10) and the buyer (player 2) indicated whether he or she would buy or not buy (accept or not accept). From the perspective of social exchange, a seller might equitably earn a higher return than a buyer. Second, in the Contest treatment, they made each seller earn the property right to be a seller by scoring higher on a general knowledge quiz than buyers. Winners were then told that they have "earned the right" to be sellers. Going back to Homans (1967), equity theory predicted that individuals who have earned the right to a higher return will be socially justified in receiving that higher return.

Figure 9.1 reproduces HMSS's Random/Divide and Contest/Exchange experimental results. Social exchange theory predicts that, in a situation in which it is equitable for player 1 to receive a larger compensation than player 2 (i.e., Contest/Exchange), (a) player 1 will offer significantly less to player 2, whereas (b) player 2 will accept any given offer with higher probability. The data in Figure 9.1 are consistent with

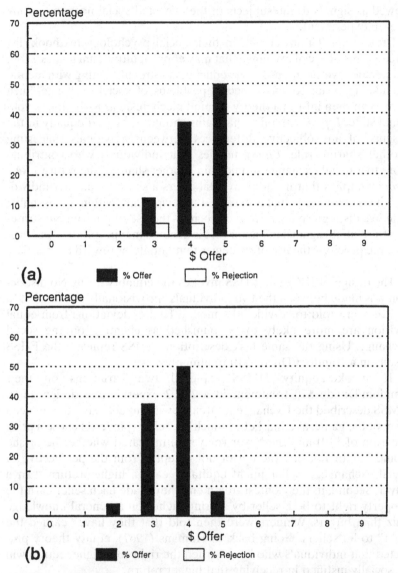

FIGURE 9.1. (a) Ultimatum; Random entitlement, FHSS instructions, Divide $10, *N* = 24. (b) Ultimatum; Contest entitlement, FHSS instructions, Divide $10, *N* = 24. (c) Ultimatum; Random entitlement, Exchange, *N* = 24. (d) Ultimatum; Contest entitlement, Exchange, *N* = 24.

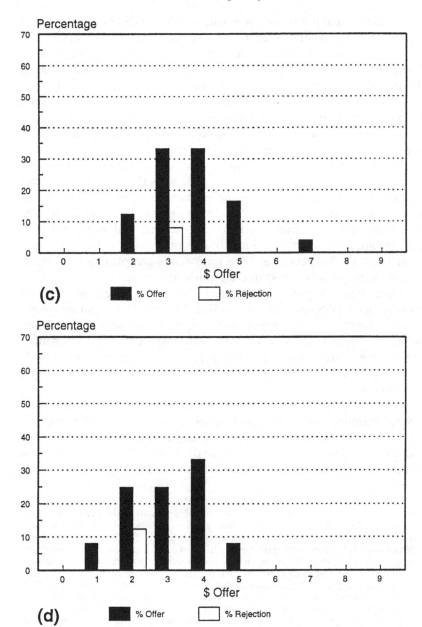

FIGURE 9.1. *Continued.*

prediction (a) and not inconsistent with prediction (b). Player 1s offered significantly less to player 2s, whereas rejection rates were statistically indistinguishable. These results suggest that the change from Random/Divide to Contest/Exchange alters the shared expectations of the two players regarding the social exchange norm operating to determine an appropriate sharing rule. Finally, the difference between Random/Divide and Contest/Exchange carries over to dictator experiments as well, indicating that the change in expectations takes place even when there is no threat of punishment from player 2.

But why do these treatments reduce offers without causing an increase in the rejection rate? One hypothesis is that both players infer one anothers' mental states – in this case expectations – from relevant information in the experiment. Mind reading implies the ability to take the perspective of another person who has common information. In this experiment, player 1 expected player 2 to find a lower offer acceptable, whereas player 2 expected, and was prepared to accept, a lower offer. At minimum, this involved a shared attention mechanism.

Observability is potentially powerful in the enforcement of social norms. Thus, FHSS recruited player 1s and player 2s to separate rooms, and the players were anonymous with respect to one another. However, subject decisions were not anonymous with respect to the experimenter. Someone was still "watching"; hence player 1s were still not entirely removed from a social exchange setting where reciprocity norms might unconsciously apply.

This led HMSS to design a double blind dictator experiment, with several features that were later changed one or two at a time, to investigate the role of social isolation in extinguishing behavior reflecting social norms (Hoffman et al., 1996a). In the double blind treatment, 64% of the player 1s take all $10; about 90% take at least $8.[6]

---

[6] Bolton et al. (1993), using a different version of the dictator game and using different double blind procedures, found no difference between their double blind and single blind treatments. The results from such treatment variations are always of interest, but claims that the experiments show that the results of HMSS do not replicate exceed what is demonstrated. When examining treatment variations on an earlier study, a second experimenter must first show that he or she can duplicate the original results using the same treatment and procedures, establishing that the results replicate with different subjects and different experimenters. Only then can the results using the new treatment, if different, be attributed to these conditions and not to the subjects, experimenter, or procedures used. Thus, HMSS replicated the procedures and results of Forsythe et al. (1994) before attempting to compare them with the results from new treatments. Given the sensitivity of the dictator game to procedures and instructions, it is important that other researchers be able to replicate such findings before changing the treatment. Eckel and Grossman (1996b) replicated the HMSS double blind experiments before conducting their interesting new treatment in which the recipient was the American Red Cross instead of another subject. Terry Burnham also replicated the HMSS double blind experiments in a study currently in process (private communication).

These results are strikingly different from the dictator results in FHSS and from the HMSS Random/Divide and Contest/Exchange dictator experiments in which subjects were observed by the experimenters. Next, in three stages, HMS varied each of the elements of the double blind dictator experiment in ways intended to reduce the "social distance" between the subjects and anyone who might see their choices. The experimental results form a predicted ordered set of distributions. As the social distance between the subject and others decreases the cumulative distribution of offers to player 2s increases. These results demonstrate the power of isolation from implied observability in the enforcement of norms of equality, equity, and reciprocity.

C.   Signaling, Trust, and Punishment in Bargaining Experiments

In this section, we review the results of two-person extensive form bargaining/trust experiments in which players move sequentially, and one player can choose to play – signal – cooperatively. Berg et al. (1995) adapted the double blind procedure to study trust and reciprocity in a two-stage dictator game. In stage one player 2 decides how much of $10 to send to player 1 and how much to keep. The amount sent triples to M before reaching player 1. In stage two player 1, acting as a dictator, decides how to split the M . Because the amount to be split is endogenous, the two players now share a common history before the dictator game is played. If reciprocity plays a significant role in promoting social exchange, then their common history should reduce the "social distance" between subjects in a two-stage dictator game. Even though, Berg et al. found significant use of trust and reciprocity, subjects in their experiments had no alternative but to rely on trust for mutual gain.

McCabe et al. (1996) studied an extensive form game in which a player could choose between two subgames, each of which could result in mutual gain. In one subgame, mutual gain could be achieved using reciprocity incentives, whereas in the other subgame mutual gain was achieved using self-interested incentives. By choosing the reciprocity subgame, the subject signaled a desire to cooperate, and each subject could earn $50. By choosing the self-interested subgame, the subject signaled a desire to play noncooperatively, and each subject earned $40. In some of these experiments, the signaling player, at a cost to himself or herself, could directly punish the other player for cheating on the implied social exchange. In the other trust experiments, there was no direct opportunity to retaliate against defection from a signal to cooperate.

1. The Constituent Games: Payoffs. Figure 9.2 shows the extensive form bargaining tree for these two constituent, or stage, games played by two persons. Player 1 begins with a move right or down at node x_1. A move right terminates the play with payoffs (35, 70), in cents, in repeat play (multiplied by 20 in single play), respectively, for players 1 and 2. If the move is down, then player 2 moves left or right at node x_2, and so on. Play ends with any move that terminates at a payoff box on the right or the left of the tree. Game 1 shows the baseline payoff structure used; game 2 is the same except for the payoffs in the boxes corresponding to plays left at nodes x_3 and x_5. McCabe et al. (1996) have studied behavior in these games under a variety of matching protocols and information treatments.

In both games 1 and 2 the right side of the tree contains the subgame perfect (SP) noncooperative outcome (40, 40), where player 2 moves right at x_6. This outcome is achieved by simple dominance, once player 2 moves right at x_2 (i.e., it is in player 1's interest to play down at x_4 and for player 2 then to play right at x_6).

In game 1, cooperative actions by the players can lead to the largest symmetric (LS) outcome (50, 50), achieved if player 1 moves left at x_3. Under complete payoff information, a move left at x_2 by player 2 can be interpreted as a signal to player 1 that player 1 should go left at x_3. (This is because 50 at LS is clearly better than 40 at SP for player 2, allowing player 1 to infer player 2's reason for playing left at x_2.) Player 1, however, can defect, move down at x_3, and force player 2, in his or her own interest, to move left at x_5 giving player 1 a payoff of 60. In fact, this is the game theoretic prediction if play occurs on the left side of the tree in game 1. In a single play, player 2 should see this, and the theoretical prediction becomes Selten's SP outcome on the right.

But a move left at x_2 in game 1 is more than a signal that player 2 wants to achieve the LS outcome (50, 50). It can also be interpreted as a potential threat to play down at x_5, punishing player 1 if player 1 defects or cheats by playing down at x_3. This action, however, is costly to player 2, because each player gets 20 if player 1 moves left at x_7. But, given the way subjects behave in ultimatum games, it is not unreasonable to assume that some subjects will move left at x_2 and then punish defections at x_3.

Game 2 contrasts with game 1 in that to achieve LS, by player 2 moving left at x_5, player 1 must resist the temptation to move left at x_3. In game 2, player 1 can cheat on the invitation to cooperate by choosing (60, 30) without the prospect that player 2 can punish player 1. Thus, game 2 allows signaling, but not punishment; it is a game of trust.

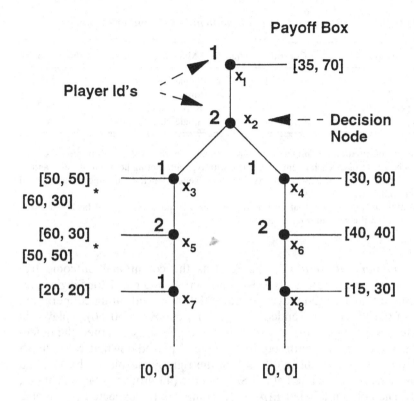

Payoff Box

Player Id's

Decision Node

[35, 70]

[50, 50]
[60, 30] *

[60, 30]
[50, 50] *

[20, 20]

[30, 60]

[40, 40]

[15, 30]

[0, 0]   [0, 0]

*   **Game 2 differs from Game 1**
    by these two payoff boxes.

FIGURE 9.2. Games 1 and 2 in extensive form.

2. Experimental Design. Table 9.1 shows four treatments that vary the protocol for matching pairs in each experiment. An experiment consists of groups of 8–16 subjects who are randomly assigned to pairs. In Repeat Single we begin the session with 16 subjects, and each person plays every other counterpart once, with their roles alternating between players 1 and 2. Under Contingent, each player indicates his or her choice at each node. Then the computer executes the play. Single means that all pairs play the constituent game exactly once for a multiple of 20 times the payoffs shown in the boxes of Figure 9.2.

Table 9.1. *Experimental design treatments and number of pairs*[a]

Designation	Constituent game	Matching protocol	Number pairs[c]
Single 1	1	Single play	26
Single 2	1	Single play	17
Repeat Single 1	1	Repeat Single play[b]	26
Single 1 Contingent[d]	1	Single play, all nodes	24

[a] Payoff information is complete – both players know both payoffs in all treatments.
[b] Each subject plays each counterpart once with type alternating between player 1 and 2.
[c] Sessions consist of at least 8 subjects, 4 pairs. In Repeat Single 1, 16 subjects each played every other subject exactly once.
[d] Contingent play means that each player makes a response at each of his/her decision nodes. Then the computer executes the play once.

3. Summary of Results. Table 9.2 lists the conditional outcome frequencies for each payoff box. Reading across data row 1 for Single 1, we observe that 13 of 30 player 2s moved left at x_2, indicating cooperation; 11 of the 13 left plays ended with player 1 choosing (50, 50); 2 player 1s defected by playing down at x_3; 1 of these player 2s accepted the defection and responded with (60, 30), whereas 1 played down at x_5 to punish player 1 who then chose (20, 20). In the right game, played by 17 of 30 player 2s, 16 of 17 ended at the SP outcome (40, 40); one play was at (15, 30). The column labeled $E(p_2 \times \text{Left})$ computes the expected profit, 46.2 cents, to player 2 from playing left at x_2, based on the relative frequencies of subsequent play by both players. $E(p_1 \times \text{Down})$ is the expected profit, 30 cents, to player 1 from defecting at node x_3. Efficiency is the percentage of the cooperative total payoff at (50, 50) that is realized by all players. Thus in Single 1, 83.8% of the cooperative surplus is collected by all pairs. At SP efficiency is 80%, so any greater efficiency implies a net social benefit from cooperative initiatives.

Result 1. *Game theory predicts that in Single 1 all plays will be in the right subgame. In fact, 43.3% are in the left subgame. In Repeat Single 1, we observe that experience does not help to achieve SP; now 58% play the left subgame. Contrary to the theory, we observe both too much attempted cooperation and too few defections on these attempts. Conditional on right branch play, however, game theory does very well in predicting the SP outcome for both games 1 and 2 in all treatments.*

Result 2. *In all treatments it is (weakly) advantageous in the expected payoff sense to play in the left subgame. This is indicated by the fact that*

Table 9.2. *Summary data; all treatments*

	Conditional outcome probabilities by treatment; for all trials										
Treatment	Left	50 50	60 30	20 20	Right	30 60	40 40	15 30	$E(\pi_2|\text{Left})$[b]	$E(\pi_1|\text{Down})$[c]	Efficiency[d] (%)
Single 1	13/30 = .433	11/13 = .846	1/2 = .5	1/1 = 1	17/30 = .567	0/13 = 0	16/17 = .41	1/1 = 1	46.2	30.0	83.8
Single 2[a]	12/26 = .462	6/12 = .5	6/6 = 1	0	14/26 = .538	0/14 = 0	14/14 = 1	0	40.0	—	86.9
Repeat Single 1	204/352 = .580	133/204 = .652	33/71 = .549	36/36 = 1	148/352 = .420	9/148 = .061	138/139 = .993	0/1 = 0	41.5	42.0	85.1
Single 1 contingent	9/23 = .391	8/9 = .889	1/9 = .111	0	14/23 = .609	3/14 = .214	11/11 = 1	0	47.8	60	88.7

[a] Note that in game 2 the play order of the outcomes (60, 30) and (50, 50) is reversed relative to game 1.
[b] Expected payoff to player 2 from playing left at x_2, given the relative frequencies of subsequent play by player 1 and 2.
[c] Expected payoff to player 1 from defecting at node x_3.
[d] Efficiency is the percent of the cooperative (50,50) total payoff that is realized by all pairs.

the expected profit to player 2 of left branch play is at least 40.0 cents in all treatments, and 40 is the payoff to player 2 at SP. Thus, right subgame play by the minority is not profitable in both *games 1 and 2.*

Result 3. *Defections by player 1 at node* x_3 *of game 1 are not profitable under the Single 1 and Repeat Single 1 treatments: the expected profit of playing down is always less than 50, the payoff to player 1 by not defecting. Thus, the punish-cheaters mental module hypothesized by Cosmides (1985) is alive. Moreover it is used only just enough to be effective, but not so much that efficiency is badly compromised.*

Result 4. *Single 1 Contingent converts game 1 from the extensive to the normal form by requiring each player's choices at all nodes of the tree to be made in advance for simultaneous play. It is equivalent to expressing all payoff path outcomes in matrix form for simultaneous choice by both players. Game theory hypothesizes that the normal and extensive forms are equivalent, but previous research has shown that this is not generally the case (Schotter et al., 1994). Comparing Single 1 with Single 1 Contingent, we see that left play declined (right play increased) in the latter. Why? Our hypothesis is that the extensive form, with sequential turn-taking moves, allows the players to engage in a move-interpreting conversation. Thus, at node* x_2, *player 2 has just received the message, "I moved down at* x_1 *because I want to do better than receive 35," from player 1. If player 2 now moves left, the message is "I am playing left because I want to forgo the (40, 40) on the right in favor of (50, 50) which is better for both of us. Also, note that if you respond by playing down at* x_3, *then I have the option of punishing you with (20, 20)." This hypothetical dialogue is disrupted with simultaneous play, although under strict rationality it is irrelevant: player 2's message is not credibly self-enforcing. But as we have seen (Baron-Cohen, 1995), mind reading allows players to infer mental states from actions and, as shown by these results, may lead them to play differently in the extensive form than in the normal form.*[7]

Result 5. *The failure of the SP predicted outcome (Result 1) motivated the study of game 2 in which the cooperative (50, 50) outcome cannot be supported by the prospect of punishment. Comparing Single 2 with Single 1 (rows 2 and 1 of Table 9.2), we see no important change in left moves by player 2s in game 2. Play in left subgame 2 produces fewer (50, 50) out-*

---

[7] Additional tests of the reciprocity hypothesis based on comparisons of the extensive form with matrix normal form are reported in McCabe, Smith, and LePore (1998). The reciprocity hypothesis also implies that SP outcomes will predominate under private information. This prediction is strongly supported in McCabe et al. (1996).

*comes (50%) than in game 1 (84.6%). This reduces the expected profit of
left play from 46.2 cents in game 1 to a break-even 40 cents in game 2.
Clearly, the strategic difference between the two games is making a difference in the game theoretic predicted direction. The more interesting
observation is that the* trust *element in game 2 is sufficient to yield cooperation for half of the pairs who play the left subgame. This is consistent
with results reported by Fehr et al. (1993) in labor market experiments and
by Berg et al. (1995) in investment dictator games. In these studies, first
movers trusted second movers to reciprocate with no possibility of
punishment.*

If you think of noncooperative game theory as applying to "foes," in
these extensive form experiments the theory accurately predicts behavior in just over half the observations. The relevance of traditional game
theory for a large segment of this population cannot be dismissed.
However, those remaining, who persist in cooperation, need also to be
explained and modeled. Their behavior is not extinguished with experience: in Repeat Single 1, the percent of play in the left reciprocity branch
increases to 58%. We conjecture that minimal elements for a complete
theory of mental phenomena in games of strategy should include (1) a
friend-or-foe detection mechanism and (2) an intentionality detector
mechanism, where the latter requires extensive form play to achieve its
full scope.

IV.   When Do People Abandon Reciprocity in Favor of
         Noncooperative Play?

The preceding examples illustrate a model of a mixture of individuals,
some of whose play reflects game theoretic principles, whereas others'
play reflects learned or innate responses involving signaling, trust,
punishment, and other ingredients of reciprocity behavior. In the latter,
the play objective serves the typical subject well: they exceed the performance of strict game-theoretic players in that surplus-improving
cooperative outcomes are more often attained than theory would
predict.

In this section, we consider an example contrary to those discussed
earlier, one in which subjects begin with their intuitive automatic
responses, discover that these responses cannot sustain good performance, and then adjust in the direction of the noncooperative rational
expectations outcome predicted by theory. In this case, subjects are given
common *information*, but this is not sufficient to induce common *knowl-*

edge in the sense of *expectations* (also see Smith et al., 1988; Harrrison and McCabe, 1992). This, we argue, is because common information leaves behavioral or strategic uncertainty unresolved. The latter is resolved over time as subjects, in successive extensive form rounds, come to have common expectations that predicted equilibrium outcomes will prevail.

McCabe (1989) reports a 6-person, 6-period, extensive form game experiment using fiat money. In successive periods, subjects use buy, sell, and null messages to trade, or not, a unit of fiat money against cash dividend paying bonds. In the last period, a bond holder should not sell because he or she would be left with worthless fiat money. Similarly, the money should not be accepted on the penultimate round and, by backward induction, should not be accepted in the first period. Although subjects have complete information on this payoff structure, trade in the first play of the sequence yields trade in each period until the last one. Repeating this constituent game ten times (common information) causes some, but not a complete, unraveling backward from the final trial. When subjects return for a second 15-trial experiment, the slow unraveling process continues, but trade persists, especially in the early trials. In a third session for 20 trials, gradually trade is further diminished and is virtually eliminated by the 15th trial.

These results can be understood in terms of a model in which people have been strongly conditioned by reciprocity experience to accept fiat money in trade because they expect others to accept money when they offer it in trade. This expectation is unconscious; they never ask themselves why they and others accept money. It is a conditional reciprocity response, which serves them effectively in daily life. They are recruited to the laboratory where the conditions for ongoing repeated exchange are not satisfied; in the end-game, intrinsically worthless money is refused in trade. This failure experience induces them to reevaluate their unconscious, accustomed response to money. Very slowly, in the limit, as play is repeated in the finite horizon environment, trade converges to zero.[8]

V.   Conclusions

The experimental game results summarized in this chapter suggest that people invoke reward/punishment strategies in a wide variety of group interactive contexts. These strategies are generally inconsistent with, but

---

[8] Similarly, Camerer and Weigelt (1988) report very slow convergence in a sequential equilibrium reputation model.

more profitable than, the noncooperative strategies predicted by game theory. However, in contrast to CT's emphasis on punishing cheaters, we observe substantial use of positive as well as negative reciprocity strategies, even in single-play games. Hence behavior is much richer and more trusting than CT's model would predict.

A punish-cheaters mechanism has the advantage, as in tit-for-tat, that it can sustain cooperation. But is a pure trust/trustworthy mechanism sustainable? Recall that the strategy C in the PD game cannot resist invasion by defectors. This is still an open question, but Carmichael and MacLeod (1995) offered a model that is encouraging. They analyzed gift exchange showing that a stable gift-giving custom, which does not depend upon the use of punishment strategies, may emerge.

Consider the following hypothetical model of the mind for human decision making. We inherit a circuitry that is modularized for solving social exchange problems. But the switches are not set; that occurs sometime in our maturation, requires no formal instruction, and is not a self-aware process. In this sense, it is like the way we "learn" natural language without being taught. The switches are set differently in different cultures, but the results are functionally equivalent across cultures; in particular there is a propensity to be programmed to try cooperation in dealing with other people who are not detected as foes. But there is variation so that we can talk about population distributions of P (the probability that a person will initiate cooperation), of Q (the probability that a person will defect on an offer to cooperate), of R (the probability a defection will be punished), of S (the probability that a person will be trusting), of T (the probability that a person will be trustworthy), and so on. These distributions of player types are an adaptation capable of changing slowly over time.

Formal education is hard because it is concerned with conscious learning, expression, and action and does not come naturally, just as written language is unnatural and hard to learn. When people are exposed to economic principles, most find it extremely hard to learn about comparative advantage, opportunity cost, gains from exchange, and Nash equilibria. Many give up, but it does not follow that if they are in an economics experiment that they will perform poorly. This is because they may be good at reading other minds and relying on their unconscious natural mental mechanisms. These mechanisms help to define reputations that are applied repeatedly across different life, and laboratory, games. A one-shot game in the laboratory is part of a life-long sequence, not an isolated experience that calls for behavior that deviates sharply from one's reputational norm. Thus, we should expect subjects to rely upon reciprocity norms in experimental settings, unless they discover in the process of participating in a particular experiment that reciprocity is punished and other behaviors are rewarded. In such cases, they abandon their natural instincts and attempt other strategies that better serve their interests.

PART III

Institutions and Markets

Introduction

The rediscovery of institutions and their economic function by many economists, working from widely divergent perspectives, is a striking feature of the development of economic thought in the past 40 odd years. Particularly noteworthy are the seminal contributions, among others, of Gordon (1954) on property rights, Coase (1960) on legal institutions and transactions, enforcement and monitoring costs, Hurwicz (1960) on exchange mechanisms, Vickery (1961) on the incentive compatibility properties (and design) of exchange rules, and recently North (1990) on the significance of institutions in economic change. In parallel with these developments, experimental economists, beginning with Chamberlin (1948), Hoggatt (1959), Sauermann and Selten (1959), Siegel and Fouraker (1960), Smith (1962), and Fouraker and Siegel (1963), were experimenting with different institutions and learning from their subjects that the institutional rules of trade were essential determinates of efficiency, prices, allocations, and the distribution of the gains from exchange. This learning was not transparent at the time but resulted from an ex post interpretation and understanding that variations in outcomes arose from variations in behavior that were mediated by different exchange rule systems.

Experimentalists have become increasingly aware that institutions matter because the rules matter, and the rules matter because they determine incentives. Institutions also provide framing, and we know from the work of Kahneman and Tversky that the framing of a decision problem can be important. An experiment defines a microeconomy governed by an institution that defines messages, the rules of message exchange, and how messages map into allocations. You can't do an experiment without creating an institution in all its nitty gritty complexity. The intimate connection between institutions and extensive form games was early emphasized by Shubik (1959) who coined the phrase "mathematical institutional economics" for the study of dynamic oligopoly games.

The eight essays in Part III were much influenced by an implicit respect for the power of institutions to control outcomes. Chapter 10 surveys some results on market mechanisms for classical environments

203

including the oral double auction in intertemporal exchange, behavior under price controls, and behavior with a monopoly seller. Also, the effect of several variations on the microstructure of double auction rules is summarized. Finally, oral bid, offer, and double auctions, as well as posted bid and offer institutions are compared. The research surveyed involves no computer-based experiments and therefore represents the end of a research epoch. Chapter 11 is also a survey but includes two-commodity double auctions showing that the properties of this institution extend to more complex environments. Among the institutions discussed is an example of exchange under a political (unanimity-voting) mechanism.

Chapter 12 presents some early evidence showing that the usual discrepancy between willingness-to-pay and willingness-to-accept payment for gambles is decreased considerably in the context of the double auction trading institution. These preliminary results were followed by further explorations by Camerer (1987) and Cox and Grether (1996) of the general question: Do people behave more rationally in repetitive institutional contexts like markets? They often do, but not always.

In Chapter 13, I and my coauthors extend the study of market contestability, among firms with scale economies, to the case of finite nonzero sunk costs. The effect of entry cost is to weaken support for certain strong forms of the contestable market hypotheses. None of the experiments support the "natural monopoly" hypothesis. These important results have since been found to be robust with respect to choice between alternative markets, and agent explicit choice of scale (Plott et al., 1994).

Chapter 14 explores extreme conditions for the validity of the competitive price model under the double auction trading institution: duopoly consistently, and monopoly often, achieve competitive equilibrium outcomes; extreme asymmetries in the distribution of surplus do not prevent convergence to competitive equilibria; multiple competitive equilibria markets yield diverse results – convergence to one of the equilibria, including the boundary, and drift from one to another.

A study of off-floor trading for one of the organized exchanges confronts a potential market failure problem (Chapter 15). Once a central exchange is organized, participants may have an incentive to free-ride on the published price discovery information by trading privately at a reduced cost of transacting. The key here is the bid–ask spread that emerges in double auction markets. If the spread does not converge to zero, traders have an incentive to, and the experiments show that they do, trade bilaterally off the exchange. This causes market disintegration, and increased price volatility as the market's information aggregation function is compromised. In the limit, the market may fail, or disappear, although this limit was not examined in the experiments.

In order to examine the off-floor trading issue, we created an environment in which the bid–ask spread did not converge to near zero, since the incentive of traders was hypothesized by exchange officials to be to split the bid–ask difference, sharing these transactions cost savings between bilateral traders. We found that the bid–ask spread systematically widened when we introduced greater supply–demand uncertainty – a result of interest in its own right in that it establishes an important behavioral characteristic of this institution.

Organized futures exchanges prevent any such market disintegration from occurring by applying heavy penalties for prearranged trades or bilateral trades outside the pits. Think of off-floor trading as involving a comparison of the transactions cost of exchange trading (exchange fees plus the bid–ask spread) with the cost of transacting off-floor, where the latter is much reduced by the existence of on-floor competitive price information – the public good provided by the exchange. The organized exchange attempts to change these incentives with penalties that increase the expected transactions cost (the probability of getting caught times the penalty) of off-floor trading. Our solution (McCabe et al., 1993) would be to eliminate the bid–ask spread with a uniform price open display double auction, but this solution is not popular among dealers whose livelihood requires a bid–ask spread. Eliminating the bid–ask spread and substituting an electronic cross reduces reliance on a cohort of dealers. Old practices die slowly in the world of electronic exchange.

Chapters 16 and 17 examine the century-old issues of (1) competition in Bertrand-Edgeworth environments and (2) the efficacy of Walrasian *tâtonnement* institutions. The first study uses numerical methods to compute mixed strategy equilibrium distributions for four-seller markets with simulated fully revealed demand. The bottom line is that although the aggregate price distributions reflect the qualitative theoretical predictions, individuals deviate greatly from the mixed strategy predictions, and exhibit too much serial correlation to satisfy the Nash requirements. As for the various Walrasian auctions studied in Chapter 17, all are less efficient than the double auction. Even the French Bourse has finally abandoned the trading mechanism that inspired Walras.

CHAPTER 10

Reflections on Some Experimental Market Mechanisms for Classical Environments
Vernon L. Smith

We must teach him what we know before we can show him what we see.

N. R. Hanson

Two themes are illustrated in the selection of experimental studies of market mechanisms for classical (pure private good) environments that will be discussed in this chapter. The first theme is perhaps best expressed in the question: Do you see what I see? Depending upon what one is looking for, what one expects to see, or which "results" are emphasized, different individuals may read or interpret differently the results of an experiment. This is a natural consequence of the desirable objective of reading, interpreting, and socializing the meaning of experimental outcomes.

Facts do not speak for themselves. As noted by N. R. Hanson (1969), facts are theory-laden. Consequently, to say that "Economists cannot make use of controlled experiments to settle their differences" (Robinson, 1977, p. 1319) is not only to make a patently erroneous statement (experimental economics is alive and well) but to misunderstand the nature of experimental evidence as well. Experimental results may generate differences at least as often as they settle differences, and they may sometimes settle some differences while simultaneously creating new differences. The theory-laden character of experimental results is well illustrated by Kaplan's (1964, pp. 153–4) report of an experiment in which rats, caged alone, were trained to obtain food pellets by pressing a lever on the opposite end of the cage. When two rats were put into the cage, and one pressed the lever, the other rat was always able to get to the pellet slot first. Eventually both rats were waiting at the food slot and neither pressed the lever. Kaplan noted that this experiment "might be taken to illustrate the breakdown of production under severe competition, the exploitation of labor, surplus value, class conflicts and I don't know what else; but plainly it proves nothing about these matters." To many of us, the experiment clearly demonstrates the dependence of any viable social organization on the principle of individual incentive compatibility.[1] But what anyone sees in such an experiment is strongly influenced by the theory (or belief system) that sensitizes one to "seeing."[2] Hence, we must always "teach him what we know before we can show him what we see." The following sections provide a summary of what I think has been established or learned by the experiments under discussion. Others may put a different interpretation on what has been learned.

A second theme concerns the distinction between two types of experiments:[3]

1. *Heuristic or exploratory experiments that probe a new field of investigation.* These experiments may be conducted merely "to see what will happen" or to distinguish between two hypotheses that are distinct enough to be tested with exploratory experiments. Exploratory experiments are so necessary as to be unavoidable if science is to investigate behavior in areas not heretofore studied experimentally.

2. *Nomothetic experiments that employ replication and rigorous control to reduce error in testing well-defined hypotheses.* Included here are both the theoretically motivated experiments (i.e., those that test hypotheses implied by a formal model or theory) and experiments designed to establish an empirical law or property conjectured from casual observation, or the results of heuristic experiments. Often the hypotheses under test are not easily distinguishable without careful experimental control and many replications.

If nomothetic experiments are the bedrock of science, heuristic experiments are its wings. Without exploratory probes of new phenomena, new scientific questions may never be asked; without rigorous experimental controls and replication, we may never be sure of what it is we know. Nomothetic experiments are the primary means by which I may come to see what you see, and heuristic probes are the primary means by which

---

[1] Evidence for the power of this principle in shaping socioeconomic organization is widespread in all human cultures. Kaplan's description of the rat experiment is reminiscent of Freuchen's (1961, p. 53) account of one of the traditions governing Eskimo hunting parties, whose prey was the dangerous polar bear. "The hunter who fixed his spear first in the bear gets the upper part (of the skin). That is the finest part for it includes the forelegs with the long mane hairs that are so much desired to border women's kamiks with." This simple well-defined property right system suggests (to many of us) an obvious individual incentive for more effective team effort.

[2] Thus, in the Eskimo example in footnote 1, others might interpret the tradition as the expression of an unselfish "fairness ethic" since the team member whose weapon makes the first strike must share all *except* the premium cut with the rest of the hunting party.

[3] See Kaplan (1964, pp. 147–54) for a stimulating discussion of different types of experiments and their scientific significance.

you may "get my attention" and cause me to entertain new scientific propositions or reexamine my belief system.

I.   Oral Double Auctions

The following sections summarize several experimental studies that use the double oral auction institution that is characteristic of the organized stock and commodity exchanges. Several variations on double-auction trading have been used by different experimenters. But common to all forms of the double auction is the condition that price quotations can be entered by both buyers and sellers. Any buyer is free to announce a bid price, and any seller is free to announce an offer price. As both bids and offers are announced, binding contracts can be formed either by a seller accepting a buyer's bid or by a buyer accepting a seller's offer. Just as all bids and offers are made known immediately to all participants, so also are the acceptances that yield contracts. Computerized oral double auctions have attempted to provide a written-bid, visual-display reproduction of these features that would be equivalent to the oral institution. Section I.D compares alternative computerized versions of the double-auction mechanism. Double-auction exchange is of special interest because it converges more rapidly to a competitive equilibrium (CE) and yields more efficient allocations than most of the exchange institutions with which it has been compared (Smith et al., 1982).

The reader is referred to Smith (1964, 1980) and to Miller et al. (1977) for examples of the experimental instructions used in typical oral auction experiments and for discussion of the payoff and other design procedures in laboratory price mechanism experiments.

A.   *Intertemporal Exchange Experiments*

The literature (Miller et al., 1977; Williams, 1979) reports two double-auction experiments in which demand cycled alternately between a low and a high level (see Figure 10.1) and a distinct group of (two) "traders" were given the exclusive right to buy in one period for resale in the subsequent period. In an "autarky" experiment, Williams (1979) used the same cyclical demand conditions but omitted the use of traders. This autarky experiment served as the baseline control experiment against which the effect of speculation could be measured empirically.

The contract prices for Williams' autarky experiment are shown in Figure 10.1. Also shown in Figure 10.1 are the corresponding period 7 prices in his speculation experiment. Figure 10.2 shows the period-by-period mean intertemporal price difference, the quantity exchanged, and

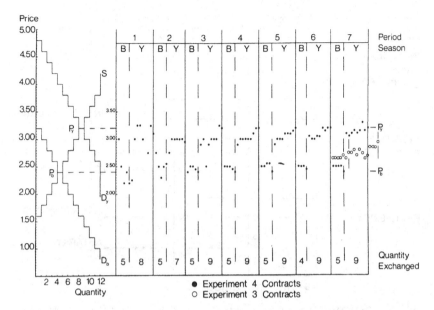

FIGURE 10.1. Double auction price contracts for cycling demand. Based on data from A. Williams (1979).

the efficiency for the Miller et al. speculation experiment (2) and the speculation (3) and autarky (4) experiments of Williams. Experiments 2 and 3 (Figure 10.2) showed a strong tendency for prices to converge to the intertemporal competitive equilibrium, whereas in the autarky experiment (4) prices tended to diverge to their respective alternating CE levels. In Figure 10.1, it is clear that in period 7 contract prices under speculation were wholly contained within the range of seasonal contract prices under autarky. As reported by Williams, the effect of speculation was to significantly reduce the interpersonal price spread, both with respect to the theoretical price difference and with respect to the achieved price difference in the autarky experiment. Similarly, in Figure 10.2 the quantity exchanged under speculation approached the intertemporal CE, and, under autarky volume approached the autarky CE. Under autarky, the total possible surplus of buyers and sellers is 92.0% of the intertemporal CE surplus. In Figure 10.2 except for period 1 in experiment 3, efficiency in every period of the speculation experiments exceeded the efficiencies in any period of the autarky experiment. The observed effect of traders was to increase the surplus of buyers and sellers, and in this process to reduce their own earnings to a minimal

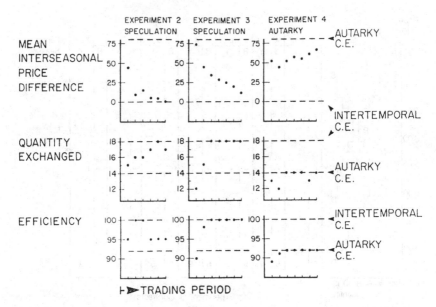

FIGURE 10.2. Mean double-auction prices, quantities, and efficiency by trading period for speculation and autarky experiments. Based on data from Miller et al. (1977) and A. Williams (1979).

level consisting primarily of the commission (5 cents) paid for each transaction.

Although these results provide strong support for classical intertemporal price theory, the state of this research is very incomplete and exploratory. The literature reports only one autarky experiment and two with speculators. Further replication of these experiments is needed to test the robustness of these results. Also, experiments with different supply and demand designs and with alternative patterns of demand and/or supply fluctuations over time are needed to test the limits of the equilibrating effect of speculation.

B.   Price Controls

Isaac and Plott (1981) have pioneered an experimental probe of the effect of price ceilings and floors on the performance of double-auction markets. Static price theory predicts that if a price ceiling (floor) is binding [i.e., if the ceiling (floor) is below (above) the free market CE price, then price will be determined by the level of the price control]. If

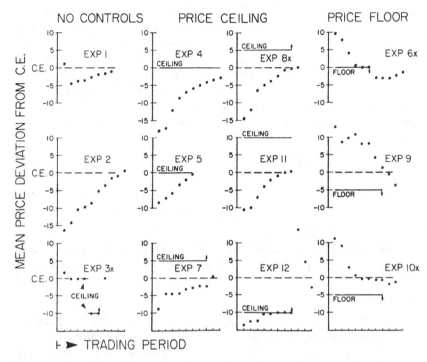

FIGURE 10.3. Mean double auction prices by trading period for no controls, price ceiling, and price floor experiments. Based on data from Isaac and Plott (1979).

the ceiling price is nonbinding [i.e., above (or the floor is below) the CE price], then the theory predicts that the controls will have no effect (i.e., the CE price will prevail). However, Isaac and Plott note that there exists an alternative collusive theory (Scherer, 1970) for nonbinding controls. The argument is that sellers may use a nonbinding ceiling price as a focal point for tacit collusion to keep prices above the CE price.

Apart from these static theories of market behavior under price controls, there is the question of how such controls might affect the dynamics of double-auction markets. Thus price controls might not affect the static CE price toward which a double-auction market converges but may affect the convergence path.

Figure 10.3 summarizes the mean deviation of contract prices from the CE price in each trading period for 12 experiments reported by Isaac and Plott (1981). Experiments 1, 2, and 3x were free markets, without price controls, except that in 3x a ceiling at the CE price was imposed in period 4, lowered in periods 5 and 6, then lifted entirely in period 7. Experiments 4, 5, 7, 8x, 11, and 12 administered a price ceiling at various levels, whereas experiments 6x, 9, and 10x administered a price floor. The *x* after the experiment number is used here to designate "experienced subjects" [i.e., subjects who had participated in a previous (but using different parameters) double-auction experiment]. In Figure 10.3, the upward-pointing arrows refer to the removal of a price ceiling following the indicated trading period, whereas a downward-pointing arrow indicates the removal of a price floor.

Isaac and Plott reported two primary conclusions and a conjecture as follows:

1. Under nonbinding price controls, market behavior is more closely approximated by the competitive model than the collusive "focal point" model.

This conclusion was supported by the price behavior of all the nonbinding control experiments in Figure 10.3. Thus, in Experiments 7, 8x, 11, and 10x, mean prices tended to approach the CE price, *not* the control price.

2. Price-controlled markets exhibit some behavioral regularities that cannot be explained in the context of the CE model.
   a. Controls at the CE price lead to market prices that diverge from the CE price.

This conclusion was not supported by the three relevant experiments (4, 5, and 6x). In each case, the average price per period was converging toward the CE price. Although average price in experiment 4 converged steadily toward the CE, prices in the tenth and final trading period were further from the CE price than were the final trading period prices in the free market experiment 2. But this was not the result in Experiments 5 and 6x, and it does not appear credible to interpret these experiments as producing a divergent price tendency.

   b. When nonbinding controls are lifted from a market, prices are changed.

It might be added that prices change in the direction of the removed control (i.e., up in the case of ceilings and down in the case of floors). In Experiments 7 and 8x, removing the ceiling after the eighth trading period causes an increase in the average price in period 9. Similarly in experiments 9 and 10x, removing the floor at the end of period 8 causes contracts to occur at lower average prices in periods 9 and 10.

c. Inefficiencies due to binding controls are greater than predicted by the standard consumer-producer surplus analysis. The amount of the lost surplus depends upon how the rationing problem, caused by the binding control, is resolved.

As evidence, Isaac and Plott (1981) noted that their Experiment 12, with a binding price ceiling, produced in every period efficiencies that were below the maximum level achievable. In their case, the short supply prevailing at the price ceiling was rationed by a first-come first-serve rule in which ties were broken by a random allocation.

d. When binding controls are removed, a sharp relatively discontinuous jump in the price level occurs.

This is evident in Experiments 3x, 6x, and 12. In Experiment 12, removing the ceiling caused a large increase as prices overshot the CE price by a wide margin. This experiment seems to illustrate a case of panic buying following the removal of a very restrictive price ceiling. The Isaac-Plott conjecture is that:

3. Nonbinding price ceilings (floors) are like a buffer that holds prices below (above) the CE price.

Isaac and Plott stated this result as a conjecture because their evidence for it is inconclusive. This is because in some experimental markets prices tend to converge from below because of "soft sellers" or from above because of "soft buyers." Consequently, in Experiments 7, 8x, and 11, for example, in Figure 10.3, it is not clear whether the slow, or incomplete, convergence from below is due to the ceiling at 5 or 10 cents above the CE price or due to soft sellers as in experiment 2 where there was no ceiling. Similarly, in Experiments 9 and 10x with a price floor 5 cents below the CE, one cannot conclusively say that the floor caused prices to converge slowly from well above the CE. If buyers were soft in these experimental groups, the observed pattern of convergence could have occurred in the absence of the price floor. One solution to this problem is simply replication (i.e., conduct N experiments without price controls and N experiments with, say, a price ceiling, where particular subject groups are allocated at random between the two treatment conditions). Suppose $m < N$ of the no-control experiments yielded prices predominantly below, and $N - m$ yielded prices equal to or above CE. If $n \leq N$ price ceiling experiments yield prices predominantly below CE, then for some n sufficiently greater than m, we would reject the hypothesis that this outcome would have occurred without the price ceiling. For example, in Figure 10.3 two (1 and 2) of the three experiments without price

Table 10.1. *Number of experiments performed under each price control condition*

Supply and demand shift in week 2 (3)	No price control in week 2 or week 3	Price control variable	
		Week 2 price ceiling 5 cents above CE week 3 price floor 5 cents below CE	Week 2 price floor 5 cents below CE week 3 price ceiling 5 cents above CE
Up (up)	1	2	1
Up (down)	1	2	1
Down (up)	1	2	1
Down (down)	1	2	1

controls produced an average price below the CE price. Consequently, the fact that all three of the experiments with a nonbinding ceiling price yielded an average price below CE does not provide significant support for the Isaac-Plott conjecture.

Smith and Williams (1981) were motivated by the Isaac-Plott price control experiments to develop a rigorous experimental design appropriate to the problem of isolating any effects of a nonbinding control on price convergence behavior. The Smith-Williams design was predicated upon the assumption that the differential bargaining strength of buyers relative to sellers is subject to sampling variation among subject groups. Their design permitted each experimental market group to serve as its own partial control in the following manner:

1. All experiments consisted of three "weeks" of trading, each week consisting of five (or four in a few experiments) trading periods. Week 1 provided the baseline set of observations with *no* price control.
2. In each experiment, following the completion of week 1 trading, supply and demand were uniformly shifted by a constant, up or down, relative to week 1. Also the assignment of the individual, shifted, unit values (and costs) was rerandomized among the buyers (sellers). Trading was then resumed in week 2. In eight experiments, a price ceiling was imposed; in four experiments a price floor was imposed, while in four there are no price controls. (See Table 10.1.) This procedure allowed any effect of the shift in supply and demand to be separated from the effect of the price ceiling or floor.
3. Following the completion of week 2, the valuations (costs) were again shifted and rerandomized. Trading was resumed in week

3 with a price floor in the eight experiments that had a ceiling in week 2, with a price ceiling in the four experiments that had a floor in week 2, and with no control in the remaining four experiments.

Certain other features of the Smith-Williams experimental design were introduced to increase control over sampling variability or to sharpen sensitivity.

1. All experiments used the PLATO computer version of the double-auction mechanism by Williams (1980). Computerized trading permitted closer control over "experimenter" effects by ensuring uniform procedures across all experiments.
2. Only experienced subjects participated in each experiment, where "experienced" means that the subject had traded in a previous PLATO double-auction experiment with different parameters and with no price controls.
3. The induced supply and demand for a typical experiment are shown on the left of Figure 10.4. In this symmetrical design, the total surplus for buyers is equal to that for sellers. Also notice that there are several intramarginal and submarginal supply and demand units within 5 cents of the CE price. This makes inefficient trades relatively easy and thereby makes possible a more sensitive measure of efficiency.

Figure 10.4 provides the contract price sequences for one of the Smith-Williams price control experiments, whereas Figure 10.5 plots prices for an experiment subject only to the supply and demand shifts. A summary of mean price per period for 12 of the experiments is shown in Figure 10.6. (Not charted are the four experiments in which the price floor was applied in week 2 and the ceiling in week 3.) The direction of shift in the demand and supply schedules for weeks 2 and 3 is indicated at the top of Figure 10.6. Thus in Experiments 30, 27, and 49, demand and supply were shifted down $(-D,S)$ in week 2 and up $(+D,S)$ in week 3. The tendency for the week 2 ceiling to lower price, and for the week 3 floor to raise price, both measured relative to the week 1 baseline, is fairly evident.

More precisely, Smith and Williams (1983) report the following regression estimates:

$$D(t) = 0.236D(t-5) + 0.464X_2^c - 2.02X_2^f + 1.089Y_2$$
$$(3.41) \qquad (2.08) \qquad (-6.03) \qquad (4.81)$$
$$R^2 = 0.55 \qquad N = 70 \qquad (1)$$

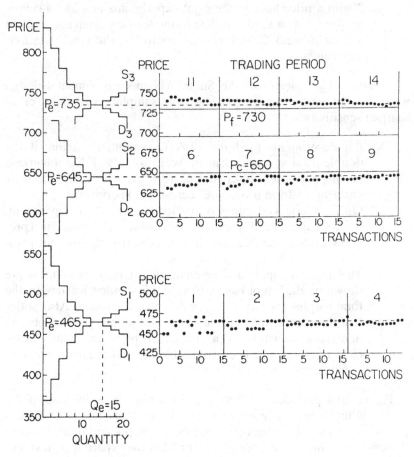

FIGURE 10.4. Experiment 26 double auction contract prices by trading period. Reproduced from Smith and Williams (1980).

$$D(t) = 0.111 D(t-10) + 2.315 X_3^c - 1.190_3^f + 0.260 Y_3$$
$$\quad (1.94) \qquad\qquad (8.47) \quad (-6.54) \quad (1.38)$$
$$\qquad\qquad\qquad\qquad R^2 = 0.74 \qquad N = 67 \qquad (2)$$

where $D(t) = B(t) - S(t)$ = Differential bargaining strength
  $B(t)$ = Buyer realized surplus in period t
  $S(t)$ = Seller realized surplus in period t
and

$$X_i^c = \begin{cases} 1 & \text{if ceiling price is imposed in week } i \\ 0 & \text{if no price control is imposed in week } i \end{cases}$$

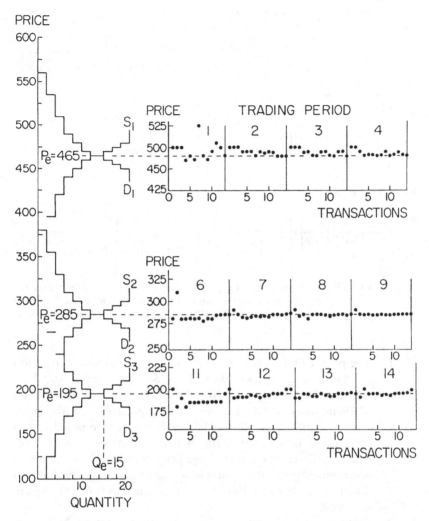

FIGURE 10.5. Experiment 57 auction contract prices by trading period.

$$X_i^f = \begin{cases} 1 & \text{if floor price is imposed in week } i \\ 0 & \text{if no price control is imposed in week } i \end{cases}$$

$$Y_i^l = \begin{cases} 1 & \text{if supply and demand shift down in week } i \\ 0 & \text{if supply and demand shift up in week } i \end{cases}$$

Equations (1) and (2) support the following conclusions:

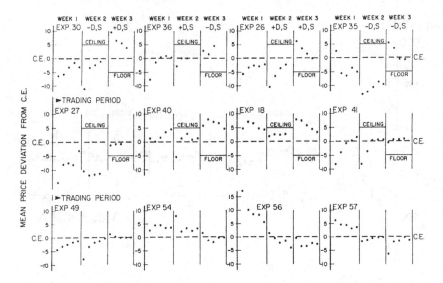

FIGURE 10.6. Per trading period mean double-auction prices for each experiment with no price control, ceiling or floor prices. Based on data from Smith and Williams (1980).

1. The price ceiling transfers about 46 cents of surplus per period from sellers to buyers in week 2 and $2.32 in week 3. The floor transfers $2.02 per period from buyers to sellers in week 2 and $1.19 in week 3. The t values (in parentheses) for the price control coefficients are highly significant. A one-tailed test is appropriate here based on the lsaac-Plott conjecture, which predicts the directional effect of the price controls. However, there is no evidence to suggest that nonbinding price controls have an effect on the ultimate *level* of contract prices as predicted by the CE price.

2. Differential bargaining strength, whether it favors buyers or sellers in a particular group, tends to persist in successive trading periods and weeks, but with decreasing magnitude.

3. A uniform shift, up or down, in demand and supply and a rerandomization of the individual limit price assignments produce some overshooting of the new equilibrium. However, the effect is smaller in week 3 than in week 2, indicating that there are probably learning effects that improve the ability of double-auction markets to track changes in supply and demand.

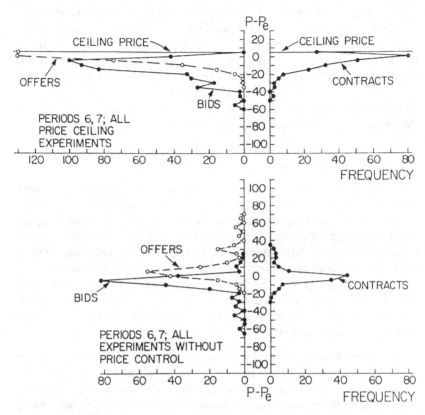

FIGURE 10.7. Price ceiling frequency distributions compared with no price controls.

In the absence of a price control, double-auction trading is characterized by a process in which sellers typically make concessions from offer prices well above the CE whereas buyers most often concede from bid prices well below the CE. This is shown by the distribution of bids, offers, and contracts in the lower half of Figure 10.7. These distributions are compiled for periods 6 and 7 from the Smith-Williams experiments in which no price controls were imposed. Observe that the bid (offer) distribution is skewed downward (upward) in favor of the buyers (sellers). Smith and Williams hypothesize that the effect of a price ceiling would be to limit the bargaining strategies of sellers more severely than that of buyers. This is because the ceiling requires sellers to begin their bargaining from a less advantageous position, whereas buyers are not similarly constrained. This is shown in the upper half of Figure 10.7. The modal offer occurs at the CE with a price ceiling in effect, but at 5 cents above the CE when no ceiling is in effect. The bid and offer distributions are not only both truncated at the ceiling, but both also tend to be shifted down relative to the corresponding distributions with no price ceiling in effect. A Mann-Whitney test shows that both of these shifts are significant, although the shift in the offer distribution is more pronounced. A similar result is found in the price floor experiments, except that the directional effects are reversed (not shown).

C.   *Monopoly Behavior*

An experiment in monopoly behavior can be viewed as a type of boundary experiment in collusive behavior. *Boundary experiments* are "associated with some set of laws and consist of fact-finding inquiries designed to fix the range of application of the laws, particularly with regard to extreme conditions" (Kaplan, 1964, p. 150). I have reported. (Smith, 1981) the results of an exploratory series of monopoly experiments using several alternative price adjustment mechanisms. In what sense are these "boundary experiments" in collusive behavior? To answer this question, consider several structural elements that might prevent successful cartelization of a market:

1. *Private uncertainty.* The members of a cartel may be uncertain as to the cost that each attaches to alternative outputs. This uncertainty may make it difficult to determine the value of a conspiracy and may provoke suspicion and mistrust among cartel members who contribute to unstable agreements.

2. *Incentive failure.* Given that individual members have sufficient knowledge of their costs, will they be motivated to reveal such costs in sufficient detail to permit a cartel solution to be identified? If not, internal deception may render the cartel agreement little or no better than if each acted independently.

3. *External uncertainty.* Uncertainty about demand and the possibility of countervailing strategic buyer behavior may make it difficult to identify or maintain a cartel market solution.

4. *Enforcement.* Given that a cartel solution can be identified and an agreement reached, are the members motivated to honor the agreement?

Is there a social "contract" effect that is self-enforcing or must there be surveillance, coupled with sanctions?

If we study monopoly under complete cost information but incomplete demand information, in effect we study the limits of collusive behavior, where *limits* refers to the extreme boundary at which we

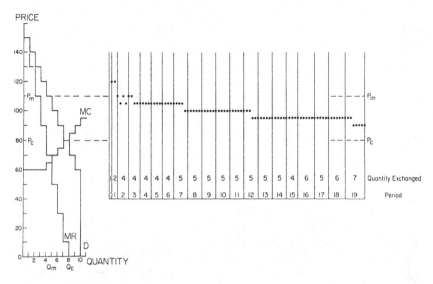

FIGURE 10.8. Double-auction monopoly experiment. Reproduced from Smith (1980).

abstract from (i.e., control for) the effect of conditions 1, 2, and 4. We ask, What sort of cartel behavior might be observed if there were ideal internal conditions and the cartel had only to cope with external (demand) uncertainty? In this sense the study of monopoly behavior is also the study of "perfect" collusive behavior. If monopolists encounter difficulties in achieving a monopoly solution because of incomplete demand information and/or strategic behavior by buyers, one could hardly be optimistic that conspirators in restraint of trade would have an easy task. Figure 10.8 plots the contract prices of one (the second) of three double-auction monopoly experiments (Smith, 1981). On the left of Figure 10.8 appears the induced demand based on five subject buyers each with assigned marginal valuations for 2 units. The seller is assigned marginal costs for 12 units as indicated by MC. Based on the theoretical demand D, the seller faces marginal revenue MR. The competitive equilibrium price is $P_c = 80$ cents and the monopoly equilibrium price is $P_m = 110$ cents. All earnings were paid in cash except for period 0, which was a practice session. Each auction period lasted for 4 minutes. In this particular experiment, the seller's average volume was about 5 units (the monopoly equilibrium quantity), but price is persistently below P_m and tends to decline throughout the experiment, as buyers effectively underreveal demand in double-auction bargaining. Although individual monopolists vary in performance, this tendency in which a monopolist

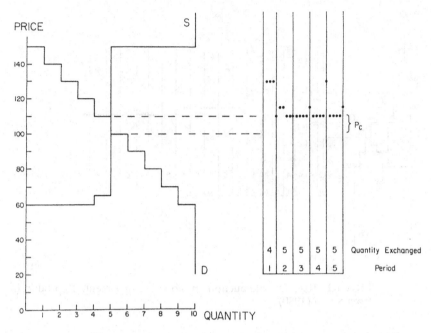

FIGURE 10.9. Five-seller double auction with monopoly supply from
Figure 10.8. Reproduced from Smith (1980).

encounters considerable difficulty in achieving the equilibrium monopoly profit is characteristic of all three of the reported double-auction
experiments (Smith, 1981).

   A monopolist only has the power to withhold sales, thereby hoping to
obtain a higher price. Buyers similarly have the power to withhold purchase in the hope of obtaining a lower price. Are some institutions, such
as the double auction, more effective than others in enabling buyers to
express this power (i.e., to underreveal demand) against a single seller?
Such tacit collusion, without a formal mechanism of agreement, has not
been observed in multiple buyer and seller double-auction markets. If
there is cultural suspicion and distrust of monopoly, this might induce a
spontaneous, countervailing form of tacit buyer collusion. One means of
testing this conjecture is to confront five buyers with the induced demand
D in Figure 10.8, but let the monopolist's MC schedule, up to the monopoly equilibrium quantity, be allocated among several sellers. One such
experiment was performed (Smith, 1981), and the results are shown in
Figure 10.9. In this multiple seller competitive experiment, there are five
buyers and five sellers. Each seller has a 2-unit marginal cost schedule

such that the theoretical supply follows the monopolist's MC in Figure 10.8 up to the fifth unit and then jumps well above the demand (see S in Figure 10.9). Consequently, we force the five-seller supply curve to correspond to the circumstances of a monopolist who rigidly limits sales to the monopoly equilibrium level (5 units). From Figure 10.9, we see that the buyers in this experiment perform more poorly as against five sellers than did the buyers in Figure 10.8 against a single seller. These results are, of course, only suggestive since an insufficient number of experiments have been conducted to obtain a good measure of sampling variability in either the monopoly experiments or the multiple seller control experiment.

In addition to the three double-auction monopoly experiments reported in Smith (1981), Williams and I have conducted two monopoly experiments (46x and 58x), using one of the PLATO computerized double-auction mechanisms developed by Williams (1980). Table 10.2 contains the mean price deviation, and (shown in parentheses) the quantity deviation from the corresponding CE levels for six experiments: The three oral auction monopoly experiments (1–3), the previous multiple-seller experiment (4), and the two PLATO experiments (46x, 58x). The mean efficiency for periods 5–10 appears at the bottom of Table 10.2. In Table 10.3 is listed the value of an index of monopoly effectiveness, for each period, and the aggregate overall periods, for each of the six experiments. M is the proportion of the difference between the seller's theoretical monopoly and competitive profits which is actually obtained by the seller. The mean prices, quantities, and values of M for the sellers in Experiments 1 and 46x show a pronounced tendency to converge to the CE or below. Average efficiency in these two experiments also approaches the high level (near 100%) typical of ordinary small-group double-auction markets. Although seller 2 shows a steady erosion in his/her selling price, M does not fall correspondingly because of the modest increase in volume. The prices in Experiment 3 fall rapidly to below the CE price in periods 5–7; in period 8 this seller succeeds in a dramatic turn-around raising the value of M to 0.44 from −0.19 in period 7. By period 12 he or she recovers nearly to the monopoly equilibrium and then starts to decline through the final period. The most effective monopolist was in experiment 58x in which M exceeds 0.90 in 6 of the 15 periods. However, due to strong buyer resistance, the cost is high. Thus sales were drastically reduced in periods 7 and 8 to achieve an M of 0.93 in period 9, and again in period 10 to achieve the higher levels of M in periods 1 1–15. Consequently, the most effective monopolist also produced the most erratic volume behavior. Experiments 2, 3, and 58x also make plain the high social cost, in terms of lost efficiency, of achieving

Table 10.2. *Deviation of mean contract price (quantity exchanged) from CE under monopoly*

Period	Oral double-auction experiments			PLATO double-auction experiments		Multiple seller
	1	2	3	46×	58×	4
1	0.375 (–4)	0.350 (–6)	0.275 (–2)	0.176 (0)	0.350 (–3)	0.20 (–1)
2	0.288 (–4)	0.275 (–4)	0.164 (–1)	0.064 (0)	0.250 (–3)	0.07 (0)
3	0.164 (–1)	0.263 (–4)	0.092 (–2)	0.031 (0)	0.188 (0)	0.06 (0)
4	0.107 (–1)	0.250 (–4)	0.050 (–2)	0.017 (0)	0.250 (–4)	0.09 (0)
5	0.081 (0)	0.250 (–4)	–0.014 (–1)	0.007 (–1)	0.217 (–2)	0.06 (0)
6	0.036 (–1)	0.250 (–4)	–0.030 (–3)	0.033 (–1)	0.150 (0)	
7	0.021 (–1)	0.230 (–3)	–0.036 (–1)	0.025 (0)	0.300 (–6)	
8	0 (–2)	0.200 (–3)	0.238 (–4)	0.013 (0)	0.250 (–7)	
9	–0.036 (–1)	0.200 (–3)	0.230 (–3)	–0.001 (–1)	0.156 (0)	
10	–0.057 (–1)	0.200 (–3)	0.217 (–2)	–0.001 (0)	0.250 (–7)	
11	–0.071 (–1)	0.200 (–3)	0.250 (–3)	0.007 (0)	0.200 (–3)	
12		0.170 (–3)	0.233 (–2)	0.005 (0)	0.210 (–3)	
13		0.150 (–3)	0.200 (–2)	–0.003 (0)	0.156 (0)	
14		0.150 (–3)	0.200 (–2)		0.183 (–2)	
15		0.150 (–4)	0.192 (–2)		0.155 (0)	
16		0.150 (–2)	0.175 (–2)			
17		0.150 (–3)				
18		0.150 (–2)				
19		0.114 (–1)				
Theoretical price (quantity) deviation from CE	0.30 (–3)	0.30 (–3)	0.30(–3)	0.30(–3)	0.30(–3)	0(0)
Mean efficiency,[a] periods 5–10	97.05	80.33	85.5	96.16	60.04	

[a] Theoretical efficiency (monopoly) is 88.5.

low monopolistic effectiveness under the double auction. In each case, average efficiency is below the theoretical monopoly level (88.5%).

D.   Alternative Forms of the Double Auction

Smith and Williams (1982) have reported the results of 21 experiments designed to provide a systematic comparison of the effect of alternative computerized double-auction trading rules and the effect of subject

Table 10.3. *Double-auction index of monopoly effectiveness*[a]

Period	Oral double-auction experiments			PLATO double-auction experiments		Multiple sellers
	1	2	3	46×	58×	4
1	0.89	0	1.19	1.04	1.19	1.07
2	0.63	0.59	0.85	0.38	0.81	1.07
3	0.85	0.56	0.37	0.19	1.11	1.04
4	0.56	0.52	0.19	0.10	0.52	1.15
5	0.44	0.52	−0.07	0.04	0.93	1.04
6	0.19	0.52	−0.22	0.17	0.89	
7	0.11	0.74	−0.19	0.15	−0.07	
8	−0.04	0.63	0.44	0.07	−0.48	
9	−0.19	0.63	0.74	−0.01	0.93	
10	−0.30	0.63	0.93	−0.01	−0.48	
11	−0.37	0.63	0.81	0.04	0.63	
12		0.52	0.96	0.03	0.70	
13		0.44	0.85	−0.01	0.93	
14		0.44	0.85		0.78	
15		0.22	0.81		0.92	
16		0.63	0.74			
17		0.44				
18		0.63				
19		0.59				
Over all periods	0.25	0.52	0.57	0.17	0.62	1.07

[a] Measured by the coefficient: $M = \dfrac{(\text{Actual profit}) - (\text{Competitive profit})}{(\text{Monopoly profit}) - (\text{Competitive profit})}$.

experience on the convergence and efficiency properties of competitive markets. Subject trades in these experiments are by means of the interactive program developed by Williams (1980) using the PLATO computer system. Two basic sets of bidding rules, each having an optional electronic bid–offer queuing system, are defined as follows:

Rule 1. *A single bid or a single offer for one unit of the exchange item is standing in the market at any time. Any such bid or offer stands for a minimum period (3 seconds), after which it can be displaced by a new bid or offer. If a standing bid or offer is accepted, PLATO then waits for a new bid or offer to be entered. Any bid or offer is rejected if it is entered before expiration of the minimum standing period for the displayed quotation.*

This bidding rule is a computerized version of an institution used for many years in the experimental study of competitive markets (Smith, 1964). Of the two basic sets of rules studied, this provides the least restriction on the negotiation process, and in this sense represents a relatively unorganized form of market. Thus, in over-the-counter telephone markets, buyers and sellers have no assurance that successive quotations will provide better price terms.

Rule 2. *Both a single bid and a single offer may stand in the market until one or the other is accepted, or until either is displaced by a new bid or offer. If one of the quotations (e.g., the bid) is accepted, it is no longer effective because it becomes a contract. The other quotation (the offer) also "dies" because (as under New York Stock Exchange rules) an auction ends with a contract, and the maker of the quotation (the offer), even if not part of the contract, is released from the (offer) obligation. After a contract, PLATO waits for a new bid and/or offer to be entered to begin a new auction. Thus, an auction can only end in a contract (except when the time allowed for each day of trading expires after the final contract of the day).*

This auction procedure corresponds to rules 71 and 72 (Leffler and Farwell, 1963, pp. 187, 190–1) of the New York Stock Exchange. Until a contract occurs, the terms of trade cannot become less favorable to a potential buyer or seller. Under Rule 2, if a trader waits for a better quotation, he or she incurs the risk that someone else will make the contract. Under Rule 1, this risk is compounded by the additional risk that the subsequent quotation will provide less favorable terms. Rule 2 imposes a converging structure on the bid–offer negotiation process that suggests a price variance reduction effect as compared with Rule 1.

Rule 1Q. *The conditions of Rule 1 are supplemented by allowing bids and offers to be entered continuously (i.e., within the 3-second standing period of the market bid or offer) and ordered chronologically in a queue. Without the queue, when a quotation dies, the person who is first in entering a new quotation gains access to the market; others must wait, try again, and probably fail. The queue lowers this opportunity and transactions cost of gaining market access.*

Rule 2Q. *As in Rule 2, market-admissible price quotations must progress so that the bid–offer spread is reduced. In addition, if a bid (offer) that is not higher (lower) than the currently standing best bid (offer) is entered, the bid (offer) is ordered lexicographically in a queue as follows: Bids (offers) are ranked first by price with higher bids (lower offers) having priority, and, second, tied bids (offers) are ordered chronologically. Price*

Table 10.4. *Number of experiments (and total number of periods of trading) classified by trading rule institution and subject experience*

Subject	Rule 1	Rule 1Q	Rule 2	Rule 2Q
Inexperienced	3	2	3	2
	(30)	(20)	(29)	(28)
Experienced	2	2	3	3
	(19)	(19)	(25)	(25)

quotes waiting in these queues can be withdrawn by the maker at any time, but once a price quote is standing in the market, it cannot be withdrawn by the maker as in Rule 1. When an auction ends with the outstanding bid or offer being accepted, then the highest bid and lowest offer in their respective queues are automatically entered into the market.

Rule 2Q combines an electronic "specialist's book" (rank-ordered queues) with the bid–ask reduction rule, prominent features of the negotiation procedure specified in New York Stock Exchange trading. This is the trading rule institution of primary interest in the Smith-Williams study, with Rules 1, 2, and 1Q representing dissected and alternative forms of this important organized exchange institution. The procedures embodied in Rule 2Q have evolved over many generations of experience on the New York Stock Exchange, and, as noted by Smith and Williams (1982), "our working hypothesis is that the survival value of a rule is manifest in measures of improved market performance." The results to be summarized here use data based on the experimental design shown in Table 10.4. In the trading sessions using inexperienced subjects, no participant had been in any previous double-auction experiment. In the experienced sessions, the subjects had all participated in at least one previous double-auction experiment using any of the four trading rule conditions. Thus, the subjects in an experienced session might have varied in the amount of their previous experience and in the rule conditions of their previous participation. The symmetric supply and demand design for all the experiments is shown on the left of Figure 10.10 (except for an inessential shift constant added to the individual unit costs and values from one experiment to another).

Figures 10.10 and 10.11 plot the contract prices, in sequence for each trading period for two illustrative experiments. In Figure 10.10 the experiment uses inexperienced subjects trading under Rule 1Q, which are the conditions that yield the weakest convergence tendency. The experiment

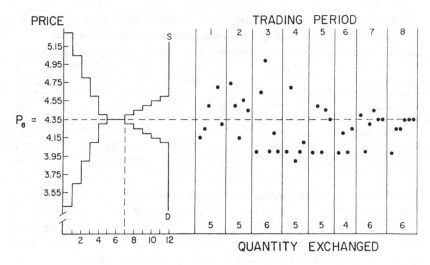

FIGURE 10.10. Time–queue double auction, inexperienced subjects. From Smith and Williams (1979).

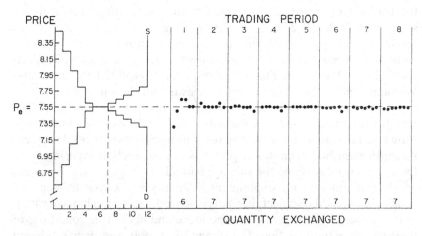

FIGURE 10.11. Rank–queue double auction, experienced subjects. From Smith and Williams (1979).

in Figure 10.11 uses experienced subjects trading under Rule 2Q, which are the conditions that exhibit the strongest convergence tendency. The effect of experience and the trading rule institution on convergence speed will be summarized in regression form. Define

t = trading period, $t = 1, 2, \ldots$

$\alpha^2(t)$ = the second moment of contract prices calculated with respect to the theoretical CE price in trading period t. Thus, if there are $Q(t)$ contracts in period t, at prices $P_k(t)$.

$k = 1, 2, \ldots, Q(t)$, then

$$\alpha^2(t) = \sum_{k=1}^{Q(t)} (P_k - P^o)^2 / Q(t) \qquad \text{where } P^0 \text{ is the CE} > \text{price}$$

The dependent variables $\alpha^2(t)$ provide a measure of price "distance" from the CE. This distance increases with both the variance of prices and the deviation between the mean and the CE price [i.e., $\alpha^2(t) = V(t) + (\bar{P}(t) - P^o)^2$]. Thus if an experimental market stabilizes, with low price variability, but near a price *other* than P^o, then $\alpha^2(t)$ may not be low.

The regressions (showing the t values for each coefficient in parenthesis) followed by the number of observations, adjusted value of R^2, and F-value for each regression, are

$$\ln \alpha(t) = -1.16 - 0.135t + 0.400 X_{1Q} - 0.920 X_s$$
$$(-7.67) (-6.46) \quad (3.35) \qquad (-7.47)$$
$$N = 99, \qquad R^2 = 0.51 \qquad F = 34.4 \tag{3}$$

where $\quad X_{1Q} = \begin{cases} 1, & \text{if Rule 1Q} \\ 0, & \text{if Rule 1} \end{cases} \quad X_S = \begin{cases} 1 & \text{if experienced subjects} \\ 0 & \text{if inexperienced subjects} \end{cases}$

$$\ln \alpha(t) = -0.918 - 0.175t - 0.138 X_2 - 0.984 X_s$$
$$(-5.99) (-8.11) \quad (-1.13) \quad (-7.88)$$
$$N = 98 \qquad R^2 = 0.56 \qquad F = 42.9 \tag{4}$$

where $\quad X_2 = \begin{cases} 1 & \text{if Rule 2} \\ 0 & \text{if Rule 1} \end{cases}$

$$\ln \alpha(t) = -1.05 - 0.184t - 0.658 X_{2Q} - 0.867 X_s$$
$$(-7.30) (-9.07) \quad (-5.93) \qquad (-7.78)$$
$$N = 102 \qquad R^2 = 0.59 \qquad F = 50.2 \tag{5}$$

where $\quad X_{2Q} = \begin{cases} 1 & \text{if Rule 2Q} \\ 0 & \text{if Rule 2} \end{cases}$

From these regressions the following conclusions may be stated:

1. All three regressions show a significant exponential convergence rate with $\alpha(t)$ declining at an average rate of 13.5–18.4% per

trading period, after the correctional effects of experience and the different trading institutions.

2. In each regression, the effect of subject experience is large and quite significant.

3. The effect of adding the queue to the unstructured (Rule 1) market is to cause a significant *increase* in the variability of prices relative to the CE price in every trading period. Smith and Williams attribute this to the effect of the queue in lowering the transactions cost associated with getting a bid or offer into the market. With the availability of the queue, a trader is assured that his quotation will work down the queue to the market. This invites relatively high offers and low bids to be entered as a means of "holding out" for a high profit. This apparent strategy works in that contract prices are relatively more variable. Without the queue, it is more difficult to get access to the market. This increases the risk of failing to make a contract and appears to put pressure on the traders to make more concessionary quotations.

4. The effect of Rule 2 relative to Rule 1 (under which the bid–offer spread must be narrowed if a bid or offer is to gain access to the market) is to decrease the variability of contract prices in every period, but this effect is not significant.

5. The effect of adding the ordered queues to Rule 2 is to cause a significant reduction in the variability of contract prices. This seems to be the result of a form of "off the floor" competition in which traders jockey for a higher priority position in the queue by replacing an earlier bid (offer) with a higher (lower) bid (offer).

6. Comparing all four institutions, Rule 2Q (i.e., the electronic "specialist's book" combined with the bid–offer reduction rules) shows the least period-by-period contract price variability, and the most rapid rate of convergence.

II.   One-Sided Pricing Institutions

Price initiatives, or quotations, in most markets are one-sided (i.e., are provided either by buyers or sellers but not both). In most retail markets, sellers post their offer prices to be accepted for some quantity, or rejected, by buyers. At the "country auction" for livestock and equipment buyers bid progressively against each other for single items offered for sale. Similarly in "sealed-bid" auctions such as the primary market for U.S. Treasury bills, buyers submit written bids for units of the security offered in fixed supply. Several experimental studies, a few of which are

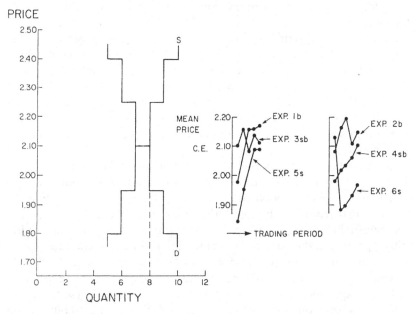

FIGURE 10.12. Comparison of per period mean prices for oral bid, offer, and double auctions. Based on data from Smith (1964).

summarized in the following sections, have attempted to determine whether these institutional considerations have an effect on either the dynamics of price formation or the stationary price levels attained in a market.

A.   Comparison of Oral Bid, Offer, and Double Auctions

Six experiments have been reported (Smith, 1964) comparing one-sided oral auctions with double oral auctions. Experiments 1b and 2b (see Figure 10.12) were conducted in which only buyers were permitted to make price quotations. A seller could either accept a given oral bid by a buyer or remain silent. Experiments 3sb and 4sb were double auctions in which buyers could make bids and accept offers while sellers could make offers and accept bids. Finally Experiments 5s and 6s were seller offer auctions in which sellers could make price offers, while a buyer could either accept a given offer or remain silent. The induced supply and demand schedules for all six experiments are shown on the left of Figure 10.12. On the right appears the mean contract price plotted by trading period for each experiment. These data exhibit a distinct tendency, after the first or second trading period, for the mean price in the bid auction to exceed that in the double auction which, in turn, exceeds the mean price in the offer auction. Hence, "silence is golden" in the sense that one-sided oral auctions lead to contracts tending to favor the silent side. In the bid auction, as buyers raise their bids competitively to induce sales, sellers learn that it is to their advantage to wait. In this sense, the silent role of sellers contributes to a form of tacit collusion. Contracts tend to rise above the CE prices, but the rise is limited by the fact that at some level sellers begin "queuing" in the sense that two- and three-way ties to accept a given bid will occur. This process is reversed in oral offer auctions.

Because the cited experiments were conducted for only five or six trading periods, it is not certain whether the results represent a temporary dynamic phenomenon or a longer-run feature of stationary equilibria. Furthermore, although the treatment effects are clearly distinguishable in Figure 10.12, and are statistically significant (Smith, 1964, pp. 193–4), they are not of dramatic proportions. The mean price differences in trading period 5 are well within the range $1.95–2.25 defined by the limit prices of the first intramarginal buyer and seller.

In the experiments reported in Figure 10.12, each buyer (seller) could contract for only one unit per trading period. There were 10 buyers and 10 sellers in Experiments 1b, 3sb, and 5s, and 14 buyers and 14 sellers in Experiments 2b, 4sb, and 6s. Plott and Smith (1978) have reported two oral bid auction experiments in which there were four buyers and four sellers each with multiple-unit contracting capacities. Both of the oral bid experiments reported by Plott and Smith (1978, pp. 143, 144) exhibit the tendency for contract prices to rise above the CE price. However, the effect, although clearly identifiable, was not large. Also, both of the Plott-Smith oral bid experiments were 99–100% efficient in every trading period. Consequently, one-sided oral auctions do not appear to misallocate resources. Their principal effect is to cause some redistribution of rent from the side quoting prices to the side with the right to accept price quotations.

B.   Posted-Price Institutions

The most common market experience of consumers in developed economies is with posted-offer pricing (i.e., sellers display or advertise fixed take-it-or-leave-it prices that are not normally subject to negotiation). There are, of course, many exceptions (e.g., the new and used automobile market), but negotiation is rare in most mass distribution retail markets. The separation of clerk from management and ownership functions has perhaps compelled posted-offer pricing ever since the general store gave way to the retail innovations of R. H. Macy and F. W. Woolworth in the last half of the nineteenth century (Marburg, 1951).[4] Although posted-offer pricing is more prevalent than posted-bid pricing, there are important markets in which buyers post bids. Examples include refiners who post bids at which they are willing to buy crude petroleum, and canners who post the prices at which they will buy fruit and vegetables from growers.

Three experimental studies (Williams, 1973; Plott and Smith, 1978; and Smith, 1980) have initiated a limited investigation of behavior in posted-bid or posted-offer markets. In these experiments, each seller (buyer) independently and privately, chooses an offer (bid). These prices are then posted (e.g., on a blackboard) where they are visible to all buyers and sellers. Then a buyer (seller), chosen at random, selects a seller (buyer), and makes that seller (buyer) a quantity offer at his or her posted price. The seller (buyer) then responds with a quantity (any portion of the quantity offered) acceptance, which forms a binding contract. If some portion of the quantity offer is not accepted, the buyer (seller) may choose a second seller (buyer) and make a quantity offer, and so on. After the first buyer (seller) has completed his or her contracting, a second is chosen at random, and so on until all have been allowed to make contracts. No price adjustment is permitted during the trading period, and no secondary market exchange is allowed after the period ends. Then a new trading period begins with the posting of a new set of prices and so on in a sequence of many trading periods. The situation is like that which occurs when Sears-Roebuck publishes a spring–winter catalog, or Macy's posts the prices on their fall garment lines with the exception that there is no subsequent follow-up sale catalog or inventory clearance sale. In this manner, one studies the institution in its purest form, uncontaminated by error-correcting, if important, supporting institutions. Any conclusions that result should, of course, be interpreted with these stark conditions in mind.

Williams (1973) conducted three pairs of experiments to compare posted offer with posted bid prices, and found in each of the three paired comparisons that the mean price when sellers post offers is significantly above the mean price when buyers post bids. The period-by-period mean price data from Williams' experiments are plotted in Figure 10.13. Offers were posted in Experiments 1s, 3s and 5s, whereas bids were posted in Experiments 2b, 4b, and 6b. The numbers in parentheses indicate the

---

[4] According to Marburg (1951, p. 527), "The one-price policy . . . became a necessity where large numbers of clerks made actual sales. . . . This policy . . . appears to have gained general favor by the late 1860's, although rural general stores still followed a multiple price or haggling system. . . ."

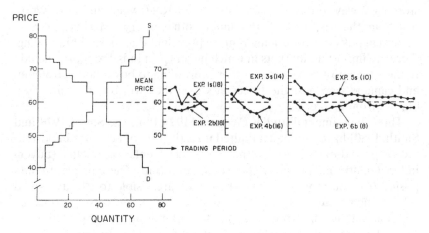

FIGURE 10.13. Comparison of mean posted seller (s) offer prices with buyer (b) bid prices. Based on data from F. Williams (1973).

number of subjects (buyers plus sellers). Thus in Experiment 1s and 2b, there were 18 subjects (9 buyers and 9 sellers). The symmetrical supply and demand schedules, with an equal number of buyers and sellers, is shown on the left of Figure 10.13. The mean price data in Figure 10.13 shows the tendency for prices to be higher when offers are posted than when bids are posted, although in Experiments 1s, 2b, 3s, and 4b these price levels appear to be converging over time. However, in the much longer trading sequence in Experiments 5s and 6b the spread in mean prices between the two pricing institutions persisted to the twentieth and final period. These experiments suggest that under posted pricing, convergence occurs from the side taking the pricing initiative, with perhaps some permanent price advantage accruing to this side. However the effects, though significant, are not large.

Plott and Smith (1978) conducted two posted-bid experiments, which essentially replicated the results of Williams. In the Plott-Smith experiments the mean price in 14 out of a total of 15 trading periods was below the CE price. But in the final trading periods of these experiments, mean observed prices deviated no more than 1–3 cents from the CE price. Efficiency averaged 95% across all periods in the two Plott-Smith experiments. This is below the near 100% efficiency for the two oral bid experiments also reported by Plott and Smith (1978) and below the efficiencies that are typical of double-auction experiments.

It appears that posted pricing operates slightly to the advantage of the posting side of the market and is somewhat less efficient than double- or one-sided oral auctions. But in the small number of experiments

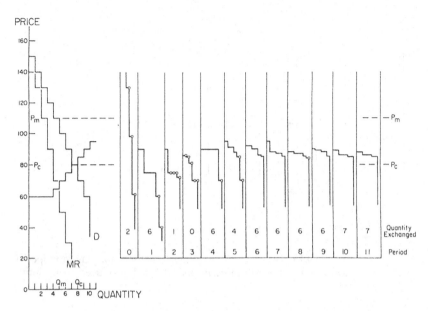

FIGURE 10.14. Buyers post bid prices to a discriminating monopolist. Reproduced from Smith (1980).

reported, these effects are not large. Clearly the competitive model is a much superior predictor of performance than a monopoly or monopsony model. Only a slight modification of CE theory seems to be suggested by the results of posted-pricing institutions.

If posted price institutions operate to the advantage of the side that takes the posting initiative, the following question can be posed. If there is but one seller, and we suppose that the seller has the freedom and perception to withhold output in an attempt to obtain a higher and more profitable price, can this exercise of monopoly power be offset, neutralized, or countervailed when exchange occurs under the posted-bid rules of trading? This question motivated three single-seller experiments reported by Smith (1981).

The demand, corresponding marginal revenue to the seller, and marginal cost are shown on the left of Figure 10.14 for one of these experiments. There are five buyers each with a capacity to buy 2 units. In this experiment, period 0 was a "trial period," with no monetary payoffs, to familiarize the participants with the procedure. In each period, the bids are shown plotted arrayed from highest to lowest. Thus in period 1, there are one bid at $.90, two at $.75, one at $.60, and one at $.40. The seller offered 2 units to the first bidder who accepted them, 2 units to each (in

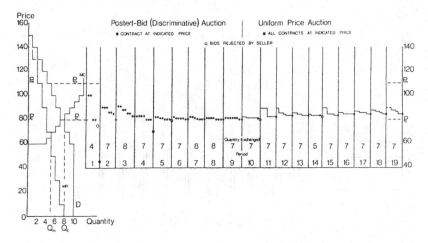

FIGURE 10.15. Buyers post bid prices to a discriminating monopolist with switch to a uniform price in period 10. Reproduced from Smith (1980).

order) of the two bidders at $.75, which were accepted, and the seller refused to offer any units to the two lowest bidders as indicated by the circles. Consequently, 6 units were exchanged in period 1. In period 2, the seller refused all bids except the highest ($.90). In period 3, the bids were increased somewhat, but not by very much, and the seller rejected them all. This produced another modest increase in the bids and the seller delivered 6 units. For period 5 and beyond, note that the bids are fairly stable, with a slight drift downward. As expected, the posted-bid rules severely constrained this seller in spite of a large cutback in units delivered against the period 2 and 3 bids. From Figure 10.14, it is seen that the distribution of price bids is relatively narrow after the first few trading periods. This is characteristic of all such posted-bid experiments. It is conjectured that this result is driven by the discriminative feature of this institution. That is, each buyer, knowing that the seller will accept the higher bids first and being required to pay what he or she bids, will have an incentive to bid only slightly in excess of the estimated level of the lowest accepted bid. These considerations suggest that if the discriminative feature of posted-bid pricing were removed, the effect would be to increase the level of the bids to the advantage of the seller.

An initial experiment to test this hypothesis is shown in Figure 10.15. In this experimental group, using five buyers and one seller, and the same valuation and cost conditions as in Figure 10.14, posted-bid discrimina-

Table 10.5. *Posted price index of monopoly effectiveness*[a]

Period	1	2	3	3 (uniform price)	Posted Offer 1
		Posted bid			
1	−0.15	0.04	0.35		0.78
2	0.06	−0.59	0.40		1
3	0.13	−0.81	0.09		0.81
4	0.15	0.41	0.04		0.89
5	0.15	0.11	0.04		1
6	0.12	0.37	0.04		1
7	0.07	0.33	0.03		1
8	0.03	0.27	0.04		1
9	0.01	0.33	0.07		1
10	−0.01	0.36		0.10	1
11	0	0.33		0.16	1
12	0.01			0.16	
13	0.06			0	
14				0.16	
15				0.21	
16				0.21	
17				0.21	
18				0.21	
19				0.21	
Over all periods	0.05	0.10	0.12	0.16	0.95

[a] For definition see Table 10.3.

tive pricing was used for the first nine periods. The bids that were accepted to form contracts are plotted as dots in the first nine trading periods of Figure 10.15. Beginning with period 10, all participants were informed that henceforth the seller, after seeing the posted bids, would announce the cut-off bid below which no bid would be accepted. Then the seller would make successive quantity offers to each of the higher bidders, in order, with the understanding that these bids would be accepted at a price equal to the announced cut-off bid (indicated by the dot in periods 10–19 of Figure 10.15). It will be noted in Figure 10.15 that, beginning with period 10, the bid distribution started to increase and continued to drift upward through the final, nineteenth, trading period.

Table 10.5 lists the period-by-period index of monopoly effectiveness for the three posted-bid experiments (Smith, 1981). The seller in

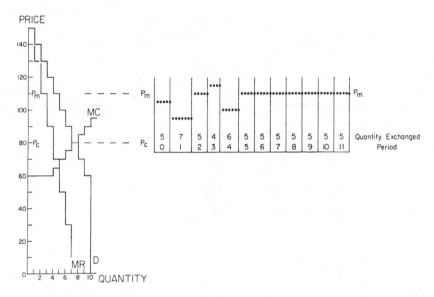

FIGURE 10.16. Monopolist posts offer price to buyers. Reproduced from Smith (1980).

Experiment 2 achieved the best final-period profit performance, which was still only about one-third of the monopoly ideal. The seller in Experiment 3 performed best over all periods, with an index of effectiveness of only 0.12. For this seller, the index rose to 0.16 after invoking the rule of a uniform price equal to the lowest bid acceptable to the seller.

These posted-bid monopoly experiments seem to support the original conjecture that the incentive to underreveal demand in the posted-bid institution would provide some decentralized restraint of monopoly power. The validity of this line of reasoning can be further tested by examining monopoly behavior under posted-offer pricing. Since posted-offer pricing operates to the advantage of sellers (Williams, 1973), this institution should be the one most favorable to the achievement of the monopoly price by a single seller. The results of one such experiment (Smith, 1981) are reproduced in Figure 10.16. After trying five posted offers, the seller in this experiment easily identified a price $1.10 as the profit-maximizing price, which was then monotonously posted in periods 5 through 11. In Table 10.5 the seller in this experiment is seen to achieve a monopoly effectiveness very close to 1. Of great interest is the fact that buyers made no attempt to underreveal demand when faced by a fixed take-it-or-leave-it price. Yet buyers persistently underreveal demand both under posted-bid pricing and in the double auction (Section I.C). Comparing the monopoly effectiveness of the double auction in Table 10.3 with that of posted-bid pricing in Table 10.5, it is clear that single sellers perform much better in the double auction than in the severely constraining posted-bid institution.

CHAPTER 11

Experimental Methods in the Political Economy of Exchange

Vernon L. Smith

Experimental methods in economics have the same scientific function that such methods have in geology and astronomy – that is, to supplement natural observations with knowledge of principles obtained from testing conjectures and formal theories under controlled laboratory conditions. Thus geologists and astronomers use principles governing the physics of matter that have been well tested in laboratory environments to help guide and interpret field observation. Likewise, experimental economists seek to establish principles of market and individual behavior in controlled laboratory environments before presuming, without evidence, that such principles can be used to interpret (or estimate parameters from) field data. Economics is noteworthy for its use of abstract theory, but rarely is such theory subjected to rigorous testing. The development of laboratory methods in the last quarter century has changed these ground rules by challenging economic theorists to submit to a new, difficult, and unaccustomed discipline, but it has also brought new standards of rigor to the data-gathering process itself by requiring the economist (like the astronomer and geologist) to assume direct responsibility for a source of data that can be replicated by other researchers. In this chapter, I hope to convey an appreciation for the scientific power and breadth of this rapidly developing methodology, which has begun to change the way economists think about their scientific mission.[1]

I. Exchange Institutions and the Creation of Wealth

Since the work of Adam Smith, political economists have hypothesized that the enormous production in modern economies originated with

---

[1] In the experiments reported here, the subjects were undergraduate volunteers who were paid $3 upon arrival for an experiment. At the end of the experiment, each subject received a cash sum equal to his or her cumulative profits earned in the experiment. These earnings averaged $15–20 in a 1- to 2-hour experiment, but varied from $2 to 50 or more for some subjects in some experiments. For a comprehensive recent survey and bibliography of experimental economics see Hoffman and Spitzer (1985b).

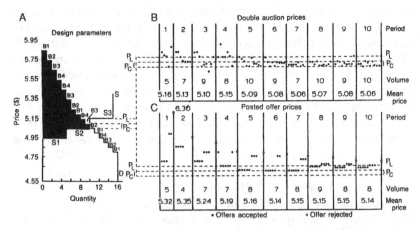

FIGURE 11.1. Comparison of double-auction and posted-offer pricing institutions. In (B) the mean price in period 10 was within the interval P_C in five of six subject groups; in (C) it was above the interval P_C for five of six subject groups.

exchange institutions that allowed human and physical capital to become specialized while supporting diversity in consumption. Smith's great insight was to see exchange as a positive sum game capable of yielding net betterment for all parties to exchange, but also to understand that this wealth-creating process was not perceived ("invisible hand") by the individual.[2] This remarkable theorem states that individuals, left to their own "betterment seeking" (which each defines in his own way), will cooperate through exchange to create wealth far exceeding what they would produce in isolation.

But what is the basis for believing that Smith's theorem has any empirical validity under the conditions postulated by its modern formulation? We have historical observations suggesting that greater wealth is associated with the use of exchange institutions, but any such association does not have the demonstration power of an experiment.

II. An Experimental Design

An example of an experimental design that provides a simple modern treatment of Smith's proposition is illustrated in Figure 11.1(A). Four

---

[2] As Adam Smith (1776; 1937, p. 423) put it, each individual "intends only his own gain, and he is . . . led by an invisible hand to promote an end which was no part of his intention."

buyers (B1, . . . , B4) can each purchase a maximum of 4 units of the commodity. Each buyer is assumed to associate decreasing marginal value to successive units of the commodity. Thus buyer B1 places a maximum value of $5.85 on the first unit consumed, $5.20 on the second, and so on, as indicated. In keeping with the hypothesis that individual circumstances are unique, each buyer is assumed to have a distinct declining marginal valuation for the commodity. In the laboratory, we want buyers to be well motivated to buy low, so we inform them that they will be paid in cash the difference between each marginal assigned value and the price paid in the market for the corresponding unit. Thus if B2 buys 2 units, one at $5.20 and a second at $5.10, he or she will earn a cash profit of 70 cents. If we arrange all 16 assigned values from highest to lowest, the result is a theoretical willingness-to-pay (inverted demand) schedule [D in Figure 11.1(A)]. Similarly, three sellers (S1, S2, and S3) have distinct (in this example, constant) marginal costs representing lower bounds on the prices at which each can profitably sell his or her respective capacity outputs (5 units). Seller S1 is most favorably situated with a marginal supply cost of $4.95 per unit, S2 is the next most eager seller, and S3 the highest cost seller. We motivate our laboratory sellers to sell high by paying them a profit equal to the difference between the actual sales price and the marginal cost of the corresponding unit. Thus if S1 sells 2 units at price $5.15, the profit is 40 cents. If we array all 15 assigned marginal costs from lowest to highest, the result is the theoretical willingness-to–accept (inverted supply) schedule, S.

This experimental design makes plain a characteristic of exchange that is easily misperceived by economic agents, namely that the buyer profits just as dependably as sellers (voluntary exchange is mutually beneficial). This is because "profit" is the surplus enjoyed by a buyer who purchases for less than his willingness-to-pay just as a seller's "profit" is the surplus obtained when units are sold for more than her willingness-to-accept. In Figure 11.1(A) the total such (consumer–producer) surplus is represented by the intersection of the area under the demand schedule and above the supply schedule [shaded in Figure 11.1(A)]. This surplus measures the maximum possible social gain created by the existence of a market institution. However, it is important to emphasize that no subject in the experiments we report has knowledge of Figure 11.1. Each subject knows only his or her own values or costs.

Any exchange institution will be efficient if the surplus shown in Figure 11.1 is realized in trade; that is, any pairing of the 10 highest valued demand units with the 10 lowest cost supply units at any vector of compatible prices will yield a set of efficient trades. However, such a pairing would be most likely to occur if the market were organized in such a way as to produce an equilibrium market clearing price, and corresponding trades, such that demand and supply are equal. In Figure 11.1(A), this is any price in the interval $P_c = (5.05, 5.10)$.

III.   The Double-Auction Pricing Institution

So far, the "environment" of exchange has been illustrated [Figure 11.1(A)], and how an exchange institution can be evaluated in terms of its ability to allow the surplus has been defined by the environment to be realized through trade. What kinds of institutions might be used to organize the exchange process? There are many; I present two that have been studied extensively: the double oral auction and the posted-offer institution. Historically, the double auction has been the preferred method of trading in the organized securities and commodity exchanges. At the University of Arizona and at Indiana University, a computerized version of this auction is used. Under the rules of this real-time institution, any buyer may enter a bid to buy 1 unit, and any seller may enter an offer to sell 1 unit. The best (highest) bid and best (lowest) offer entered are displayed publicly to all traders as the standing bid and offer. Any other bids entered are ordered in a queue from highest to lowest, and any other offers are ordered from lowest to highest. Waiting bids and offers are not displayed; they represent an "electronic book" corresponding to the specialist's book on the New York Stock Exchange. The maker of any such bid or offer may withdraw it at any time. But a "standing" bid or offer cannot be withdrawn by the maker. Any new bid (offer) may become the new standing bid (offer) if it is higher (lower) than the currently standing bid (offer). Thus bids and offers must improve the "bid–ask" spread to become standing. Any-time a standing bid (offer) is accepted by a seller (buyer), we have a binding contract at that price. Because it is not possible in field environments for agents to know the maximum buying prices of buyers or minimum selling prices of sellers, in the typical laboratory market each trader is informed only of his own value or cost situation. However, all traders are continuously informed as to the public information (bids, offers, contracts) provided by the auction institution.

The contract prices in sequence for each of ten trading periods are charted in Figure 11.1(B). Each period lasted 300 seconds, with each subject assigned the same set of values (costs) in each period. Except for learning, each trading period is a pure replication of the market environment in Figure 11.1(A). In this design, in addition to the competitive equilibrium price set $P_c = (5.05, 5.10)$ based on the supply response of the two intramarginal sellers, S1 and S2, we also have the "limit price" equilibrium, P_L, determined by seller S3 whose cost defines the external supply margin. Any attempt by sellers S1 and S2 to cooperate in boosting prices above the competitive range will be limited by the profitable entry of S3 at any price above P_L. Of six experiments with this design, only one, using inexperienced subjects, stabilized at prices slightly below P_L; the remaining five stabilized in the set P_c. Consequently, under double-auction trading with two intramarginal sellers, price discipline is only weakly dependent on an external supply margin to limit price increases.

Several hundred experiments by different researchers with many variations on the design in Figure 11.1(A) have established the robustness of the static competitive equilibrium prediction with the double-auction institution (Smith, 1982). For example, the use of middlemen, a group of agents who buy from producers in one market and resell to the buyers in a distant second market, does not alter the equilibrium tendencies illustrated in Figure 11.1(B) (Plott and Uhl, 1981). Similarly, if demand or supply or both follows a regular alternating period or seasonal cycle, and a third class of agents is given the right to speculate (buy in low price periods for resale in high price periods), a tendency to converge toward intertemporal competitive equilibrium is observed (Williams and Smith, 1984). This latter result has been found to extend to the case in which buyer-induced values (demands) are random (Plott and Agha, 1983). Although static competitive price theory predicts these empirical tendencies in the double-auction institution, it does not help us to understand the rich dynamic convergence patterns revealed in a number of experimental studies. For example, the tendency for prices to converge from above [Figure 11.1(B)] is a general characteristic of double-auction trading when the surplus (profits) of buyers exceeds that of sellers, whereas convergence tends to be from below if sellers' surplus exceeds that of buyers (Smith and Williams, 1982). Static price theory makes no statement about these empirical regularities. Similarly, experiments with a price ceiling just above P_c, which is therefore not binding and has no effect on the static equilibrium price, in fact yields a reduced speed of convergence, and the convergence path is from below (Isaac and Plott, 1981; Smith and Williams, 1981). Furthermore, when such a price ceiling is removed after the market has stabilized, we observe an explosive temporary rise in prices before they converge back toward P_c (Isaac and Plott, 1981). Efforts to model double-auction trading as a dynamic process (Wilson, 1985) may ultimately provide a better understanding of these results.

In another line of experimental research, alternative institutions of exchange have been studied to determine in what sense, if any, institutions matter. In Figure 11.1(C), the results of an experiment that replicates the environment of Figure 11.1(A) are illustrated but with different subjects trading under posted-offer pricing rules (Smith, 1976b; Plott, 1986). Under these rules, in each period each seller selects a private take-it-or-leave-it price offer that is then posted (displayed on each agent's computer screen), and buyers queue up to make individual purchases in sequence. Prices under posted offer tend to be higher, converge more slowly and less reliably, and produce less efficient trades than under double auction [Figures 11.1(B, C)]. We see in Figure 11.1(C) a tendency for the market to stabilize at prices just below P_L defined by the supply cost of S3. In 5 of 6 experiments using different subjects, the mean price exceeded P_c in period 10.

IV.   A Multiple Market Double Auction

Each buyer's maximum bid prices for successive units are design constants in Figure 11.1(A). However, field environments are characterized by multiple markets that, in general, are interdependent. This interdependence is captured in the case of two substitute commodities, where x_i and y_i, defined on the nonnegative orthant, are the quantities of each that are purchased by individual i. A buyer is hypothesized to behave as if he has a preference ordering $u^i(x_i, y_i)$, which is increasing and concave in (x_i, y_i). The buyer's budget constraint is $x_i P_x + y_i P_y \leq T_i$, where (P_x, P_y) are the commodity prices and T_i is the buyer's expenditure limit. Classical theory[3] derives the demand functions $x_i = d_x^i(P_x, P_y)$ and $y_i = d_y^i(P_x, P_y)$ for each i, and from the additivity (noninteraction) hypothesis the market demand functions are $X = D_x(P_x, P_y) = \Sigma_i d_x^i$ and $Y = D_y(P_x, P_y) = \Sigma_i d_y^i$. In a laboratory experiment, we motivate subjects to behave as if they had preferences $u^i(x_i, y_i)$ by guaranteeing to pay $V^i(x_i, y_i)$ dollars in U.S. currency if i purchases the bundle (x_i, y_i) where V^i is some particular increasing, concave functional form. We also endow the subject with a fixed budget of T_i "tokens" (the exchange medium). So long as our subject strictly prefers more money according to some (unobserved) increasing function $U_i(V^i)$, then $u^i = U_i[V^i(x_i, y_i)]$ becomes the subject's "as if" preference function, and we can calculate the demand functions from $V^i(x_i, y_i)$ and the token endowment, T_i.[4] It should be emphasized that the individual interdependent demand functions d_x^i and d_y^i, derived from a particular payoff function V^i, do not define firm maximum

---

[3] Each i is assumed to be motivated to adjust his purchases so as to solve the problem: maximize $u^i(x_i, y_i)$ subject to the budget constraint. Standard Lagrange methods lead to the marginal rate of substitution (derivative) condition $u_x^i / u_y^i = P_x / P_y$, which together with the budget constraint (normalized by setting $T^i = 1$) yields demand functions as indicated in the text.

[4] Because $u_x^i / u_y^i = V_x^i / V_y^i = P_x / P_y$, if $U_i' > 0$, it follows that the demand functions can be calculated from V^i independently of the particular utility of money function U_i.

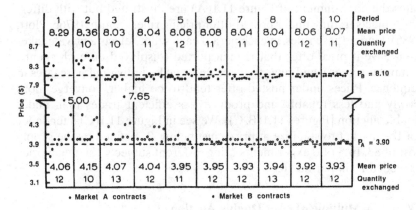

FIGURE 11.2. Double-auction pricing in two interdependent markets. In 10 of 15 experiments, the mean price deviates by less than 5 cents from the competitive equilibrium price in both markets in period 10.

willingness-to-pay limit prices as in the single-market representation in Figure 11.1(A). In the two-market model, i's demand prices P_x for successive units of x are different depending upon the actual price realizations for P_y. Hence, the demand for either commodity is an opportunity cost demand – that is, what one is willing to pay for units in one market depends upon the value of the alternative opportunity of spending one's limited token income in the other market. This defines a more difficult social task for Smith's "invisible hand" (Smith, 1776; 1937).

The market is completed by adding sellers with specified separable marginal cost functions $s_x^j(P_x)$ and $s_y^j(P_y)$, giving the additive total supplies $S_x(P_x) = \Sigma_j s_x^j$ and $S_y(P_y) = \Sigma_j s_x^j$. In an experiment, the functions $V^i(x_i, y_i)$ or $s_x^j(P_x)$ and $s_y^j(P_y)$ are presented to each subject in the form of tables defined on integer values of units purchased or sold. Market clearing prices (P_x^c, P_y^c) and quantities (X^c, Y^c) are defined by the equilibrium conditions: $X^c = D_x(P_x^c, P_y^c) = S_x(P_x^c)$ and $Y^c = D_y(P_y^c, P_y^c) = S_y(P_x^c)$. Each subject is given information only on his or her own tabular presentation of V_i or s_y^j. No subject has knowledge of these equilibrium prices, although some versions of classical theory have made the implausible and indefensible assumption that economic agents are completely informed.

All contract prices for a typical experimental economy consisting of six buyers and six sellers trading simultaneously in two markets are illustrated in Figure 11.2. The parameters of the induced preference function $V = \delta(\alpha x^\rho + \beta y^\rho)^{1-\rho}$, token endowments, and seller costs were selected to give equilibrium prices $(P_x^c, P_y^c) = (8.10, 3.90)$ and exchange quantities $(X^c, Y^c) = (12, 12)$. The convergence tendencies in this experiment are similar to the results of 15 experiments reported by Williams et al. (1986). The most important feature of these results is that the high predictive power of demand theory in the single-market setting extends to the budget-constrained interdependent two-market setting.[5] Subject traders, in effect, solve a set of simultaneous nonlinear equations using double-auction trading rules, without being aware that this is the market consequence of their behavior.

V.   Bubbles and Crashes in Stock Market Trading

Experimental methods have been used to examine the intrinsic value dividend theory of stock price determination (Smith et al., 1988). One objective of this research was to see if "bubbles and crashes" in stock market prices could be observed in the laboratory and, if so, to characterize their dynamic behavior over time. The environment is one in which subject agents ($n = 9$ or 12) are each given endowments of cash and shares (e.g., \$2.25 and three shares, \$5.85 and two shares, and \$9.45 and one share in one experimental design). At the end of each of 15 trading periods (using double-auction exchange rules) a dividend in cents, drawn from a distribution, for example, $\tilde{d} = (0, 8, 28, 60)$ with equal probability and expected value $E(\tilde{d}) = (0 + 8 + 28 + 60)(1/4) = 24$ cents, is paid on each share held in the account of each investor. Investors also receive any capital gains (losses) occurring on any share sold to another investor at a price higher (lower) than the price paid for it. Note that all value arising from share ownership in this market is derived from dividends. Net capital gains summed across all investors must be zero. The intrinsic value dividend theory of share prices states that the market price of a share will tend to a level representing the (discounted) expected sum of all future dividends. In the laboratory, investors are given complete probabilistic information on the dividend structure and know in each period the expected cumulative dividend value of a share.

In the preceding example, this value is $15E(\tilde{d}) = \$3.60$ in period 1 before the first dividend payment, \$3.36 in period 2, \$3.12 in period 3, and so on to 24 cents in period 15, as indicated by the horizontal lines

---

[5] This result is particularly significant because of the direct evidence from choice surveys showing that most people do not treat the implicit cost of forgone opportunities on a par with explicit incurred costs (see Thaler, 1980). Many other studies (see Coursey et al., 1987) support the proposition that revealed behavior in the context of markets differs from that found in psychological choice surveys, with the former more consistent with rational choice theory than the latter.

for each period in Figure 11.3. To date we have observed 13 of 21 market experiments that exhibit a price bubble and crash similar to the one shown plotted in Figure 11.3. Four of the 21 experiments, all with experienced investors (who had participated in one or more previous experiments), converged more or less quickly to near the intrinsic value dividend price and followed its decline to the end.

The following price adjustment hypothesis characterizes the dynamics of these markets: $\bar{P}_t - \bar{P}_{t-1} = -E(\tilde{d}) + \beta(B_{t-1} - O_{t-1})$, $\beta > 0$, where $\bar{P}_t - \bar{P}_{t-1}$ is the change in mean prices from period $t - 1$ to t, B_{t-1} is the number of bids entered in $t - 1$, and O_{t-1} is the number of offers. The expression for lagged excess bids is $B_{t-1} - O_{t-1}$ and is postulated to provide a surrogate measure of the excess demand for shares arising from investors' endogenous capital gains expectations. The hypothesis is that mean price changes consist of an intrinsic value dividend component, $-E(\tilde{d})$, plus an excess demand component due to capital gains expectations, which is linearly increasing in lagged excess bids. The regression estimate of this equation is shown in Figure 11.3 for that experiment. All 13 bubble–crash experiments yield estimates $\hat{B} > 0$, 10 of which are significantly greater than zero. Furthermore, in only 1 of the 13 experiments is the intercept $\hat{\alpha}$ significantly different from $-E(\tilde{d})$. Consequently, the intrinsic value dividend theory, as an equilibrium concept, cannot be rejected, although it must be rejected as an instantaneous predictor of the mean price.

VI.   Single-Object Auctions

The distinct concepts of an environment, institution, and behavior that underlie all market experiments are most easily illustrated in single-object auctions. In this theory (Smith, 1982), an environment consists of a list of agents $\{1, \ldots, N\}$, a list of commodities or resources $\{1, \ldots, K\}$, and certain characteristics of each agent i [e.g., the agent's value preferences (utility) u^i, resource endowment r^i, and knowledge endowment k^i]. Agent i is characterized by the vector $E^i = (u^i, r^i, k^i)$ defined on the K-dimensional commodity space. A microeconomic environment is defined by the vector $E = (E^1, \ldots, E^N)$, that is, the set of circumstances that are hypothesized to condition agents' interactions through institutions. The superscript i identifies the individual but also implies that these circumstances are in their nature personal. It is the individual who likes, works, knows, and makes. Institutions define the "property" right rules (human rights to act) by which agents communicate and exchange commodities within the limits and opportunities inherent in E. Because markets require communication to effect exchange, the rules governing message

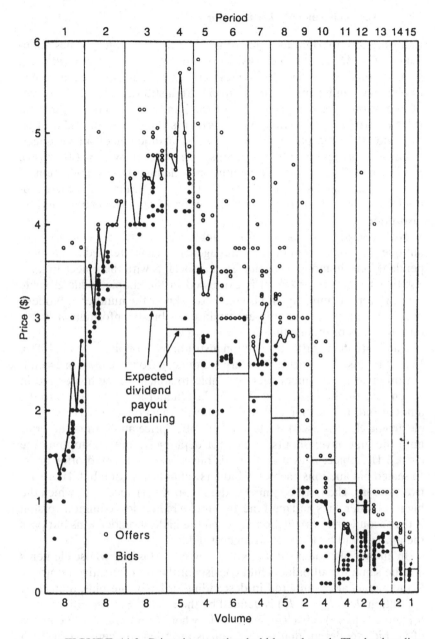

FIGURE 11.3. Prices in a market bubble and crash. The broken line connects successive bids (offers) that were accepted to form contracts. The step function indicates that the expected dividend value of a share declines each period by the expected one-period dividend value (24 cents). The least-squares prediction equation for the change in mean price in successive periods based on excess bids is $\bar{P}_t - \bar{P}_{t-1} = -0.12 + 0.063 (B_{t-1} - O_{t-1})$. The standard error of the intercept is 0.16 and of the slope is 0.016.

rights are as important as rights to goods. An institution specifies a language $M = (M^1, \ldots, M^N)$ consisting of message elements $m = (m^1, \ldots, m^N)$, where M^i is the set of messages that can be sent by i (e.g., the range of bids that can be entered by a buyer). An institution also defines a set of allocation rules $a = [a^1(m), \ldots, a^N(m)]$ and a set of cost imputation rules $c = [c^1(m), \ldots, c^N(m)]$, where $a^i(m)$ is the commodity allocation to i and $c^i(m)$ the payment by i, each as a function of all messages. Each agent's rights (and obligations) are defined by $I^i = (M^i, a^i(m), c^i(m))$, and a microeconomic institution is defined by the collection of these human rights characteristics, $I = (I^1, \ldots, I^N)$. Finally, a microeconomic system is defined by the conjunction of an environment and an institution, $S = (E, I)$.

Now consider an auction for a single object such as a painting or antique vase, as an example of S. Let agents be characterized by an independent, certain monetary value each associates with the object $V_1, \ldots, V_N$; that is, the vector (u^i, r^i) is expressed in the simple reduced value form, V_i, for one unit. Agent i is assumed to know the number of bidders, N, and V_i, but possesses only uncertain probabilistic information, $P(V)$, on the values of others; that is, $E = (V^i, P(V), N)$.

There are many different auction institutions (Coppinger et al., 1980). In the "English" (e) auction bids are announced from the floor in ascending order until the auctioneer is unable to solicit a new higher bid in which case the item is awarded to the last bidder at a price equal to the amount bid. In the "Dutch" (d) auction the auctioneer (in Holland an electronic clock is used) starts at a high offer price and lowers the price until the first buyer shouts "mine" (or depresses a button stopping the clock). The object is awarded to this buyer at the accepted offer price. In sealed bid auctions each of N bidders submits a written bid. There are two versions: The most common is the first-price (f) auction in which the highest bidder wins and pays the amount he bids. A less common version is the second-price (s) auction in which the highest bidder wins but pays the amount bid by the second highest bidder.

In all four auction institutions, the language M is bids whose elements are the same for all bidders and consists of the set of positive numbers. If the agents are numbered in descending order of the bids, then the f institution, $I_f = (I_f^1, \ldots, I_f^N)$ is defined by the rules $I_f^1 = [a^1(m) = 1, c^1(m) = b_1]$ and $I_f^i = [a^i(m) = 0, c^1(m) = 0]$, $i > 1$, where $m = (b_1, \ldots, b_N)$ consists of all bids tendered; that is, one unit is awarded to agent 1 (the high bidder), who pays his bid b_1, while all others receive and pay nothing (we assume no access fee for bidding). In contrast, for the s auction, $I_s = (I_s^1, \ldots, I_s^N)$, where $I_s^1 = [a^1(m) = 1, c^1(m) = b_2]$ and $I_s^i = [a^i(m) = 0, c^i(m) = 0]$,

$i > 1$; that is, the unit is awarded to agent 1 who pays the second high bid b_2.

A microeconomy is driven by the choices of agents in M. In the static description of an economy, agent behavior can be defined as a function (or correspondence), $m^i = \beta(E^i|I)$ carrying the characteristics of i into a choice m^i, conditional upon the rights specified by the institution I. Given the behavior of each agent, the rules of the institution determine the outcomes $h^i(m) = h^i(\beta(E^1|I), \ldots, \beta(E^N|I))$ and similarly for $c^i(m)$. Thus agents choose messages, but institutions (the social rules) determine allocations. A theory of agents' behavior deduces a particular β function from assumptions about $S = (E,I)$. In the s auction, it is a dominant strategy to bid one's value; that is, $b_i = \beta(V_i|I_s) = V_i$, for all i. A bid below V_i increases the risk of losing the auction without changing the price paid, whereas a bid above V_i risks having to pay more than V_i. The predicted result is that $b_1 = V_1$ is the winning bid and agent 1 pays the price V_2. Similarly, in the e auction, agent 1 will eventually exclude agent 2 by raising the standing bid to V_2 (or somewhat above) and obtain the item at this price. Thus theory asserts that the e and s auctions are isomorphic institutions.

Experimental studies of the e and s auctions (in which, say, the values V_i are assigned at random, and the winning bidder is paid $V_1 - b_2$ in U.S. currency) show that the two auction institutions are approximately equivalent (Coppinger et al., 1980). English auction prices tend to be slightly above V_2, and s auction awards tend to be at prices slightly below V_2. This is because discreteness leads to some overbidding in the e auction, whereas in the s auction not all subjects perceive that it may be in their self-interest to bid value. However, over time in a sequence of auctions, many of the subjects in this latter category "learn" to follow the dominant strategy. Both types of auctions are very efficient – some 95–97% of the awards are to the person with the highest item value.

The f and d auctions are technically the most interesting of all these institutions because each agent's optimal strategy depends upon the strategies followed by the others. Vickrey (1961) proved that if each agent maximizes expected surplus ($V_i - b_i$) in an environment with $P(V) = V$ (the V_i are drawn from the linear distribution function on $[0, 1]$), then a distinct noncooperative bidding strategy for the environment $E_i = (V_i, P(V) = V, N)$, is for each i to bid $b_i = \beta(V_i, P(V) = V, N|I_f) = (N - 1) V_i/N$ in an f auction. This strategy defines a noncooperative equilibrium in the sense that if all of any $N - 1$ bidders use this strategy, then this strategy will maximize the expected profit of the remaining bidder.

It is easy to prove (Cox et al., 1982) that the f and d auctions are iso-morphic. Thus each bidder should plan to accept the standing offer in a d auction when it falls to $b_i = (N - 1) V_i/N$. This is because the real time d auction is noninformative; that is, each i's knowledge that at each instant no buyer has yet accepted the standing offer will not yield an incentive to change the f auction bidding rule.

Experimental studies of f and d auctions for $E_i = (V_i, P(V) = V, N)$, where $N = 3, 4, 5, 6$, and 9, have established that d auction mean prices are somewhat lower than f auction prices, but in both auctions the mean prices are too high to be consistent with the Vickrey risk neutral model (Cox et al., 1982). This last result in f auctions motivated the constant relative risk averse model (CRRAM) (Cox et al., 1982; 1988) based on the hypothesis that each i bids as if to maximize expected utility using the utility-of-surplus function $u_i = (V_i - b_i)^{r_i}$, where r_i is an element of (0, 1]. This leads to the linear equilibrium bid function $b_i(V_i) = (N - 1)V_i/(N - 1 + r_i) \geq (N - 1) V_i / N$, which explains the overwhelming tendency of bidders (92%) to bid above the risk-neutral bid. An astonishing property of bidding behavior (the subjects are absolutely naive in the sense of knowing nothing about bidding theory) is the great consistency with which most individuals submit bids showing high linearity with randomly assigned values (Cox et al., 1988). An example of a typical subject's bidding behavior is illustrated in Figure 11.4. Furthermore, subjects bid higher in groups with larger N as predicted by the equilibrium bid function. From a sample of 33 subjects who returned for a second experimental session, only 20% reveal linear bidding behavior that is statistically distinguishable from their previous session. The same test of the null hypothesis that the N bidders competing in the same auction are using the same linear bid function is rejected for 60% of the groups, which supports the proposition that individuals bid as if they had distinct risk attitudes, r_i. However, contrary to the theory, about 22% of the subjects' empirical bid functions have statistically significant intercepts. One modification of the theory that accounts for this is the postulate that $u_i = (V_i - b_i + w_i)^{r_i}$ if $V_i - b_i + w_i \geq 0$, and $u_i = 0$, otherwise. If for any i, $w_i < 0$, the interpretation is that there is a threshold amount of money $|w_i|$ potentially to be obtained before the individual will enter a serious (nonzero) bid. When $V_i \leq |w_i|$ the individual bids zero. Hence, linear regression may yield a significantly negative intercept. If for any i, $w_i > 0$, the individual is postulated to attach commodity value, or a utility of gambling, $u_i = (w_i)^{r_i}$ to winning the auction. Such an individual may even bid in excess of (low) assigned values of V_i in an attempt to "win" even if this involves a negative surplus, $(V_i - b_i)$. This extension of the theory is testable (although w_i is not observable)

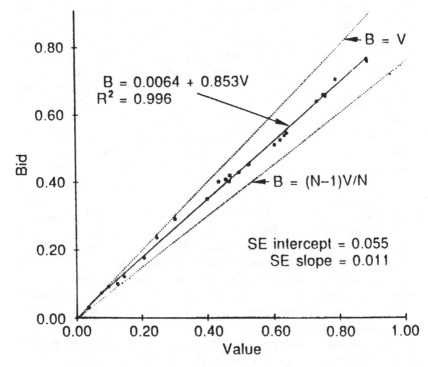

FIGURE 11.4. Bidding behavior for a typical subject in an auction with $N = 4$ bidders. Bids, B, within the triangle defined by the rays, $B = V$ and $B = (N - 1)V/N$ (the risk-neutral bid function), which vary linearly with value, are consistent with subjects bidding as if risk averse with utility that is log linear in monetary rewards.

in the sense that we can run experiments in which individuals are paid (charged) a lump sum $w_i' > 0$ ($w_i' < 0$) in addition to being paid ($V_i - b_i$) conditional on being the high bidder. The extended model predicts a parallel upward (downward) shift in the estimated bid function. These developments in the study of bidding illustrate a progressive research program in which there is continuing interplay between experimental testing and theory extensions that seek to increase the empirical content of the theory.

VII.   Exchange in Political Institutions

The theory of induced preference (Smith, 1976a) has been used to drive innovative extensions of the methods of experimental economics to the study of political behavior. The extensions are based on the observation that the arguments of a reward function V^i can be common outcomes to all i, say $V^i(X_1,X_2)$ in the case of two "public goods" with outcome quantities (X_1,X_2) to all participants. Also the extensions exploit the fact that the institution may be a traditional political institution, which means simply that the messages, m_i, are votes for (or against) outcomes proposed through that institution. Under one institution, a committee of N members may reach agreement on an outcome (X_1,X_2) in a plane by direct majority rule referenda with no agenda restrictions on the order in which proposals are voted on. When preferences satisfy a certain condition on symmetry, it is possible to identify a distinct majority rule equilibrium (X_1^*,X_2^*) , which has the property that it is stable against all proposals to move; that is, every proposal to move to some other point (X_1,X_2) will be defeated by majority vote when the rules resemble Roberts Rules of Order. The experimental results strongly support this theoretical model as against numerous other theories of political choice that have been proposed (Fiorina and Plott, 1978). However, a majority rule equilibrium exists only under special conditions on preferences. When these conditions are not satisfied, we get a (an indeterminant) cycle. So how can majority rule outcomes be obtained with the high frequency that we observe in committees and elections? One hypothesis is that determinancy results because of the use of an agenda that structures the decision procedure and avoids cycles. This has been demonstrated experimentally in an environment with and without a majority rule equilibrium, in which the institution imposes an agenda that defines a particular sequence of pairwise comparisons to be selected by majority rule (Levine and Plott, 1977). Furthermore, it is shown that the final outcome chosen can be changed predictably by using a different agenda whether or not an equilibrium exists. In a third institution, an electorate of N members uses a plurality voting rule to select among $(n = 2, 3)$ candidates who announce "platform" positions in the (X_1,X_2) plane in response to periodic polls during a "campaign" (Plott, 1982b). Outcomes tend to support the majority rule equilibrium in two-candidate elections, but not in three-candidate elections where plurality applies. Still a fourth institution asks each of N voters to "bid" on each of n propositions by stating the amount he or she is willing to pay or requires to be compensated if the proposal passes, the winning proposal being the one with the largest unanimously approved nonnegative sum of the individual bids (Smith, 1977). Consider three propositions and six voters (Table 11.1). Each voter knows only his or her own value. Note that there is no majority rule equilibrium in this environment; P2 beats P1, P3 beats P2, and

Table 11.1. *Voter valuation with three propositions and six voters*

Proposition	Voter valuation (dollars)						Total
	1	2	3	4	5	6	
P1	5	−30	−30	25	25	0	−5
P2	60	5	5	−10	−10	55	105
P3	−20	45	45	0	0	−25	45

P1 beats P3 by a vote of 4 to 2 in each of these pairings. Yet P2 and P3 each yield a positive net gain for the electorate with P2 easily having the largest net social value, provided the losers, voters 4 and 5 are compensated by the gainers. Four of five experiments with cash-motivated undergraduate subjects using the preceding bidding institution reached a stopping rule equilibrium (unanimous consent signaled by a vote following each trial) in a maximum of 10 trials in two experiments, and a maximum of 6 trials in three experiments.

VIII. An Experiment in Law and Economics

I will close with a brief report on an important recent discovery in bargaining behavior (Hoffman and Spitzer, 1985b). According to the Coase theorem (Coase, 1960) in law and economics, parties capable of harming one another, but who can negotiate, will bargain to an efficient outcome whichever side has the legal right to inflict damage. Experimental results are uniformly consistent with this prediction. However, the "controller" subject who is endowed with this legal right by means of a coin flip invariably fails to extract the full individually rational share of the bargaining surplus that is predicted by game theory. Instead, the bargainers share the surplus equally, suggesting a "fairness" ethic. Hoffman and Spitzer hypothesized that subjects do not perceive an asymmetric property right as "legitimate" if it is awarded by a random coin flip. They proceeded to replicate their bargaining experiments, but with a treatment difference that awarded the controller condition to the subject who won a game of skill before the experiment. Now the controller may perceive that the position of advantage has been earned. The results are striking in that more than two-thirds of the controllers obtain individually rational shares of the joint surplus, whereas under the random assignment treatment none did.[6]

[6] I thank J. Cox, J. Ledyard, G. Suchanek, J. Walker, and A. Williams with whom I have worked on a number of experimental studies from which I have drawn illustrative examples in this chapter, and the National Science Foundation for financial support over many years, beginning in 1962, for experimental research in economics.

CHAPTER 12

Individual Rationality, Market Rationality, and Value Estimation

Peter Knez, Vernon L. Smith, and
Arlington W. Williams

Direct experimental tests of expected utility theory (EUT), in which subjects are asked to choose among alternative gambles or to make judgments as to their willingness-to-pay (WTP) and/or willingness-to-accept (WTA) payment for a gamble, have not been kind to EUT. As noted in the survey by Slovic and Lichtenstein (1983), the results of these interrogations are remarkably consistent in a wide variety of contexts and are robust under examinations designed to determine the effect of monetary incentives, experience, and other factors that might have accounted for the discrepancy between subject responses and the predictions of EUT. On the other hand, experimental studies of individual and market behavior based upon EUT models of market decision making have yielded results showing high consistency with the predictions of these models (see the references in Smith, 1982). Are individual revealed preferences in some market contexts more likely to be "rational" (consistent with EUT) than individual responses to choices among alternative prospects?

Several studies designed to solicit WTP and WTA responses for a variety of goods have found a wide disparity between the "buying price" and "selling price" measures of individual value (see the study and the citations therein by Knetsch and Sinden, 1984; hereafter K-S). Values of WTA obtained in this way are frequently an order of magnitude greater than values of WTP although theoretically WTP and WTA "should" differ by no more than a presumed "small" income effect. These results should not be dismissed by economists on the grounds of poor subject motivation because the experiments include some (see those in K-S) that have carefully introduced actual monetary payments and cash compensations and have not relied on hypothetical choices.

These results are explained by K-S (and by most of the authors of such studies) in terms of the Kahneman and Tversky (1982) "framing" paradigm in which people reveal that they are less willing to spend wealth that they consider to be part of their endowment than wealth not so considered. We would emphasize that such behavior is "irrational"

257

only in the narrow sense of EUT as a behavioral hypothesis, which may not only be a poor predictor of individual choice but may also not be a satisfactory guide to action. For example, the differential treatment of wealth that has become part of one's endowment may have important survival value, which is imprinted in decision behavior. However, K-S (p. 508, footnote 3) reported one, perhaps significant, experiment in which they did not get the usual WTA-WTP disparity. In this experiment, cash payments and offers for a lunch made to respondents entering an office cafeteria showed a much smaller, statistically insignificant, disparity. In this case, the respondents were about to participate in a familiar market for the commodity being evaluated.

On this same theme, an important new study by Coursey and Schutze (1987) uses a repetitive series of Vickrey (second-price) auctions to determine market WTA and WTP prices for entitlements to an unfamiliar item, which they compare with hypothetical measures of WTA and WTP. They found that, although individual bids in the first of a sequence of Vickrey auctions show a large WTA-WTP disparity, ending bids, after a series of auctions, yield no such disparity. Their interpretation is that marketlike learning experience yields results that are not inconsistent with the "rational" economic model. Because the motivation for such models is to articulate a theory of market behavior, we would argue that the Coursey and Schutze work raises fundamental questions as to the appropriate context in which tests of the observable implications of economic theory are to be carried out. In this emphasis, we are not denying the reality of what Kahneman and Tversky have called framing effects. Such effects are identifiable both in the hypothetical and the reward-motivated contexts in which they have been measured. What we are questioning is the uncritical *interpretation* of the implications of this research for the theory of markets (Arrow, 1982). According to this interpretation, the results of direct studies showing that individual participants are subject to framing effects implies that markets are inefficient. We think this interpretation is incorrect (see Smith, 1985) for two reasons.

1. It confuses individual rationality, in the sense of EUT, with market rationality, in the sense of allocative efficiency. Market efficiency is a proposition about allocations given demand behavior, whereas EUT leads to propositions about rational demand behavior. Thus EUT could have very poor predictive power, but given this EUT-inconsistent demand environment, markets might be highly efficient. Also, an essential feature of markets is that price is determined by the marginal traders, and

the presence of nonmarginal traders who are EUT irrational does not imply that market prices are EUT irrational.

2. Direct studies of framing have concentrated on inconsistencies in individual responses to questionnaires or in one-shot buying and selling decisions in which individuals do not have the opportunity to participate in an ongoing market. If individuals modify their opinions and their decisions in the light of this experience, these effects will not be reflected in the instruments that have been used in framing studies. We would argue that although such studies have relevance to measuring people's preference attitudes, they provide no basis for extrapolation to behavior in markets. Most (but not all) experimental markets show some learning effects over time with equilibrium behavior quite different from start-up behavior.

In this chapter, we report the results of two series of experiments designed to address two research questions: (1) if we ask subjects WTP and WTA questions concerning a security that yields a random dividend from a known probability distribution, and that will be traded in a market, do these responses, even if inconsistent with EUT, provide "good" predictors of the mean market price generated by trading among these same subjects? By a good predictor, we mean that it does at least as well in predicting the mean market price as does the rational expectations equilibrium (REE) theory of such a market. (2) If trading is repeated over several consecutive market periods, and we apply the WTA-WTP questionnaire instrument between each of these trading periods, do we observe any trend in effect on subject responses in this context?

I   Experimental Design and Results, Series I

The first group of experiments on which we report were not designed to study WTP and WTA. These experiments were designed to study the efficient markets hypothesis (or REE) in the context of asset trading under double-auction contracting rules, where an asset's value is derived from a random dividend distribution (for a more complete discussion, see Smith et al., 1988). In these experiments, 9 (or 12) subjects participate in a sequence of 15 consecutive trading periods for an asset whose dividend probability distribution is common knowledge. At the end of each trading period, all shares receive the dividend realized for that period. In period 1, each share represents a prospect that will yield 15 realizations from the given distribution; in period 2 a share can claim 14 remaining realizations; and so on until the final period when only one realization remains. Each subject begins period 1 with an endowment of cash and securities. The expected (dividend) value of a share in period 1 is $3.60 (15 periods times the expected dividend per period, $0.24), or, in some designs, $2.40. This is the REE price based on expected value as the "intrinsic worth" of a share (the REE price adjusted for risk-averse or risk-preferring behavior may be below or above this expected dividend value). Each subject ends the 15-period experiment with his or her initial cash endowment plus the sum of all dividend realizations plus (minus) any net capital gains (losses) from trading shares during the 15 periods.

After completing an initial series of 12 experiments of this type, we applied a WTA-WTP instrument in our subsequent 14 experiments (Series I). After each subject had completed the asset market instructions and been informed of the dividend structure and of his or her initial endowment, but before the opening of the first trading period, the following two questions were administered: (1) Given your endowment of $———— cash (i.e., working capital) and ———— asset units, what would be the minimum price you would be willing to accept in order to sell 1 unit of your inventory in the trading period about to begin? ————. (2) Given your endowment of $———— cash (i.e., working capital) and ———— asset units, what would be the maximum price that you would be willing to pay in order to buy 1 unit of this asset in the trading period about to begin? ————.

The results of our 14 Series I experiments are shown in Table 12.1, which lists the buyer and seller surpluses and the predicted market price (P_w) based on the WTA-WTP interrogations, as well as the actual mean transaction price $(\bar{P})$ for all trades in period 1. Price P_w equates supply and demand, where supply is the WTA responses ordered from lowest to highest, and demand is the WTP responses ordered from highest to lowest. Our results are summarized as follows.

1. We first asked if the mean price deviations in period 1, $p_r = \bar{P} - P_r$ (measured in deviations from the normalizing REE price, P_r) differ between the prior series of 12 experiments that did not apply the WTA-WTP interrogation and the 14 Series I experiments that did. Because these sample mean deviations are $0.46 and $0.70, respectively, and their difference is not statistically significant ($t = 0.56$), interrogation appears not to affect prices.

2. Buyers' surplus tends to exceed sellers' surplus, which implies that there is more diversity among intramarginal limit buy prices than among corresponding limit sell prices. However, this dif-

Table 12.1. *Market rationality series I results*

Exp.	Surplus seller:buyer	WTA, WTP price, P_w	Mean price, $\bar{P}$
116	2.9:11.1	1.47	1.53
117[a]	2.1:8.8	1.00	1.74
118	4.4:4.0	1.90	2.10
119[b]	0.5:2.0	3.00	5.44
125[b]	2.4:2.3	2.00	2.55
128[b]	3.1:1.1	1.62	1.85
139[b]	0.6:4.1	0.60	0.42
141[a]	4.3:12.3	1.62	2.32
142[b]	5.2:11.9	2.32	3.78
143[b]	8.1:2.9	3.59	3.42
146[b]	1.4:10.2	1.00	2.67
148[b]	6.1:2.8	2.62	3.55
149[b]	3.8:2.7	2.75	3.40
150[b]	2.5:0.4	3.50	3.40

Note: Exp. denotes experiment.
[a] Denotes $P_r = 2.40$; otherwise $P_r = 3.60$.
[b] Denotes experienced subjects.

ference is not significant $[t(26) = 1.6]$. Since WTA and WTP reflect expectations about future price increases and the concomitant capital gains, it would appear that such expectations varied considerably among subject trader groups.

3. Comparing the predictive error of the WTA-WTP equilibrium price, $p_w = \bar{P} - P_w$, with that of the REE price, $p_r = \bar{P} - P_r$, we reject the null hypothesis that $\sigma_r^2 = \sigma_w^2$ in favor of $\sigma_w^2 < \sigma_r^2$ ($F = 2.45$). Hence the WTA-WTP data do much better in predicting the mean trading price than the widely touted intrinsic value or REE theory of stock prices.

4. In each experiment we have complete data on all the bids and/or offers submitted by each subject, allowing us to compare actual bids with WTP_i and actual offers with WTA_i. Examining these data, we find that the lowest offer made was below the stated WTA_i for 14% of the subjects, whereas the highest bid entered was above the stated WTP_i for 46% of the subjects. We conjectured that buyers were more willing to abandon their WTPs because they sensed a possible rising market in period 1 and were going for capital gains. Most of the markets would subsequently confirm this prediction (see Smith et al., 1988).

II.   Experimental Design and Results, Series II

In a Series I experiment, the first market period requires evaluating a complicated compound gamble. Furthermore, because it is the first of a 15-period sequence of trading periods, it may be quite important in yielding expectations information for each agent. Hence a subject with well-articulated WTA and WTP attitudes based only on dividend information, endowment, and "thinking about it," may alter those attitudes drastically upon observing the first few trades that reveal something about the behavior of others. Consequently, our second series (II) of three experiments each consisted of 4 or 6 single trading periods for an asset in which all subject endowments were *reinitialized* at the beginning of each period of trading. This pure replication design controls, on any first-period trading, effects due to capital gains expectations across periods (but not, of course, within a period). In these experiments, a single draw at the end of one period of trading is made from a binary probability dividend distribution $(p_1, d_1; p_2, d_2) = (\frac{1}{2}, \$0.50; \frac{1}{2}, 2.00)$, with expected value \$1.25. If we define E = (cash, shares) as the endowment vector, there are three agent classes, E_1 = (\$4.50, 1), E_2 = (\$3.25, 2), and E_3 = (\$2.00, 3) with three subjects in each class comprising a nine-trader market. Hence the expected value of each agent's endowment is \$5.75 in each of the independently initialized trading periods in an experiment. Except for the effects of learning, each trading period is a pure replication of the market for a single binary gamble. In this environment, we also administered the two questions stated in Section I.

The results of our three Series II experiments consisting of 16 independent single-period markets, each preceded by a WTA-WTP interrogation, are shown in Table 12.2. Our results are summarized as follows.

1.   The WTA-WTP schedules for both the Series I and II experiments typically reveal frequent inconsistencies with EUT. For example, in period 1 of experiment 133, subjects 3 and 7 report WTPs that equal or exceed the maximum possible payoff' (\$2). However, these violations of simple dominance are not repeated. In spite of the EUT inconsistencies, the period 1 market-clearing price of \$1.25 can hardly be classified as irrational.

2.   Comparing Tables 12.1 and 12.2, both seller and buyer surpluses tend to be smaller in Series II (period 1) than their counterparts in Series I. This is consistent with the expectation that moving from a compound to a single one-draw gamble will reduce the diversity in both the WTA and WTP measures of individual

Table 12.2. *Market rationality series II results*

Exp.: period	Surplus seller:buyer	WTA, WTP price, P_w	Mean price, $\bar{P}$
129: 1	1.9:0.9	1.25	1.66
2	1.3:0.9	1.25	1.39
3	0.9:0.5	1.62	1.60
4	1.2:0.3	1.50	1.41
133: 1	2.2:2.9	1.25	1.30
2	2.0:0.2	1.42	1.51
3	0.4:0.3	1.47	1.52
4	0.5:0.2	1.50	1.58
5	1.0:0.3	1.50	1.51
6	0.2:0.0	1.50	1.58
137: 1	1.9:3.1	1.12	1.43
2	1.2:0.5	1.50	1.49
3	1.0:0.2	1.40	1.40
4	0.5:0.2	1.40	1.26
5	0.7:0.4	1.30	1.18
6	0.3:0.5	1.20	1.21

Note: $P_r = 1.25$ in all experiments.

value. In Table 12.2, sellers' surplus is larger than buyers' surplus in all but three trading periods.

3. In 10 of 16 periods, P_w is a better predictor of $\bar{P}$ than P_r, but the repeat trials with the same subject group in each experiment yield a sample that is too small (three independent sets of observations) for a meaningful test.

4. If in each trading period we compare WTA_i with actual offers and WTP_i with actual bids for each subject, we find that for 34% of the subjects, the lowest offer made was below their stated WTA_i, and for 47% the highest bid was above their stated WTP_i. The abandon with which subjects violate their own WTA-WTP responses suggests that the latter may serve only as a pretrade bargaining objective from which there is frequent deviation.

5. Standard (risk-averse) theory suggests that for any i, WTA_i will equal or exceed WTP_i. We counted the number of individuals who violated this inequality in their period-by-period WTA-WTP responses. The number of violations in successive trading periods of each Series II experiment are as follows: Experiment 129: 0, 0, 0, 0; Experiment 133: 3, 2, 1, 2, 3, 0; Experiment 137: 5, 2, 1, 0, 2, 1. By this measure of rationality, it appears that

replication of the interrogation followed by market experience tends to reduce the incidence of EUT inconsistent responses, with most of the reduction occurring in period 2.

III.   Conclusions

The following conclusions appear to be justified by the preceding experiments: (1) The WTA-WTP interrogation itself does not have a significant effect on the subsequent observed mean contract price of an asset. (2) In Series I, based on the WTA-WTP data, buyers' and sellers' surpluses do not differ significantly. (3) Subjects often submit actual offers below their stated WTAs, and/or bids above their stated WTPs (14–47% of the responses), suggesting perhaps as L. J. Savage once said, "It is difficult to be honest with one's self about prices generally" (1962, p. 165). (4) Although these WTA-WTP responses are frequently abandoned by subjects, the equilibrium predicted prices, P_w, that result are not bad predictors of the mean observed contract prices, in the sense that P_w is closer to the mean price than the "intrinsic" value REE price, P_r. (5) Over time in Series II there is a considerable decrease in subject violation of the risk-averse rationality prediction WTA $\geq$ WTP.

Extensive studies of the consumption-leisure *revealed* choice behavior of mice, rats, monkeys, pigeons, and people in repeat purchase environments (Battalio et al., 1981, p. 623) yield steady-state results consistent with the Slutsky-Hicks model of maximizing behavior. For the animal studies, there is no presumption of cognitive calculating choice, yet this presumption is *implicit* in tests of EUT based on subject responses to one-shot choices among gambles and/or word problems. We do not deny that EUT is in trouble standing as a clearly nonfalsified theory of decision making under uncertainty, but we would urge suspension of scientific judgment until this evidence has been further examined in repetitive marketlike environments. In any case, there is no justification for the normative and judgmental conclusion that EUT violations imply that either individuals are incompetent or markets are inefficient. What may be in doubt is EUT as an attempt to give formal meaning to the concept of rationality.

CHAPTER 13

Market Contestability in the Presence of Sunk (Entry) Costs

Don Coursey, R. Mark Isaac, Margaret Luke, and Vernon L. Smith

The core of the contestable markets theory is the hypothesis that, with completely free entry and exit, a market that exhibits economies of scale – the traditional "natural monopoly" cost structure – will not exhibit monopoly behavior, even if only a single producing firm is observed in the market (Demsetz, 1968a; Bailey, 1980; Bailey and Panzar, 1980; Baumol and Willig, 1981; Baumol, 1982; Baumol et al., 1982). That is, in the absence of any other restrictions on entry and exit, scale economies alone do not constitute an effective barrier to entry. Coursey et al. (1983: hereafter CIS), have reported the results of a series of experiments in which each of two firms has identical decreasing marginal cost and the same capacity, but demand is insufficient to accommodate (profitably) any output in excess of the capacity of either firm. The conditions of these experimental markets further provide the "hit-and-run," zero sunk costs (Baumol, 1982; Baumol et al., 1982) of the contestable markets hypothesis. In CIS, these results are compared with those from an uncontested market with one monopoly firm (i.e., a market in which sunk costs are effectively infinite for a potential entrant). The CIS experiments strongly support the contestable markets hypothesis, namely that to observe approximately competitive behavior by a single producing firm with substantially decreasing costs, it is sufficient that (a) sunk costs are zero and (b) there are two contesting firms acting noncooperatively in the sense that there is no explicit nonprice communication between them that leads to collusive restriction in supply. Furthermore, it is necessary that (c) the producing firm's market be contested by at least one other firm with the same cost structure. This follows from the observation that competitive outcomes tend to prevail when there are two contesting firms, but monopoly outcomes tend to prevail when there is one uncontested seller.

The purpose of the research reported here is to broaden the CIS study to examine the competitive discipline of contested markets where sunk cost is neither zero nor infinite. Several authors have conjectured that sunk costs might weaken the discipline of contested markets, and CIS have established that, behaviorally, the competitive discipline does fail in the polar case in which the sunk cost of a potential entrant is infinite.

In Section I, we explore further the notion of sunk costs as a barrier to entry. In Section II, our experimental design and its relation to the theory are presented along with some hypotheses. Section III is a brief description of the posted-offer trading institution employed, whereas Section IV discusses the use of programmed buyer responses versus subject buyers as a treatment variable. Section V contains the experimental results and interpretation, and Section VI summarizes the findings and proposes some general conclusions.

I.   Sunk Costs, Conjectural Variations, and Entry Barriers

In enumerating the assumptions of a theory of market performance, there is a distinction to be made between structural and behavioral assumptions. The former include characteristics of the production or cost technologies available, market or other limitations on the potential number of producing firms, and formal or informal rules under which exchange contracts are negotiated (the trading institution). The latter include such attributes as the risk attitudes of sellers and interfirm expectations (conjectural variations). In testing a theory using experimental methods, it is appropriate to begin with an experimental design in which the structural conditions are reproduced as faithfully as possible in the laboratory. If the theory is then "falsified," relative to any competing theories, by the experimental evidence, one or more of the behavioral assumptions of the theory may be in question. If the theory is not "falsified" by the experimental evidence, then it is natural to explore the robustness of this result with respect to changes in the structural variables of the theory.

In the previously reported tests of the contestable market hypothesis, the structural conditions specified by the theory (costless entry and exit) were met precisely for a market with a "natural monopoly" cost structure and two contesting firms. The behavioral assumptions about sellers' expectations have two functions: They complete the contestable markets hypothesis, and they allow for the construction of alternative hypotheses. The contestable market hypothesis argues that the structural conditions allow for what Baumol calls "hit-and-run" entry. That is, any situation in which an incumbent firm attempts to price at a level generating positive profits will induce entry, even if there is a conjecture that the profit opportunities are transient. The CIS article presented alternative scenarios (based on different conjectural variations) which predicted other outcomes (tacitly supported cartel-like pricing and unimpeded monopoly behavior by a surviving firm). The data from the experiment falsified the alternative hypotheses and supported the contestable markets hypothesis.

Because CIS found support for the contestable markets hypothesis under the conditions specified in the theory, the present research turns to the search for potential boundaries of falsifiability. Specifically, we explore the effect of sunk costs on the previous design with two contesting firms.

We shall use the term *sunk costs* in a manner consistent with the definition used by Baumol and Willig (1981).[1] The significance of a sunk cost is that it is a fixed opportunity cost of the *entry* decision (i.e., sunk costs can be avoided by a decision not to enter a particular market). The concept is to be distinguished from fixed costs that are independent of any operating decision. Fixed costs that are not sunk (e.g., the fixed cost of aircraft usable on any route) are independent of the decision to supply any particular market. Hence, sunk costs may be a deterrent to entry in any particular market, but once incurred, they do not affect profits over the life of the sunk investment.

Consider a market with a natural monopoly cost structure but with zero cost of either entry or exit. The contestable market hypothesis states that even where only one firm is observed serving the market, that firm is devoid of monopoly power. What happens under exactly the same conditions if firms must incur positive sunk entry costs? Several authors have asked this or a similar question in the contestable markets literature. Bailey and Panzar say that "the difficulty [potential barriers to entry] arises from the presence of sunk costs, *not* economies of scale" (1980, p. 128). Baumol and Willig provide two conjectures. First, they argue that the need to incur sunk costs can create barriers to entry: "The risk of losing unrecoverable entry costs, as perceived by the potential entrant can be increased by the threat (or the imagined threat) of retaliatory strategic or tactical response of the incumbent" (1981, p. 418). Second, in a footnote, they suggest that, with different expectations on the part of the potential entrant, the need to sink costs could enable a potential entrant to overcome other barriers to entry: "The entrant who deliberately incurs substantial sunk costs ... may thereby make it far more difficult for the incumbent to dislodge him" (Baumol and Willig, 1981, p. 419). Schwartz and Reynolds suggest that "once we deviate even

---

[1] Definition: Let $C(q, s)$ represent the short-run cost function applicable to an output rate of q units per period sold in some market for s time periods in the future. The $K(s)$ is the sunk cost of access to this market for s periods if $C(q, s) = K(s) + G(q, s)$, where $G(0, s) = 0$.

Table 13.1. *Parameter summary for market contestability*

Parameter description	Value
Number of buyers	5
Number of sellers	2
Price of sellers' permit, K	$2.00
Length of sellers' permit validity, s	5 periods
Monopoly price (normalized)[a] = P_m	$ 1.15
Monopoly quantity = Q_m	6
Competitive prices (normalized)[b]	[0.04, 0.15]
Competitive quantity	10
Seller quasi rent per period at P_m, Q_m	4.00
Seller quasi rent per period at P_m, Q_m, less 1/5 permit cost	
Seller working capital endowment[c]	15.00
Buyers' surplus per period at P_m, Q_m	3.75
Seller quasi rent per period at $P = .04$, $Q = 10$	0.40
Seller quasi rent per period at $P = .04$, $Q = 10$, less 1/5 permit cost	
Buyers' surplus at $P = .04$, $Q = 10$	12.35

[a] This is actually the lower of two equal-profit monopoly prices. The other is $1.40.
[b] The lower bound on competitive price is taken to be the smallest price supporting $Q = 10$ and covering variable costs plus 1/5 permit costs. If the requirement of covering permit cost were excluded $P_c \in [0, 0.15]$.
[c] This cash endowment was awarded unconditionally to each seller. It provided capital for the purchase of permits and to cover losses on sales, but it could be retained if a seller elected not to purchase permits.

slightly from the strict assumptions of perfect contestability, pricing and entry decisions depend upon the nature of firm interactions" (1983, p. 489). These and similar conjectures regarding the way in which sunk costs might affect the performance of an otherwise contestable market motivate the new series of experiments reported later.

II.   Experimental Design, Hypotheses, and Research Strategy

The aggregate demand and marginal cost schedules (identical to those used in CIS) are shown in Figure 13.1. Marginal unit cost and values are measured in deviations from the average variable cost of unit 10, AVC(10). Table 13.1 provides a parameter summary for the experimental design.

The sunk costs were imposed by requiring that a firm purchase an entry permit as a condition for being allowed to post a price. The permits cost $2 each and, once purchased, were valid for five consecutive periods.

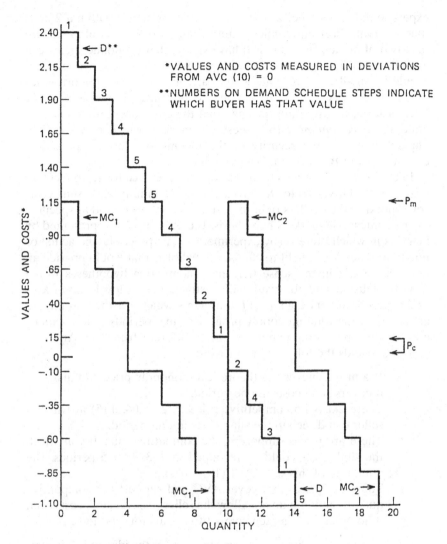

FIGURE 13.1. Market parameters.

In terms of the Baumol and Willig (1981) definitions, each of the firms considering buying a permit faced a short-run planning horizon (s) equal to five periods and a level of sunk entry costs (K) equal to $2. These values of K and s were chosen for the following reasons: Experience had shown that one could expect to obtain a maximum of about 25 experimental market periods of posted-offer exchange within a 2-hour time interval.[2] Previous studies (Smith, 1962, and Isaac et al., 1985, are only two of numerous examples) have shown that economic agents can exhibit "convergent" behavior with repeated decisions. Therefore, s should be small enough to allow the participants several opportunities to evaluate entry–exit responses in the presence of the sunk costs. Furthermore, s must not be so small that the entry decision precludes a multiperiod *commitment* to contest the market, which may carry an implied threat to the security of the incumbent (see the preceding quotation from Baumol and Willig, 1981, p. 419).

Likewise, there was a wide range of possible choice for K. In fact CIS tested two polar values for K, zero and positive infinity. Zero sunk costs correspond to the costless right to post a price in any period as specified by the contestable markets hypothesis. The other pole is represented by markets in which there is (by experimenter fiat) precisely one actual or potential seller. We sought to choose a level of K that would provide an informative test in the sense that many competing hypotheses would be both plausible and observationally distinct. At very low levels of K (1 or 2 cents) or at very high level (at amounts which, for the entrant, are greater than the total monopoly profit over five periods), these experiments would be testing hypotheses little different from CIS. An entry cost of $2 yields the following properties:

1. If a firm achieves the theoretical monopoly price and quantity, it covers sunk costs in one period.
2. There exists no competitive price $P_c \in [0.04, 0.15)$ at which a seller could recoup the sunk costs in one period.
3. There are prices supporting the competitive quantity at which the sunk costs could be recouped in 2, 3, 4, or 5 periods. The minimum of this set is $AVC(10) + 0.04$.
4. There are prices that cover AVC and support the competitive quantity but that do not allow the seller to cover sunk costs even if he or she sells all ten competitive units for 5 periods.

Because of the prominence in this literature of the idea of an "incumbent" seller as differentiated from an "entrant," such a distinction among sellers was operationalized in this design. By a toss of a coin before each experiment, one seller was allowed the choice of being a seller of type A or type B. (The loser of the coin toss became the type not chosen by the winner.) Seller A was incumbent in that he or she was required to

[2] Subjects knew an approximate maximum amount of time they would participate in the experiment, but there was no common knowledge of the end period.

begin the experiment by purchasing seller permits for periods 1–5 and 6–10. The incumbent was a protected monopolist in periods 1–5. Seller B could observe the market prices and his or her own cost technology in periods 1–5, and was allowed the option of contesting the market by purchasing permits in any period beginning with period 6. Seller A could choose to continue to contest the market by purchasing a new permit in period 11 or any period thereafter.

To guard against differences in behavior in this design (compared with CIS) due to the wealth effects of requiring participants to pay for entry permits, the up-front "working capital" endowment of sellers was increased by $10 (the maximum possible permit expenditure in a 25-period experiment) from $5 to $15.

In this design, we identified six types of behavior that we hypothesized might be observed after period 5 (when the market becomes contestable):

1. *Natural monopoly.* The market outcomes are at or near monopoly levels, with a single surviving firm satisfying all demand. This could occur through either of two routes: (a) The incumbent firm successfully threatens the entrant, by blocking entry or by driving the entrant out; or (b) the entrant commits sunk costs and then proceeds to drive out the incumbent by undercutting his prices.

2. *Tacit collusion.* Both firms enter the market and price consistently at noncompetitive levels.

3. *Contestable markets hypothesis.* Both firms enter the market and price within (or near) the competitive range.

4. *Limit pricing* (contestable markets hypothesis). Either the incumbent or the entrant exits the market, but the producing firm continues to price at the competitive level, thereby discouraging entry. We interpret this hypothesis as a subcase of the contestable markets hypothesis, since the emergence of a limit price is a direct consequence of the fact that the market is contested. It is, however, distinguishable from the contestable markets hypothesis in that it requires one of the firms to make an exit decision. Contrary to the traditional limit pricing literature, this behavioral mode need not be associated with a price policy consciously intended to limit entry but is a consequence of the market-contesting process.

5. *Unstable prices* (monopoly or contestable markets hypothesis). Either the incumbent or the entrant exits the market. The producing firm gains short-term positive profits by raising prices

toward the monopoly level. The increased prices present a profit opportunity that eventually attracts the other firm to enter. If prices subsequently decline, one firm may again exit, followed by an increase in price, thus leading to unstable or cyclical behavior. In a finite experimental market, the experiment might end near the monopoly or competitive outcome, and in this sense the unstable price hypothesis may contain either the monopoly or competitive outcomes as subcases.

6. *Market collapse.* Both firms exit the market and stay out. They are able, thereby, to retain the capital that would be extended to incur entry costs.

It may be helpful in understanding our methodological approach to the study of contestable markets to discuss (a) the state of our experimental knowledge before undertaking the sunk-cost experiments and (b) our research strategy contingent on the outcome of the initial series of 6 sunk-cost experiments. From the experiments reported by CIS, we knew that the contestable markets hypothesis was strongly supported with zero sunk cost ($K = 0$), and that the monopoly outcome was supported when there was only one firm whose market was protected from any possibility of being contested by a second firm ($K = \infty$). Consequently, we supposed that there must be (at least one) finite value for K in the interval $[0, \infty]$ at which we would observe a switchover from competitive to noncompetitive outcomes. In designing any program of experimental research it is important to consider alternative possible outcomes, to evaluate their implications, and to develop a contingent research strategy. In the present context, this means that attention focuses on the value of K, which theory tells us is of qualitative importance, but it does not tell us how to choose. Our research plan was to begin with $K = \$2$, a "reasonable" value having the properties enumerated earlier. We conjectured that the contestable market result *might be* relatively *fragile*, so that sunk costs of $K = \$2$ might yield a predominance of noncompetitive outcomes supporting the alternative hypotheses 1 and/or 2. In that event, our research plan would have called for additional experiments with $K < \$2$ to determine the value of K below which the contestable markets hypothesis was supported. Alternatively, we conjectured that the contestable market result *might be* relatively *robust* so that at $K = \$2$ we might continue to observe strongly convergent competitive outcomes supporting hypothesis 3. In that case our research plan would have called for additional experiments with $K > \$2$ to search for the boundary of contestability. A third alternative was that with $K = \$2$ we might observe mixed results, either with outcomes supporting hypothesis 5 or outcomes distributed across several other hypotheses. This last category of results would suggest that for sunk costs $K = \$2$ the discipline of contestability is diminished, but that its weakening is relatively "continuous" rather than being manifest as a discrete jump at some K in the interval $[0, \infty]$. In particular, if outcomes are distributed across several of the hypotheses, it suggests that when contestability is weakened, the scope for nonstructural variables to influence outcomes increases (as suggested by the earlier quotation from Schwartz and Reynolds, 1983). Thus, individual variations in expectations may no longer be swamped by the power of costless entry. Because our results were best described by this third alternative (see Section V), we decided not to expend additional resources to examine further the effect of K on this multifarious result (subject payoffs alone average in excess of \$150 per experiment). Instead, we addressed the internal question of whether our results for $K = \$2$ might be a result of strategic buyer behavior or the expectation of such by sellers (see Section IV). That is, given that $K = \$2$ has a treatment effect distinct from $K = 0$ and $K = \infty$, we asked whether this result might interact with a potentially important aspect of buyer market behavior.

III. The PLATO Posted-Offer Procedure

Most retail markets are organized under what has been called the "posted-offer" institution (Plott and Smith, 1978). As we define it in this institution, each seller independently posts a take-it-or-leave-it price at which deliveries will be made in quantities elected by each individual buyer subject to seller capacity limits. These posted prices may be changed or reviewed frequently, infrequently, regularly, or irregularly, but in any case a central characteristic of this mechanism is that the posted price is not subject to negotiation.

The experiments reported here used the posted-offer mechanism programmed for the PLATO computer system by Jonathan Ketcham (for a more detailed description see Ketcham et al., 1984). This program allows subject buyers and sellers, sitting separately at PLATO terminals, to trade for a maximum of 25 market "days" or pricing periods. The display screen for each subject shows his or her record sheet, which lists a maximum of 5 units that can be purchased (sold) in each period. For each unit, the buyer (seller) has a marginal valuation (cost) that represents the value (cost) to him or her of purchasing (selling) that unit. These controlled, strictly private, unit valuations (costs) induce individual, and aggregate market, theoretical supply and demand schedules (Smith, 1976a, 1982). That is, in an experiment, buyers (sellers) earn cash rewards equal to the difference between the marginal value (selling price) of a unit and its purchase price (marginal cost). Sales are "to order" in the sense that there are no penalties, there is no carry-over of inventories, associated with units not sold (or units not purchased). Consequently, the assigned marginal valuations and costs induce a well-defined flow of supply and demand conditions.

Each period begins with a request that sellers select a price offer by typing a price into the computer keyset. This offer is displayed privately on the seller's screen. The seller is then asked to select a corresponding quantity to be made available at that offer price. The maximum number of units a seller can offer corresponds to the number of the last unit whose cost is not greater than the offer price. The minimum number of units a seller can offer corresponds to the number of the first unit whose cost is not greater than the offer price. (The seller, however, is required to offer at least one unit; a seller cannot post a price for zero units.) This procedure permits individual induced marginal costs to be declining, constant, or increasing. If the seller faces declining marginal costs, as in the experiment reported later, these minimum and maximum quantity constraints prevent his or her choices from being such that a loss is guaranteed, but if price is below the first unit's marginal cost, a loss will be made on the first units sold, which must be more than offset by profits on later units if an overall profit is to be earned in the period.[3] Because it is costly in terms of time and effort for a seller to calculate the profit that any given offer may provide, especially with declining costs, PLATO always informs the seller of the potential profit (loss) if all offered units are sold. When a seller is satisfied with the selected price and quantity, he or she presses a touch-sensitive "offer box" displayed on the screen. This action irrevocably places that seller's offer into the market. Before touching the offer box, the seller may change the price or quantity as many times as desired. Each seller sees the prices posted by the other seller only after both have entered their offers.

The screen viewed by the buyer displays one "price box" for accepting units offered by each seller. After all sellers have entered their offers, each seller's price is posted in those buyer's acceptance boxes. PLATO then randomly orders the buyers in a buying sequence, and the first is informed that he or she may now purchase the good. A buyer, once selected, can purchase from any seller. To purchase a unit from a selected seller, the buyer presses the box corresponding to that seller, and then depresses a "confirm" key on the keyset. Repeating this sequence causes a second unit to be purchased, and so on. A buyer is allowed to purchase up to his buying capacity from any seller or sellers. However, a buyer

---

[3] Thus, in Figure 13.1 if a seller posts a price $P = \$0.45$, the minimum quantity that can be offered is 3 units and the maximum is 10 units. At this price, the seller earns a positive profit only if sales are at least 7 units.

cannot purchase a unit whose price is greater than the unit's marginal valuation and cannot buy from a seller who has sold all of the units offered. When a seller's last available unit is sold, the price appearing in the buyer's box for that seller is replaced with the message "out of stock" on the buyer's screen. After the first buyer has finished making purchases, the next buyer in random order may begin purchasing, and so on. The period ends when the last buyer completes this buying mode.

All participants in these experiments were "experienced" in the sense that all had previously participated in other experiments using the PLATO posted-offer trading institution, although they participated in different groups and with a different market design. Both with and without computer organization of markets, an occasional subject will display a gross misunderstanding of the rules or of the mechanics of the process (CIS, 1983; Isaac et al., 1985). We saw absolutely no evidence of any such problems in the experiments reported here.

There is no difference in physical surroundings or computer interaction depending upon whether a seller has purchased an entry permit. This was done to minimize any extraneous incentives to purchase or not to purchase a permit. A seller who chooses not to purchase an entry permit remains at his terminal and watches the progress of the market. Since this is a posted-offer market, sellers with and without permits are equally passive in computer terminal responsibilities once the market has opened to the buyers.

It is important to emphasize that buyers and sellers have only limited information. All unit values (costs) assigned to individual buyers (sellers) are strictly private, known only to the subject (and the experimenter). Each buyer sees all the sellers' price offers but not the quantities available at these prices. In the experiments reported later, sellers see the prices posted by each other (after both prices have been "locked in" and the trading period opens), but the PLATO computer program allows this information to be suppressed. Finally, buyers (sellers) know only their own purchases (sales) and profits.

IV. The Role of Buyers

We report the results of 12 experiments. In the first six experiments (70, 79, 82, 87, 96, and 97)[4] the role of the buyers is exactly as reported in CIS

---

[4] The contestable markets experiments reported in this article were not conducted sequentially but were interspersed with a variety of other posted-offer experiments conducted for other studies. In this report, we retain the original sequential numbering that we use for all posted-offer experiments. Thus, Experiment 70 was our 70th PLATO posted-offer experiment, but it was our first contestable market experiment. With this numbering we can readily access the data for any experiment in response to questions or requests from readers (see the last sentence in footnote 7).

(using the computer procedures reported in the previous experiments). These 6 experiments serve as the most direct test of the effect of sunk costs in comparison with the CIS experiments.

After completing these 6 experiments, we still had observed no experiments yielding the standard natural monopoly outcome. We asked ourselves, was it possible that this could be owing to strategic (non-fully-demand-revealing) behavior on the part of buyers? An implicit assumption of contestable market theory is that buyers reveal demand. An examination of the data shows that buyer withholding of demand occurred at a very low rate (1.24% of full revelation quantity). This is almost identical to the low level of the CIS contestable duopolies (1.16%) and much less than the CIS monopoly experiments (9.14%). It seems unlikely that such low rates of demand underrevelation could have any effect on seller behavior. However, two possibilities could mitigate this conjecture. (1) Low rates of demand underrevelation, if strategically timed (e.g., when prices are increased), might affect behavior disproportionately to their occurrence. (2) Seller behavior may be influenced by the *expectation* that buyers will withhold demand at the higher prices. Consequently, we conducted six additional experiments in which demand was fully revealed, and this was *known* to the sellers. In these six experiments (113–116, 118, and 119), the decisions of the buyers were programmed into the PLATO system, with the program automatically providing full demand revelation. That this computerized response would take place, and that the "buyers" would purchase "all that was profitable to them at the given prices" was explained to the sellers, so that it was not credible for sellers to harbor even the expectation that demand might be underrevealed.

V.   Results and Interpretation

Table 13.2 provides a classification of experimental price outcomes for the 4 monopoly and 6 contestable market experiments reported in CIS and the 12 sunk-cost experiments conducted for this chapter. The price behavior for each experiment is classified according to which of the six hypotheses (discussed in Section II) the observed behavior supports. Each experiment is also classified according to a price observation that is measured by the ruling (low) seller price in the reference period. This reference period is period 18 in the CIS experiments and period 23 in the sunk-cost experiments. Because the incumbent firm's market is uncontested in the first 5 periods of the sunk-cost experiments, period 23 is the 18th contestable market period and is, therefore, comparable to period 18 of the CIS experiments. Where appropriate, we distinguish

Table 13.2. *Classification of outcomes by hypothesis and treatment condition for market contestability (experiment number in parentheses)*

	Subject buyers make purchase decisions			Programmed buyers reveal demand, $K = \$2.00^b$
Hypothesis supported	$K = +\infty^a$ (CIS)	$K = 0^a$ (CIS)	$K = \$2.00^b$	
(1) Natural monopoly				
Strong $\hat{P} \geq P_m$	2 (36, 46)	0	0	0
Weak $\hat{P} \geq \dfrac{P_c^* + P_m}{2}$	4 (35, 36, 46)	0	0	0
(2) Tacit collusion				
Monopoly: $\hat{P} \geq \dfrac{P_c^* + P_m}{2}$	N.A.	0	0	0
Strong competitive (contestable markets hypothesis): $\hat{P} \leq P_c^*$	N.A.	0	0	1 (116)
Weak competitive (contestable markets hypothesis): $\hat{P} \leq \dfrac{P_c^* + P_m}{2}$	N.A.	0	0	2 (116, 119)
(3) Contestable markets hypothesis Strong $\hat{P} \leq P_c^*$	0	4 (45, 47, 51, 42)	2 (96, 97)	2 (113, 115)
Weak $\hat{P} \leq \dfrac{P_c^* + P_m}{2}$	0	6 (37, 45, 47, 48, 51, 52)	3 (70, 96, 97)	2 (113, 115)
(4) Limit pricing (contestable markets hypothesis)	N.A.	0	1 (82)	0
(5) Unstable prices				
monopoly: $\hat{P} \geq \dfrac{P_c^* + P_m}{2}$	N.A.	0	0	0
Strong competitive (contestable markets hypothesis): $\hat{P} \leq P_c^*$	N.A.	0	2 (79, 87)	1 (118)
Weak competitive (contestable markets hypothesis): $\hat{P} \leq \dfrac{P_c^* + P_m}{2}$	N.A.	0	2 (79, 87)	2 (114, 118)
(6) Market collapse	N.A.	0	0	0

[a] P = ruling price in period 18.
[b] P = ruling price in period 23 (the 18th period in which the market is contestable).

277

strong and weak forms for the reference period price prediction of each alternative hypothesis. Thus, according to the natural monopoly hypothesis, only one firm survives; the strong form of the hypothesis predicts a price closer to the monopoly than to the competitive price set, $\hat{P} \geq (P_c^* + P_m)/2$.[5] The tacit collusion hypothesis is also interpreted in terms of these strong and weak forms, except that both forms remain active in the market. Similarly, the strong form of the contestable markets hypothesis predicts prices in the competitive equilibrium set, $\hat{P} \in [0, P_c^*]$, whereas the weak form predicts price closer to the competitive than to the monopoly price set, $\hat{P} \leq (P_c^* + P_m)/2$. Note that these different interpretations of the theoretical hypotheses are not mutually exclusive; outcomes satisfying the strong form of the contestable markets hypothesis must also satisfy the weak form, but not vice versa. The unstable price hypothesis refers to the pattern of price behavior over the entire experiment, although the reference period outcomes yield observations that are either weakly or strongly competitive and, therefore, support the contestable markets hypothesis. In effect, the only difference between the outcomes we observed under hypotheses 3 and 5 is that the former reflected a strong (essentially monotone) convergence to the competitive level.

Table 13.3 summarizes the results of binomial tests of the contestable markets hypothesis from all 22 experiments. In these tests, the null hypothesis corresponds to a naive random model of behavior in which prices have a uniform distribution over the range from the lowest competitive price to the highest monopoly price (0 to $1.40). Thus, the strong version of the contestable markets hypothesis postulates that $0 \leq \hat{P} \leq P_c^* = \$0.15$, which occurs with probability $\theta_0 = 0.15/1.40 = 0.107$ (i.e., the "hit" region of the contestable markets hypothesis is the subinterval $[0, 0.15]$ contained in the feasible price range $[0, 1.40]$). The weak version of the contestable market hypothesis predicts that $0 \leq \hat{P} \leq (P_c^* + P_m)/2 = \$0.65$, which occurs with probability $\theta_0 = 0.65/1.40 = 0.464$ under the null hypothesis. Under each version of the contestable markets hypothesis Table 13.3 reports tests of the null hypothesis that $\theta = \theta_0$ (all feasible prices up to the monopoly price are equally likely), against the contestable markets hypothesis that $\theta > \theta_0$ (prices in the contestable markets hypothesis range are more likely than predicted by the naive model), where θ is the binomial probability that any one observation will support the contestable markets hypothesis.

From Table 13.3, it is seen that neither version of the contestable

---

[5] P_c^* is the highest price in the range of competitive equilibrium prices. P_m is the lower of the two monopoly prices.

Table 13.3. *Binomial tests of the contestable markets hypothesis by structural treatment condition*

Form of hypothesis	Uncontested market; infinite entry cost			Contested market; entry cost = 0			Contest market; entry cost = $2		
	x	n	α	x	n	α	x	n	α
Strong contestable markets hypothesis $\hat{P} \le P_c^*$ $\theta_0 = 0.107$	0	4	1.00	4	6	.0016	6	12	.0008
Weak contestable markets hypothesis $\hat{P} < \dfrac{P_c^* + P_m}{2}$ $\theta_0 = 0.464$	0	4	1.00	6	6	.01	12	12	.0001

θ_0 = null binomial probability from assumption that (normalized) prices are uniformly distributed between 0 and $1.40. The null hypothesis is that $\theta = \theta_0$ against the contested markets hypothesis alternative that $\theta > \theta_0$.
$\hat{P}$ = ruling price in period 23.
P_c^* = highest competitive price ($0.15).
P_m = lowest monopoly price ($1.15).
x = number of experiments supporting given version of the contestable markets hypothesis.
n = total number of experiments.
α = binomial probability of x or more experiments supporting the contestable markets hypothesis if true probability = θ.

markets hypothesis is supported when a single firm is protected from any possibility that a competitor will enter. Hence, if experiments with zero or finite positive entry costs provide support for the contestable markets hypothesis, this result will be attributable to the disciplinary function of free entry. Table 13.3 also shows that there is significant support for rejecting the null hypothesis when the market is contested by two firms. The "weak" version of the contestable markets hypothesis is supported by all 18 contested market experiments whether entry costs are zero or $2. The fact that the weak version of the contestable markets hypothesis receives somewhat stronger support than the strong version in the 18 contested experiments shows that structure alone (economies of scale, entry cost level, and two potential suppliers) is not sufficient to yield precisely the competitive outcome. Dynamic or expectational elements have measurable effects in raising prices. The resulting increase in prices is small, however, and the contestable market hypothesis is essentially correct in comparison with the "natural monopoly" theory for the entry conditions that have been studied.[6]

Based upon the classification of experimental outcomes in Table 13.2, we offer the following qualitative observations.

Observation 1. The presence of sunk costs, in an amount that permits a positive net profit in the top of the competitive equilibrium price range, does not prevent entry. In all 12 new experiments, the B seller entered the market in period 6. In the 13 cases in which a seller exited, and had an opportunity to reenter, the seller did reenter in every case.

Observation 2. There is evidence that sunk costs cause some weakening of the competitive discipline of contestability. In most cases this weakening appears to be temporary. Thus, in 6 of our 12 experiments there were price "run-ups," corresponding to temporary episodes of tacit collusion or the exiting of a firm, which were *not* observed in the CIS experiments with zero entry cost. This is illustrated in Figures 13.2(b, d) by the price charts for Experiments 79 and 119.[7]

---

[6] Dan Alger of the Federal Trade Commission reviewed an earlier draft of this chapter and suggested a Bayesian report based on the data of Table 13.3. Let θ have a uniform prior distribution (a member of the class of beta distributions). Because the beta and binomial likelihood distributions are natural conjugates, the posterior distribution of v is beta. Using our data, Alger calculates the posterior probability $\Pr(\theta > 0.5)$ for each treatment and each version of the contestable markets hypothesis as follows:

Hypothesis	$k = +\infty$	$k = 0$	$k = \$2$
Strong CMH	0.031	0.77	0.50
Weak CMH	0.031	0.992	0.999

This report is more conservative than our tests in Table 13.3 for the strong version of the contestable markets hypothesis, because we (implicitly) assumed that support for the contestable markets hypothesis is a priori unlikely (all feasible prices equally likely), which corresponds to using a nondiffuse beta prior in a Bayesian report.

[7] Each of the charts in Figure 13.2 graphs prices and total quantity exchanged over the trading periods of the experiment. Trading period quantities sold are identified by seller category: A (for the original incumbent) or B (for the original potential entrant). Dark circles on the vertical price scale indicate offer price of the nontrading seller during each period. Recall that the potential for contesting begins only in period 6 and that the market is not necessarily contested in later periods. We have indicated by shading under the price bar those periods in which both firms were owners of active entry permits. Data similar to those in Figure 13.2 are available for all 18 reported experiments upon direct request to the authors.

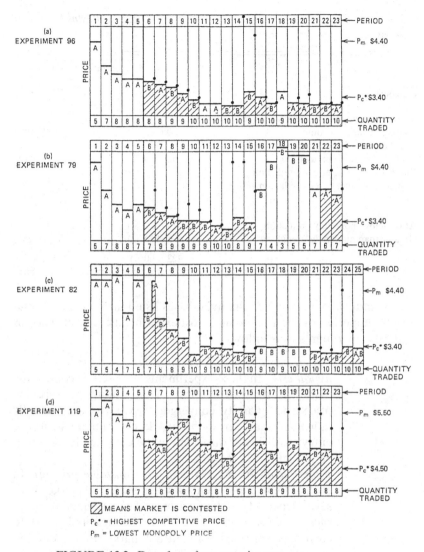

FIGURE 13.2. Data from four experiments.

Observation 3. There is a tendency for observed quantities to be closer to the competitive prediction than is the case for measures of market efficiency. This is shown in the tabulations in Table 13.4. This difference is due to the efficiency loss from duplication of the sunk costs when two firms purchase permits. This duplication is part of the cost of achieving a competitive discipline when there are positive entry costs.

Table 13.4. *Quantity and efficiency outcomes for 222 contestable periods*

Outcome	Performance criteria	
	Quantity	Efficiency
Closer to monopoly prediction than to competitive prediction	69 (31.1%)	124 (55.9%)
Equal distance between the monopoly and competitive predictions	52 (23.4%)	4 (1.8%)
Closer to the competitive prediction than to the monopoly prediction	101 (45.5%)	94 (42.3%)
Total	222 (100%)	222 (100%)
At or below monopoly prediction	27 (12.2%)	43 (19.4%)
Greater than monopoly prediction	195 (87.8%)	179 (80.6%)
Total	222 (100%)	222 (100%)

Observation 4. No one of the six hypotheses listed in Table 13.2 is uniformly supported by the 12 new sunk-cost experiments. A brief synopsis of these experiments is as follows:

> *Experiments 70, 96, 97, 113, and 115 (contestable markets hypothesis).* In these experiments, both sellers contest the market in the vast majority of the trading periods. The price and quantity convergence patterns are virtually indistinguishable from the six CIS experiments with zero entry cost. This is illustrated in the chart for Experiment 96 in Figure 13.2(a).
>
> *Experiments 79, 87, 114, and 118 (unstable pricing).* In each of these experiments, a seller exited the market after several periods of low prices and the remaining seller raised the price close to or above the monopoly level. In each case, the seller who left the market then reentered and the price declined. This pattern is illustrated by Experiment 79 in Figure 13.2(b).
>
> *Experiment 82 (limit pricing).* As in Experiments 79, 87, and 114, there was a sequence of contested periods with prices at or near the competitive range. Seller A exited for 5 periods, yet the incumbent *never* raised price outside of the competitive range (although prices rose to the top position of this range and seller B was earning positive

profits). This appears to be "limit pricing" and is illustrated in Figure 13.2(c); it represents the competitive case with one firm.

Experiments 116 and 119 (tacit collusion). In these experiments, both sellers contested the market in all periods after the fifth. Yet the prices do not show the tendency to decline monotonically toward the competitive range as exhibited in the CIS experiments. In each case, the sellers are able to coordinate one or more increases in prices, but the effort is temporary and the price coordination is unstable. In the end, prices are closer to the competitive than to the monopoly price. [See Figure 13.2(d).] This behavior is consistent with an attempt to obtain "tacit collusion," although these cases do not confirm the hypothesis that such collusion will be a success. Because this behavior was not observed by CIS with zero entry cost, it is plausible to conjecture that entry costs may have some "commitment" effect that supports temporary episodes of tacit cooperation.

Observation 5. Certain hypotheses found no observational support. There was never any collapse of the market. Nor was there any indication that the combination of scale economies and intermediate-level sunk costs ever facilitated a permanently effective, monopoly-sustaining barrier to entry. Of 222 potentially contested periods, the observed market price was closer to the competitive range than to the theoretical monopoly price in 144 (64.86%) periods (see Table 13.4).

Observation 6. The failure to observe a sustained natural monopoly outcome appears not to be a result of strategic behavior by the five buyers. This outcome continued to be absent when we switched to the second series of (6) experiments in which sellers knew that buyer responses were programmed to yield passive, simple maximizing behavior. We did, however, observe an increase in the number of partially successful attempts to achieve a "tacit cartel" (two in the second series, none in the first). This suggests a qualitative effect in the form of reduced competition when human buyer subjects are replaced by programmed simple maximizing responses. A comparison of mean price difference in periods 18–23 in the two series of experiments reveals that the mean price was 9 cents lower for the experiments with human buyer subjects. But this price difference was not significant ($t = 1.072$ based on the assumption that the period-by-period prices are independent, and $t = 0.506$ treating each experiment as an independent observation). Consequently, in Table

13.3 the two series of experiments are pooled for the binomial test. This small, statistically insignificant difference might be the result of one or more of the following: (i) random (subject) sampling errors; (ii) the effect of the 1.24% underrevelation of demand; and (iii) seller anticipation of the possibility of buyer withholding of demand, even if it only rarely occurs.

VI.   Conclusions

On the basis of the ruling price in the 18th period in which the market is contested, the effect of an entry cost is to weaken support for the strong form of the contestable markets hypothesis. Thus, with entry cost $K(0) = 0$, CIS reported that 4 of 6 experiments supported the strong contestable markets hypothesis. With $K(5) = \$2$, we found that 6 of 12 experiments supported the strong contestable markets hypothesis. Further, according to this measure, entry cost had no effect on support for the weak form of the contestable markets hypothesis: CIS found that 6 of 6 experiments supported the weak contestable markets hypothesis with zero entry cost, and we found that 12 of 12 experiments supported the weak contestable markets hypothesis when $K(5) = \$2$. A comparison based on ruling prices in any single reference period, however, fails to capture the dynamics of the contesting process, which is perhaps the most striking aspect of the observations generated in the new series of experiments. In the CIS experiments with zero entry cost, the price convergence paths were essentially monotone in all six cases, although individual experiments differed with respect to their speeds of convergence to the competitive range. In the 12 experiments reported in this chapter, we found that entry cost has a pronounced effect on market performance over time, with only 5 experiments replicating the strong convergence property of the CIS experiments. The remaining 7 experiments, although in the end supporting the weak form of the contestable markets hypothesis, exhibited modes of behavior supporting the unstable price hypothesis, the limit price hypothesis, and transient episodes of the tacit collusion hypothesis. We think it is significant that in 12 "trials" not a single outcome supported the natural monopoly, tacit collusion (except in transient form), or market collapse hypotheses. Thus, the disciplining power of market contestability remains impressive, even where entry cost weakens that power enough to produce a wide diversity of dynamic patterns of interaction over time.

The results of these experiments may also have something to say about the way we think about the development and testing of hypotheses in industrial organization behavior. To those who expected that we would necessarily end up with a single correct industrial organization "story," these results might be somewhat surprising. Yet, all the various predictions of seller behavior are based upon different behavioral assumptions that are specific to the characteristics of the economic decision makers. Sometimes (as in the case of zero entry cost) the results are rather robust with respect to the risk preference conjectural variations, expectations, and other characteristics of the individuals. But there is no reason to believe that this must be the case in different market structures.

Readers familiar with traditional industrial organization research may notice a similarity in this discussion to the distinction between "structure" and "conduct" in determining market performance. If market "structure" means the observable, environmental variables such as numbers of buyers and sellers, presence or absence of entry costs, and scale economies, then these results suggest an interesting interpretation. Some aspects of market structure "matter," as is demonstrated by the change in market dynamics with the addition of entry costs. Also, some forms of structure may not matter (e.g., economies of scale). But structure, even where it matters, is not necessarily deterministic, thereby suggesting problems for those who would wish industrial organization research to restrict consideration to the reduced-form links between structure and performance which bypass issues such as expectations formation. Although we cannot directly observe such concepts as expectations or conjectural variations, we can see variation in experimental outcomes among different contesting duopolists within a fixed structure (positive entry costs, increasing returns) and conclude that there are residual effects owing to agent characteristics. The intellectual challenge for industrial organization is to articulate falsifiable interpretations of such behavioral concepts as "expectations," which allow direct tests of the hypothesis that such concepts account for the variability of outcomes within a given structure.

CHAPTER 14

The Boundaries of Competitive Price Theory: Convergence, Expectations, and Transaction Costs

Vernon L. Smith and Arlington W. Williams

"Boundary experiments are explicitly associated with some set of laws and consist of fact-finding inquiries designed to fix the range and application of the laws, particularly with regard to extreme conditions" (Kaplan, 1964, p. 150). In the laboratory experiments reported here, we probed three distinct boundaries of the application of the law of supply and demand in markets organized as double auctions. This "law" of competitive market behavior predicts that prices will occur at a level where the quantity supplied by sellers (positively related to price) is equal to the quantity demanded by buyers (negatively related to price). Any price where quantity demanded equals quantity supplied is referred to as a competitive equilibrium (CE) price; the corresponding exchange volume is referred to as the CE quantity. The specific design parameters utilized in our experimental markets were chosen to address the following research questions.

1. In trading between b buyers and s sellers, how small must s be to invalidate the application of the law of supply and demand as a predictor of market outcomes?
2. In a market where the law of supply and demand predicts that all gains from exchange will be earned by only one side of the market (either buyers or sellers), will actual contract prices converge to the price predicted by the law of supply and demand? What minimal compensation will subjects on the other (zero profit) side of the market need to induce them to participate in trade?
3. In a market where any feasible price is also a CE price (generated by an unorthodox box-shaped supply and demand configuration where the quantity demanded equals the quantity supplied at all prices between the upper and lower bounds of the box), will contract prices tend to stabilize on one of these equilibria? If not, will contract prices attain a stable distribution, drift in an orderly manner, or fluctuate erratically?

286

I.   Experimental Procedures

The basic contracting institution utilized in all of the markets reported below is the PLATO computerized double-auction mechanism described in detail by Williams (1980) and Smith and Williams (1983). This exchange procedure is referred to as a "double" auction because both buyers and sellers have the ability to enter price quotes into the market. Market participants enter price quotes (bids to buy or offers to sell) for one commodity unit by typing in a number on their keyset and then touching a box-shaped area on their display screen. Any buyer (seller) is free to accept a seller's (buyer's) price quote by touching a box labeled "ACCEPT." A binding contract is formed if the acceptor touches another box labeled "CONFIRM" within 5 seconds. After a contract is confirmed, the transaction is recorded in both the buyer's and seller's private record sheets. All bids, offers, and subsequent contracts are public information (i.e., appear on all subjects' display screens).

The technique of "induced valuation" is utilized to define a supply and demand structure in experimental markets. (For more information on induced valuation techniques, see Smith, 1976a, 1982, or Plott, 1982a, 1986.) For each unit traded, the buyer earns the difference between the unit's "resale value" (assigned by the experimenter) and the contract price; the seller earns the difference between the contract price and the unit's "production cost" (assigned by the experimenter). Resale values thus represent the maximum a buyer is willing to pay for one commodity unit, whereas production costs represent the minimum a seller is willing to accept for one unit of the commodity. In many of the experiments reported here, a small ($0.05 or $0.10) "commission" was paid per trade to induce the exchange of marginal (zero profit) units. Commissions are intended to compensate subjects for any minimal transaction costs (physical and mental effort) associated with executing a trade and thus cannot be used to cover losses (i.e., buyers trading slightly above resale value or sellers trading slightly below production cost). In fact, the computer does not allow buyers (sellers) to enter or accept price quotes above (below) a unit's resale value (production cost) without first reading a loss warning message and bypassing it. Assigned values and costs were strictly private information in the sense that they were revealed only to the individual buyer or seller.

Ordering all buyers' assigned resale values from high to low generates the market "induced demand array"; ordering all sellers' assigned production costs from low to high generates the market "induced supply array." The intersection of these step-functions defines a CE price and quantity. For example, looking ahead to the left side of Figure 14.1, the

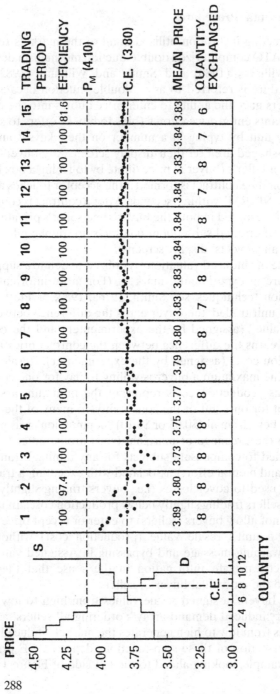

FIGURE 14.1. Duopoly experiment D1.

intersection of the supply and demand arrays occurs at \$3.80 with a quantity exchanged of 8 units (assuming that the marginal unit trades).

Each market experiment reported here occurred over a sequence of trading periods, with each trading period lasting 360 (or, in some experiments, 300) seconds. Subjects were drawn from the undergraduate and graduate student populations at the University of Arizona and Indiana University. Most of the experiments used "experienced" subjects in the sense that each had participated in at least one previous PLATO double auction using entirely different market parameters. Upon arriving at the PLATO lab, each participant was paid \$3 (in a few early experiments \$2) for keeping the appointment and then randomly assigned to a computer terminal. The double-auction program then randomly assigned each terminal to a buyer or seller condition, presented instructional material, and executed the actual experiment storing the data for later recall and analysis. At the end of the experiment, subjects were paid privately in cash the amount of their individual earnings in the experiment.

II.   Experimental Results: Duopoly and Monopoly

A substantial body of evidence suggests that markets organized under double-auction trading rules converge "rapidly" to a CE price when there are as few as four sellers and four buyers. Suppose that we maintain the number of buyers at some level greater than 4 but reduce the number of sellers to 2 (duopoly) or even 1 (monopoly). For what number of sellers will the CE outcome fail to be approached?

Table 14.1 lists some of the basic design features for four duopoly and five monopoly experiments. The left sides of Figures 14.1–14.9 show the induced valuation (D) and cost (S) arrays and the resulting CE price and quantity for these nine experiments. The monopolist's profit-maximizing price is indicated by a dashed line and labeled P_M on the right side of each figure. (P_M corresponds to the price that maximizes the sum of the two sellers' profits in the duopoly experiments.) Figures 14.5–14.9, corresponding to the five monopoly experiments, also display the marginal revenue (MR) array used to determine P_M. To profit maximize, the monopolist must trade all Q_M units for which the additional sales revenue (MR) exceeds the additional production cost (i.e., marginal profit is positive) and charge a price equal to the Q_Mth step on the demand array. It is important to note that, in order to calculate this single-price monopoly optimum, the seller must somehow identify the market demand curve and then have the analytical sophistication to know how to use this information to identify P_M. This is an unlikely scenario because the monopolist was not explicitly given the market

Table 14.1. *Design parameters for duopoly (D) and monopoly (M) experiments*

Experiment	No. of buyers	Commission per trade	Buyers' profit per period at CE	Sellers' profit per period at CE	Sellers' profit per period at P_M
D1	5	$0.05	$2.80	$1.00 ($0.50 per seller)	$2.40 ($1.20 per seller)
D2x	6	$0	$2.80	$1.90 ($0.95 per seller)	$3.30 ($1.65 per seller)
D3x, D4x	10	$0.10	$5.60	$2.20 ($1.10 per seller)	$4.90 ($2.45 per seller)
M1x, M2x, M3x, M4xs, M5x	5	$0.10	$2.80	$1.10	$2.45

Notes: x experiment suffix denotes all experienced subjects; xs experiment suffix denotes experienced seller only; profits are calculated exclusive of any trading commissions; CE profits for D2x are calculated at the midpoint of the CE range.

demand array induced on buyers. Of more realistic interest is whether a double-auction monopolist is able, through some search process over time, to extract profits that are at, or "near," the level that occurs when Q_M units are sold at a fixed price of P_M.

To the right of the induced S and D arrays in the figures is a chart of contract prices in their sequential order of occurrence in each successive trading period. Also shown for each period are three descriptive statistics summarizing market performance: the mean contract price, quantity exchanged, and efficiency. Efficiency is the percentage of the theoretical gains from exchange (at a CE) that are actually earned by subjects through trading in the experiment. Efficiency is 100% only when all units with resale values greater than the CE price and all units with production costs less than the CE price are exchanged (as is predicted by the law of supply and demand).

In duopoly experiment D1 using inexperienced subjects (five buyers, two sellers) shown in Figure 14.1, the mean price fluctuates within 4 cents of the CE price from periods 5 through 15. At no time (after the first two) are contract prices near the monopoly optimum price of $4.10. Efficiency is 100% in all but two periods. In duopoly experiment D2x using experienced subjects (six buyers, two sellers) shown in Figure 14.2, price fluctuates within 6 cents of the midpoint of the range of CE prices (3.20–3.30) in all but the first two periods. Efficiency is greater than 95% in all but four trading periods. Note that the quantity exchanged and

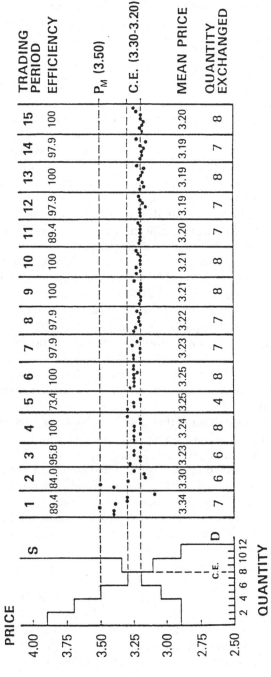

FIGURE 14.2. Duopoly experiment D2x.

291

efficiency is slightly lower in D2x (106 units in 15 periods) than in D1 (114 units in 15 periods). We conjecture that the reduced trading volume in D2x is due to the absence of the 5 cent commission payment that applied in experiment D1.

In duopoly experiments D3x and D4x we increased the number of buyers to 10 and increased the CE volume to 16 units. All 24 subjects in these two experiments were experienced and a $0.10 commission was paid to both the buyer and seller for each unit traded. The 2 sellers in D3x (Figure 14.3) are able to hold prices above the CE in the first four trading periods. In periods 5–13, prices appear to have stabilized at or slightly below the CE. With the exception of the first period, efficiency is 97% or greater on a trading volume of 15 or 16 units per period. The sellers in experiment D4x (Figure 14.4) are somewhat more successful in holding prices above the CE, but after seven trading periods the mean price falls within 5 cents of the CE. Efficiency is 97% or greater in periods 2–12 on a volume between 13 and 16 units per period.

The results of our duopoly experiments suggest that the convergence of market prices to a CE predicted by the law of supply and demand is not qualified when the number of sellers is reduced to only two of equal (or approximately equal) circumstances. In these four experiments, contract prices are not *exactly* equal to the CE prediction, but they are far closer to the CE than to the joint-profit-maximizing (monopoly) prediction. We hasten to add that the results of only four experiments are hardly sufficient to establish an empirical law of behavior; more duopoly experiments using different subject groups and market parameters would be required.

Having tentatively established that double-auction markets with only two sellers continue to exhibit convergence to the CE, we now focus on the "ultimate numbers boundary" by running experiments with only one seller. Figures 14.5–14.9 display the results of five monopoly experiments each with 5 buyers competing against the single seller. With the exception of experiment M4xs, all the monopoly experiments used subjects with prior experience. In M4xs, the seller was experienced, but the buyers were inexperienced. The sellers in these experiments were deliberately chosen on the criteria of (1) experience in several previous experiments and (2) an exhibited pattern of "toughness" in pursuing their self-interest.

The seller in experiment M1x (Figure 14.5) performed well as a monopolist in the first trading period. Her first four contracts were only 5 cents below the monopoly profit maximizing price (P_M) of $4.10. She then sold at successively lower prices inducing lower valuation buyers to trade. Period 1 efficiency was 100% with a CE trading volume of eight

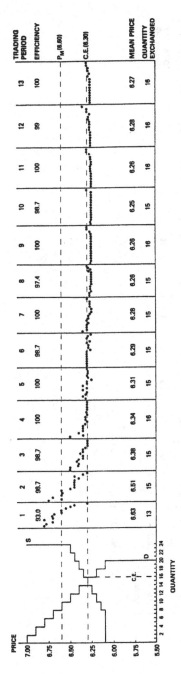

FIGURE 14.3. Duopoly experiment D3x.

293

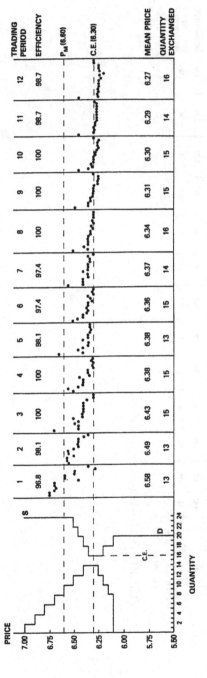

FIGURE 14.4. Duopoly experiment D4x.

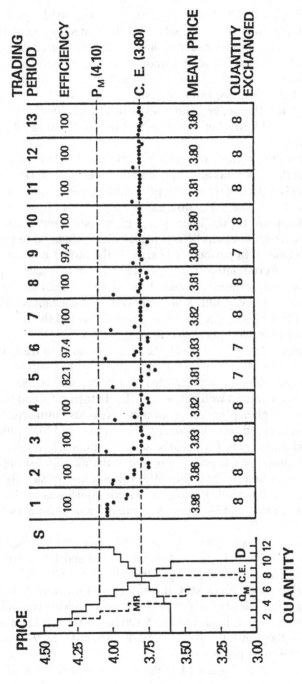

FIGURE 14.5. Monopoly experiment M1x.

units. The seller's ability to "price discriminate" generated a pure redistribution of CE profits to her benefit. However, in subsequent trading periods, she was unable to effect a similar pattern of trades. The discriminative price cutting in the first trading period "spoiled the market" in the sense that, in period 2, buyers held out for contracts closer to the lower prices they saw in the last four contracts in period 1. It was downhill thereafter for the seller, who traded at essentially the CE from periods 9 through 13. Market efficiency was nearly 100% in all periods except the fifth.

A tougher selling pattern was seen in experiment M2x (Figure 14.6). In this market the seller was able to maintain prices close to (P_M) for the first five periods, with discriminative price cutting resulting in high efficiency in periods 3, 5, and 6. The discriminative price cutting again results in buyers holding out for the lower prices in periods 7 and 8. The seller refused to concede, the result being only 2 units exchanged in period 7 and 1 unit exchanged in period 8. In period 9, the buyers conceded, and the result was a discriminative, 100% efficient pattern of trades. In period 10, the buyers again refused to trade at the higher prices, and the seller refused to concede, the result being only one unit exchanged. For the remaining periods 11–15, efficiency was above 88%, and the mean price remained more than 15 cents above the CE price.

In experiment M3x (Figure 14.7), the seller was able to trade 6 units at prices generally well above the CE in periods 1–5. In period 6, buyers initially held back demand waiting for lower prices, and the seller conceded with a first contract well below the CE. He then returned to offering units in the higher price range of most previous contracts; buyers underrevealed demand resulting in only three trades and 51% efficiency for the period. In periods 7 and 8, the seller "softened," and prices fell to, and then below, the CE price. In period 9, the monopolist appeared to change strategy, holding firm with offer prices above or slightly below P_M, until late in the period. Trading in periods 10–15 was in the range between the CE price and P_M with the mean price in periods 14 and 15 falling toward the CE.

In experiment M4xs (Figure 14.8) period 1 prices started well above P_M, and then fell to the CE on a volume of 7 units and 100% efficiency. In periods 2–9, prices generally ranged from P_M to the CE with a downward intraperiod trend. As in M1x, the monopolist was unable to maintain this discriminative pricing pattern. The mean price eventually fell from $0.13 above the CE in period 6 to $0.06 below the CE in period 12. Efficiency was 100% in all but two periods (when it was 97.4%) on a volume of 7 or 8 units per period.

In experiment M5x (Figure 14.9) the seller was able to hold prices

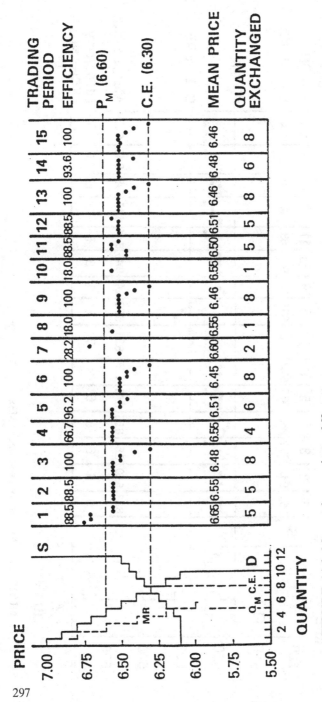

FIGURE 14.6. Monopoly experiment M2x.

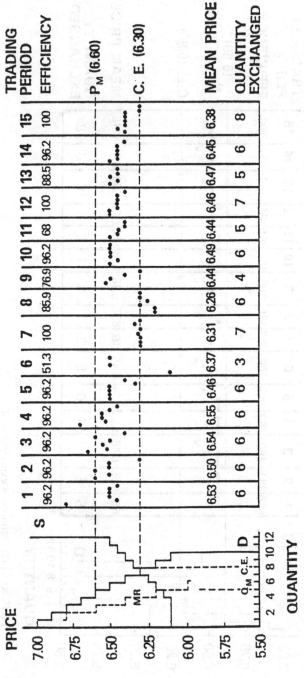

FIGURE 14.7. Monopoly experiment M3x.

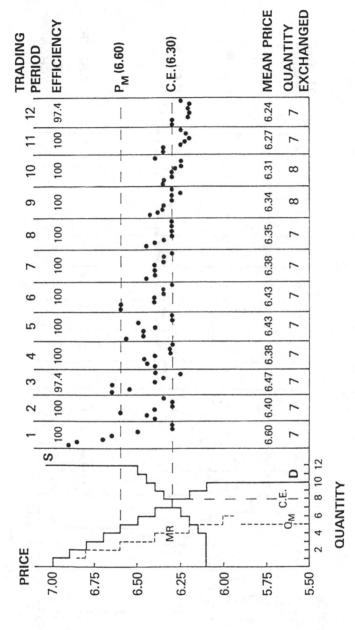

FIGURE 14.8. Monopoly experiment M4xs (experienced seller, inexperienced buyers).

299

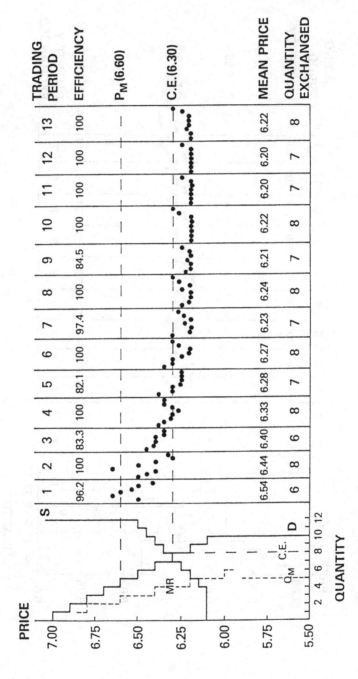

FIGURE 14.9. Monopoly experiment M5x.

Table 14.2. *Index of monopoly effectiveness for duopoly and monopoly*

Trading period	Duopoly experiments				Monopoly experiments				
	D1	D2x	D3x	D4x	M1x	M2x	M3x	M4xs	M5x
1	0.49	0.41	1.46	1.32	1.04	1.19	1.00	1.56	1.01
2	−0.03	0.01	1.13	0.90	0.38	0.81	0.86	0.52	0.84
3	−0.43	−0.16	0.42	0.71	0.19	1.11	1.01	0.86	0.39
4	−0.29	−0.07	0.22	0.45	0.10	0.52	1.06	0.42	0.16
5	−0.17	−0.46	0.03	0.39	0.04	0.93	0.65	0.69	−0.08
6	−0.08	0	−0.06	0.31	0.17	0.89	−0.22	0.67	−0.16
7	0.02	−0.15	−0.09	0.38	0.15	−0.07	0.03	0.41	−0.35
8	0.17	−0.19	−0.21	0.24	0.07	−0.48	−0.22	0.25	−0.37
9	0.15	−0.24	−0.24	0.06	−0.01	0.93	0.19	0.21	−0.44
10	0.22	−0.22	−0.26	0	−0.01	−0.48	0.81	0.07	−0.48
11	0.23	−0.27	−0.23	−0.04	0.04	0.63	0.40	−0.18	−0.50
12	0.20	−0.32	−0.16	−0.20	0.03	0.70	0.81	−0.31	−0.49
13	0.16	−0.31	−0.18		−0.01	0.93	0.52		−0.44
14	0.18	−0.32				0.78	0.63		
15	0.07	−0.26				0.92	0.48		
Mean	0.06	−0.017	0.14	0.38	0.017	0.62	0.53	0.43	−0.07

above the CE in only the first four periods. The mean price in this market fell from $0.24 above the CE in period 1 to $0.08–0.10 below the CE in periods 9–13. Efficiency was 96% or greater in 10 of 13 periods. Thus, in 3 of the 5 monopoly experiments, prices stabilized at, or just below, the CE.

The results of these computerized double-auction monopoly experiments are similar to the results of three oral double auctions reported by Smith (1981). Some, but not all, monopoly sellers succeed in lifting prices above the CE price. The negotiation of prices much above the CE is accompanied by frequent underrevelation of demand by buyers and considerable loss in efficiency.

Table 14.2 summarizes seller performance using the following index of monopoly effectiveness (first introduced in the paper reprinted as Chapter 10, this volume) for the monopoly and duopoly experiments reported earlier:

$$M = (\pi - \pi_c) / (\pi_m - \pi_c)$$

where π is realized seller profit (excluding any commissions) in some period or periods; π_c and π_m are, respectively, the seller profit at the CE and the monopoly optimum (P_M, Q_M). Note that $M = 0$ if seller profit is exactly equal to the CE prediction; $M > 0$ (<0) if seller profit is above (below) the CE prediction; $M = 1$ if the single-price monopoly optimum profit is obtained; and $M > 1$ if some discriminating monopoly profit is obtained.

None of the duopolists or monopolists are generally successful at obtaining full monopoly profits (although the seller in M3x is more than 75% effective in the final three periods). Based on these results, we conclude that the CE model appears to provide a satisfactory prediction of actual market outcomes with as few as two sellers (and four or more buyers) trading under double-auction institutional rules. When the number of sellers is reduced to one, the predictive ability of the CE begins to break down with some monopolists being able to hold prices above the CE. However, under double-auction rules, monopolists are generally unable to hold prices near P_M and extract full single-price monopoly optimum profits.

It is important to realize that these results should not be assumed to be robust with respect to alternative exchange institutions or information conditions. For example, a move to "take-it-or-leave-it" posted-offer pricing, explicit revelation of the demand array to sellers, or allowing sellers to communicate (form a conspiratorial cartel) could all significantly enhance the ability of duopolists and monopolists to extract monopoly profits. Smith (1981) and Isaac et al. (1984) have examined posted-offer monopoly experiments and both posted-offer and double-auction seller conspiracy experiments, respectively. These studies tend to confirm that both posted-offer exchange rules and seller communication lead to more frequent breakdowns of the CE model. Also see Plott (1986) for a more general discussion of the posted-offer pricing institution.

III.   Experimental Results: The "Swastika Design"

An alternative boundary of the CE convergence property of double auctions is associated with inducing market supply and demand arrays that are so bizarre, if not pathological, that one might easily conjecture that the CE would be a poor predictor of market outcomes. One such case, which we call the "swastika design," is illustrated on the left of Figure 14.10. This design is described by the following general market demand (D) and supply (S) conditions:

$$D = \bar{D} \quad \text{if } P \leq P_d \quad D = 0 \quad \text{if } P > P_d \tag{1}$$

$$S = \bar{S} \quad \text{if } P \geq P_s \quad S = 0 \quad \text{if } P < P_s \tag{2}$$

where $\bar{D}$, $\bar{S}$, P_d, and P_s are positive constants. That is, a total of D units with an induced value of P_d are allocated across buyers, and a total of S units with an induced cost of P_s are allocated across sellers. For trade to occur, we must have the condition that $P_d > P_s$. For $\bar{D} \neq \bar{S}$, there is no well-defined market-clearing CE price (where the quantity supplied equals the quantity demanded) because the quantities supplied and demanded are unequal constants rather than increasing and decreasing functions of price as is traditionally assumed. Competitive price theory, however, still predicts that the market equilibrium is where the supply and demand arrays intersect. Thus, for $\bar{D} > \bar{S}$, we have a CE price of P_d and a CE volume of $\bar{S}$ with excess demand of $(\bar{D} - \bar{S})$ at all feasible prices. In this case, because the buyers' induced value (P_d) is also the CE price prediction, the law of supply and demand predicts that all gains from exchange will go to the sellers. For $\bar{S} > \bar{D}$, we have a CE price of P_s and a CE volume of $\bar{D}$ with excess supply of $(\bar{S} - \bar{D})$ at all feasible prices. In this case, all gains from exchange at the CE will go to buyers. Clearly, such markets push the CE model to an "earnings inequity" boundary.

The swastika experiments reported here were implemented using four buyers, four sellers, and two basic $\bar{D}$ and $\bar{S}$ conditions each having $P_d - P_s = \$1.10$. In the first condition (A), we had $D_A = 11$ and $S_A = 16$ generating a CE with 11 units traded at a price of P_s. In the second condition (B), we had $D_B = 16$ and $S_B = 11$ generating a CE with 11 units traded at a price of P_d. As in the previously reported monopoly and duopoly experiments, all value and cost assignments were strictly private information, and no communication was allowed between subjects. Units were distributed as evenly as possible among the buyers and sellers. For example, when $D = 16$, each of the four buyers had 4 units potentially traded; when $D = 11$, three buyers had 3 units potentially traded and one buyer had only 2 units.

The left side of Figure 14.10 illustrates both conditions A and B for the case where $P_d = \$5.50$ and $P_s = \$4.40$. Condition A (B) results in the full $12.10 exchange "surplus" per period going to the buyers (sellers) at the CE. In addition, each buyer and seller in the first six swastika experiments (S1x–S6x) were paid a commission of $0.10 per trade in order to minimally motivate purchases at P_d and sales at P_s, thereby making credible the price quantity conditions given in Equations (1) and (2). Hence, at a CE price of $4.40 (Condition A in Figure 14.10) sellers earned only the $0.10 commission per trade whereas buyers earned a "surplus" of $P_d - P_s = \$1.10$ per trade plus the $0.10 commission per trade. Note that efficiency was 100% only if all 11 units were exchanged (regardless of how actual negotiated contract prices distributed the $1.10 per trade between the buyer and seller).

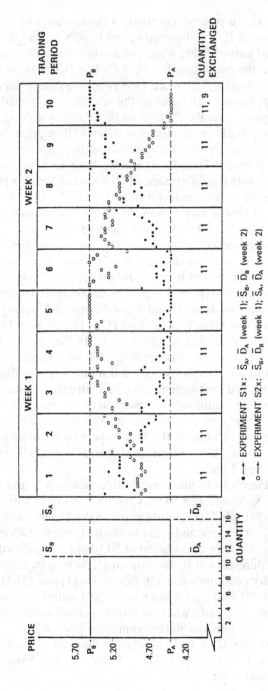

FIGURE 14.10. Experiments S1x and S2x, $0.10 commission.

304

It is reasonable to conjecture that the extreme earnings inequality generated by this supply and demand design might severely retard, if not inhibit entirely, market convergence to the CE prediction. However, earlier oral (noncomputerized) double auctions using this basic design (but with a \$.05 commission and no change in $\bar{S}$ and $\bar{D}$ conditions) displayed fairly rapid convergence to the CE (Smith, 1965). We report here a series of computerized double auctions using the swastika design. In Experiments S1x, S3x, and S5x, there were five periods of trading (periods 1–5 = "week 1") under condition A followed by five periods of trading (periods 6–10 = "week 2") under condition B. These experiments are paired in Figures 14.10–14.12 with Experiments S2x, S4x, and S6x, which utilized identical initializations except that trading in week 1 was under condition B and in week 2 under condition A. Each experiment employed a different group of experienced subjects. The three experiment pairings correspond to specific initializations of P_d and P_s (holding $P_d - P_s = 1.10$) in order to disguise the CE price across experiments. In addition, each pairing utilized a slightly different rule governing the progression of price quotes in basic double-auction trading. (See Smith and Williams, 1983, for a discussion of alternative bidding rules in the PLATO double auction. Because market behavior appears to be unaffected by bidding rule changes using the swastika design, it is not included as a focus of this chapter.)

It is important to note that the $\bar{S}$ and $\bar{D}$ shift, which occurred between periods 5 and 6, was quite subtle; the participants received the same numeric-induced values/costs on their private record sheets but a slightly smaller (or larger) quantity of units potentially traded. We hypothesized that, even if a market converged to the CE in week 1, the subtlety of the change in market conditions combined with the radical swing in the CE prediction to the opposite end of the feasible price set might inhibit CE convergence in week 2.

We also report two experiments (S7, S8) using the swastika design in which no commissions were paid. These experiments (using inexperienced subjects and no change of market conditions after period 5) were conducted in an effort to estimate the minimum profit required to induce exchange (transaction cost) in PLATO double-auction trading. With a zero commission, if the mean contract price stabilizes at some level P (above P_s in condition A or below P_d in condition B), then the difference between P and the CE prediction is a measure of the revealed subjective cost of transacting. If Experiments S1x–S6x (using the \$0.10 commission) converge to the CE price, then one would expect experiments S7 and S8 to converge to a price range within \$0.10 of the CE price unless inexperienced subjects tend to reveal higher transactions

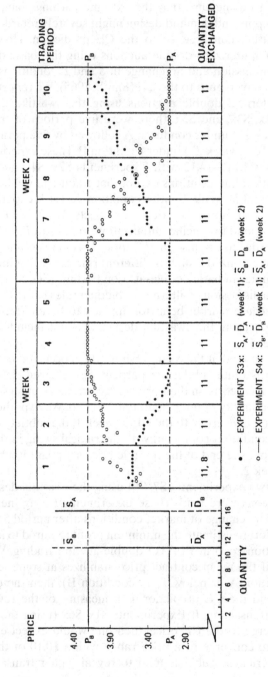

FIGURE 14.11. Experiments S3x and S4x, $0.10 commission.

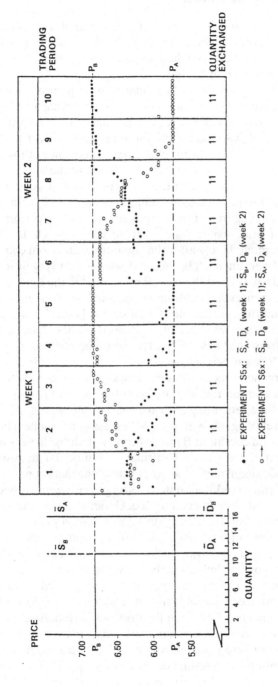

FIGURE 14.12. Experiments S5x and S6x, $0.10 commission.

costs than experienced subjects. Given the task complexity associated with computerized double-auction trading, this is a distinct possibility especially in the early periods when inexperienced subjects are still learning to become proficient traders.

The right side of Figures 14.10–14.12 chart the sequence of contract prices for the three pairs of swastika experiments employing a $0.10 commission. Note that even though $P_d - P_s$ is held constant at $1.10, the specific values of P_d and P_s vary across the three pairings. A clear tendency for CE convergence was evident in all six experiments in both weeks 1 and 2. Week 1 prices tended to start near the middle of the feasible price set and then began moving toward the CE. The speed of convergence during week 1 varied somewhat across subject groups, but all the markets were clearly approaching the CE after four or five trading periods.

The strength of price expectations formed during week 1 is quite evident in period 6 immediately after the "quantity shift" from condition A to condition B. Experiments S3x, S4x, and S6x showed very little price variation in period 6 in spite of the radical movement in the CE. The subtlety of the change in market conditions appears to have created a purely expectational equilibrium at the "old" CE price. The power of such firmly entrenched expectations was further evidenced by the tendency for prices to *diverge* from the "new" CE after the initial contract in period 6 of Experiments S1x and S5x and in period 7 of Experiment S4x.

The CE convergence process in these markets appears to rely quite heavily on the information revealed by price (bid or offer) competition that occurs in the time remaining after the full 11 units were traded in a given period. The set of agents with the five "excess units" (sellers in condition A and buyers in condition B) were prone to indulge in very active offer cutting (condition A) or bid raising (condition B) in order to attempt to trade additional units. The other side of the market was forced to remain "silent" (they could not enter or accept price quotes) because all 11 of their units had already been traded. Under these circumstances, end-of-period competition frequently drove unaccepted price quotes to the CE (sellers' offers fall to P_s under condition A and buyers' bids rise to P_d under condition B). It is interesting to note that participants frequently failed to recognize immediately the value of this market information. Initial contract prices in a period following such a flurry of competition were often considerably higher (condition A) or lower (condition B) than the final price quote in the previous period. As evidenced by the period 8–10 contract price sequences, subjects eventually modified their expectations, and prices moved rapidly toward the new CE.

Figure 14.13 displays the sequence of contract prices for swastika experiments S7 (condition A) and S8 (condition B) which had *zero*

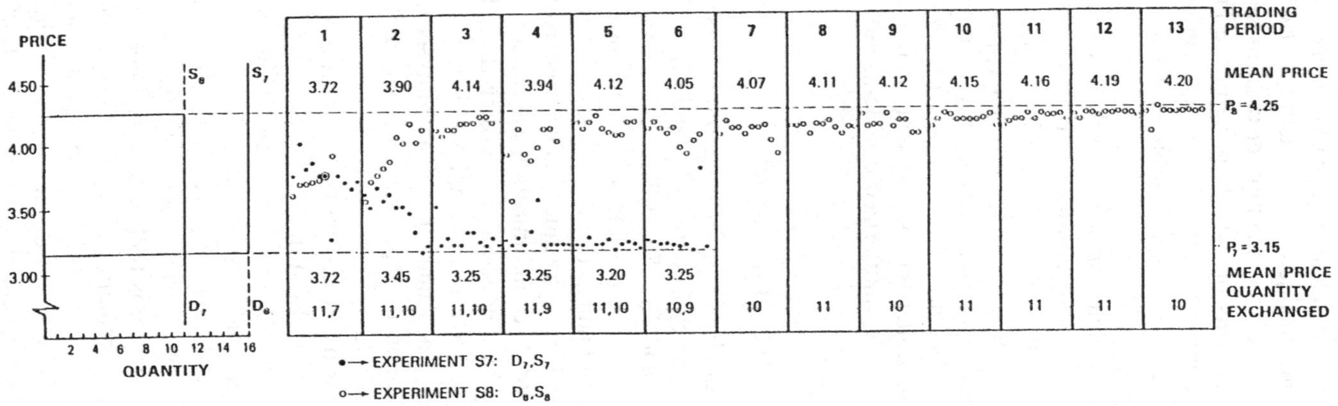

FIGURE 14.13. Experiments S7 and S8, no commission.

309

trading commission, experienced no change in market conditions after period 5, and used inexperienced subjects. Experiment S7 (which was aborted after six trading periods due to a computer crash) generated a mean contract price within 10 cents of the CE price in the final four periods (3–6). Experiment S8 approached the CE somewhat more slowly than S7, but it also had a mean contract price within 10 cents of the CE price during the final four periods (10–13).

The results of the eight experiments presented in this section suggest that the CE convergence property of double auctions is robust with respect to the gross "earnings inequity boundary" embodied in the swastika market design. Furthermore, this basic result appears to be unaffected by whether the earnings inequity favors buyers or sellers. In addition, Experiments S7 and S8 lend tentative support to the conclusion that, for this subject population, 10 cents represents an upper bound for the cost of transacting in our computerized double-auction trading environment.

IV.   Experimental Results: The "Box Design"

In this section we present five double auctions using four buyers and four sellers in a market design defined by Equations (1) and (2) for the case where $\bar{S} = \bar{D} = 11$, $P_s = \$5.50$, and $P_d = \$6.60$. The supply and demand arrays corresponding to these conditions, which we call the "box design," are illustrated on the left side of Figures 14.14–14.18. Consistent with all previous experiments reported here, assigned values and costs were strictly private information, and no communication was allowed outside the information flows defined by double-auction trading rules. The five experimental replications of the box design employed identical market parameters and trading rules. Each market had an entirely different subject group. With the exception of experiment B3, all subjects had previous double-auction experience.

Our interest in this design is motivated by the fact that any price in the set of feasible prices $[P_d, P_s]$ is also a market-clearing CE price if a trading commission at least equal to transactions cost is paid. The law of supply and demand, as it is traditionally applied, has no criteria for selecting any particular member of this set of CE prices. In the absence of any excess demand or excess supply to drive price toward some market-clearing level, one simple conjecture is that some initial contract price will occur based on the relative bargaining strength of the specific buyers and sellers in the experiment and that this first contract will determine all subsequent prices. If subjects are homogeneous, one would predict that the first contract would occur near the CE midpoint. In this case, buyers' and sellers' group earnings would be approximately equal. We offer this hypothesis (as a special case of H1 stated below) as well as three alternative hypotheses (H2, H3, H4) describing the general behavior of these markets. [The box design is similar to Edgeworth's (1881; 1932, p. 46) example of the following market with indivisibilities: There are an equal number of masters and servants and only one servant can work for one master. Also, see Stigler's (1957, pp. 8–9) discussion.]

H1: *Strong Stability.* Contract prices will stabilize on one of the CE prices within the closed set $[P_d, P_s]$ depending on the bargaining characteristics of a particular subject group. This hypothesis implies a behavioral equilibrium that yields a near-zero variance price series such as that observed in swastika experiments S3x, S4x, and S6x. We interpret this hypothesis as being consistent with a rational expectations equilibrium where subjects come to have common expectations regarding an "acceptable" contract price. Buyers (sellers) are unwilling to negotiate upward (downward) away from this price such that contract prices and expectations become mutually supportive.

H2: *Weak Stability.* Contract prices will attain some stationary equilibrium distribution in $[P_d, P_s]$. This hypothesis implies a behavioral equilibrium where the mean contract price is subject only to random sampling variation from period to period around some population mean determined by the bargaining characteristics of a particular subject group. We interpret this hypothesis as being consistent with a weaker form rational expectations equilibrium where common expectations settle on some mean price with observed contract prices exhibiting relatively small random fluctuations around this price due to subjective variations in transaction costs and dynamic bargaining strategies.

H3: *Orderly Drift.* Contract prices will exhibit an "orderly drift" in the sense that they will not attain a stable equilibrium distribution in $[P_d, P_s]$ nor will they fluctuate erratically within or across trading periods. This hypothesis implies relatively low intraperiod price variance around a mean price that exhibits trends or perhaps cycles across trading periods.

H4: *Chaotic Instability.* Contract prices will fluctuate erratically within $[P_d, P_s]$ showing little or no tendency toward intraperiod stability.

Figure 14.14 displays the sequence of contract prices for box experiment B1x. This market provides support for H3 (Orderly Drift). The mean contract price exhibited no tendency to stabilize over 15 periods

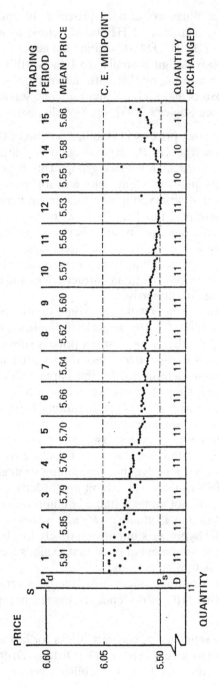

FIGURE 14.14. Box experiment B1x.

of trading. Prices drift steadily downward approaching P_s ($5.50) in period 11. In period 12, after 10 units had traded at a level consistent with period 11 prices, the seller holding the last available supply unit entered an offer considerably above the level of recent contracts. This seller refused to concede, and in the final seconds of the trading period the buyer with the remaining demand unit conceded by accepting the "high" offer. This same sequence of events occurred in period 13 (except that this time the seller failed to trade 1 supply unit resulting in 10 rather than 11 trades in the period). These actions had the effect of reversing the downward trend in price expectations. In period 14, and again in period 15, other sellers began standing firm with higher offers, buyers capitulated, and the contract prices moved rapidly upward.

Figure 14.15 displays the data from experiment B2x where prices drifted upward until period 6 to a level well below P_d ($6.60) and then showed a small downward drift. In this experiment, following period 10 we lowered the individual value and cost assignments by a constant ($2.50) and resumed trading in period 11. We conjectured that this might lock prices in at P_d (now $4.10) because this upper bound of the new feasible price set was well below the level of prices in all previous trading periods. Contrary to this conjecture, the subjects appear to have simply "rescaled" their price expectations based on the downward shift in their assigned values and costs. Except for an increase in the variance of period 11 prices, the downward drift in the mean price continued through period 15. Thus, experiment B2x provides obvious support for H3.

The sequence of contracts in experiments B3 (using inexperienced subjects) and B4x is displayed in Figures 14.16 and 14.17, respectively. These two experiments are generally supportive of H2 (Weak Stability). The distribution of prices in experiment B3 (Figure 14.16) appears to have stabilized near $6.13 in trading periods 8–12. The price distribution in periods 8–15 of experiment B4x (Figure 14.17) also appears to have approximately stabilized, but in a price range very close to P_s rather than near the CE midpoint as in Experiment B3. The initial movements of the mean price toward P_s are reminiscent of Experiment B1x, although the B4x price series displayed greater variance and more rapid convergence toward P_s. Unlike B1x, prices in B4x did not begin to drift upward after "bottoming out" near P_s.

Experiment B5x (Figure 14.18) is the only box design experiment that is sufficiently stable to be interpreted as consistent with H1 (Strong Stability). The mean contract price in B5x was $6.18 over the last nine periods (6–14) with very little variance in individual contract prices. Although prices were never truly constant, 93 of the 97 contracts formed

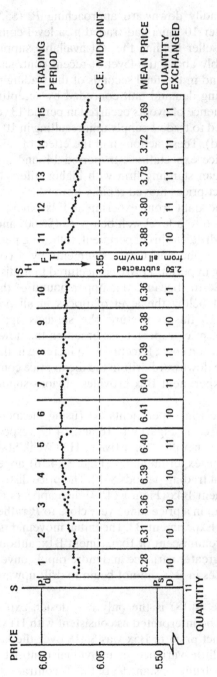

FIGURE 14.15. Box experiment B2x.

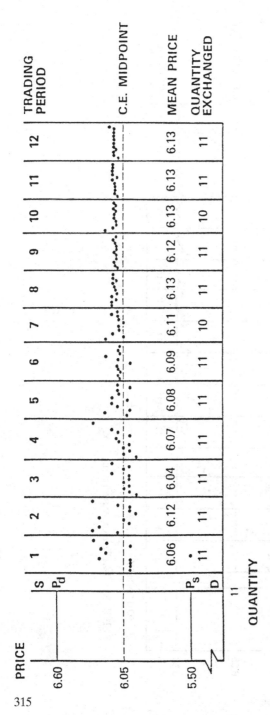

FIGURE 14.16. Box experiment B3.

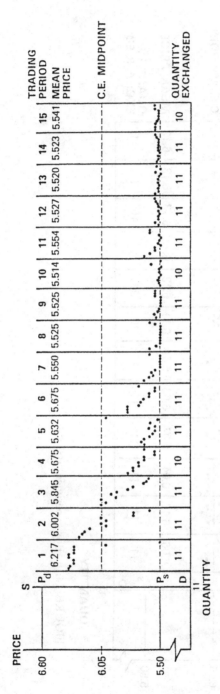

FIGURE 14.17. Box experiment B4x.

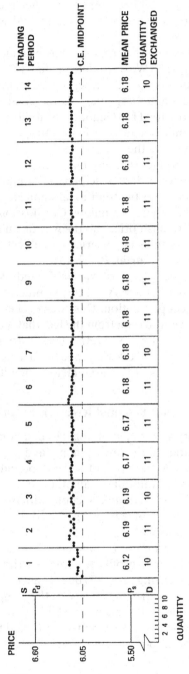

FIGURE 14.18. Box experiment B5x.

317

during periods 6–14 were at either $6.17 or $6.18 (the other four were at $6.19 and $6.20), and all prices were between $6.15 and $6.20 in periods 2–14.

The results of these five box design experiments thus provide mixed support for H3 (Orderly Drift), H2 (Weak Stability), and H1 (Strong Stability). Which of these hypotheses best describes a particular market appears to be determined by the innate bargaining characteristics of the subject group. We find no support for H4 (Chaotic Instability) nor for the extreme form of H1 that requires a zero variance intraperiod price series. Furthermore, we do not observe the immediate price stability that might be conjectured based on the fact that any initial contract price is also a CE. We do, however, observe orderly disciplined trading in spite of the fact that the box design eliminates the traditional stabilizing effects of excess supply and demand when there is a unique CE. It is somewhat surprising that buyers were able to push prices all the way down to P_s in two of the five box experiments (both using experienced subjects) but in none of the experiments do prices occur at P_d. This result is generally consistent with previous evidence reported by Smith and Williams (1982), suggesting that there may exist a very subtle asymmetry in bargaining strength within this subject population. This "weak seller effect" is conjectured to be cultural in origin, arising from the fact that most subjects' prior market experiences are as buyers in retail markets (organized under posted-offer trading rules). The box design appears to magnify the price and earnings-distribution effects of this asymmetry when it exists.

V.   Summary of Conclusions and Potential Research Extensions

This study has utilized laboratory experimental double-auction markets to explore three distinct boundaries of the law of supply and demand as a predictor of market outcomes: a "number of sellers" boundary, an "earnings inequity" boundary, and a "multiple equilibria" boundary. Our results can be summarized as follows: (1) double auctions with two sellers (duopoly) and four or more buyers display convergence to the competitive equilibrium; (2) double auctions with a single seller (monopoly) and five buyers generate a marked deterioration of the predictive ability of the competitive model, but prices and profits tend not to rise to the single-price monopoly profit-maximizing level; (3) double auctions using the swastika design, in which all gains from exchange at the competitive equilibrium go entirely to one side of the market, exhibit convergence to the competitive equilibrium when a $0.10 commission is paid to minimally motivate the exchange of zero-profit units; (4) using zero commissions in the swastika design generates convergence to a price band within \$0.10 of the competitive equilibrium suggesting that \$0.10 is an upper bound of subjective transaction costs in double-auction trading; (5) double auctions using the box design, in which any feasible contract price is also a competitive equilibrium price, tend to display either an "orderly drift" or converge to a stable, low variance price distribution.

All these conclusions are inevitably conditioned by a host of experimental parameters that were not allowed to vary in this study. Several of these parameters are obvious treatment variables for future research designed to examine the robustness of the experimental results presented here. Primary among these are the trading institution, subject information regarding the underlying market structure, and intersubject communication.

In duopoly markets, will the CE convergence result hold if the two sellers are allowed to communicate and form conspiratorial agreements? How would changing trading institutions or giving sellers full demand information affect market outcomes in both monopoly and duopoly? Will monopolists or duopolists who understand the traditional analytical determination of Q_M and P_M be able to negotiate such outcomes in actual experimental markets? Previous research offers evidence on some of these questions (e.g. Isaac et al., 1984) but much remains to be done.

Using the swastika design, will trading institutions other than the double auction generate CE convergence in spite of the severe profit inequities at the CE? Will the CE convergence property be enhanced, retarded, or eliminated if subjects have complete information on the underlying market parameters? Several noncomputerized double-auction experiments conducted by Smith (1980) suggest that, in the swastika design, more information may actually inhibit CE convergence. This suggests that subtle factors such as judgments of "fairness" and complex intertemporal strategies may emerge as the participants, information sets are increased.

The box design has potential for use in situations where the experimenter wishes to empirically test for, and purposefully magnify, any subtle asymmetries in bargaining strength or behavioral instabilities that might be the result of a particular trading rule, information condition, reward structure, or subject population. In addition, a formal model explaining any empirical regularities or robust stability properties exhibited in the box design will require insights into expectation formation and trading dynamics that go beyond the traditional use of market supply and demand curves to predict a static competitive equilibrium.

CHAPTER 15

Off-Floor Trading, Disintegration, and the Bid–Ask Spread in Experimental Markets

Joseph Campbell, Shawn LaMaster, Vernon L. Smith, and Mark Van Boening

This study has its origin in a series of meetings between the authors and various futures market exchange officials. Our interest was in identifying one or more research questions, arising in the ordinary operation of an exchange, that might be capable of examination using experimental methods. We wanted the scrutiny of exchange officials and their assistance in helping to define a set of questions that we thought would be researchable by laboratory experimentation. Initially we discussed a wide range of issues, including the problem of "off-floor" trading, which ultimately was the research focus that we mutually agreed would be a good starting candidate. We selected this problem for a number of reasons.

1. All futures and stock exchanges have rules that prohibit the members of an exchange from engaging in unauthorized off-floor trades.[1] Consequently, the problem is of general interest within the securities industry, and we are able to ask whether such rules are warranted by the results we obtain in laboratory experimentation.
2. Off-floor trading in futures markets is known to occur in spite of penalties that have been levied on exchange members who violate these rules. This suggests that there exist endogenous incentives strong enough to overcome the penalty strictures intended to prevent such trading activity.
3. The frequency of occurrence, as well as an understanding of the circumstances of individual violations, is not known precisely by exchange officials. The fact that off-floor trades are prohibited and punishable as a major offense, and therefore are clandes-

---

[1] For example, rule 520 of the Chicago Mercantile Exchange (1985), states that "All trading for future delivery in commodities traded on the Exchange must be confined to transactions made on the Exchange floor in the designated trading area during trading hours. ... Any member violating this rule shall be guilty of a major offense."

tine, makes it impossible to gather systematic field data on off-floor trades. Essentially, experimental evidence is the only feasible source of observations on off-floor trading.
4. Off-floor trading illustrates a research problem that has not yet received attention in the published literature of experimental economics: If an individual voluntarily elects to forgo trade in an organized market and to trade instead by bilateral bargaining with another individual, then we have an example of endogenous choice between two institutions of exchange.
5. Finally, we judged that we would be able to develop a set of experimental procedures and designs that would make the off-floor trading problem researchable by laboratory methods.

I. Related Background Literature

The question of whether it is socially desirable to permit off-floor private trades is best understood by recognizing that securities and futures trading involves three different markets: the market for securities, the market for dealer services (see Schwartz, 1988, pp. 427–8, for a discussion of these two), but also the market for the services of exchanges. Prior to 1975, the Securities and Exchange Commission had supported the industry's cartel for fixing minimum commission fees. This price fixing was rendered viable to the extent of enforcement of the rules prohibiting off-exchange trading. The Securities Acts Amendments of 1975 sought two important changes: to eliminate all unjustified competitive constraints in securities trading and to mandate the development of a National Market System. The result of the first proscription was to remove the fixing of commissions. This has resulted in a substantially more competitive market for *dealer services* and in lower commission rates. The mandate for a National Market System has resulted in the Intermarket Trading System linking the national and regional exchanges; also we now have an over-the-counter automated quotation and trading system. This has increased competition in the market for *exchange services* [see Hamilton, 1987, 1988, for studies regarding the trading of New York Stock Exchange (NYSE)-listed securities on the regional exchanges; also Garbade and Silber, 1979].

These changes, which have increased dealer competition and market integration, have left unresolved the question, should off-floor trading be permitted on a given exchange? Schwartz (1988, p. 498) suggests that "... off-board trading restrictions appear to have some justification ..." because traders benefit socially (lower bid–ask spreads, price efficiency) from order consolidation. But because of a "public good" problem, individual incentives may not be compatible with order consolidation. Our explicit interpretation is as follows: contracts listed on an exchange are successful trading instruments only to the extent that they accommodate trading activities of agents that were previously unavailable (e.g., the Standard and Poor futures index), or only available at the higher transaction cost of a disintegrated market (e.g., the original over-the-counter trading of stock puts and calls). But upon listing a new contract, an exchange also provides a central place where interested traders meet, making it possible to trade off-floor at minimum search cost and to use the available competitive price information to lower negotiation cost. Hence off-floor trades based on the bid–ask spread may be cost efficient for certain traders who complement each other through reputation or block-trading frequency.

But why should off-floor trading qualify market performance? Cohen et al. (1985) use a queuing theory model of trading to show that disintegration (relative to order consolidation which maintains price priority in double-auction trading) produces wider bid–ask spreads and increased price volatility. Using simulation methods, similar results are obtained by these authors when time priority is violated. Our computerized exchange maintains a strict price priority rule with tied bid (or offer) prices ranked by a time priority rule. Both price and time priority are violated in our experiments when traders negotiate off-floor bilateral contracts. Under a clearing-house regime, Mendelson (1987) demonstrated that fragmentation (disintegration) reduces the expected volume and expected gains from exchange while increasing the price variance faced by traders. Although our market is a continuous auction, these predictions receive qualitative support by our results.

II.　　Design Considerations and Motivation

The research questions we investigated did not spring full-blown at the project's inception; they evolved, and were articulated gradually over a series of experiments interspaced between feedback discussions with exchange officials. After our initial discussions, we designed an experiment intended to provide an explicit exogenous transactions fee differential between on-floor computerized double-auction trading of single units and off-floor private bilateral block trades. This served as our first, baseline 1, experiment (1 in Table 15.1) showing clearly what everybody expected, namely that the a priori predicted division of trades between the two institutions would occur in the laboratory using reward-motivated subjects. This experiment provided a vehicle for focusing the next round of discussions on the elements driving off-floor trading as conjectured by exchange officials. A number of questions emerged from

Table 15.1. *Experimental design for off-floor trading experiments*

Experiment number	Market size	Off-floor trading	P_e by period	Value/cost assignment	Number of periods
Baseline 1 (transaction cost):					
1	6 buyers 6 sellers	6-unit blocks	Constant	Constant	15
Baseline 2:					
2, 3, 4	5 buyers 5 sellers	None	Constant	Random	15
7, 8	5 buyers 5 sellers	None	Random	Random	15
Treatments:					
5x	5 buyers 5 sellers	Single units	Constant	Random	15
6x	5 buyers 5 sellers	Single units	Random	Random	15
9x, 10x	5 buyers 5 sellers	3-unit blocks	Random	Random	14
11xx	5 buyers 5 sellers	3-unit blocks	Random	Random	15

this and subsequent discussions. Will the phenomenon of off-floor trading be observed in an environment in which there are *no* explicit transactions cost saving and *no* block trades? How much off-floor trading occurs relative to on-floor trading? Does off-floor trading persist with experience over time? The challenge here was to create an environment in which the decision to trade off-floor was entirely endogenous, unmotivated by exogenous conditions. Is the extent and persistence of off-floor trading influenced by design treatments that increase the (naturally emerging) bid–ask spread? This latter question resulted from the conjecture of exchange officials that off-floor trades were motivated by the mutual gains at prices inside the bid–ask spread. If off-floor trades are observed in the weakly motivating environment of single-unit trading, will such trades increase when subjects can trade blocks of units off-floor?[2] These questions led to the design and execution of the five new baseline 2 experiments and five treatment experiments listed in Table

---

[2] Of course, block trades can be executed on all exchanges, traditionally under a rule that prohibits all-or-none bids or offers (see Chicago Mercantile Exchange, 1985, Rule 523 and New York Stock Exchange 1987, pp. 2061–2). Of course, no such restriction would apply in rule-violating off-floor negotiation. Ironically, rules prohibiting all-or-none bids and offers might provide an incentive for violating rules against off-floor trading.

15.1. An x following an experiment number (e.g., 5x) refers to the use of once-experienced subjects, whereas xx refers to twice-experienced subjects; otherwise subjects are inexperienced. Three of the baseline experiments (2–4) used an environment in which the static supply and demand equilibrium was unchanging over the 15 periods of trading; two experiments (7, 8) used an environment in which the equilibrium was shifted randomly in each of the 15 periods of trading. In these baselines, no off-floor trading opportunities were provided. The objective was to test our conjecture that the naturally emerging bid–ask spread in the static environment would be narrower than the bid–ask spread that emerged in the random environment. The purpose was to establish that we had indeed created two environments with different endogenous bid–ask spreads that were *independent* of the occurrence of off-floor trading. This provided baseline controls for comparison with subsequent "treatment" experiments in which subjects were given the opportunity to make bilateral trades off-floor. In the treatment experiments, we ask: (1) Will subjects trade off-floor? (2) Will off-floor trades be greater in the random than in the static supply and demand environment? (3) Will off-floor trading in the random environment be greater for block trades than for single-unit trades?

Because our results provided generally affirmative answers to these questions, in our final experiment (11xx), we collected data designed to answer the question: Do off-floor trades occur at prices that are predominately inside the bid–ask spread standing at the time of execution? If so, this is confirmatory evidence that the motivation for off-floor trades is to split the gain measured by the bid–ask spread.

III.   Experimental Design and Trading Mechanisms

A.   *Experimental Design*

We used standard monetary reward procedures to induce controlled supply and demand schedules in each period of every market experiment (see Smith, 1976a). Our experimental design used the schedules shown in Figure 15.1; these were known to the experimenter, but were *not* known by any subject. From Experiments 2–11xx (Table 15.1), the induced supply and demand, measured in deviations from the center of the set of competitive equilibrium prices, are shown in Figure 15.1(b). There are 5 buyers and 5 sellers. Three of the buyers (B_i, B_k, B_n) each had a capacity to buy up to 6 units, whereas two of the buyers (B_j, B_m) had a capacity to buy up to 3 units in any single trading period. Symmetrically, three sellers (S_i, S_k, S_n) could sell up to 6 units and two (S_j, S_m)

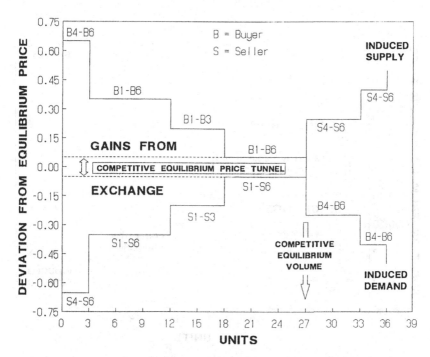

FIGURE 15.1(a). Supply and demand for Experiment 1.

could sell up to 3 units. Any particular buyer (seller) subject was assigned randomly to one of the step positions (i, j, k, m, n) at the beginning of each of the 3 weeks (5-day trading periods) in an experiment. A buyer's profit was determined by computing the difference between his or her assigned value and purchase price in the market for each unit bought. In Figure 15.1(b), if the equilibrium price is $3.00, then B_i has 6 units valued at $3.40. If a unit was purchased at $3.05, then B_i made a profit of $3.40 − $3.05 = $0.35 on that unit. Consequently, B_i had a well-defined maximum willingness-to-pay of $3.40 for each unit. The cumulative profit on all units purchased in all 15 periods was paid in cash to each buyer at the end of the experiment. Thus the incentive of each buyer was to buy as low as possible, but to balance this gain against the increased uncertainty of making a trade at lower prices. A seller's profit was computed by subtracting his or her assigned cost from the selling price of each unit sold. If S_k was the seller of the unit at price $3.05 to buyer B_i in the preceding example, then the seller's profit was $3.05 − $2.80 = $0.25. The

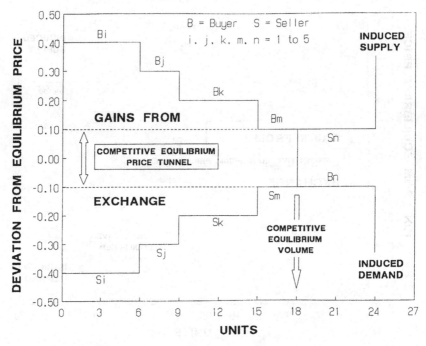

FIGURE 15.1(b). Supply and demand for Experiments 2–11xx.

maximum possible profits that could be earned by the 10 subjects in an experiment was simply the area between the supply and demand schedules, which is shown as "Gains from Exchange" in Figures 15.1(a, b), since this measures the maximum aggregate gains from exchange achievable through market trade. Market efficiency is well defined as the ratio of the total profits actually realized in any trading period to the maximum profits shown in Figure 15.1(b). A market is 100% efficient if and only if 18 units trade, and buyer B_n and seller S_n trade none of their units.

In Experiments 6x–11xx (Table 15.1), subjects were not only assigned randomly by 5-day weeks to the steps shown in Figure 15.1(b), but in addition a random constant (positive or negative) was added each period to all buyer values and all seller costs. Consequently, in these experiments, the competitive equilibrium price was shifted randomly each period. This provided increased price and transaction uncertainty relative to those experiments (2–5x) in which only the step assignments were randomized.

In our first baseline 1 experiment, the value and cost assignments to buyers and sellers remained constant over the entire 15-period trading horizon. The resulting supply and demand arrays are shown in Figure 15.1(a). In this experiment all on-floor "electronic" trades were subject to a 25-cent-per-unit "commission" fee. The supply and demand schedules in Figure 15.1(a) are computed net of the 25-cent charges levied on the buyer and seller in each trade.[3]

B.   The PLATO Double-Auction Mechanism

In each experiment, exchange trading occurs via our PLATO double-auction computer software program written by Arlington Williams (1980). The screen display for a subject (buyer 5) in Experiment 11xx is shown in Figure 15.2. The upper panel of the screen contains buyer 5's private record sheet for all transactions in week 2 (periods 6–10). In period 6, buyer 5 had the capacity to buy a maximum of 6 units, each valued at $6.83, but bought only 2 units via PLATO – the first for $6.60, yielding a profit of $0.23, the second for $6.67 giving a profit of $0.16. Buyer 5 in week 2 had the position B_k shown in Figure 15.1(b) on the step that is $0.20 above the equilibrium price; that is, the equilibrium price was $6.63 in period 6 and $4.23 in period 7. Just below the record sheet appears the standing bid (offer), which is *public* information for all subjects. All traders could see that currently a buyer had a standing bid to buy at $4.12, and a seller had a standing offer to sell at $4.43. Any buyer was free to accept the standing offer by touching the outlined box area labeled "accept offer"; he/she then had up to 5 seconds to confirm by touching the box area labeled "confirm contract." Similarly any seller could touch his/her "accept bid" box then confirm. The resulting contract is binding, and the auction for 1 unit ends. PLATO then waits for a new bid and offer from the "floor," if there are no bids or offers stored in the "electronic book." The box on the left allowed a subject to enter a new bid (offer). Suppose buyer 5 desired to place a new bid at $4.35, then he/she typed this number on the keyboard and confirmed that it appeared (privately) to the right of the arrow pointed at the $ symbol.

---

[3] In the static environment of baseline 1 [Figure 15.1(a)], the bid–ask spread converged to minuscule levels. In order to test the key hypothesis of the study, we needed a design for the subsequent experiments in which the bid–ask spread would converge to a wider level than we had observed in Experiment 1. This led us to widen the tunnel of competitive equilibrium prices [cf. Figures 15.1(a, b)] in addition to introducing the random supply and demand environment.

WEEK 2	TRADING PERIOD (columns)				
RECORD SHEET for BUYER 5	6	7	8	9	1Ø
Unit 1 resale value	6.83	4.43			
Unit 1 purchase price	6.6Ø				
Profit	Ø.23				
Unit 2 resale value	6.83	4.43			
Unit 2 purchase price	6.67				
Profit	Ø.16				
Unit 3 resale value	6.83	4.43			
Unit 3 purchase price					
Profit					
Unit 4 resale value	6.83	4.43			
Unit 4 purchase price					
Profit					
Unit 5 resale value	6.83	4.43			
Unit 5 purchase price					
Profit					
Unit 6 resale value	6.83	4.43			
Unit 6 purchase price					
Profit					
Total Profit for Period	Ø.39				

A BUYER BIDS $4.12   A SELLER OFFERS $4.43

| ENTER BID | ≫$ | | ACCEPT OFFER | | CONFIRM CONTRACT |

Contracts: 4.45, 4.44, 4.42, 4.35, 4.36, 4.28
Trading Period 7 now in progress. SECONDS REMAINING: 28

FIGURE 15.2. PLATO screen display for a buyer.

By pressing the touch-sensitive box labeled "enter bid," this number, adjacent to the arrow, disappeared and reappeared publicly as the new standing bid replacing the previous bid at $4.12.[4]

We want to emphasize that bids, offers, and acceptances are executed quickly on PLATO. There is no delay like that occurring in negotiating

---

[4] Note that the PLATO mechanism uses many of the New York Stock Exchange rules. As we see in this example, a standing bid (offer) is subject to an improvement rule: Any new bid must be higher and any new offer must be lower than the current standing bid and offer (see NYSE, 1987, Rules 70, 71). All bids and offers outside the standing bid–ask spread are placed in a price priority rank-queue or "electronic book"; tied prices are sec-

a trade off-floor using the procedures described later. All our traders are principals operating for their own accounts; there are no dealers or specialists trading for the account of others. The bid–ask spread, if and when it exists at any time during an experiment, is entirely a naturally occurring endogenous event. The experimenters have no *direct control* over the bid–ask spread; only the possibility of indirect control via the introduction of induced supply and demand uncertainty in the environments.

At the bottom of the screen under the touch-sensitive boxes, the last several contracts (up to a maximum of 8) are listed in their historical sequence. Below this line of contracts the subject is reminded that period 7 is now in progress, and that the number of seconds remaining is 28. In the experiments reported here, each period is of length 240 seconds.

C. Off-Floor Bilateral Bargaining

After reviewing the PLATO instructions in all off-floor trading experiments, supplemental instructions were read aloud while subjects followed their own printed handout sheets. In each period, subjects could trade the units on their screen either in the PLATO market or off-floor. Buyers and sellers were seated alternately so that each buyer (seller) had a seller (buyer) on each side with whom they could trade off-floor. Each buyer (seller) was given bid (offer) tickets upon which they could write a bid (offer). If a buyer (seller) wished to submit a bid (offer) off-floor, he/she held the ticket in the direction of the seller (buyer) to whom he/she wished to submit the bid (offer). One of four experimenters then placed the ticket on the appropriate subject's table, and the subject marked the ticket either "accept" or "reject." The ticket was then returned forthwith to the person who submitted it. Off-floor trades and profits were recorded manually in tables supplied to each subject.

The seating arrangements and parameter randomization determined potential off-floor trading partners. In these experiments, we made no attempt to match high-volume (i.e., 6-unit) buyers and sellers. In the off-floor block-trading experiments, subjects could trade units off-floor in blocks of three. This means that agents endowed with only 3 units would trade their entire endowment if they traded off-floor; others might trade 3 units off and 3 units on, or all 6 on (or off) the floor.

ondarily ranked by a time priority rule. Bids and offers once standing cannot be withdrawn [see NYSE, 1987, Rule 72(e)], but those in the queue can be canceled at any time by the maker. The standing bid (offer) is public, but the queue is not (see NYSE, 1987, Rule 115).

It should be noted that off-floor trading must inevitably take more time than electronic trading, and this would tend to inhibit off-floor trading although less so for block trades. But this is true for naturally occurring markets as well as for our experimental markets. Our procedures were designed to minimize the mechanical (not negotiation) effort required to make off-floor trades because we did not want such trades to be unduly influenced by artifactual mechanical difficulties.[5]

IV.   Experimental Results

A.   *Off-Floor Trading to Save Transactions Cost*

It is evident that if block trades off-floor can effect savings in transactions cost, this can provide an external incentive to choose bilateral off-floor exchange over electronic exchange. In Experiment 1, 12 subjects were assigned randomly to the normalized value/cost positions shown in Figure 15.1(a). Each subject had the right to trade 6 units. The trading fee of $0.25 on all PLATO trades was automatically deducted from each buyer and each seller's profit on each transaction. Net of commission fees, the equilibrium price range, normalized on the competitive equilibrium price, was (−0.05, 0.05) and the corresponding volume was 27 units.

Supplemental instructions informed all subjects that after period 5 some buyers and sellers would have the option of executing 6-unit block trades outside PLATO at a flat commission fee of $0.80. Thus if a subject traded 6 units per period in the PLATO market, total commission fees would be $1.50 as opposed to $0.80 if those 6 units were traded off-floor. Prior to each period (after period 5), three buyers and three sellers were allowed to submit off-floor block trade contract proposals to one another via an experimenter. If a proposal was accepted, the buyer and seller involved traded all six units at a standard contract price determined by

---

[5] A referee posed the following substantive issue: "Was there any attempt to see how the thickness or thinness of the market affected off-floor exchange? If the PLATO market is thin (i.e., time between trades is lengthened), is there a greater probability of trading off-floor?" Because the answer to the first question is no, we have no empirical data for answering the second question. But an assumption underlying our experimental design was that market volume might indeed affect off-floor trading. Hence Experiments 2–11xx all controlled for this using supply and demand designs with an equilibrium exchange volume of 18 units per period. Because each period lasted 240 seconds, the average time (theoretically) between trades is 13.3 seconds, which was the same for all experiments. One could study this factor in a controlled manner by increasing the length of each of the induced price limit steps in Figure 15.1(b) by some multiple, 2, 3, etc., that would increase volume by the same amount and reduce average time between trades proportionately.

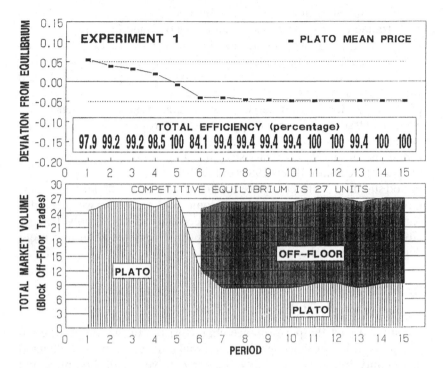

FIGURE 15.3. Baseline 1 experiment: block off-floor trading at reduced fee.

the average PLATO price in the period.[6] The mean price, PLATO and off-floor volume, and total market efficiency in each period are shown in Figure 15.3. The average PLATO price was always within the competitive range, and the total (PLATO plus off-floor) volume was always within 3 units of the equilibrium level. In periods 7–15, all subjects with the opportunity to trade off-floor did so. The prediction was for 18 units to trade off-floor, and for 9 units to trade via the PLATO terminals. In

---

[6] This "standard-contract," average-floor-price, rule was imposed by the experimenters to represent the kind of informal agreement that might arise among block traders for after-hours trading. After preliminary discussions, Experiment 1 was developed as the pilot experiment we used to focus our dialogue with exchange officials to demonstrate one set of incentive conditions under which off-floor trading might occur and to calibrate their thinking with ours on the potential for using experimental methods. It also provided pilot experience for the experimenters in a new area of research. Once we saw how to fashion the procedures for the auxiliary market, we eliminated the idea of a "standard contract," and allowed all off-floor trades to be freely negotiated.

period 6, one buyer did not accept an off-floor proposal and only 12 units were traded off-floor. Because mean prices declined in each of the first six periods, it was reasonable for this buyer to expect that by trading on-floor he might beat the standard mean contract price applying to off-floor trades. After period 6, PLATO prices were nearly constant and within the competitive range even though two-thirds of the volume was off-floor. The failure to observe a degradation in market efficiency with 60% of all trades off-floor simply illustrates the robustness of the double-auction institution in producing competitive outcomes in *stationary* environments. This has been demonstrated in hundreds of experiments over the years (see Smith, 1976b, 1982; and Williams, 1980). The use of an after-period standard contract to price off-floor trades controlled for any interference between off-floor and electronic trading. When we relax this control and also introduce greater uncertainty in the supply/demand environment, as in the experiments reported next, we shall find more degradation in market efficiency.

B.   *Establishing the Performance Characteristics of Baseline*
      Environments Without Off-Floor Trading

We studied next the performance characteristics of two different environments with differing degrees of external induced supply and demand uncertainty. In Experiments 2–4, the competitive equilibrium price and quantity were constant over all periods, whereas in Experiments 7 and 8 the competitive equilibrium price level shifted at random each period. Our a priori prediction was that the second condition would yield greater price volatility than the first. We also expected the bid–ask spread, when it existed, to widen under the second condition relative to the first. A measurement problem with the latter prediction is that contracts may and often do occur without a defined bid–ask spread, or before that spread has a chance to narrow. Thus, a bid could be entered and accepted before an ask price was established. Figure 15.4 provides charts of mean prices by period for all the baseline 2 experiments, and summaries of mean volume and efficiency by period across each of the two groups of experiments.[7]

Table 15.2 lists the mean volume per period, mean price deviation,

---

[7] Notice the tendency of the mean price to lie in the lower half of the tunnel in both treatments. The hypothesis that the mean prices are greater than or equal to 0 is rejected at the 0.01 level [$t(14) = -32.3$ constant, -5.98 random]. The ability of buyers in double-auction trading to extract a larger share of the surplus has been noted before (see Smith and Williams, 1982). Although explanations have been conjectured (subjects are more likely to have experience as buyers than as sellers), the cause is unknown. The experienced sessions reported later in Sections IV.C and IV.E exhibit less bias in favor of buyers. In the baselines, the equilibrium volume was traded 24 times, but 100% efficiency

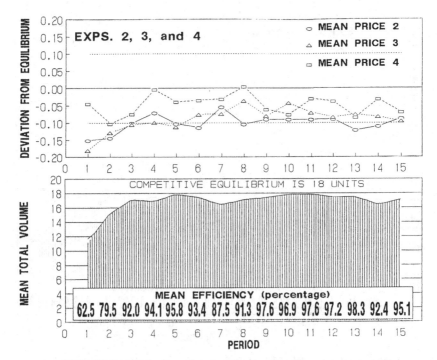

FIGURE 15.4(a). Baseline 2 experiments with constant equilibrium.

price variance, mean square error of prices (variance relative to predicted equilibrium), and the mean and median observed bid–ask spread at the time of contract for all PLATO trades. The same data (except for the spread) are listed for all off-floor contracts. Finally, the fraction of total volume that occurs off-floor and market efficiency are listed in the last two columns. All statistics are computed across all periods and contracts in each experiment. We measure "the spread" in two ways. First, when a bid was accepted to form a contract but no ask was entered, we define the standing offer as $9.99, the maximum possible price that PLATO will accept; if there was an offer price being accepted, but no bid, we defined the "standing bid" as $0.01, the minimum possible price that PLATO will accept. In this way we were able to utilize all the information content of our data; it required only the weak assumption that

was reached only 6 of those times. A necessary and sufficient condition for 100% efficiency is that *all* intramarginal units trade. The relatively low prices allow trading of extramarginal units, resulting in less-than-complete realization of the maximum gains from exchange (profits).

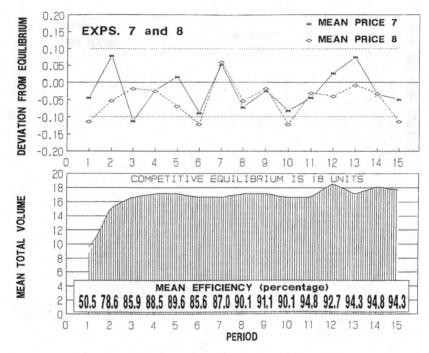

FIGURE 15.4(b). Baseline 2 experiments with random equilibrium.

any seller would be willing to sell at $9.99 and any buyer would be willing to buy for $0.01. Defining the spread in this way for outlier cases led to some large erratic observations under all treatment conditions. In order not to weight such observations unduly, we used the median as the measure of central tendency. Second, when there was either no bid or no ask at the time of contract, we excluded the observation and computed the mean spread using the remaining observations.

From Table 15.2, comparing the constant and random environments (Experiments 2–4 with 7–8), the latter increases the price variance, mean square error, and the mean and median spread, all by a factor of about two. Further comparisons are provided in Section IV.F.

C.   Will Off-Floor Trades Occur When Single Units Can Be Traded?

From these results, we were satisfied that we had successfully created two environments with differing bid–ask spreads. Recall that the importance

Table 15.2. *Summary data, all off-floor trading experiments*

Experiment	PLATO Contracts						Off-Floor Contracts				All Contracts	
	Mean volume per period	Mean price[a]	Price variance	Mean square error[b]	Mean spread	Median spread	Mean volume per period	Mean price[a]	Price variance	Mean square error[b]	Fraction of volume off-floor	Trading efficiency
Baseline 1:												
1 (periods 1–5)	25.6	0.03	0.0014	0.0022	0.11	0.05	—	—	—	—	—	0.99
1 (periods 6–10)	8.8	-0.05	0.0000	0.0021	0.01	0.01	17.40	-0.05	0.0000	0.0021	0.66	0.98
Baseline 2:												
Constant												
2	16.9	-0.10	0.0023	0.0125	0.25	0.14	—	—	—	—	—	0.94
3	16.1	-0.09	0.0035	0.0109	0.16	0.10	—	—	—	—	—	0.89
4	16.7	-0.05	0.0056	0.0077	0.13	0.10	—	—	—	—	—	0.92
Random												
7	15.9	-0.02	0.0169	0.0173	0.36	0.24	—	—	—	—	—	0.86
8	16.8	-0.05	0.0154	0.0176	0.28	0.18	—	—	—	—	—	0.89
Off-floor trading:												
Single units:												
Constant:												
5x	15.5	-0.05	0.0021	0.0042	0.05	0.02	1.73	-0.03	0.0023	0.0029	0.10	0.97
Random:												
6x	14.8	-0.02	0.0048	0.0051	0.13	0.06	2.47	-0.01	0.0059	0.0059	0.14	0.96
Blocks, random:												
9x	11.6	-0.04	0.0063	0.0077	0.12	0.09	4.50	-0.05	0.0052	0.0072	0.28	0.91
10x	13.9	0.01	0.0023	0.0023	0.09	0.05	3.64	0.01	0.0053	0.0072	0.21	0.98
11xx	9.3	0.02	0.0087	0.0091	0.13	0.10	7.00	0.05	0.0072	0.0093	0.43	0.90

[a] Mean prices are expressed as deviations:

$$\bar{P} = \frac{1}{Q}\sum_{i=1}^{Q}(P_i - P_{CE})$$

where Q is total contracts, P_i is the ith contract price, and P_{CE} is the midpoint of the set of competitive equilibrium prices.

[b] Mean square error is the variance of price deviations from the competitive equilibrium:

$$MSE = \frac{1}{Q}\sum_{i=1}^{Q}(P_i - P_{CE})^2$$

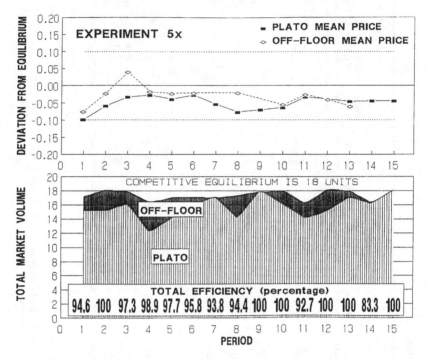

FIGURE 15.5(a). Single-unit off-floor trading; constant equilibrium.

of this resides in the fact that we exercised no direct control over the naturally occurring bid–ask spread. Given two environments with differing levels for the bid–ask spread we ask: Will we observe off-floor trading? Will we observe more off-floor trading in the environment known independently to yield a wider bid–ask spread?

In both questions, we restricted off-floor trades to the single-unit condition judged to provide the weakest incentive to trade off-floor. We were skeptical as to whether off-floor trades would occur in these environments. Our skepticism grew out of the fact that for a trader to opt for off-floor trading he or she had to substitute a market with a lesser trading opportunity for one with a greater trading opportunity. Any off-floor bid (offer) could always be entered more quickly on PLATO and exposed to a larger number of potential acceptors. The disadvantage of such action might be to "spoil" the market by advertising *to all* a willingness to trade at a concessionary price. Making the bid (offer) off-floor maintains privacy *without* forgoing the option of returning to the floor.

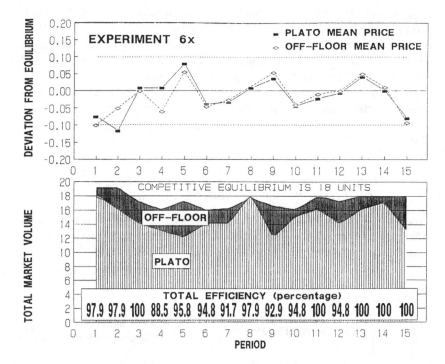

FIGURE 15.5(b). Single-unit off-floor trading; random experiments.

Figure 15.5 charts the mean price deviation and volume by period both off-floor and on PLATO for Experiments 5x and 6x. As shown in Table 15.2, the price variance and mean square error are greater in 6x than in 5x for both PLATO and off-floor contracts; the mean and median spread are both greater in 6x than in 5x. Note that the spread data for 5x and 6x are not comparable with 2–4 and 7–8 because of differences in subject experience (see footnote 10). Finally, the mean off-floor volume increases from 1.7 to 2.5 going from the constant to the random environment.

D.   Does Off-Floor Volume Increase with Block Trading?

Having established that off-floor trades occur under the weak endogenous incentive condition of single-unit trades, we turned to a replication of the random equilibrium environment but with block trading. The hypothesis was that off-floor trading volume would increase in this environment with block trading. We conducted two replications (9x and 10x), with different groups of once-experienced subjects, as in Experiment 6x. The results are charted in Figure 15.6. Comparing Experiments 9x and 10x with Experiment 6x in Table 15.2, the mean off-floor volume is increased with the introduction of block trading from 2.5 in 6x to 4.5 and 3.6, respectively, in 9x and 10x. The volatility and spread data suggest that these measures are not systematically affected by the introduction of block trading.

E.   Do Off-Floor Trades Persist with Increased Experience at Prices Inside the Standing Bid–Ask Spread?

We next wanted to examine the persistence of off-floor trading with increased experience and to obtain direct evidence that off-floor trades occur at prices within the bid–ask spread.

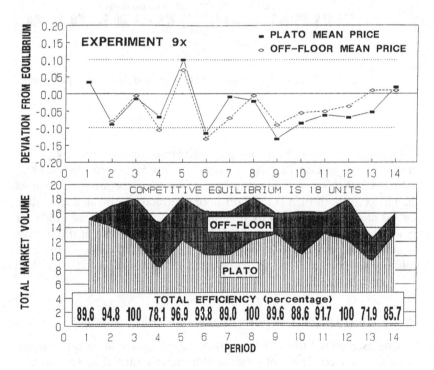

FIGURE 15.6(a). Block off-floor trading; random equilibrium.

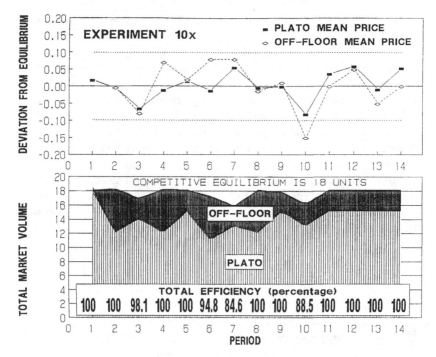

FIGURE 15.6(b). Block off-floor trading; random equilibrium.

Our final experiment used 10 subjects recruited from the pool of subjects who had participated in Experiments 9x and 10x. They were therefore experienced in two of the previous 15-period experiments reported here. We thought such experienced subjects would be able to handle the additional recording demands we placed upon them. In particular, with our monitoring assistance, we thought a subject would be able to record quickly the PLATO clock time at which a bid (offer) was tendered to an adjacent trader, and that the receiving trader could record the PLATO clock time at which the bid (offer) was accepted or rejected. In fact, this extra procedural task worked smoothly with little apparent interference in the process. This procedure is illustrated by the display in Figure 15.2. Note that buyer 5 faces a standing bid–ask of $4.12 to $4.43, with 28 seconds remaining. At time 28, buyer 5 conveyed a bid to seller 4, stating a willingness to buy a 3-unit block at $4.35 (8 cents below the standing offer and 23 cents above the standing bid). At time 20 seller 4 checked "accept" on the form and returned it to buyer 5. These two traders made a timely trade for 3 units and still had 20 seconds left for additional trading effort.

From Figure 15.7 and Table 15.2, comparing Experiment 11xx with Experiments 9x and 10x, we note a substantial increase in off-floor volume, an increased bid–ask spread, and an increase, both on and off-floor, in the variance and mean square error of price deviations. Thus off-floor trading not only persisted but increased with experience. Within Experiment 11xx, off-floor trading also increased over time (Figure 15.7), as subjects became more experienced in repeat period trading.

Table 15.3 reveals that (1) a preponderance of accepted off-floor trade proposals are inside the bid–ask spread at the time of submission and at the time of acceptance; (2) the number of accepted proposals, the number rejected, and the mean bid–ask spread all tend to increase

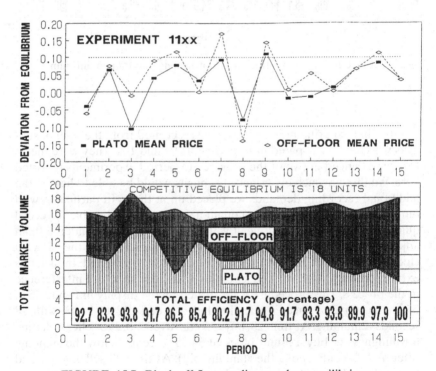

FIGURE 15.7. Block off-floor trading; random equilibrium.

across the 3 weeks of the experiment; and (3) rejected proposals are much more likely to be outside the mean spread, but note that the number of rejected proposals is far larger than the number accepted.

F.   Regression Tests of Hypotheses

Using dummy independent regression variables for the baseline and treatment conditions, and observations from 10 experiments, we shall report Ordinary Least Squares (OLS) estimates and hypothesis tests for the questions posed in the previous discussion. The OLS regressions,

Table 15.3. *Experiment 11xx off-floor activity relative to standing PLATO bid–ask spread[a]*

Periods	N	Mean spread	Submission number			Mean spread	Response number[b]		
			In	Out	Ind		In	Out	Ind
Accepted proposals:									
1–5	10	0.166	7	2	1	0.195	6	3	1
6–10	10	0.186	9	1	0	0.138	7	3	0
11–15	5	0.329	14	0	1	0.239	14	0	1
Subtotal	35	0.241	30	3	2	0.197	27	6	2
Rejected proposals:									
1–5	145	0.237	55	77	13	0.259	57	71	17
6–10	138	0.291	63	64	11	0.259	57	68	13
11–15	140	0.323	80	54	6	0.307	73	56	11
Subtotal	423	0.284	198	195	30	0.275	187	195	41
All proposals:									
1–5	155	0.232	62	79	14	0.254	63	74	18
6–10	148	0.283	72	65	11	0.250	64	71	13
11–15	155	0.324	94	54	7	0.301	87	56	12
Total	458	0.280	228	198	32	0.269	214	201	43

[a] Spread is the difference between standing PLATO bid and offers.
[b] In and out refers to the number of off-floor contract prices inside or outside, respectively, the relevant spread. Ind means indeterminant; there was no standing bid and/or offer at the time of the off-floor contract. In period 5 there was no standing offer on PLATO at the time of an off-floor contract but the contract price was less than the standing bid; this trade is recorded as outside the spread.

Table 15.4. *OLS estimation of treatment effects and pairwise comparisons in off-floor trading*

Independent variable	PLATO contracts				All Contracts
	Price variance[a]	Spread[b]	Median spread[a]	Fraction of volume off-floor[a]	Market efficiency[a]
C	0.003	0.180	0.150	—	0.914
	(0.0009)	(0.0111)	(0.0188)		(0.0134)
R	0.014	0.316	0.270	—	0.875
	(0.0011)	(0.0135)	(0.0230)		(0.0165)
OSC	0.001	0.053	0.044	0.101	0.966
	(0.0016)	(0.0194)	(0.0325)	(0.0277)	(0.0233)
OSR	0.002	0.130	0.081	0.144	0.965
	(0.0016)	(0.0203)	(0.0325)	(0.0277)	(0.0233)
OBX1	0.002	0.101	0.072	0.242	0.943
	(0.0012)	(0.0157)	(0.0238)	(0.0203)	(0.0170)
OBX2	0.005	0.126	0.119	0.426	0.904
	(0.0016)	(0.0256)	(0.0325)	(0.0277)	(0.0233)
R^2	0.380	0.080	0.271	0.543	0.109
N	148	2.083	148	−73	148

	C ≥ R	C ≥ R	C ≥ R		R ≥ C
C vs. R[c]					
H_0	C ≥ R	C ≥ R	C ≥ R	—	R ≥ C
t	-7.57 [0.000]	-7.80 [0.000]	-4.06 [0.000]	—	1.82 [0.281]
U	-5.96 [0.000]	-12.0 [0.000]	-4.01 [0.000]	—	2.39 [0.034]
OSC vs. OSR[c]					
H_0	OSC ≥ OSR	OSC ≥ OSR	OSC ≥ OSR	OSC ≥ OSR	OSC ≥ OSR
t	-0.44 [0.499]	-2.71 [0.499]	-0.82 [0.499]	-1.10 [0.411]	0.03 [0.499]
U	-2.234 [0.038]	-6.40 [0.038]	-2.38 [0.038]	-1.31 [0.287]	0.17 [0.499]
OSR vs. OBX1[c]					
H_0	OSR ≥ OBX1	OSR ≥ OBX1	OSR ≥ OBX1	OSR ≥ OBX1	OSR ≥ OBX1
t	0.33 [0.505]	1.13 [0.999]	0.23 [0.504]	-2.85 [0.008]	0.75 [0.499]
U	-0.03 [0.499]	-1.11 [0.499]	0.14 [0.499]	-2.93 [0.002]	-0.04 [0.501]
OBX1 vs. OBX2[c]					
H_0	OBX1 ≥ OBX2	OBX1 ≥ OBX2	OBX1 ≥ OBX2	OBX1 ≥ OBX2	OBX1 ≥ OBX2
t	-1.49 [0.276]	-0.83 [0.499]	-1.17 [0.487]	-5.37 [0.000]	1.34 [0.368]
U	-1.96 [0.100]	-2.95 [0.006]	-2.12 [0.069]	-3.95 [0.000]	2.19 [0.057]

Note: Standard errors are in parentheses. Bonferroni *p*-values are in brackets. H_0: the null hypothesis is that the coefficient of the variable on the left is not smaller than the coefficient of the variable on the right (e.g., $C ≥ R$ for price variance).

[a] One observation per period per experiment. Estimated coefficient is mean value per period for the given treatment.

[b] One observation per period per PLATO contract. Estimated coefficient is mean value for the given treatment. Spread is the difference between the standing PLATO bid and offer. Of the 2189 PLATO contracts, 106 occurred when there was either no standing bid or no standing offer.

[c] *t* is calculated from OLS results. *U* is the Mann-Whitney *z*-variate calculated from pairwise rank sums.

evaluating the marginal effects of the treatments on the price variance, spread, per period median spread, efficiency, and fraction of volume off-floor are shown in the top panel of Table 15.4. In each case, the dependent variable was regressed on the baseline dummy variables C (= 1 for a constant competitive equilibrium environment; 0 otherwise) and R (= 1 for a random CE environment; 0 otherwise), as well as the off-floor treatment variables OSC (= 1 for single-unit constant CE; 0 otherwise), OSR (= 1 for single-unit random CE; 0 otherwise), OBX1 (= 1 for block trading once-experienced; 0 otherwise), and OBX2 (= 1 for block trading twice-experienced; 0 otherwise).

Appearing in the lower panel of Table 15.4 are the Bonferroni t-values and the nonparametric Mann-Whitney U-statistic for joint tests of the a priori ordering of the regression coefficients.[8] For example, in the base-lines, the prediction was that the median spread would be wider and efficiency lower for R than for C; that is, the R environment was expected to yield wider spreads, and for the gains from exchange to be lower. Therefore the null hypothesis was that the median spread regression coefficient for C was greater than that for R. The Bonferroni t is (−4.06) for this comparison, and the negative sign indicates that the R coefficient (0.27) exceeds the C coefficient (0.15). This was corroborated by the non-parametric Mann-Whitney U-test. Comparing the random (OSR) with the constant (OSC) environment for off-floor single-unit trading, the spread coefficients exhibited the predicted order, and in the U-test the difference was significant.[9] In contrast, there was no significant difference between the spread for block (OBX1) and for single-unit (OSR) trading, or between twice- (OBX2) and once- (OBX1) experienced traders. The efficiency coefficients declined monotonically as we proceeded down the treatments from C to OBX2; as predicted, two of the pairwise comparisons were significant using the Mann-Whitney U, and none were significant using the Bonferroni t-values. Finally, in the upper right panel of Table 15.4, we note that the coefficients for fraction of off-floor trading increase, as predicted, with the successive off-floor treatments. The lower right panel shows that block trading significantly increased off-floor trades relative to single-unit trading, and the effect of experience was to further significantly increase off-floor trading. Finally,

---

[8] Because we were conducting multiple comparisons of coefficients estimated from the same data set, we used the Bonferroni t-test (see Miller, 1981). In this application, we report one-tailed t-values because the original experimental design allowed an a priori prediction of the sign of coefficient differences.

[9] Direct comparison between the coefficients of C or R and those of OSC or OSR are not meaningful because the latter used experienced subjects, whereas the former used inexperienced subjects. We only made comparisons after controlling for experience, because we expected experience to reduce spreads and price volatility.

in the upper left panel of Table 15.4, the coefficients for price variance in the constant relative to the random environment have the predicted direction and significantly so, as shown in the lower left panel of Table 15.4.

V.   Discussion and Conclusions

Our primary objective in this chapter was to investigate the incentive conditions under which the phenomenon of off-floor trading might occur. We began with the simplest and most transparent environment that might induce traders to leave an organized exchange to engage in bilateral private trades: an environment in which the rate structure provided lower transactions cost for block trades off-floor than unit trades on-floor. This environment parallels that of U.S. financial markets before 1975 when the schedule of minimum brokerage fees did not properly reflect the cost of block trades, and this helped to support the "third market" in off-exchange trades. In Experiment 1, off-floor trading was permitted after period 5, and in periods 7–15, we observed the predicted number (18) of off-floor trades. It is clear from this experiment that by providing an off-floor cost advantage to all (or most) traders one might precipitate a type of market failure in which ultimately the on-floor trades were so thin that it would no longer provide competitive price information to facilitate off-floor bilateral bargaining. This experiment illustrated the important principle that on-floor brokerage commissions must be competitive with the off-floor costs of direct negotiation if market disintegration is to be avoided.

The environment of Experiment 1 was that of stationary induced supply and demand schedules, with each trader assigned unchanging limit supply or demand prices. In this repeated static market, the naturally occurring bid–ask spread converged toward the minimum possible spread of 1 cent. In fact, the median observed spread was only 1 cent (Table 15.2) across trading periods 6–10. It followed that if we were to study the incentive of traders to contract off-floor at prices inside the bid–ask spread, then it would be essential that we create an environment in which the naturally occurring bid–ask spread converged to a larger level. We conjectured that this would be the case in supply/demand environments in which (1) the buyer (seller) induced value (cost) assignments were rerandomized repeatedly and (2) a random constant was added (or subtracted) repeatedly to all values and costs to effect random shifts in supply and demand. We tested our conjecture in three experiments (2–4) using condition 1, yielding a constant competitive equilibrium price, and two experiments (7–8) using conditions 1 and 2, yielding a random competitive equilibrium price. In the constant environment, with only random reassignment of traders to value-cost steps, we observed a much wider bid–ask spread than in Experiment 1: a median spread of 10–14 cents, in Experiments 2–4 compared with 1 cent in periods 6–10 of Experiment 1. Under conditions 1 and 2, which added a random shifting competitive equilibrium price, the median observed bid–ask spread widened further to 24 and 18 cents, respectively, in Experiments 7 and 8 (Table 15.2).

These findings, even though they are ancillary to the primary objective of the chapter, have important implications for modeling the bid–ask spread in double-auction trading institutions. Traditional theories of the bid–ask spread are of two kinds: (1) The bid–ask spread is a transactions cost of the dealer or a specialist for providing the services of immediacy (see Demsetz, 1968b), and (2) the bid–ask spread is due to the existence of traders with information superior to that of the specialist (see Copeland and Galai, 1983; and Glosten and Milgrom, 1985). One should be aware that these models provide *sufficient* not necessary conditions for the existence of a positive bid–ask spread. That they are not necessary is shown by the hundreds of experimental double-auction markets, and our baseline 2 experiments reported here, in which a positive bid–ask spread persists; yet these are principals markets, without intermediate dealers or specialists, and the transactions cost is minuscule. In many of these experiments, all individuals have identical (although uncertain) information on the value of the securities traded (see Smith et al., 1988). Yet one observes a bid–ask spread. A third theory is based on establishing that ". . . the probability of a limit order executing does not rise to unity as the price at which the order is placed gets infinitesimally close to a counterpart (bid or ask) market quote" (Cohen et al., 1981, p. 300). In terms of this theory, our success in inducing a wider bid–ask spread by increasing uncertainty in the environment can be attributed to the fact that we shifted the probability of a limit order executing.

The next step in our research was to allow off-floor trading using constant versus random supply and demand shifts, and single-unit versus block trading, as treatment variables (with no explicit trading cost in either the electronic or off-floor transactions). Comparing experiments with off-floor single-unit trading in the random environment with those in the constant environment, we found more off-floor trading in the former than in the latter (Table 15.2), but the difference was not statistically significant (Table 15.4). We attribute the increase in off-floor trading with the random environment to the fact that the bid–ask spread is wider than in the constant environment. But this is not documented because we collected no data on the extent to which off-floor trades occurred within the spread in Experiments 5x–10x.

Comparing experiments using off-floor single-unit trading with those having block trading (both using the random environment) we observed more off-floor trading with blocks than with single units (Table 15.2), and the difference was significant (Table 15.4). The reason for this appears to be straightforward: In our experimental environment, the subjective cost of an off-floor trade (the effort in writing a bid or an offer, deciding which of two adjacent traders to give it to, and then delivering the quotation) is the same for a 3-unit block as for a single unit. Consequently, an elementary transactions cost argument predicts more units will trade off-floor under block trading than under single-unit trading.

Our last experiment (11xx) used twice-experienced subjects and recorded the standing bid–ask spread at the time each off-floor block bilateral trade proposal was made, and again at the time when the proposal was either rejected or accepted. In this experiment, 27 of 35 off-floor (3-unit block) trades, or 77%, were inside the bid–ask spread at the time of acceptance. This supports the hypothesis that the primary motivation for such trades is to split the gains inherent in the standing bid–ask spread, although there may exist block-trading advantages, such as reduced uncertainty of execution, at prices outside the spread. Furthermore, comparing off-floor trading using twice-experienced subjects with that for only once-experienced subjects, we note a significant increase in off-floor trading with experience (Tables 15.2 and 15.4). Consequently, the phenomenon is not an artifact of trader inexperience. We think this is because, with experience, traders become more skilled in moving back and forth between the two markets and are able to handle the demands of off-floor negotiation with less effort.

Finally, across treatments that are associated with an increase in off-floor trading, we observed a monotonic decline in market efficiency (Table 15.4). This is evidence in favor of the hypothesis that off-floor trading is socially undesirable. [The fact that the decline is not significant (Table 15.4) in the pairwise comparison of *adjacent* treatments moderates this conclusion, although this result might be altered with increased sample size.] But the results of this research are best interpreted as providing only weak support for market degradation in the presence of off-floor trading. Hence, off-floor trading may be less of a problem for the social objective of maximizing the gains from exchange than it is for the exchange firm that loses volume to bilateral traders who free-ride on the public price information generated by the exchange.

CHAPTER 16

Bertrand-Edgeworth Competition in Experimental Markets

Jamie Brown Kruse, Stephen Rassenti,
Stanley S. Reynolds, and Vernon L. Smith

Oligopoly markets have been the topic of extensive theoretical and experimental research. Oligopoly market models with price setting firms provide the opportunity to explore price formation in ways that are not possible using a quantity choice (Cournot) formulation. In particular, one can consider the implications of various equilibrium and disequilibrium models of seller-pricing behavior. This study explores capacity-constrained price-setting behavior in a four-seller laboratory environment. We focus on patterns of prices that arise over a relatively long time horizon (60 periods) and examine the effect of three different levels of aggregate production capacity and three levels of information about demand and rivals' costs.

Rivalry among price-setting sellers has been investigated in several prior experimental studies that have used the posted-offer environment. Prior posted-offer experiments examined a number of issues: the effects of changes in the number of sellers, the effects of the amount of information provided to sellers, the role of subject experience, the extent of market power for sellers, and the effects of changes in the market exchange institution itself. Results from many of these posted-offer experiments are discussed in Ketcham et al. (1984; hereafter KSW) and in survey articles by Plott (1982a) and Holt (1989). Experimental price and quantity outcomes have typically been compared to the competitive equilibrium, the collusive prediction, and the quantity-Cournot prediction.

Theoretical analysis of price-setting rivalry began with Bertrand's duopoly analysis of price-setting firms and the subsequent extension of Edgeworth (1925) that considered the role of production capacity constraints. Rivalry among firms that set prices, produce at constant marginal cost up to a capacity constraint, and offer a homogeneous product is typically referred to as Bertrand-Edgeworth (BE) competition. Game-theoretic analyses of single-period models of BE competition appeared in Beckman (1965) and Levitan and Shubik (1972). Allen and Hellwig (1986), Dasgupta and Maskin (1986),

348

Davidson and Deneckere (1986), Osborne and Pitchik (1986), and Vives (1986) and extended the static, game-theoretic analysis in various ways. Results from these analyses indicated that, in many cases, pure strategy equilibria in prices do not exist. This led game theorists to offer mixed strategy equilibria as an explanation of price formation under BE competition. Repeated interaction of sellers under BE competition was analyzed in Brock and Scheinkman (1985), Benoit and Krishna (1987), and Davidson and Deneckere (1990). These papers focused on the roles that the number of sellers and their capacity constraints play in the enforcement of collusive pricing schemes.

Most prior posted-offer experiments were not designed in a way that permits results to be compared to predictions from the full range of theories of BE competition. For many prior posted-offer experiments, pure strategy Nash equilibria do not exist, and mixed strategy equilibria in prices were typically not computed.[1] Given the designs used in most prior posted-offer experiments, numerical computation of equilibrium mixed strategies would be a formidable task.[2] Also, the role of excess capacity held by sellers was typically not considered as a treatment variable in prior experiments. In the industrial organization literature, excess capacity has been identified as a key factor influencing the viability of tacit collusion for price-setting sellers.

In this study, we report results from a series of experiments that were designed to (i) capture essential features of BE competition and (ii) permit game-theoretic equilibria to be computed as a basis for comparisons with the data. These experiments allow us to evaluate the predictive power of theories of BE competition in a controlled experimental laboratory setting. Competing hypotheses about price-setting behavior are based on four principal theories: competitive equilibrium (CE) pricing, Edgeworth cycles in prices, mixed strategy Nash equilibrium (NE) in prices, and tacit collusion. The experiments that we report were designed to provide more information about capacity-constrained pricing behavior and to learn what existing theories contribute to our understanding of pricing behavior.

---

[1] The recent experimental study by Davis et al. (1990) is an exception. They investigate market power of sellers in a posted-offer environment and provide explicit calculations of the mixed strategy NE in prices for their design.

[2] Holt and Solis-Soberon (1993) illustrate how one can calculate mixed strategy NE in prices for the type of step demand and cost structures that are often used in experiments. They show how these calculations become progressively more complex as more steps and more heterogeneity among agents is introduced.

I.   Experimental Background

A number of experimental studies over the past 25 years have tested the predictive implications of pure strategy noncooperative (Nash) equilibrium theory in a variety of institutional contexts. The first such tests, using data from 17 experiments, were reported by Fouraker and Siegel (1963) in their classic work on bargaining behavior. These experiments compared the observational support for Nash equilibrium, competitive, and monopoly theory under three different institutions: (i) price leadership bilateral monopoly, (ii) Bertrand price-setting duopoly and triopoly, and (iii) Cournot quantity-setting duopoly and triopoly. We focus on institution (ii) because this is a variation on "posted-offer" oligopoly pricing.[3]

In Fouraker and Siegel's Bertrand price-adjuster experiments, the oligopolists each posted a take-it-or-leave-it price (there were no capacity constraints so the NE corresponds to the CE). Demand was then simulated (with fully revealing buyers), with the low-priced seller getting the entire market and tied price sellers sharing the market equally. These experiments were run under conditions of private information, in which subjects were informed of their own payoff schedule but not the payoff schedule(s) of their rival(s), and under public information, in which subjects were informed of payoff schedules for all participants. In these repeat transaction experiments, strong support for the pure strategy Nash (-competitive) equilibrium is observed under private information duopoly and triopoly. This support is weakened in the direction of the monopoly outcome under public information duopoly, but not under public information triopoly. That is, the triopoly condition dominates the information condition yielding Nash (-competitive) outcomes.

In summary, the Fouraker and Siegel posted-offer oligopoly experiments generally yielded strong support for the "complete information," pure strategy Nash equilibrium concept in environments with *private information* but not necessarily in environments with (common) public payoff information. These experimental results indicated that a complete information Nash equilibrium for a single-play model can provide good predictions for repeated trial (market period) environments in which agents have only private information.

In Ketcham et al. (1984) the performance of the posted-offer institution was compared to the double oral auction in two different experimental designs. These were private information experiments – a seller

---

[3] For a more complete discussion of the Fouraker and Siegel experimental results, see Smith et al. (1982, pp. 64–5).

knows only his own cost schedule, a buyer knows only his own redemption values. Each seller posted a price and a maximum number of units offered for sale in each period. Most of the experiments were run for 25 market periods. In design I (four buyers, four sellers) posted prices tended to converge to the CE (this CE is not a NE) as in the Fouraker and Siegel experiments; a NE is not computed for this design. In design II (four buyers, three sellers) a pure strategy NE existed and was computed. Posted prices tended to deviate from the CE in the direction of the NE in the design II experiments.

Davis et al. (1990) reported on a series of two-seller and three-seller posted-offer experiments with computer-simulated buyers. Their experiments were designed to investigate the impact of static market power; static market power exists when static NE prices exceed the CE price. Sellers were fully informed about buyer demand. A random stopping rule was used after period 15 in these experiments. Static market power leads to higher prices for both two- and three-seller experiments, with a significant effect for three-seller experiments. Their results for market power experiments were generally unsupportive of the mixed strategy static NE; median prices in two-seller experiments tended to be below their predicted values, and median prices for three-seller experiments tended to be above their predicted values. Davis et al. found some evidence of tacit collusion in each of their treatments. However, collusion is typically imperfect with prices below the monopoly price.

Alger (1987) also reported on a series of two- and three-seller posted-offer pricing experiments with simulated buyers. Most experiments involved private information – subjects knew their own costs but were not informed about rivals' costs or about demand. The focus of Alger's study was a search for a behavioral equilibrium in the experimental data. An experiment was terminated only after a series of market outcomes were observed that satisfied the operational definition of equilibrium (this was essentially a condition that prices stabilize over several market periods). As a consequence of this termination rule, some experiments were run for a large number of periods (e.g., 120 periods). Most prior posted-offer experiments had been run for a fixed, maximum number of periods (e.g., 20 periods). Alger found that market prices plotted over time tend to be U-shaped; prices typically fall in initial periods, then rise in later periods, finally stabilizing at a price level above the CE. Disequilibrium prices were found to be significantly different from equilibrium prices.

Alger's results for experiments with long time horizons are similar to results reported by Stoecker (1980) and Friedman and Hoggatt (1980) for duopoly experiments with experienced subjects. Convergence to the

CE was not the characteristic result; prices were more likely to be near the (quantity) Cournot price or the joint profit maximizing price.[4]

II.   Experimental Design, Procedures, and Predictions

A group of four subjects participated as sellers in each multiperiod posted-offer experiment. The four sellers in an experiment had identical average costs of production and identical capacity constraints. These average cost and capacity conditions were held constant over all market periods of an experiment. Aggregate demand was composed of many computer-simulated buyers.

The experiments are divided into five cells (or groups) based on two primary treatment conditions: the amount of information provided to subjects and the aggregate capacity. This is illustrated as a "cross design" in Table 16.1.

There were three levels of information provision. In PRIVATE information experiments, subjects (sellers) were informed about their own average cost and capacity but were not informed about their rivals' costs and capacities nor were they informed about market demand. In MIXED information experiments, subjects were told all sellers' costs and capacities but were not informed about market demand. In PUBLIC information experiments, subjects were given information about all sellers' costs and capacities and about aggregate demand.

There were three levels of aggregate seller capacity. In LOW capacity experiments, each seller had 145 units of capacity. In MEDIUM capacity experiments, each seller had 185 units of capacity. HIGH capacity experiments were run with 225 units of capacity per seller. HIGH capacity experiments were designed so that there was substantial excess capacity at the competitive equilibrium (with price equal to the constant average cost, AC), as illustrated in Figure 16.1. In both MEDIUM and LOW capacity experiments, the competitive price was above AC, and sellers fully utilized their capacity in a competitive equilibrium (see Figure 16.1).

Subjects for the experiments were recruited from undergraduate economics and business classes at the University of Arizona. Each subject was paid $3 for arriving on time for the experiment. Subjects were told

---

[4] But in the experimental studies of Alger (1987), Davis et al. (1990), Stoecker (1980), and Friedman and Hoggatt (1980), fully revealing demand behavior was simulated, while in Ketcham et al. (1984) all buyers were human subjects. Brown-Kruse (1991) has reported experiments comparing the effect of real as opposed to simulated buyers. Mean price paths were significantly higher when buyer behavior was simulated than when subject buyers were used, suggesting that the reported instances of tacit collusion may depend upon simulated fully revealing demand behavior.

Table 16.1. *Bertrand-Edgeworth experimental design[a]*

| | | Capacity level | | |
		Low $K = 145$	Medium $K = 185$	High $K = 225$
	Private		MRI1	
			MRI2	
			MRE1	
			MRE2	
			600	
Information	Mixed	LMI1	MMI1	HMI1
provision		LMI2	MMI2	HMI2
		LME1	MME1[b]	HME1
		LME2	MME2	HME2
		1000	600	400
	Public		MUI1	
			MUI2	
			MUE1	
			MUE2	
			600	

$n = 4$ sellers
K = production capacity per seller
AC = 5 pesos per unit of output, for output up to K
$m = 100$ (simulated) buyers

$D(p) = \sum_{j=1}^{m} d_j(p) = 5094p^{-1.15}$ = market demand

[a] A four-character string identifies each experiment. The first character indicates a capacity level from the set (Low, Medium, High). The second character indicates the information provision (Private, Mixed, Public). The third character indicates subject experience (Inexperienced, Experienced). The final character is an index number for the experiment.
[b] The exchange rate of pesos per dollar is listed at the bottom of the box for each treatment condition. The exchange rate for experiment MME1 was 400 pesos per dollar.

that the experiment would run for up to 2 hours. A typical experiment lasted about 1 hour and 15 minutes.

Four experiments were run for each of the five cells in Table 16.1. Two of the four experiments in each cell were run with inexperienced subjects. The other two experiments in each cell were run with experienced subjects; experience means previous participation in one or more of the posted-offer experiments in our design.[5]

[5] Subjects who had previously participated in a MIXED or PUBLIC information experiment were not chosen for another experiment with a lower provision of information.

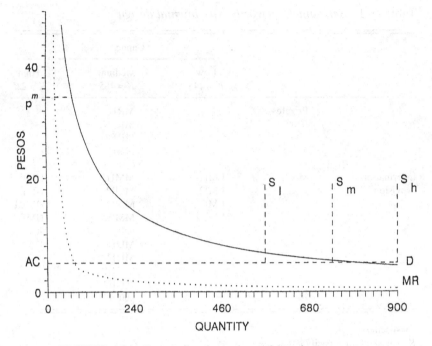

FIGURE 16.1. Demand and supply configurations.

The experimental design and market parameters are summarized in Table 16.1. Prices, costs, and profits were denominated in experimental "pesos." The names of the experiments and the exchange rate used are listed in each cell.

The buyer side of the market was identical for all experiments. A large number ($m = 100$) of computer-simulated buyers were used. Each buyer followed a demand-revealing purchasing rule. Inverse demand for an individual buyer was of the form,

$$P_j = \alpha_j q_j^{-1/\eta} \qquad (j = 1, \ldots, 100) \tag{1}$$

The α_j parameters were assigned according to draws from a log-normal distribution to reflect a distribution of income across the simulated buyer population. A single drawing of 100 α_j parameters was used for all experiments. The aggregation of individual demand maintained the property of constant own price elasticity in the market demand,

$$D(p) = \theta\, p^{-\eta} \qquad \eta = 1.15 \qquad \theta = \sum_{j=1}^{100} \alpha_j^\eta = 5094.0 \tag{2}$$

A random ordering of buyers was drawn at the start of each market period. Buyers at the front of the queue chose the seller with the lowest price. If this seller had sufficient capacity to satisfy all buyers at the posted price, then all purchases were from this seller. If $D(p_i) > K_i$ (where seller i had the lowest price p_i, and had capacity K_i), then some buyers must go to the seller with the second lowest price. If the seller with the second lowest price did not have enough capacity to satisfy the remaining buyers, then buyers further back in the queue went to the seller with the third lowest price, and so on.

If buyers were atomistic, then sales for seller i would be x_i (see Allen and Hellwig, 1986),

$$x_i = \min\left[K_i, \max\left(0, \left(1 - \sum_{P_j < P_i} \frac{K_j}{D(P_j)}\right) D(P_i) \frac{K_i}{\sum_{p_s = p_i} K_s} \right)\right] \quad (3)$$

This queuing scheme rations up to the fraction,

$$\left[1 - \sum_{p_j < p_i} K_j / D(p_j)\right]$$

of all buyers to sellers who had chosen price p_i. For example, suppose that $p_1 < p_2 < p_3 < p_4$ and $K_1 < D(p_1)$. Then the fraction of buyers $[1 - K_1/D(p_1)]$ is available to purchase from seller 2.

In our experiments sales to seller i can deviate from x_i in (3) because we allowed only sales of discrete units and because buyers are not atomistic. However, (3) provides a good approximation to actual sales because many units of output are traded in the market and because each of the 100 buyers represented a small fraction of total demand.[6]

Experiments were run for up to 60 market periods.[7] Subjects were not informed about the number of periods in the experiment. There were two main reasons for having more market periods than most prior posted-offer experiments. First, we wanted to have enough periods to be able to construct frequency distributions of prices for individual sellers and perform statistical tests on the distributions. Second, Alger's (1987) results suggested that in some environments posted prices during the first 20 or 25 periods may not be representative of results over a longer sequence of periods. We did not attempt to use a termination rule based

---

[6] An alternative experimental design would be to use the sales function (3) directly, rather than specify demands for individual buyers. Our approach of specifying individual buyer demands has the advantage of permitting parallel experiments using human buyers, at some point in time.

[7] All experiments except MMI1 have 60 periods. Experiment MMI1 was terminated after period 54 because of a computer error.

on some operational equilibrium definition. Our experimental environment was one in which we would not necessarily expect prices to stabilize (see the discussion of Edgeworth cycles and mixed strategies later in Sections II.B and II.C).

Each subject (seller) made a single decision in each market period; namely, which price to post. A seller did not choose a maximum quantity to sell, as in most previous posted-offer pricing experiments. The capacity constraint (set by the experimenter) took the role of the quantity limit. After prices were posted and all buyers finished making purchases, each seller observed all prices posted for the period, his or her sales and profit for the period, and total market sales for the period. The history of posted prices for the previous seven periods was also displayed on each subject's computer screen. The instructions for sellers appear in Appendix I.[8]

Several types of theoretical predictions might explain the behavior of sellers in our experiments. Operational versions of these predictions are described next.

A.   Competitive Pricing

The competitive theory predicts that each seller sets the market clearing price, p^c. Market clearing prices were 5, 5.35, and 6.62 pesos for HIGH, MEDIUM, and LOW capacity experiments, respectively. Competitive pricing yielded positive profits for sellers in the LOW and MEDIUM capacity treatments and zero profit in the HIGH capacity treatment. Setting a competitive price was not a best response to competitive pricing by all other sellers in any of the treatments; the CE is not a static NE for our experiments. Because competitive pricing does not involve mutual best responses for sellers in a single period, sellers in our experiments had static market power as Holt (1989) defines the term.

For some experimental designs, posted-offer experiments have exhibited prices that converged to p^c over time from above. For example, this was a feature of results from design I experiments reported in Ketcham et al. (1984) (recall that the CE was not a NE for those

---

[8] The instructions in Appendix I reproduce the computer screens that the subjects observed at the beginning of an experiment. The instructions refer to a production facility that is jointly owned by the sellers. This wording was to facilitate parallel experiments in which sellers share some production costs. Seller costs and capacities are not shared or interdependent in the experiments reported in this study. Subjects were also given supplementary verbal instructions and were given the chance to ask questions about their instructions. The verbal instructions repeated the information about the random buyer queuing routine.

experiments).[9] This pattern of convergence can emerge with as few as three or four sellers. The competitive model is generally thought of as a model of limited or incomplete information; a competitive seller knows his or her own AC and capacity but need not know payoff information for other market participants. Thus, competitive pricing is most likely to emerge when subjects have limited information, as in our PRIVATE and MIXED information treatments.

B. Edgeworth Price Cycles

A duopoly model of capacity-constrained, price-setting firms was first formulated and analyzed by Edgeworth (1925).[10] Edgeworth examined a multiperiod model in which each seller sets a price in the current period based on the expectation that its rival will maintain its price from the previous period. Edgeworth predicted that a pattern of cycling in prices over time would emerge in some cases. If sellers start with high prices (e.g., near the monopoly level), then each seller initially has an incentive to undercut its rival's price. However, there is some threshold price such that if a rival's price is below the threshold, a much higher price (the monopoly price, when buyers are randomly ordered) is more profitable than undercutting. After both sellers raise their prices, the price undercutting process begins again. Market prices thus evolve in cycles.

Edgeworth's duopoly theory was easily extended to our four-seller environment. A multiple-seller version of the theory predicts that each seller sets an optimal price in a period given the expectation that each of its rivals maintains his or her actual price from the previous period. We use this "naive price expectations" assumption to generate Edgeworth price predictions for the four sellers in each period after the first period of an experiment. A key difficulty with the Edgeworth cycle theory is that it is a disequilibrium theory in which expectations are inconsistent or irrational. Each seller would continually find that his or her price expectations do not match the rival's actions. In spite of this theoretical difficulty, there is evidence of Edgeworth price cycles in the

[9] However, earlier posted-offer pricing experiments differed in some important ways from the current experiments. For example, in design I of KSW (1984), a relatively small number of discrete units are traded, a small number of human buyers are used, heterogeneous sellers have differing marginal cost schedules, and these experiments had a maximum duration of 25 periods.

[10] A game-theoretic analysis of an Edgeworth duopoly model appears in Maskin and Tirole (1988). Their analysis assumes an alternating choice framework in which each seller sets a price in every other period. This framework is not directly applicable to our experimental study.

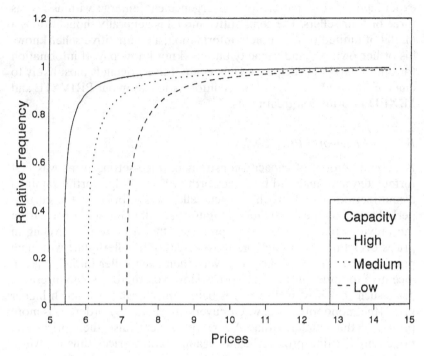

FIGURE 16.2. Mixed strategy Nash equilibrium price distribution for three capacity levels.

posted-offer duopoly experiments reported on in Isaac and Smith (1985, p. 339).

C.   Mixed Strategy Nash Equilibrium in Prices

The cycling pattern described by Edgeworth may be interpreted as the failure of existence of a pure strategy NE in prices (for the single-period, complete-information game). For the environments we consider, pure strategy NE in prices do not exist. Total capacity of sellers exceeds monopoly output and is less than the capacity that would generate the marginal cost-pricing Bertrand result for each capacity-level treatment.

In Appendix II, we develop a computational procedure for finding the symmetric mixed strategy NE for the symmetric, four-seller game. This procedure is applied to the parameters for each capacity level. The mixed strategy NE cumulative distribution functions for the three capacity levels are illustrated in Figure 16.2. In each case, the lower bound of the price support for the equilibrium mixed strategy is within 1 peso of the corresponding competitive price. Also, each distribution is very steep at its lower bound, with more than 80% of price draws predicted to be within 1 peso of the lower bound. Median predicted prices for the mixed strategy NE are 5.48, 6.16, and 7.24 pesos, for the HIGH, MEDIUM, and LOW capacity environments, respectively.

The mixed strategy NE is derived in the context of a one-shot game model. One way to test this prediction would be to gather data from many single-period experiments with a different set of seller subjects in each experiment. For example, this might be done by rotating a large pool of subjects in and out of groups with four sellers per group, so that each seller faces new rivals in each period. We are interested in a different issue. Oligopolistic pricing rivalry in naturally occurring markets usually involves a fixed group of sellers making repeated price decisions. We are interested in whether the mixed strategy NE can provide useful price predictions in repeated trial environments with a fixed group of sellers. Clearly, the NE mixed strategy is also an equilibrium for an environment with repeated play over a sequence of periods, such as our experimental environment. (A repeated play environment may admit additional Nash equilibria – this issue is addressed in our discussion of tacit collusion.) We interpret the symmetric NE mixed pricing strategies as providing predictions of frequency distributions of sellers' prices. A frequency distribution of prices for a seller in an experiment can be constructed from data gathered over a sequence of market periods. A repeated play environment also permits a richer set of alternative hypotheses (Edgeworth price cycles, tacit collusion, etc.) than that of one-shot experiments.

A literal interpretation of the mixed strategy NE is that it applies to a one-shot game in which each player has complete information about the payoffs of all players. We ran our MEDIUM capacity experiments for three types of information conditions: PRIVATE, MIXED, and PUBLIC. Experimental evidence described herein suggests that the NE for the one-shot complete information game may provide good predictions for repeated trial experiments in which subjects have limited payoff information (as in our PRIVATE and MIXED information experiments).

D.   Tacit Collusion

There are no opportunities for explicit communication between seller subjects in our experiments. However, subjects may be able to achieve high prices and profits through some type of tacitly collusive price-signaling behavior. The highest total profit for a group of sellers is achieved at the monopoly price of $p^m = 38$ pesos for each experiment (see Figure 16.1). Demand and cost parameters were chosen so that there was a large separation (in percentage terms) between competitive and monopoly prices for each experiment. This feature of the experimental design yields a large support for mixed strategy NE prices and helps to separate the Edgeworth cycle and mixed strategy NE predictions.

Our experimental design involved substantial excess capacity at the monopoly price. The ratio of excess capacity at the monopoly price to total market capacity ranged from 87 to 91% in our experiments. This means that if sellers set a common price equal to the monopoly price and one seller undercuts the monopoly price then that seller will experience a fourfold gain in sales and profits. Tacit collusion that involves monopoly pricing would be unlikely if subjects believed the experiment may end soon because of the large gains from undercutting the monopoly price.

Tacit collusion may involve prices and profits that are below monopoly levels but above noncooperative levels. Subjects in our experiments interact over a long sequence of market periods with an unknown stopping time. Suppose that the subjects in an experiment share a common, subjective probability equal to $1 - \delta$ that the experiment will stop after the current period. The theory of repeated games indicates that if the continuation probability δ is not too small, then a variety of tacitly collusive outcomes can be supported as noncooperative Nash equilibria of the repeated game. For example, Benoit and Krishna (1987) analyzed a repeated game of seller price choice in which sellers have fixed capacity constraints.[11] One type of equilibrium they considered was a stationary perfect equilibrium in which sellers charge constant prices along the equilibrium path. This pricing outcome is supported as a perfect equilibrium with trigger strategies that specify reversion to mixed strategy NE pricing if deviations from the stationary path are observed. The continuation probability δ must be high enough so that no seller has an incentive to cheat by undercutting the stationary price, if stationary prices are to be an equilibrium outcome.

For our experiments there is a minimum subjective continuation probability that would be required to support some level of tacit collusion with stationary pricing (i.e., stationary pricing that yields profit per seller above the corresponding mixed strategy NE profit). This minimum prob-

---

[11] Benoit and Krishna (1987) use surplus maximizing buyer rationing rather than the random buyer rationing rule that is used in our experiments. Thus, their results, such as Proposition 4 on stationary price paths, do not apply directly to our model. Benoit and Krishna also consider the choices of investment in production capacities by sellers.

ability varies with the level of capacity.[12] For LOW capacity experiments, δ must exceed 0.64. For MEDIUM capacity experiments, δ must exceed 0.56. For HIGH capacity experiments, δ must exceed 0.48. These values for δ indicate that subjects would not need to have high subjective continuation probabilities in order to sustain some level of tacit collusion. The minimum subjective continuation probabilities required to sustain monopoly pricing are higher because the gains from defection are greatest when all sellers set the monopoly price. The minimum continuation probabilities for monopoly pricing are as follows: $\delta > 0.85$ for LOW capacity, $\delta > 0.81$ for MEDIUM capacity, and $\delta > 0.78$ for HIGH capacity.

Prior pricing experiments with this type of repeated interaction have sometimes yielded results consistent with tacit collusion; recall Alger's (1987) experiments with two or three sellers. However, the attainment of tacitly collusive prices by sellers who are not permitted to communicate with one another involves a difficult coordination problem. In practice, this coordination problem may be substantially more difficult when there are four sellers than when two or three sellers serve the market.

If tacit collusion does occur, we would expect it to involve a relatively simple pricing pattern, such as constant equal prices for all sellers or some type of price rotation scheme (e.g., two pairs of sellers take turns being the low price sellers in alternating periods). Complex pricing patterns that yield tacitly collusive profit levels are possible in principle, and it may be possible to support them as noncooperative NE of the repeated game. However, it would be extremely difficult for sellers to coordinate a complex pricing pattern without communicating with one another because of difficulties in interpreting defections from the tacitly collusive path.

The likelihood that collusive prices are observed should depend on both the information and capacity-level treatments. The provision of more information about demand and sellers' costs should aid sellers' pricing coordination and raise the likelihood of successful tacit collusion. Thus, the tacit collusion hypothesis yields the prediction that average market prices rise as we go from PRIVATE to MIXED to PUBLIC information conditions.

---

[12] This minimum probability is found as follows. First the "no cheating" condition is $\delta > (\bar{\pi}_d - \bar{\pi}) / (\bar{\pi}_d - \pi^0)$, where $\bar{\pi}$ is the payoff per period from stationary pricing in a tacitly collusive outcome, $\bar{\pi}_d$ is the maximum payoff from defection from $\bar{\pi}$ and π^0 is the expected payoff in the mixed strategy NE. Second, find the minimum δ that satisfies the no cheating condition for each value of $\bar{\pi}$ between π^0 and one firm's share of monopoly payoffs. Third, search for the smallest subjective probability δ over all of the δ-values that were identified in step 2. Recall that each δ-value identified in step 2 has a corresponding average collusive payoff per seller and a defection payoff.

The level of capacity may also influence the stability of (tacitly) collusive agreements. The standard view is that more excess capacity weakens a collusive agreement. The argument for this is that if firms carry substantial excess capacity then each firm has a strong incentive to cheat because it can greatly expand its sales with a small price cut.

An alternative view is advanced by Davidson and Deneckere (1990) in their analysis of the Benoit-Krishna model. They argue that one should also consider how excess capacity affects the ability of sellers to retaliate against cheating. While greater capacity may increase the short run gain from cutting price, it also permits rival sellers to retaliate more effectively and impose greater long run losses on any seller that cheats. Thus, higher capacity levels raise the likelihood of successful tacit collusion. This argument is the basis for conditions that are required to sustain monopoly pricing as a perfect equilibrium in our experimental setup. Lower capacity levels require a higher minimum subjective continuation probability in order to sustain monopoly pricing.

III.   Experimental Results

Summary statistics for prices (mean, median, sample variance around the mean, trend) for 20 experiments appear in Table 16.2.[13] Statistics were computed for three intervals (beginning, middle, and ending periods) and for all periods of each experiment. Two primary conclusions can be drawn from the summary statistics and from observation of the raw price data.

1.   All the experiments exhibited a pattern of downward movement of prices over the first 20 to 25 periods. The trend growth rate of mean seller price is negative for the first 20 periods of every experiment. This pattern is broadly consistent with pricing data from prior posted-offer experiments (see e.g., Ketcham et al., 1984). However, prices typically do not reach the competitive price level by the end of this initial phase of price cutting. For six of the experiments (LME1, LMI2, HME2, MRI1, MRE2 and MUI1), this downward price pattern continues for the duration of the experiment. Note that experience of subjects does not seem to play a role in determining whether or not prices continue to fall during an experiment. Out of the six experiments identified as having falling prices throughout, three involved inexperienced subjects and three involved experienced subjects.

---

[13] The raw price data for all 20 experiments are available from the authors by request.

Table 16.2. *Bertrand-Edgeworth summary statistics for price data*

Experiment	Periods	Mean price	Median price	Sample variance	Total growth
MRI1	1–60	8.64	8.12	36.35	−2.5
	1–20	10.53	9.11	103.64	−6.2
	21–40	8.26	8.13	0.17	−0.7
	41–60	7.12	7.05	0.06	−0.7
MRI2	1–60	9.45	7.25	46.01	−2.1
	1–20	13.96	9.75	107.41	−6.1
	21–40	7.46	7.35	0.47	0.4
	41–60	6.94	6.88	0.29	−0.8
MRE1	1–60	7.15	6.78	9.92	0.5
	1–20	7.58	6.96	19.50	−0.5
	21–40	6.67	6.03	4.72	0.8
	41–60	7.20	6.68	5.36	1.2
MRE2	1–60	7.82	7.53	8.53	−2.1
	1–20	8.98	8.07	22.32	−5.6
	21–40	7.33	7.18	1.00	−0.5
	41–60	7.13	7.19	0.38	−0.4
LMI1	1–60	10.89	8.25	125.07	−0.9
	1–20	9.07	8.57	1.85	−2.3
	21–40	13.79	8.00	255.08	5.9
	41–60	9.80	8.00	180.37	−6.3
LMI2	1–60	8.13	8.15	0.18	−0.2
	1–20	8.29	8.35	0.47	−0.1
	21–40	8.17	8.16	0.01	−0.1
	41–60	7.94	7.96	0.02	−0.3
LME1	1–60	7.59	6.98	36.26	−2.4
	1–20	9.01	7.73	106.57	−6.9
	21–40	6.99	6.98	0.03	−0.3
	41–60	6.76	6.75	0.05	−0.1
LME2	1–60	8.23	7.89	2.16	−0.7
	1–20	8.42	8.22	1.00	−2.0
	21–40	8.36	7.82	3.46	0.0
	41–60	7.91	7.70	1.93	−0.1
MMI1	1–54	7.78	6.99	41.19	2.4
	1–20	6.79	6.50	0.54	−1.3
	21–40	7.06	6.80	0.43	0.8
	41–54	10.22	8.51	151.32	9.2
MMI2	1–60	9.32	6.75	149.45	2.4
	1–20	7.30	6.99	1.31	−1.6
	21–40	6.73	6.54	0.57	−0.5
	41–60	13.93	6.75	417.82	9.2

Table 16.2. (*Cont.*)

Experiment	Periods	Mean price	Median price	Sample variance	Total growth
MME1	1–60	6.95	6.10	37.69	−2.6
	1–20	7.75	6.15	110.33	−8.1
	21–40	6.45	6.10	1.00	1.2
	41–60	6.63	6.10	1.70	−1.2
MME2	1–60	7.40	7.00	1.13	−0.7
	1–20	7.68	7.20	1.72	−2.1
	21–40	7.30	7.10	0.74	−0.3
	41–60	7.23	6.90	0.85	0.1
HMI1	1–60	7.30	5.89	80.21	−0.6
	1–20	6.64	6.22	2.00	−2.6
	21–40	8.65	5.68	236.23	−0.2
	41–60	6.61	5.69	1.67	0.9
HMI2	1–60	8.10	6.87	40.38	−2.6
	1–20	9.39	7.49	76.96	−7.3
	21–40	6.65	6.62	0.21	−1.2
	41–60	8.28	5.99	41.16	0.6
HME1	1–60	7.28	5.89	48.06	−4.6
	1–20	7.93	6.25	115.58	−4.4
	21–40	6.29	5.68	12.02	4.5
	41–60	7.61	6.00	16.27	−4.5
HME2	1–60	6.51	5.35	39.31	−2.9
	1–20	8.69	7.13	111.26	−7.8
	21–40	5.55	5.30	0.30	−1.2
	41–60	5.28	5.33	0.12	0.0
MUI1	1–60	12.39	9.78	60.46	−2.6
	1–20	18.32	17.75	118.98	−6.2
	21–40	9.91	9.44	7.37	−0.6
	41–60	8.95	8.27	2.84	−0.3
MUI2	1–60	10.13	6.92	157.21	−1.5
	1–20	10.62	7.13	102.83	−5.2
	21–40	10.74	6.82	215.07	−0.3
	41–60	9.02	6.92	155.87	0.1
MUE1	1–60	7.21	6.75	36.61	−0.7
	1–20	7.14	6.84	1.18	−2.3
	21–40	6.81	6.75	0.09	−0.2
	41–60	7.67	6.50	109.28	0.3
MUE2	1–60	7.56	6.75	50.37	1.5
	1–20	7.75	6.58	109.09	−0.1
	21–40	6.92	6.55	1.65	0.2
	41–60	8.04	6.86	40.97	4.3

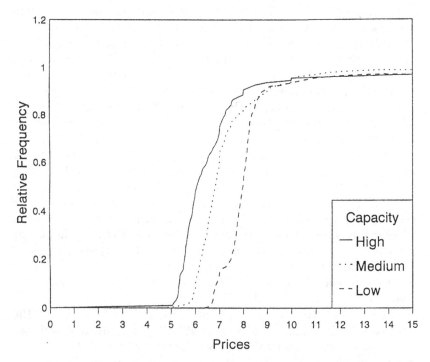

FIGURE 16.3. Cumulative price distributions from experiments for the MIXED information condition (seller' costs and capacity are public knowledge but demand is private).

2. The majority of the experiments exhibited a pattern of upward and downward price swings by two or more sellers that began during the middle periods of the experiment. The sample variance of prices is relatively high in the middle third or the final third of a number of experiments. In several cases, this pattern of price swings persists for the remainder of the experiment; that is, prices do not necessarily stabilize over time.

The impact of the amount of capacity held by sellers is illustrated in Figure 16.3, which shows the cumulative distributions of actual prices for HIGH, MEDIUM, and LOW capacity levels for prices in all MIXED information experiments. The distributions of prices for lower capacity experiments were to the right of distributions for higher capacity experiments, as one would expect.

We investigated the effects of all of the exogenous treatment conditions on prices by using an analysis of variance (ANOVA) procedure. The ANOVA statistics were calculated by running an Ordinary Least Squares (OLS) regression with price as the dependent variable and dummy variables specified to represent the experimental treatment conditions. The regression was run for all the price data after trading period 1 collected in 20 experiments. Three capacity dummy variables spanned the space of capacity treatments. There were dummies for two of the information conditions: PRIVATE and PUBLIC. The MIXED information condition was the omitted category. In our analysis of the data, we found that subject inexperience had effects that interacted with capacity and information conditions. We specified five dummy variables for subject inexperience, so that inexperience was interacted with the five possible combinations of capacity level and information provision in our experiments. These dummy variables are listed as INEXP followed by two letters; the first letter indicates capacity (L, M or H) and the second letter indicates information (M, R or U). Subject experience was the omitted category. PERINV is an explanatory variable equal to the inverse of the trading period.

The ANOVA regression results are reported in Table 16.3.[14] The positive and significant coefficient on PERINV is consistent with our earlier observation that there is a downward trend in prices for the early periods of all twenty experiments. The coefficients on the capacity dummy variables are all statistically significant. The hypothesis that these three coefficients are equal can be rejected at the 1% level in favor of the alternative hypothesis that they are ordered so that higher capacity is associated with a lower coefficient.

The coefficient for PRIVATE is positive but not statistically significant. This means that PRIVATE information experiments had prices that were higher, but not significantly higher, than MIXED information experiments. PUBLIC information raises prices by 0.44 pesos on average, compared to the MIXED information condition. However, this effect is not statistically significant.

The coefficients on the five-subject inexperience dummy variables are all positive. This means that experiments with experienced subjects had *lower* prices than experiments with inexperienced subjects. Prior experience with this posted-pricing environment did not enable subjects to achieve higher prices. All the coefficients for inexperience were significantly greater than zero (at the 5% level).

---

[14] The ANOVA regression explains only part of the observed price variability. This is not surprising given the pricing instability predicted by the Edgeworth cycle and mixed strategy NE theories for this environment.

Table 16.3. *Bertrand-Edgeworth OLS results for ANOVA price regression*

Variable	Coefficient estimate (t statistic)
LOW capacity	7.220
	(24.15)
MEDIUM capacity	6.472
	(21.65)
HIGH capacity	6.155
	(20.59)
PRIVATE information	0.436
	(1.06)
PUBLIC information	0.441
	(1.07)
INEXP-LM	1.817
	(4.42)
INEXP-MM	1.644
	(3.95)
INEXP-HM	0.873
	(2.12)
INEXP-MR	1.371
	(3.34)
INEXP-MU	3.586
	(8.72)
PERINV	7.308
	(6.53)
4696 observations; adjusted R^2 = 0.630	

Note: Based on data beginning in period 2.

We also checked for the presence of experiment-specific (or cohort) effects in the data. A regression equation was specified that included all the independent variables listed in Table 16.3 plus a set of dummy variables that represented individual experiments. We ran an F test for the hypothesis that the coefficients of these experiment-specific dummy variables are all zero. This hypothesis was rejected at the 1% significance level. This indicated the presence of cohort effects in the data. We also ran an ANOVA regression for price data using the average price for the first five periods in an experiment as an additional explanatory variable. We wanted to see if the cohort effects could be explained on the basis of the average price that a cohort began with. Cohort effects were diminished with this specification but were still present; the F test was significant at the 1% level.

We now examine how well the competing hypotheses of price formation stack up against the data. The competitive model provides, at best, a very incomplete explanation of the price data. There were two experiments (LME1 and HME2) in which prices converge to the competitive equilibrium price from above. In the other 18 experiments, prices remained above the competitive price.

Edgeworth price predictions were derived by calculating a seller's profit-maximizing price given the expectation that rival sellers maintain their prices from the previous period. This approach permitted us to compute predicted Edgeworth prices after period 1 for each seller in each experiment. To assess the extent to which actual prices adjusted to predicted Edgeworth prices, we first estimated a linear equation for each seller in which the dependent variable was the current period price minus the previous period price and the independent variables were the current predicted Edgeworth price minus the actual previous period price and the lagged value of this independent variable. The form of the estimating equation captured the case of complete and immediate adjustment to the predicted Edgeworth price (for some coefficients) as well as cases of partial or zero adjustment to the predicted Edgeworth price. We then performed tests of significance for the coefficients that characterize adjustment to predicted Edgeworth prices. The estimating equation and a summary of results of significance tests are reported in Table 16.4.

The first test reported in Table 16.4 measured the significance of both explanatory variables in accounting for a seller's price adjustments. For 63 out of 80 sellers, the explanatory variables (which are based on current and lagged predicted Edgeworth prices) had a significant effect (at the 0.05 level) on actual price adjustments. The null hypothesis of the second test was that the actual price adjusted completely and immediately to the predicted Edgeworth price. This null hypothesis is rejected for 70 out of 80 sellers.

The null hypothesis of the third test is that the first adjustment coefficient is zero. This hypothesis is rejected for 55 out of the 80 seller subjects in favor of the one-sided alternative that the coefficient is positive. The large number of rejections for the second test showed that few sellers adjusted their prices completely and immediately to the predicted Edgeworth price. The results of the third test showed that most subjects adjusted their prices partially in response to the current predicted adjustment to Edgeworth prices. The null hypothesis of the fourth test is that the coefficient for lagged predicted adjustment was zero. This can be

Table 16.4. *Results of OLS regressions for adjustment to predicted Edgeworth prices*

Estimating equation:

$$P_{it} - P_{i,t-1} = \beta_0 + \beta_1 (P_{it}^E - P_{i,t-1}) + \beta_2 (P_{i,t-1}^E - P_{i,t-2})^a$$

Results for subject-specific regressions:

Null hypothesis	Number of subjects whose behavior allows rejection of the null hypothesis at the 0.05 level (out of 80 subjects)
(1) $\beta_1 = \beta_2 = 0$	63
(2) $\beta_0 = 0; \beta_1 = 1; \beta_2 = 0$	70
(3) $\beta_1 = 0^b$	55
(4) $\beta_2 = 0^b$	12

Coefficient estimates when all subjects are pooled[c]	
β_0	−0.572
	(0.112)
β_1	0.291
	(0.010)
β_2	−0.174
	(0.010)

Adj. $R^2 = 0.158$; 4616 observations

[a] P_{it} is the price set by seller i in period t. P_{it}^E is the Edgeworth predicted price for i in t, based on rivals' prices in period $t - 1$.
[b] The alternative hypothesis is that the coefficient is positive.
[c] Standard errors are in parentheses.

rejected for only 12 out of 80 subjects. That is, the once-lagged predicted Edgeworth adjustment did not have a significant effect on current price adjustment for most subjects.

We also estimated the Edgeworth adjustment equation specified in Table 16.4 for the pooled sample with all subjects. The estimated coefficients (see Table 16.4) illustrate the response to predicted Edgeworth prices averaged over all subjects in all periods. The results are consistent with the idea of partial adjustment that emerged from the subject-specific regressions. A representative subject would be predicted to adjust his or her price by an amount equal to 29% of the difference between the Edgeworth prediction and the current price. The extent of a subject's adjustment would diminish somewhat over time if the Edgeworth prediction stays fixed because the estimated β_2 is negative.

Our interpretation of the mixed strategy NE prediction is that each seller's price was drawn from a common distribution ϕ^* in each period; that is, predicted prices were independent, identically distributed random variables. We ran a vector autoregression for each experiment in order to test the hypothesis that mean prices in a period were independent of prices in previous periods. A VAR(2) specification was used with current period prices for the four sellers as a vector of dependent variables and once- and twice-lagged price vectors as independent variables. The results of the VARs indicate that actual prices are not realizations of independent, identically distributed random variables. By using F tests, we reject the hypothesis that mean prices in a period are independent of prices in previous periods for each experiment (i.e., lagged prices do contribute to the explanatory power of the VAR for each experiment).[15] We also checked whether this failure of independence was due to a dependence only on own lagged prices or whether it was due to dependence upon both own lagged prices and lagged prices of rivals. By running chi-squared tests, we rejected the hypothesis that current prices depended only on own lagged prices, for each experiment (at the 0.05 level). Lagged prices of rivals contributed to the explanatory power of the VAR for each experiment. This was consistent with the results from the Edgeworth regressions in which we found that most subjects adjusted at least partially to the predicted Edgeworth price, which was based on lagged prices of rival sellers.

The results from the VARs suggest that actual prices do not conform to period-by-period draws from the mixed strategy NE distribution. Actual prices depended on past prices in some way that is not captured by the static NE theory. However, we were still interested in whether the mixed strategy NE distribution captured qualitative features of the aggregate price data. A comparison of the (symmetric) mixed strategy NE distributions in Figure 16.2 and the price frequency distributions in Figure 16.3 indicates some similarities between the aggregate price frequencies and the mixed strategy NE predictions.[16] In most experiments,

---

[15] We also ran the VAR(2) regressions with an explanatory variable equal to the inverse of the trading period. These regressions permit us to test for independence from past prices after taking into account a time trend in the data. We reject the hypothesis that mean prices in a period are independent of lagged prices for each experiment, based on these regressions.

[16] The Kolmorogov-Smirnov (KS) test provides a statistical test of the hypothesis that a sample of observations comes from a particular continuous theoretical cdf. This test requires that data represent independent draws from some common distribution. The VAR(2) tests suggest that the independent draws assumption is violated. Nevertheless, we ran a KS test of the hypothesis that prices are drawn from the mixed NE distribution for each subject in our experiments. The hypothesis that prices are drawn from the mixed strategy NE distribution is rejected for all subjects in our experiments.

Table 16.5. *Bertrand-Edgeworth profit comparisons*

	PRIVATE MEDIUM	MIXED LOW	MIXED MEDIUM	MIXED HIGH	PUBLIC MEDIUM
Benchmark profit per seller:					
CE	65.2	234.2	65.2	0.0	65.2
Expected static NE	199.8	310.3	199.8	97.2	199.8
Monopoly pricing	640.9	640.9	640.9	640.9	640.9
Actual average profit per seller[a]:					
Inexperienced subjects	332.7	366.0	265.0	207.4	362.6
Experienced subjects	312.9	316.4	236.6	157.6	263.7
All subjects	322.8	341.2	250.8	182.3	313.1

[a] Average profit in pesos per seller per period. Actual dollar payoffs to subjects were determined by an exchange rate that was fixed at the beginning of the experiment.

a high percentage of prices are in an interval that begins within about a peso above p^c and ends 3 to 4 pesos above p^c. This is the price interval where the mixed strategy NE distribution places the greatest probability weight. However, the aggregate frequency distributions for price data tend to lie to the right of the corresponding mixed strategy NE distributions, indicating that actual prices tended to be higher than predicted mixed strategy NE prices.

The experimental results are clearly inconsistent with monopoly pricing. The summary statistics in Table 16.2 show mean and median prices that are far below the monopoly price of 38.3 pesos for all experiments. Given the very high levels of excess capacity when sellers choose the monopoly price, this result is not too surprising.

The results appear to support a type of tacit collusion that yields prices and profits that are above the noncooperative level and below the monopoly level. The median price for the last 20 periods exceeds the noncooperative NE median price in 17 out of 20 experiments (see Table 16.2). Table 16.5 reports profit comparisons. Average profit per seller exceeds the corresponding noncooperative static NE profit for each of the treatment categories reported in Table 16.5. If one looks at the last half of each experiment, average profit per seller exceeded the noncooperative static NE profit in 18 out of 20 experiments.

The impact of capacity levels on prices was consistent with the standard view of how excess capacity affects tacit collusion. The ANOVA regression results indicated that higher capacity levels are associated with lower prices (see also Figure 16.3). The data were inconsistent with the Davidson and Deneckere (1990) prediction that greater excess capacity makes collusive pricing more likely. This prediction relies on the ability of sellers to find a joint profit-maximizing level for prices and to sustain this price level by punishments of low pricing. Sellers occasionally set high prices in our experiments, but there were no episodes of sustained monopoly pricing by all sellers.

The tacit collusion theory predicts that greater provision of information to sellers will raise prices. The ANOVA results offer little support for this. Price in PUBLIC information experiments were higher, but not significantly higher than prices in MIXED information experiments.

Although the price and profit results described here are supportive of the tacit collusion hypothesis in some respects, it is less clear that tacit collusion provides a good explanation for the observed results. Tacitly collusive behavior is based on the idea that sellers recognize their mutual interdependence and mutual interest in high prices. This recognition would motivate each seller to avoid price cuts that would lead to further price cuts by rivals. Price cuts would be utilized only to punish "cheaters."

There was little evidence that sellers set stable high prices (i.e., above the median noncooperative price) in the experiments. Although all four sellers did set high prices in a trading period for some experiments, these high prices were quickly followed by successive rounds of price cuts. There was also no evidence of simple price rotation schemes designed to achieve high profits.

There were efforts by sellers in some experiments to signal rivals by setting high prices. For example, seller 3 set the following sequence of prices in the middle periods of experiment LMI1: $\{25, 50, 75, 50, 50, 50\}$. This sequence of high prices set by seller 3 appears to be a signal for rivals to raise their prices. The last five prices in this sequence were well above seller 3's myopic best responses, so seller 3 was forgoing profitable opportunities to cut her price. However, this signaling by seller 3 did not help the group of sellers achieve stable, high prices. Even though one rival seller did raise his price to 50 pesos during this sequence, the other sellers raised their prices only partially to this level, and prices unraveled several periods later so that all prices fell below 9 pesos.

The appearance of profit levels above the noncooperative profit benchmark may be a result of a disequilibrium adjustment process rather than a result of tacit collusion. In order to illustrate this point, suppose four sellers each set prices according to the estimating equation for adjustment to predicted Edgeworth prices in Table 16.4. We chose parameter values $\beta_0 = -0.572$, $\beta_1 = 0.291$, $\beta_2 = -0.174$ and an error term with standard deviation of 3 pesos, for each seller's price adjustment (these are the parameter values estimated from the pooled sample). We ran a simulation of price adjustment for 60 periods for the MEDIUM capacity case, with initial prices set equal to marginal cost for each seller.

Average profit per seller in the simulation was 529.1 pesos per period. This profit level is well above the noncooperative profit benchmark of 199.8 pesos per period.[17] This simulation is not advanced as an accurate description of individual seller behavior in the experiments. Rather, it is intended to illustrate how a myopic partial adjustment process that responds to past prices of rivals can lead to profits that are substantially higher than noncooperative profits in this environment.

The impact of subject experience provides indirect evidence against the tacit collusion hypothesis. The ANOVA results indicate that prices were higher for inexperienced subjects than for experienced subjects. Subjects with no prior experience in this price-setting environment had difficulty in tacitly coordinating their decisions to achieve high prices. If successful tacit collusion was the basis for observed prices and profits, then we would expect groups of experienced subjects to achieve higher profits and prices than inexperienced groups. Experienced subjects should have a better understanding of the advantages of high prices and a better understanding of how to achieve tacit coordination.[18]

IV.   Summary and Conclusions

The Bertrand-Edgeworth model describes competition among a group of price-setting sellers, each of whom faces a production capacity constraint. We report on a series of 20 experiments that were designed so as to capture essential features of BE competition. These experiments permitted us to evaluate the predictive power of four different theories of BE competition: Competitive equilibrium pricing, Edgeworth cycles in prices, mixed strategy Nash equilibrium in prices, and tacit collusion. Our experimental results indicated that each of the four theories helps to explain some aspects of the data. However, none of these theories was completely consistent with the experimental data.

Average seller price was decreasing over time for the first 20 periods

---

[17] These average profit results are robust with respect to changes in initial prices and to minor adjustment parameter changes.

[18] The cohort effects that we reported in our ANOVA results and the variety of pricing patterns observed in the experiments are supportive of the presence of repeated game effects in the data. The Folk theorem for repeated games tells us that many different pricing patterns can be sustained as noncooperative equilibrium play if subjects possess a high subjective continuation probability. Equilibrium play of this type requires that sellers understand the strategies employed by rival sellers and that deviations from equilibrium play are met by a series of punishment actions that are part of equilibrium strategies. While repeated game effects may be the explanation for the cohort effects in the data, we think it is at least as likely that disequilibrium adjustments that vary across experiments are behind the cohort effects. The results on subject experience argue against an explanation based on sophisticated equilibrium play.

of each experiment. However, with the exception of two experiments, prices did not converge to the CE over time.

Observed pricing did not conform to our interpretation of the Edgeworth cycle theory. The hypothesis of complete adjustment to predicted Edgeworth prices was rejected for 70 out of 80 sellers. However, the hypothesis of partial adjustment to predicted Edgeworth prices was not rejected for a majority of subjects. In addition, many of the experiments exhibited upward and downward price swings of the sort predicted by the Edgeworth cycle theory.

Pricing was not consistent with the mixed strategy NE distribution. Observed pricing violated intertemporal independence and tended to exceed predicted mixed strategy NE prices. The qualitative nature of price dispersion for aggregate data was similar to the dispersion predicted by the mixed strategy NE; most prices were in a fairly small interval above the CE price, with a "tail" extending to the monopoly price.

Observed price and profit levels were consistent with tacit collusion. Median prices and average profit were above the corresponding (static) mixed strategy NE predictions in each experiment. However, the observed patterns of pricing within individual experiments were less supportive of the hypothesis that behavior was tacitly collusive. There was neither evidence of sustained high prices by all sellers within an experiment nor evidence of simple price rotation schemes to achieve tacit collusion. Whenever a group of sellers managed to achieve high prices, this was quickly followed by a price-cutting episode.

None of the four theories that we considered provided a single, comprehensive explanation of the experimental price data. This points to a need for the development of a theory that is capable of explaining the variety of pricing patterns that were observed. The observed pricing results seemed most consistent with some type of disequilibrium process of price adjustment. The Edgeworth cycle theory, which posits a disequilibrium adjustment process, was the only one of the four theories we considered that predicted the sort of time dependence and price cycles that appear in the data. Our regression results indicated that even though few subjects adjusted their prices completely to predicted Edgeworth prices, most subjects adjusted their prices by a positive fraction of the predicted Edgeworth price change.

A modified version of the Edgeworth cycle theory may provide a good model of disequilibrium price formation. Modifications that may prove to be useful include changes in the specification of expectations of rivals' prices, adding price inertia or partial adjustment to optimal price choices, and adding "experimentation" in price choices or "noisy" price adjustment.

Appendix I INSTRUCTIONS FOR SUBJECTS – ON PLATO COMPUTER SYSTEM

This is an experiment dealing with market decision making. Funds for this experiment have been provided by a research grant. If you consider your alternatives carefully and make effective decisions you may earn a CONSIDERABLE AMOUNT of MONEY, which will be paid to you IN CASH at the end of this experiment.

From this point on, all references to money will be in terms of "PLATO pesos." At the conclusion of this experiment, you will be paid in cash at the rate of $1.00 U.S. for every 1,000 PLATO pesos you have earned during the experiment. Note that you will maximize your cash payment at the end of the experiment by earning as many PLATO pesos as you can. During the experiment, your accumulated wealth in pesos will be displayed.

Press -NEXT- to continue

To aid in conducting this experiment and distributing the profits at its end, please type in your NAME at the arrow, and then press the -NEXT- key. (If you make a mistake, press the -ERASE- key to erase one character at a time, or press the -EDIT- key to erase an entire entry.)

Stephen Rassenti

Stephen Rassenti, you will be known as seller #4 during this experiment.

Press -NEXT- to continue

The experiment that follows will be conducted for a sequence of many periods. During each period sellers are able to produce and market a fictitious good that buyers may then choose to purchase.

In this experiment, the buyers will be simulated by a computer. Each period these simulated buyers – some rich and some poor – will be placed in a queue (lined up) in random order. In that order, buyers will make purchases from sellers based on price and availability of the good. In other words, when a given buyer's turn comes up, this buyer will purchase from the seller that has available capacity at the lowest price.

Press -NEXT- to continue

Although sellers are free to post whatever selling price they choose, they provide the good to the buyers through a single, jointly owned, production facility. As a seller, you incur a cost of producing and selling the good. Your production cost is based on the number of units purchased from you. Your production cost during this entire experiment is 5 pesos PER UNIT. You will have the capacity to produce a maximum of 145 units of the good in each period.

The sequence of events in each period is:

1. Submit your selling price for the good. (You may use a decimal point to submit fractional prices ... e.g., 11.61 pesos.)
2. Sellers' prices are displayed to buyers.
3. Buyers take turns purchasing the good.
4. Your PLATO record displays the following:
   (a) How many units you sold;
   (b) Your revenue, cost, and profit;
   (c) Your accumulated wealth;
   (d) All other sellers' prices;
   (e) The total trade in the market.
5. The next period begins.

We are waiting for 1 subjects to finish the instructions. Please be patient!

P25	P26	P27	P28	P29	P30	P31	Seller #1
145	145	145	145	145	145	145	k = Capacity
8.21	8.17	8.18	8.16	8.16	8.17		p = Unit price
15	145	17	145	145	145		u = Units Sold
123	1,185	138	1,183	1,183	1,185		r = Revenue
75	725	85	725	725	725		pc = Prod. cost
48	460	54	458	458	460		Period profit
8,447	8,907	8,961	9,419	9,877	10,337		Wealth
							Other Sellers
145	145	145	145	145	145	145	Capacity (2)
8.20	8.19	8.17	8.16	8.20	8.17		Unit price (2)
145	145	145	145	145	145	145	Capacity (3)
8.18	8.17	8.16	8.16	8.15	8.16		Unit price (3)
145	145	145	145	145	145	145	Capacity (4)
8.19	8.18	8.17	8.25	8.25	8.20		Unit price (4)
450	448	452	453	449	452		Total trade

Type in your unit price for period 31.

Appendix II COMPUTING MIXED STRATEGIES FOR A SYMMETRIC, FOUR-SELLER GAME

Let $\pi(p;\phi)$ be the expected profit to a seller who charges a price p when each of his three rivals plays the mixed strategy cumulative distribution function ϕ. The support of ϕ is $[p^0, p^m]$ where $p^0 \cdot p^c$.

$$\pi(p;\phi) = (p-c)\min\{K, D(p)\}(1-\phi(p))^3 + 3(p-c)[1-\phi(p)]^2$$
$$\times \int_{p^0}^{p}\min\left\{K,\max\left[0,D(p)\left(1-\frac{K}{D(q)}\right)\right]\right\}\phi'(q)dq$$
$$+ 3(p-c)[1-\phi(p)]$$
$$\times \int_{p^0}^{p}\int_{p^0}^{p}\min\left\{K,\max\left[0,D(p)\left(1-\frac{K}{D(q)}-\frac{K}{d(r)}\right)\right]\right\}\phi'(q)dq\phi'(r)dr$$
$$+ (p-c)\int_{p^0}^{p}\int_{p^0}^{p}\int_{p^0}^{p}\max\left\{0,D(p)\left(1-\frac{K}{D(q)}-\frac{K}{D(r)}-\frac{K}{D(s)}\right)\right\}$$
$$\times \phi'(q)dq\phi'(r)dr\phi'(s)ds \tag{A1}$$

This expected profit is the sum of four terms. The first term is the profit to this seller if p is the lowest price times the probability that the other three sellers all set a higher price. The second term is expected profit to this seller when p is the second lowest price. Note that $[1 - K/D(q)]$ is the fraction of buyers allocated to this seller when the lowest price is $q < p$. The third term is expected profit when p is the third lowest price. Finally, the fourth term is expected profit for this seller when p is the highest price.

Equation (A1) may be rewritten as follows:

$$\pi(p;\phi) = (p-c)\min\{K, D(p)\}(1-\phi(p))^3 + 3(p-c)[1-\phi(p)]^2$$
$$\times \int_{p^0}^{p}\min\left\{K,\max\left[0,D(p)\left(1-\frac{K}{D(q)}\right)\right]\right\}\phi'(q)dq$$
$$+ 3(p-c)[1-\phi(p)]$$
$$\times \int_{p^0}^{p}\int_{p^0}^{p}\min\left\{K,\max\left[0,D(p)\left(1-\frac{K}{D(q)}-\frac{K}{d(r)}\right)\right]\right\}\phi'(q)dq\phi'(r)dr$$
$$+ (p-c)\int_{p^0}^{p}\int_{p^0}^{p}\int_{p^0}^{p}\max\left\{0,D(p)\left(1-\frac{K}{D(q)}-\frac{K}{D(r)}-\frac{K}{D(s)}\right)\right\}$$
$$\times \phi'(q)dq\phi'(r)dr\phi'(s)ds \tag{A2}$$

If ϕ is a Nash equilibrium strategy then π must be constant for all p in $[p^0, p^m]$. Let p_3 be the price that is implicitly defined by $D(p_3) = 3K$. If $p^0 < p_3$ then Equation (A2) may be rewritten as follows for p $\varepsilon(p^0, p_3)$:

$$
\frac{(p^0 - c)K}{(p - c)D(p)}
$$

$$
= \frac{K}{D(p)}\left\{1 - \phi(p)^3 + 3\phi(p)[1 - \phi(p)]^2 + 3\phi(p)^2[1 - \phi(p)]\right\}
$$

$$
\times \int_{p^0}^p \int_{p^0}^p \int_{p^0}^p \left(1 - \frac{K}{D(q)} - \frac{K}{D(r)} - \frac{K}{D(s)}\right)\phi'(q)dq\phi'(r)dr\phi'(s)ds \tag{A3}
$$

The constant profit level in (A2) is equal to $(p^0 - c)K$. After integrating the expression on the right-hand side of (A3) and rearranging terms we have the following equation for p $\varepsilon(p^0, p_3)$:

$$
\int_{p^0}^p \frac{\phi'(q)}{D(q)}dp = \frac{\left(\dfrac{p - p^0}{p - c}\right) + \left(\dfrac{D(p) - K}{K}\right)\phi(p)^3}{3D(p)\phi(p)^2} \tag{A4}
$$

Now differentiate both sides of (A4) with respect to p. After simplifying the expressions that result from this differentiation, the following ordinary differential equation (ODE) emerges:

$$
\phi'(p) = \frac{\dfrac{(p^0 - c)}{(p - c)^2} + \dfrac{D'(p)\phi(p)^3}{K} - \dfrac{D'(p)(p - p^0)}{D(p)(p - c)} - \left(\dfrac{D'(p)\phi(p)^3}{D(p)}\right)\left(\dfrac{D(p) - K}{K}\right)}{\phi(p)^2\left(4 - \dfrac{D(p)}{K}\right) + \dfrac{2(p - p^0)}{\phi(p)(p - c)}} \tag{A5}
$$

This ODE defines the Nash equilibrium mixed strategy f over the interval (p^0, p_3), as long as $p^0 < p_3$.

The mixed strategy ϕ is defined over the remainder of the price support as follows. Differentiating (A2) with respect to p and holding π constant provides a necessary condition that ϕ must satisfy over all of its support. [If ϕ is piecewise differentiable, then this differentiation is admissible except on a set of points of measure zero. The other functions of p on the right-hand side of (A2) are continuous and piece-wise differentiable in p.]

$$-(p^0 - c)KZ(p) = [1 - \phi(p)]^3 Y'(p) - 3\phi'(p)[1 - \phi(p)]^2 Y(p)$$

$$+3\phi'(p)[1 - \phi(p)]^2 Z_2(p,p)$$

$$+3[1 - \phi(p)]^2 \int_{p^0}^{p} \frac{\partial Z_2(p,q)}{\partial p} \phi'(q)dq - 6\phi'(p)[1 - \phi(p)]$$

$$\times \int_{p^0}^{p} Z_2(p,q)\phi'(q)dq$$

$$-3\phi'(p)\int_{p^0}^{p}\int_{p^0}^{p} Z_3(p,q,r)\phi'(q)dq\phi'(r)dr + 3[1 - \phi(p)]$$

$$\times \int_{p^0}^{p}\int_{p^0}^{p} \frac{\partial Z_3(p,q,r)}{\partial p} \phi'(q)dq\phi'(r)dr$$

$$+6\phi'(p)[1 - \phi(p)]\int_{p^0}^{p} Z_3(p,q,p)\phi'(q)dq + 3\phi'(p)$$

$$\times \int_{p^0}^{p}\int_{p^0}^{p} Z_4(p,q,r)\phi'(q)dq\phi'(r)dr \qquad \text{(A6)}$$

where $Z(p) = [D(p) + (p - c)D'(p)] / [(p - c)D(p)]^2$
$Y(p) = \min\{1, K / D(p)\}$
$Z_2(p,q) = \min\{K / D(p), \max\{0, 1 - K / K(q)\}\}$
$Z_3(p,q,r) = \min\{K / D(p), \max\{0, 1 - K / D(q) - K / D(r)\}\}$
$Z_4(q,r,s) = \max\{0, 1 - K / D(q) - K / D(r) = K / D(s)\}$

An equilibrium distribution function $\phi(p)$ must satisfy the integrodifferential equation (A6) and the boundary conditions, $\phi(p^0) = 0$, $\phi(p^m) = 1$.

We have developed a computational procedure that permits numerical approximation of the symmetric, Nash equilibrium mixed strategy function ϕ. First, choose a value for p^0 between p^c and p_3. Second, approximate ϕ over the interval $[p^0, p_3]$ by solving the ODE of (A5). Third, divide the interval $[p_3, p^m]$ into a large number of subintervals and solve for $\phi'(p)$ at the right-hand edge of each subinterval by using (A6). The solution for ϕ' at the right-hand edge of a subinterval provides an approximation of ϕ over the next subinterval. This iterative process is repeated until a value for $\phi(p^m)$ is found. If $\phi(p^m)$ is equal to 1 then the procedure is finished. If $\phi(p^m)$ is less than 1, then a smaller value for p^0 is selected and steps 1–3 above are repeated. If $\phi(p^m)$ exceeds 1, then a larger value for p^0 is selected, and steps 1–3 are repeated.

This computational procedure was utilized for each of the three capacity levels in our experimental design. In each case, the value for p^0 that was selected was between p^c and p_3. The computed value of $\phi(p^3)$ exceeded 80% for each capacity level. That is, over 80% of the mixed strategy cdf was calculated using the ODE defined in Equation (A5).

CHAPTER 17

An Experimental Examination of the Walrasian *Tâtonnement* Mechanism

*Corinne Bronfman, Kevin A. McCabe, David
P. Porter, Stephen Rassenti, and Vernon L. Smith*

Joyce (1984) reports the results of experiments with a Walrasian *tâtonnement* auction that show that the mechanism is stable, exhibits strong convergence properties, and generates efficiencies that average better than 97%.[1] He also found that when subjects could see part of the order flow (excess demand), prices tended to be lower. His experiments consisted of a stationary environment where subjects were provided single-unit supply and demand functions. We assess the robustness of his results in a more general multiunit per subject setting; and we systematically investigate the effect of various rules about order flow information and message restriction rules on the performance of the Walrasian mechanism.

Our experiments are motivated by several considerations.

1. When there are both buyers and sellers in the market, each of which has one unit to buy or sell, the only Nash equilibria of the Walrasian *tâtonnement* mechanism are those that support the competitive equilibrium outcome. Furthermore, a Walrasian *tâtonnement* process can be designed that has a dominant strategy equilibrium where each participant reveals value or cost (see McAfee, 1992). The design imposes constraints on participant messages; specifically, at the announced price at *t*, if excess demand is positive (negative), any seller (buyer) not registering a sell (buy) order at *t* cannot register an order at time *t* + 1. Without this improvement rule, the dominant strategy equilibrium outcome no longer exists. But even with this improvement rule, the dominant strategy revelation property does not hold when demands and supplies are multiunit, since a participant may influence price without being entirely out of the market. When suppliers and demanders have multiple units to trade, theory provides little guidance in market design or the appro-

---

[1] Efficiency is defined as the percent of theoretical producer plus consumer surplus realized by a trading mechanism.

priate price-adjustment rules by which to organize a Walrasian *tâtonnement*.

2. The results reported in Noussair (1992) and Joyce (1991) also raise questions about the robustness of Joyce's results. He shows that the isomorphism between the English auction (which gives full order flow information) and a uniform price sealed-bid auction (which gives no order flow information) does not hold when multiple units are to be allocated to each participant. It is desirable, therefore, to study this case and the role of supply and demand information in the performance of the *tâtonnement* auction.

3. With prices sensitive to reported supply and demand, the price adjustment process[2] in a *tâtonnement* auction typically results in a Nash equilibrium in which participants underreveal demands and supplies (see Hurwicz, 1972; Otani and Sicilian, 1990). We ask whether these theoretical considerations are borne out by observation and whether changes in the order flow information and restrictions on traders' messages affect allocations in a Walrasian *tâtonnement*.

I.   Relevance to Financial Markets

In addition to the theoretical interest in the Walrasian mechanism's performance, its efficiency in field implementations has been questioned. For example, at the opening on the New York Stock Exchange (NYSE), the specialist in each security calls out prices until he or she finds the price that maximizes the volume of matched buy and sell order quantities submitted over the electronic system and those held by floor traders actively participating in the auction at the specialist's post. If there is excess demand (supply), and if the specialist is not prepared to absorb the imbalance, the price is adjusted upward (downward). As each new price is called, traders modify their orders to reflect their changed willingness to trade at that price. Amihud and Mendelson (1991) and Stoll and Whaley (1990) establish empirically the increased volatility of opening prices. These results are consistent with the findings in this chapter that the institution is not robust, and that the outcome is particularly sensitive to strategic manipulation. Because rules matter in the performance of a mechanism, it is important to investigate the impact of different implementations of the Walrasian mechanism on market efficiency.

---

[2] Price is adjusted in the direction of excess demand (downward if there are more sells than buys, upward if there are more buys than sells).

The relevance of our experimental tests of the *tâtonnement* mechanism to issues in financial markets is easily clarified. Even though the standard perfectly competitive paradigm of a large number of buyers and sellers trading a homogeneous good may appear to be met in financial markets, in fact, there are important differences.

The most important difference is the significant role of institutional traders who trade quantities that are large relative to average daily trading volume in any particular security. The "upstairs market," where trades are negotiated by representatives of the various brokerage houses, facilitates the trading of some of this volume. But there is also a significant volume traded during the day on the floor of the exchange itself. To reduce the effects of market power and front-running on their trading costs, institutions act strategically when they price, time, and (most important for the *tâtonnement* experiments) size their desired trade. If they were to reveal their trading plans, they would expect to pay a significant premium (or sell at a large discount).

This strategic behavior is particularly evident at the NYSE opening where floor traders present at the specialist's post reveal portions of the orders they hold as the specialist actively searches for the price to open the market. The first half hour following the opening is known to be very volatile and active as traders attempt to buy or sell those volumes that were not (or could not have been) traded at the opening price (see Bronfman and Schwartz, 1992).

The need to minimize the negative own impact of large institutional order on price has been reflected in the operations of the once-a-day call auction of the Arizona Stock Exchange (AZX). The AZX has instituted a hidden reserve book along with its standard open book in which market participants can observe stock prices and aggregate volumes of the orders that have been submitted. The reserve book allows large traders to hide a portion of their orders that are revealed to the market only if and when there is a counterside order for a similar quantity.

There are also quantity response procedures that have been developed in the futures markets that effectively allow traders to "underreveal" their desired trades. Some mechanisms work better than others. Most important, the small-numbers problem does not go away as the number of traders is increased at any point in time because it is the balance of buys and sells that allows a large volume to be traded without market impact. If one side reveals, there is an incentive for the other side to withhold (underreveal) if they can affect the price at which a portion of their order will trade, then hopefully leak out the remainder of the order over the remainder of the hour, or day, without affecting the trading price. If an order is large relative to average daily trading volume, then the potential price effect does not reflect underlying buy and sell conditions (if all traders were present in the market as in Walras' world) but rather the effect of transitory market illiquidity. Therefore a premium (or discount) must be accepted if the market is to absorb the order.

Our experimental design is intended to replicate only certain generic conditions in these markets in the field, namely the presence of traders who trade in significant volume and an auction organized around a quantity response that results in a price adjustment.

Control over supply and demand conditions and the information provided to traders is impossible in the field, and therefore minimal conditions for studying the role of auction rules in price discovery are not possible. The use of laboratory methods employing monetary incentives allows underlying demand and supply conditions to be induced so that equilibrium price and quantity exist and are known to the experimenter. Given the induced supply and demand environment, we can assess the performance of a pricing institution (auction rules) as measured by the efficiency of allocations. In addition, we can compare the strategic withholding behavior of subjects with fully revealing strategies. Our experiments are completely computerized, allowing for greater control in differentiating private and public information and enforcing different message restrictions on subjects.

In our experiments, the underlying supply and demand conditions are not stationary for each market period. This environment provides a difficult test of the efficiency of price discovery and quantity allocation for a Walrasian *tâtonnement* mechanism. We also provide evidence on the performance of the Walrasian process under different levels of "transparency" (market information).[3] For the Walrasian mechanism, this translates into providing information on the current buy and sell orders in the market and potential price movement. It is not known whether such information can assist or hinder the market. In addition to the transparency issue, we also investigate the properties of bid–offer restriction rules that may facilitate orderly price discovery.

Our results show that all versions of the computerized multiple-unit Walrasian auction produce prices consistent with the competitive equilibrium prediction, but strategic withholding at these prices results in efficiencies lower than those provided by a continuous double auction. Among all the Walrasian auction designs we tested, the treatment in which full order flow information is provided and in which there are no bid–offer restrictions yields the highest efficiency. As theory would predict, there is a strong correlation between per-unit profit and the

---

[3] Transparency is defined as the amount of real-time information on quotes, transaction prices, and volume that is disclosed.

amount of underrevelation by players. Finally, unlike the result found by Joyce, we find no significant strategic behavior differences between buyers and sellers.

II. Experimental Environment and Walrasian Auction Design

We first consider a simple experimental environment developed by Joyce (1984) in his examination of the Walrasian auction. We then describe our multiunit nonstationary supply and demand environment and computerized implementation of the Walrasian auction process.

A. Baseline

Consider the following environment faced by n buyers and n sellers of a single commodity. Each buyer has a value for a discrete single unit. Each seller has the capacity to supply only one discrete unit to the market for a specified cost. Given the values and costs of the potential market participants, a supply and demand array can be constructed as in Figure 17.1, which we will call environment E1.

In this simple environment Joyce implements a specific Walrasian auction as follows:

1. An initial price $P_0 > 0$ is selected by an auctioneer.
2. Either (a) with all participants present in the same room, each buyer and seller indicates to the auctioneer whether he/she wants to buy or sell a single unit at the announced price by raising his/her hand [however, only the auctioneer knows if a particular subject is a buyer or seller; that is, each trader's identity (buyer or seller) is his own private information]; or (b) buyers and sellers are in separate rooms. (Thus, buyers can observe the number of buy orders, and sellers can observe the number of sell orders during each iteration and infer the opposite side's demand and supply at the end of each iteration.)
3. If the number of buyers demanding a unit equals the number of sellers supplying a unit at that price, the process stops.
4. If there was an imbalance of supply and demand at that price [i.e., excess demand $E(P)$ is nonzero], the auctioneer updated the price using the following formula:

$$\Delta P = \begin{cases} \$0.5E(P) & \text{if} |E(P)| > 1 \\ \$ZE(P) & \text{if} |E(P)| = 1, \end{cases}$$

where $Z < \$.05$ is decided by the auctioneer.

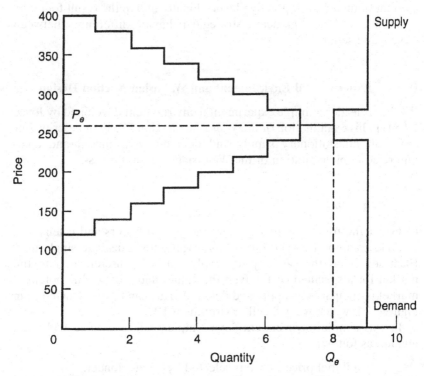

FIGURE 17.1. Demand and supply environment E1.

   In all cases, current buy or sell messages are not constrained by past
messages (there is no improvement rule), and the price adjustment rule
is linear. However, there is a strong restriction placed on each participant's message; he or she can only register demands and supplies for one
unit.

B.   *Nash Equilibrium Strategies with Single-Unit Demands
       and Supplies*

When individuals have demands or supplies for one unit, nonrevelation
is a risky strategy because, should the market clear, the individual will
fail to make a profitable transaction. If there is complete knowledge concerning values and costs, then in a nonrepeated process of this type, any
pure-strategy Nash equilibrium must be at (Q_e, P_e). This follows because
at any outcome different from (Q_e, P_e) individuals using a nonrevealing
strategy who are not part of the allocation would do better by revealing.

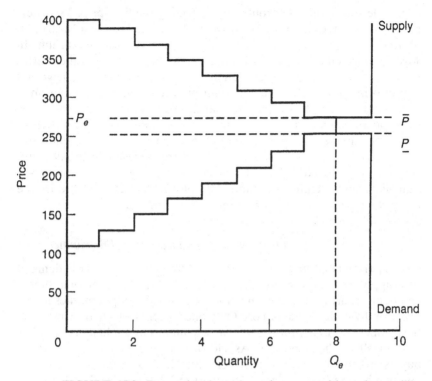

FIGURE 17.2. Demand and supply environment with a price equilibrium tunnel (multiple competitive equilibria).

In particular, with the arrays given in Figure 17.1, revelation is a Nash equilibrium. However, suppose that the market environment is as pictured in Figure 17.2. Then, if $P_0 > \underline{P}$, a Nash equilibrium is where one (or several) demander(s) with value greater than $\underline{P}$ does(do) not reveal until price is at $\underline{P}$ and all sellers reveal. A similar result can be found for the case when $P_0 > \bar{P}$; sellers with cost less than $\bar{P}$ do not reveal until price is at $\bar{P}$. With full information on the order flow, the actual price determined in the auction period will be affected by the relative bargaining power of buyers and sellers, and to some extent, the initial price P_0 will affect each side's ability to manipulate the outcome. However, with single-unit demands and supplies, the only Nash equilibria are those in which the outcome is in the equilibrium "price tunnel," and all valuable units are traded.

If there is incomplete information about supply and demand, then individual participants must balance the probability of failing to make a profitable trade with the profits from affecting the final price by under-revealing. In this case, the competitive outcome need not be a Nash equilibrium, and thus ex post inefficiencies can occur in equilibrium. In Joyce's study, efficiency averaged over 97%. Under the treatment 2(b), prices were significantly lower than under treatment 2(a). This suggested that information on the actual amount of excess demand is important.

From this example, we can see that the Walrasian mechanism allows strategic manipulation, and that information about the composition of excess demand is important in determining an outcome. The questions that motivate our research are (i) Which rules result in greater efficiency? (ii) How well does the mechanism perform when there are significant opportunities to manipulate prices? (iii) How well does the mechanism perform in a nonstationary environment?

C.   Multiunit Nonstationary Supply and Demand Environment

Our experiments utilized five buyers and five sellers. The basic demand and supply configuration is provided in Figure 17.3. The aggregate supply and demand arrays are step functions, where each step identifies a particular individual's value or cost. Only one trader is assigned to a step on these functions. In addition, each participant has multiple units to bid or to offer all on the same step. As shown in Figure 17.3, there are three buyers (B1, B3, B5) and three sellers (Sl, S3, S5) endowed with 6 units, and two buyers (B2, B4) and two sellers (S2, S4) endowed with 3 units. Thus there are 24 buy and sell units in the market; of these, 18 are potentially tradable in the equilibrium price tunnel (450, 470).

During an experiment, buyers remained buyers and sellers remained sellers, period to period, although two important changes occurred each period. First, the equilibrium prices were changed by parallel and equal shifts in the aggregate demand and supply arrays. In particular, from period to period, a random constant from the interval [100, 490] was added to (or subtracted from) each step on the aggregate demand and supply functions. In period 4, the steps were as shown in Figure 17.3.

Second, within each period, buyers are assigned (by a random rotation procedure) to one of the demand steps (B1–B5), and sellers are assigned to one of the supply steps (S1–S5). Each period they are assigned to a new step. For example, buyer 1, who in period 4 was endowed with the right to resell up to 6 units at a price of 500, could find himself or herself on a step with 6 units but with no tradable units within the equilibrium price tunnel, as is buyer 5 in Figure 17.3. Alternatively, he or she could be on a step with only 3 units, as is buyer 4.

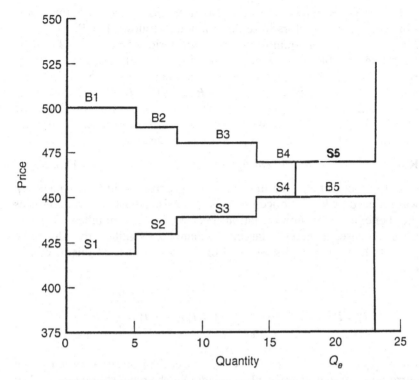

FIGURE 17.3. Environment E2 with shifting supply and demand: shown for period 4.

This experimental environment, which we call E2, allows us to assess the performance of the Walrasian auction where participants have multiple units and where relative competitiveness is variable period to period. This environment has been used in previous experimental studies (see Campbell et al., 1991, and McCabe et al., 1992, 1995), and clearly stresses the price discovery process. The environment, from the participant's perspective, is changing each period, so relying on past market experience can hinder price discovery.

D.   *Walrasian Auction Design and Computerized Implementation*

A Walrasian *tâtonnement* must specify the following five rules in order to implement the auction.

Rule 1. *The process must determine a starting or initial price* P_0.

For each experiment, we selected a set of initial prices from three possible vectors. The vectors were determined as follows: Let $P^e = (P_1^e, \ldots, P_n^e)$ be the vector of equilibrium prices for periods $i = 1, \ldots, n$. Let θ_i be a random variable drawn from the interval $[-50, 50]$ for each $i = 1, \ldots, n$. Let v_i be a random variable drawn from the interval $[-25, 25]$. The first vector of initial prices was $P_0^1 = (P_1^e - \theta_1, \ldots, P_n^e - \theta_n)$; the second initial price vector was given by $P_0^2 = -P_0^1$; the third vector was given by $P_0^3 = (P_1^e - v_1, \ldots, P_n^e - v_n)$. We used these initial price vectors to investigate the effect of the opening price on price discovery.

Rule 2. *The price adjustment function* γ,[4] *where* $P_t = P_{t-1} + \gamma(D_{t-1}, S_{t-1})$.

After each set of four iterations the previous adjustment factor, γ, was reduced by half.[5] Notice that this piecewise adjustment rule reduces the benefits from nonrevelation because as the number of iterations increases, it takes a larger imbalance to significantly adjust the price. In our experiments, we used the following form of this piecewise rule:

$$P_t = P_{t-1} + rn\left\{4\left[\frac{1}{2\left(1+\left\|\frac{t}{4}\right\|\right)}\right][D(P_{t-1}) - S(P_{t-1})]\right\}$$

where $\|y\|$ denotes the greatest integer less than or equal to y, t is the current iteration in the period, and $rnd(y)$ is the nearest integer to y. For example, in iteration 11 with an announced price of 200 and reported excess demand of 10, the price next period will be 207. Unlike the experiments conducted by Joyce, our experiments are computerized and thus there is no human auctioneer judging the "appropriate" price changes.

Rule 3. *Joyce (1984) and Noussair (1992) both note that information supplied to participants concerning the composition of excess demand can have a pronounced effect on the outcome of a* tâtonnement *process. In our experiments, we consider two alternative information structures: minimum information and complete order flow information. Under the minimum information treatment, subjects are informed (on their computer screens) of the current iteration price, the adjustment factor for the current iteration, the number of seconds remaining for the current iteration, and*

---

[4] We define $D_t = [D_0(P_0), D_1(P_1), \ldots, D_t(P_t)]$, $S_t = [S_0(P_0), S_1(P_1), \ldots, S_t(P_t)]$ as the aggregate supply and demand reports for each price iteration up to P_t and D_t^i, S_t^i are the individual supply and demand reports for each price iteration up to P_t. We will represent the true demands and supplies with the lowercase letters, d_t, s_t, d_t^i, s_t^j.

[5] We define an iteration as the time between two successive price changes and a *period* as the time between two successive allocations.

*a full history of past iteration prices and past order flow imbalances.
However, they are given no information on any imbalance at the current
price.*

Our second treatment provides subjects with order flow information
as well. In addition to the information in the minimum information treatment, subjects are provided at each iteration with the real-time updated
buy and sell orders as they arrived during the current price iteration, and
what the next iteration price would be, based on the current imbalance
information. Allowing participants to see the exact real-time composition of buy and sell imbalances should affect the price discovery process.
The effect of order flow information on efficiency will also depend on
the underlying environment under study. In this study, we assess the
impact of this order flow information on the speed of price discovery
using a stochastic environment.

Rule 4. *A message restriction specification limits the messages that can
be sent.*

This rule restricts the potential buy and sell orders that can be placed
during iteration t as a function of past responses. In all replications,
we placed the following restrictions on the messages participants could
send at each iteration: (i) Individuals could not sell short or buy on
margin. Thus, individuals were not permitted to offer more units than
their maximum capacity or demand more units than they had positive
values. (ii) Once an order was sent to the market it could not be
canceled.

In several replications, we put additional restrictions on subject messages. We imposed an improvement rule that required a buyer who was
willing to purchase m units at a price Y to be willing to purchase at least
m units at prices lower than Y. Similarly, a seller who was willing to sell
n units at price Z must have been willing to sell at least n units at prices
above Z. A buyer who was willing to buy 2 units at a price of 325 could
not state a willingness to purchase only 1 unit at a price of 290. The
motivation for this rule was to restrict manipulation and obvious
misrevelation.

This rule does not prevent withholding. Thus a subject who was
willing to buy 2 units at 325 is not precluded from revealing later in the
period that in fact he is willing to buy 3 units at 325. A seller who
was willing to sell only 1 unit at 340 can in the end agree to sell 4 units
at 340. The rule is flexible enough to permit subjects to explore their
influence on the market. We refer to this as the bid–offer improvement rule.

UNIT		Period			
		10	11	12	13
1	Value	400			
	Price				
	Profit				
2	Value	350			
	Price				
	Profit				
3	Value	200			
	Price				
	Profit				
4	Value	100			

Iteration D-S P (BUY)	Potential Price	Your current buy order:
2 -2 385(1) 1 5 360(2)	375	1 units
	Adjustment Factor: 2	Profitable Units: 1
	Buys Sells 17 16	

FIGURE 17.4. Computer display screen showing buyer values (upper panel) and market state variables for the Walrasian mechanism.

Rule 5. *The stopping rule used in our experiments has two dimensions. First, during an iteration, the time remaining to submit an order was endogenous. A clock was set at 15 seconds when the iteration price was posted. Any new order quantity submitted at the price reinitialized the clock to 15 seconds. This rule provided an implementation of a "soft close" procedure. A soft close enforces a unanimity requirement in that no one can guarantee himself or herself the last say. The second dimension dealt with the exact close of the market period. We closed the market period, at trial t*, when $P_{t*} = P_{t*-1}$ or $E(P_{t*}) = 0$. Notice that given our price adjustment rule, this stopping rule does not imply that $E(P) = 0$. Thus, if at t*, $E(P_{t*}) \neq 0$, we ration by time priority.*

III.   Experimental Design

Figure 17.4 shows the computer screens that subjects were viewing. Order flow information is provided in the lower middle box. Under the minimum information treatment, the only information provided in this box is the current iteration price (this is referred to as Potential Price on

Table 17.1. *Walrasian mechanism experimental treatments*

Message restriction	Information	
	Minimal	Order flow
No	4	5
Yes	3	3

Note: All of our treatments were conducted by using the piece-wise linear price adjustment rule described in this section.

the subject's screen). In all treatments, past trials and imbalances are recorded in the lower left-hand box, and the subject's current submitted quantity (and the number of profitable units at the current price) are recorded in the lower right-hand box.

Table 17.1 provides an overview of the experimental treatments and the number of experiments conducted per cell in our design. The design consists of two factors (improvement rule and order flow information) that are either present or not in each experiment. The experimental instructions are available on request.

IV.   Experimental Results

A.   *The Simple Environment*

In order to test the computer implementation of the Walrasian *tâtonnement* mechanism, we conducted two experiments using the E1C environment described in Figure 17.5. This environment is similar to the E1 environment used by Joyce. These two replications allow us to check our procedures and compare the results of our computerized *tâtonnement* with the oral auction version reported in Joyce.

In Joyce and our environment, subjects were endowed with single-unit supplies and demands, and there was a 20-cent range defining the competitive equilibrium price. Price above the midpoint of this tunnel gives greater surplus to sellers, and price below gives it to the buyers. In our experiments, the tunnel was defined by subject valuations and costs; in Joyce's design, it was created by providing subjects with a 10-cent commission for each trade. In both experiments, subjects were paid the difference between their limit price and the market-clearing price (plus the commission in Joyce).

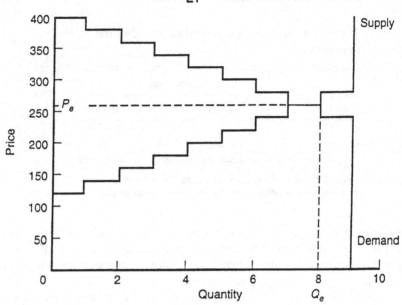

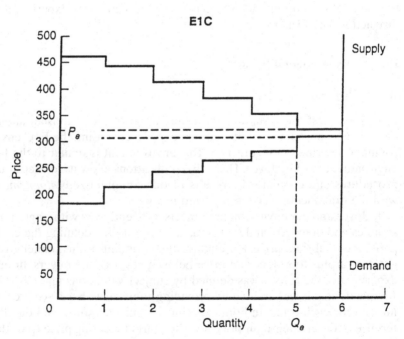

FIGURE 17.5. Single-unit per person supply and demand environment.

Table 17.2. *Walrasian mechanism mean efficiency by periods for E1C and E1*

	E1C	E1
Periods 1–6	85.3	98.9
Periods 7+	97.7	96.3

Table 17.2 shows the mean efficiency (percent of the maximum producer plus consumer surplus generated) for periods 1–6 and periods 7+ for both the E1 and E1C environments.

Result 1. *Comparing periods 1–6 with periods beyond period 6 shows that efficiencies significantly increase with E1C, but there is no significant change with E1.*

Support. The *t*-statistic is 2.25 for E1C and –1.64 for E1.

We also tested for differences in efficiency between the oral auctions conducted by Joyce and our computerized auction and found that they are not different for periods 7+. The strong period effect in the computerized treatment relative to the oral implementation is consistent with the results found in Williams (1980), where convergence to the competitive equilibrium price was slower with a computerized versus an oral implementation of a continuous bid–offer trading system.

Result 2. *There is no significant difference in efficiency between the E1 and E1C cases.*

Support. The *t*-statistic for periods 7+ is 0.605.

In terms of price formation, there is no difference between the computerized and the oral implementation. Prices lie in the equilibrium price tunnel, near the midpoint (see Figure 17.6). Hence, these data support the Nash competitive equilibrium prediction for single-unit demand and supply.

Result 3. *There is no significant difference in the distribution of prices between the E1 and E1C cases.*

Support. For periods 7+, the *t*-statistic is 1.83 (p-value = 0.07).

B.   *Baseline and Treatment Effects*

For the remainder of this chapter, we will use the following abbreviations for the treatments in our design: FINI = full information with no

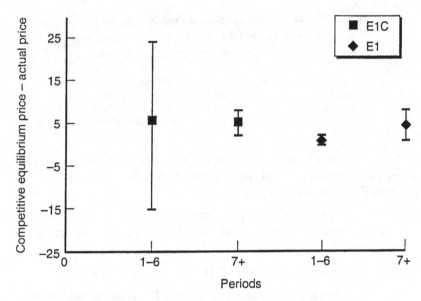

FIGURE 17.6. Mean and 95% confidence intervals for all prices in environments E1 and E1C.

bid–offer improvement; NINI = no information with no bid–offer improvement; FII = full information with bid–offer improvement; NII = no information with bid–offer improvement.

Figure 17.7 shows the efficiency distribution (boxplots) for each of the four treatments in our implementation of the Walrasian auction in the E2 environment. The boxplots show the median (the dot), interquartiles (the box), the 10th and 90th percentiles (bars below and above each box). In addition to the Walrasian treatments, we report the results of six baseline double auction (DA) experiments using the E2 environment. A double auction is a real-time continuous process in which traders submit bids and offers with the bid–offer spread determined by a standard bid–ask improvement rule. The double auction has been used extensively in experimental studies of markets and has the robust capacity to implement the competitive equilibrium outcome.

Notice that the double auction has a very tight distribution, whereas the Walrasian treatments have a large dispersion in efficiency.

Result 4. *The double auction outperforms each of the Walrasian auction designs we tested. FINI performs best among the Walrasian auction treatments.*

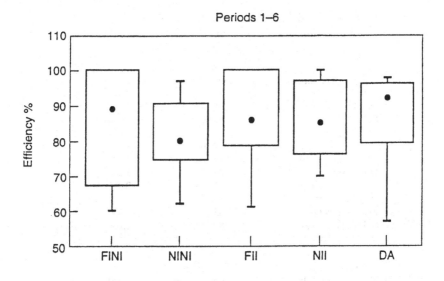

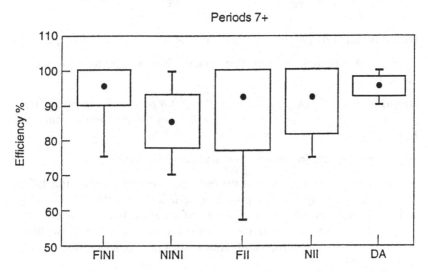

FIGURE 17.7. Quartilebox plots for the distribution of efficiency in Walrasian treatments and double auction. Median shown as dot.

Support. An analysis of variance was based on the following dummy variable regression:

$$\text{Efficiency} = \alpha_1 \text{DA}^*\text{Periods}(1-6) + \beta_1 \text{FINI}^*\text{Periods}(1-6) + \cdots$$
$$+ \alpha_2 \text{DA}^*\text{Periods}(7+) + \beta_5 \text{FINI}^*\text{Periods}(7+) + \cdots + \varepsilon$$

Table 17.3. *Walrasian mechanism analysis of variance estimates on efficiency*

Independent variable	Estimated coefficient	Standard error
DA*Periods (1–6)	85.344	1.663
FINI*Periods (1–6)	83.000	1.358
NINI*Periods (1–6)	80.720	3.036
FII*Periods (1–6)	83.667	3.030
NII*Periods (1–6)	85.125	2.629
DA*Periods (7+)	94.619	1.358
FINI*Periods (7+)	91.718	2.062
NINI*Periods (7+)	84.031	2.526
FII*Periods (7+)	85.082	2.630
NII*Periods (7+)	88.147	2.209

Table 17.3 supplies the outcome of this regression and the associated statistics.

Result 5. *Each treatment yields an increase in efficiency in later periods.*

Support. Additional support is provided by the results reported in Table 17.3.

Result 6. *The following efficiency rankings, for periods 7+, show that only the FINI treatment approaches the efficiency of the double auction.: DA ≥ FINI ≥ NII = FII = NINI.*

We summarize the following comparative static results.

  (i) Conditional on having no bid–offer restriction rule, full information helps in obtaining more efficient allocations.
  (ii) Conditional on only minimal information being provided, the improvement rule helps in obtaining more efficient allocations. However, the level of efficiency does not approach that of FINI or DA.

With respect to price formation, Figure 17.8 shows the price dispersion relative to the competitive equilibrium price tunnel. From the boxplots, it is easy to see that each treatment results in prices that lie within the tunnel (−10, +10). However, the low efficiencies reported in Table 17.3 show that the supply-and-demand match is not correct, and they suggest the presence of significant underrevelation on both sides of the market: If either side underreveals to gain an advantage, the other side underreveals to neutralize that advantage.

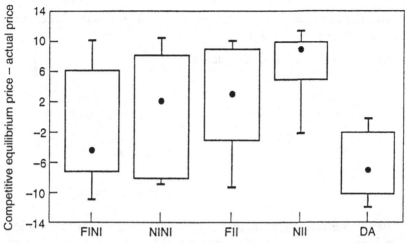

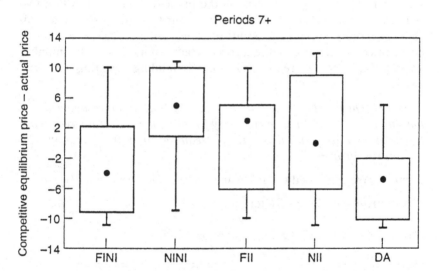

FIGURE 17.8. Box plots for distribution of price deviations from competitive equilibrium by treatment.

To see if the final price is dependent on the initial price P_0, we estimate the following equation for each treatment for periods 7+:[6]

$$\text{(Revelation price} - \text{Actual price)}$$
$$= \alpha + \beta \text{ (Revelation price} - \text{Initial price)} + \varepsilon$$

[6] Revelation price is defined as the price that would have occurred if every participant acted as a price taker in the market.

Result 7. *In no treatment does the initial price have an effect on the final price obtained in the market.*

Support. The estimates are as follows:

Treatment	a	Standard error	b	Standard error
FINI	−2.65	1.61	−.0256	.0578
NINI	3.69	1.45	−.0290	.0486
FII	−0.84	1.93	−.0560	.0860
NII	0.26	1.28	.0330	.0520

Before we investigate individual behavior, we consider the relationship between the number of iterations and the efficiency of each treatment. Under price-taking behavior, the process should stop within two iterations. This rarely happened in any of our treatments so that significant misrepresentation was occurring. Since subjects are trying to discover price and determine the terms of trade, an increase in the number of iterations may increase strategic withholding resulting in lower efficiencies.

Result 8. *The number of iterations required to match supply and demand has an insignificant effect on efficiency for all of the Walrasian treatments. Significantly more price iterations are required to clear the market with the improvement rule.*

Support. We estimated the following regression (for periods 7+).

$$\text{Efficiency} = \alpha + \beta\,(\text{Iterations}) + \varepsilon$$

The average per-period estimates are as follows:

Treatment	α	Standard error	β	Standard error	Number of Iterations
FINI	96.9	3.97	−0.83	0.54	6.30
NINI	89.3	4.27	−0.89	0.52	6.77
FII	90.4	5.72	−0.56	0.50	8.57
NII	77.7	4.65	1.18	0.52	9.75

Result 8 reflects the difficult strategic problem faced by traders in a Walrasian auction. When there is no order flow information and trading strategies are constrained in subsequent iterations by the improvement rule (NII), slow revelation of demand reduces risk insofar as it allows subjects to assess their relative competitiveness. However, such under-revelation can result in an inefficient market clearing.

C. Individual Behavior

Three types of individual behavior can be identified in our experiments:

1. *Overrevelation.* A buy or sell response that can result in a marginal loss in profit if the process stops (i.e., for each iteration t and participant i at the price P_t):[7]

    $$D_t^i(Pt) > d_t^i(Pt)$$
    $$S_t^j(Pt) > s_t^j(Pt)$$

2. *Underrevelation.* A buy or sell response that is less than the number of units that are profitable at the current price:

    $$D_t^i(Pt) < d_t^i(Pt)$$
    $$S_t^j(Pt) < s_t^j(Pt)$$

3. *Revelation.* A buy or sell response that contains all profitable units and no unprofitable units at the current price:

    $$D^it(Pt) = d^it(Pt)$$
    $$S_t^i(Pt) = s_t^j(Pt)$$

For each treatment, less than 3% of responses are consistent with overrevelation. For periods 7+, the number of responses that are consistent with overrevelation is less than 1%. If we focus only on cases in which positive profits can be made at the current price, there can be no cases of overrevelation since we have imposed short-selling restrictions. Thus, under the condition of positive profits, Table 17.4 shows the percent of responses consistent with underrevelation. It shows that both buyers and sellers underreveal nearly a third of the time. In FII, over 65% of the buyer responses are consistent with underrevelation.

Notice that under our improvement rule, in later periods, once a buyer (seller) has revealed a willingness to purchase (sell) x units at a particular price, he or she is required to purchase (sell) that many units at a lower (higher) price; therefore, underrevealing at the beginning of a period is the only way to obtain strategic bargaining room later in a

---

[7] Recall that uppercase letters represent actual aggregate supply and demand responses, whereas lowercase letters represent true demand and supply functions.

Table 17.4. *Walrasian mechanism percent underrevelation responses by type, treatment, and periods*

	Periods 1–6		Periods 7+	
Treatment	Buyers	Sellers	Buyers	Sellers
FINI	33	38	31	35
NINI	33	34	37	26
FII	37	33	66	38
NII	39	31	40	37

period. Consequently, the improvement rule fosters underrevelation by motivating people to begin their bargaining from a more advantageous position.

Table 17.4 suggests that underrevelation is common. Indeed, there are no cases in which a subject always reveals in every iteration and period of an experiment. However, if we consider only the final outcomes of a period in an experiment, we can investigate the distribution of underrevelation by subjects. For periods 7+, we determined the sum of the units underrevealed in the last iteration of a period by each subject in a treatment. Figure 17.9 plots the percent of underrevealed units by sellers and buyers on the last iteration in periods 7+.

Result 9. *By the end of a period, nearly half of all buyers reveal and a third of all sellers reveal. In general, underrevelation is concentrated among a few of the participants.*

If we focus on the underrevelation cases and determine what influences the amount underrevealed, theory shows that an underrevealing strategy is undertaken because the forgone profit on the unrevealed units is more than compensated for by the lower/higher price paid/received for the accepted units. Thus, there should be an effect on the amount of a subject's underrevelation based on per-unit profit. The following equation was estimated for each treatment (for period 7+):

$$\text{\# units underrevealed} = \alpha + \beta(\text{per-unit profit})$$
$$+ \gamma(\text{buyer/seller dummy}) + \varepsilon$$

We would predict that $\alpha < 0$, $\beta > 0$ and $\gamma = 0$. Table 17.5 presents the estimates of this equation.

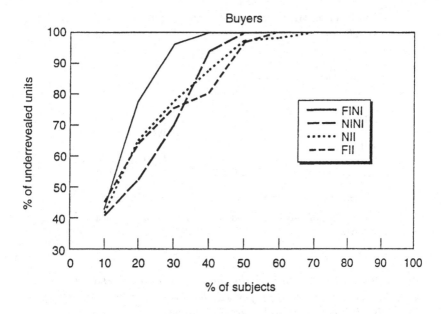

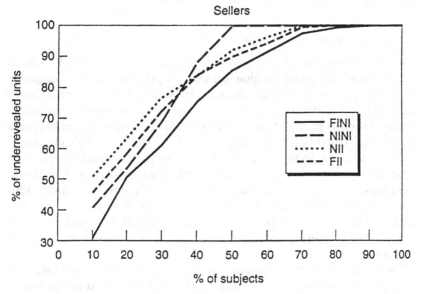

FIGURE 17.9. Percentage distribution of buyers (upper panel) and of sellers (lower panel) who underreveal on the last iteration in periods 7+.

Table 17.5. *Walrasian mechanism under-revelation estimates*

Treatment	α	β	γ	R^2
FINI	−4.75	0.057	0.27	0.34
	(15)	(0.0049)	(0.21)	
NINI	−4.29	0.0520	0.30	0.28
	(16)	(0.0057)	(0.23)	
NII	−4.14	0.0301	0.05	0.18
	(0.17)	(0.004)	(0.24)	
FII	−4.36	0.056	−0.42	0.40
	(0.16)	(0.006)	(0.23)	

Note: Standard error is listed in parentheses under each estimate.

Result 10. *For all treatments, the amount of underrevelation is significantly affected by per-unit profits. The level of underrevelation is not significantly different between buyers and sellers.*

V.   Summary

Walras's knowledge of the operations of the Paris Bourse and his need for a price adjustment mechanism that, in principle, could coordinate general equilibrium price adjustments led him to invent the mechanism in Walras (1871; 1954). Its theoretical appeal was to define a virtual, or "fictitious play" process that allowed the dispersed information of agents to be aggregated before binding contracts would occur. This characteristic allowed one to finesse the complexity of path-dependent processes that result when contracts can occur out of equilibrium and no doubt accounts for the extensive theoretical study of its dynamic and stability properties. While the *tâtonnement* had been found to be theoretically unstable in multiple markets, its potential for application to single-market calls, in securities and other markets remained an open question.

Joyce was the first to examine this mechanism empirically (some 100 odd years after Walras's work) and found that it performed well in single-unit per person environments using a human auctioneer. We find that all versions of the computerized multiple-unit Walrasian auction perform less efficiently than the continuous double auction. The full-information version, however, with no restrictions on bid–offer behavior, performs best. Because the Paris Bourse used a Walrasian process until recently, and it has a similar long application to the London bullion price "fixing" (Jarecki, 1976), why, given its relatively poor efficiency properties, has it been so durable? A likely possibility is that it works in field applications because it uses a live auctioneer, better informed and more flexible than a computer algorithm, whose presence threatens obvious manipulatory behavior, and who is able to avoid backtracking or to minimize its effects. An alternative possibility is that mechanisms survive in the field for historical and other reasons unrelated to efficiency.

With the decline of interest in general equilibrium theory and the concomitant ascendancy of work in game theory, other auction mechanisms, popular throughout the world of commodity and financial markets, have been exposed to theoretical and empirical examination. A comparison of alternative call market mechanisms shows clearly that oral bid mechanisms, such as the Vickrey (1976) version of the multiple-unit English auction perform badly relative to the one-sided convergence characterized by the English clock auction (McCabe et al., 1991). This result is robustly corroborated in two-sided auctions using the "Dutch English" (DE) clock mechanism (McCabe et al., 1992). In the latter, a price clock is started high; buyers report their demand quantities (total Q_D), and sellers report their supply quantities (total $Q_S > Q_D$). As the clock price ticks down, buyers enter additional demand and Q_D increases, sellers exit some supply and Q_S decreases, until $Q_D = Q_S$ and Q_S units are sold to the active buyers. In the DE procedure, buyers who enter must commit; sellers who exit cannot reenter. If there is an overshoot, the penultimate trial becomes binding, and the long side is rationed. Consequently, DE is like a Walrasian adjustment process but with tighter controls on exit/entry – a Walrasian auction with a heavy-handed auctioneer, if you like. An obvious disadvantage of DE is that if new disrupting information arrives during a call, the committed traders cannot escape.

The principles here seem clear. Efficiency and strategy-proofness can be enhanced by restricting the message space of traders. Prices are called exogenously, responses are restricted to exit/entry commitments that are binding, and backtracking is ruled out. An alternative to requiring commitment is to levy a charge for pulling your bid or offer. This provides an incentive to commit, but room for escape. It can lead to a "premature" stop with rationing or a "failed" market. The latter of course may be desirable when it causes an appropriate restart of the auction ex post new information.

The charge approach to the incentive problem is used effectively by the Arizona Stock Exchange. The AZX charges a commission for a trade, but you pay it if you pull your bid (offer), and pay it again if you reenter.

The AZX is a uniform-price double-auction call market with open display of all bids and offers in real time. Currently the call is held once daily for 2 hours, with New York exchanges closing after the first hour. This mechanism was found to be as efficient as the continuous double auction in the stochastic environment examined by McCabe et al. (1993) and in this study.

The results of our examination of the Walrasian mechanism show that it lacks robustness in environments in which multiunit demands and supplies are present, and there is little depth at the margin so that under-revelation has a direct influence on price. The examined process tends to generate a sequence of approximately correct price signals supported by both sides strategically underrevealing.

PART IV

Stock Markets and Bubbles in the Laboratory

Introduction

One of the more robust, and uneasily controversial sets of results emanating from laboratory research is the phenomenon of stock market bubbles. The controversy is uneasy, suppressed, and even a little embarrassed, precisely because of this robustness. Following their original presentation and exploration (Smith et al., 1988), the bubbles results were replicated by many experimentalists (see Sunder, 1995, for a survey and references), including ourselves (see Chapter 18 in this volume; King et al., 1993; Porter and Smith, 1995). The newcomers were as skeptical as my coauthors and I were originally. It was fascinating to watch others go through the pangs of reappraisal that we had experienced; some have avoided this reappraisal through denial of the observations. This is unfortunate because it is clearly a disequilibrium phenomenon, no more perplexing than the observation that double-auction supply and demand markets do not converge instantly to the competitive equilibrium. In the stock markets, convergence just takes longer than theorists expect.

The environment is one in which N (usually 9 or 12) subjects are given endowments of cash and shares such that all have the same expected initial wealth endowment. At the end of each of a finite number of trading periods T (common information to all subjects), a dividend is drawn from a discrete distribution, whose parameters are common information to the subjects. The expected per-period dividend $E(\tilde{d})$ is computed and reported to all subjects, and, at the end of each period, the "holding value" of a share is computed and announced. The latter is the expected value of the remaining dividend draws, or the number of periods remaining times the per-period expected dividend. Thus, the subjects are well-informed on the opportunity cost of trading a share at any time, know that others have the same information, and are reminded each period that the fundamental value of a share declines from $TE(\tilde{d})$ to zero at the rate $E(\tilde{d})$ per period.

This environment produces the following stylized pattern of results:

1. Inexperienced subjects (students, corporate managers, and over-the-counter traders) in period 1 tend to trade at prices below

409

fundamental value, $TE(\tilde{d})$. Prices rise in subsequent periods to levels above declining fundamental value. This price bubble then breaks sometime before the last period, with prices falling rapidly, but closing near fundamental value in period T or a few periods earlier. Trading volume is high with a substantial portion of the floating supply turning over in each period.

2. When once previously experienced subjects return for a second session, the price bubble is repeated, sometimes rising faster, but crashing sooner, with the price path deviating from fundamental value less than in the first session, and trading volume reduced.

3. When twice previously experienced subjects return for a third session, prices follow fundamental value much more closely, and trading volume is very low.

4. Across the sequence of trading periods, price changes from period to period are explained (predicted) by a regression equation of the form

$$\overline{P}_{t+1} - \overline{P}_t = \alpha + \beta(B_t - O_t) + \varepsilon_t \tag{1}$$

where P_t is the mean (or closing) price in period t, $B_t(O_t)$ is the number of bids (offers) to buy (sell) submitted in period t under the rules for continuous double-auction trading, ε_t is random error, the estimate of $\beta > 0$ is significantly greater than zero, and $\alpha < 0$ is not significantly different from $-E(\tilde{d})$. Thus the per period changes in price can be divided into three additive components: (a) a decline due to the using up of a dividend drawing right, (b) an increase (decrease) representing excess demand arising from endogenous capital gains expectations, measured by excess bids (offers), and (c) random error.

The excess bids equation provides more reliable forecasts of price changes than does the subjects' consensus forecast (mean of the individual subject forecasts of next period's mean price). This forecasting quality perhaps underlies the success and persistence of claims of "front running" in financial markets wherein large brokers are able to monitor the incoming flow of public orders, sense the emergence of excess demand for particular securities, and make trades for their own accounts in advance of price movements. Specialists on the organized exchanges are similarly positioned but, in principle, are constrained by rules whose objectives are to prevent specialist front running.

It has been discovered that the excess bids dynamic also applies to price bubbles occurring in experimental foreign exchange markets (Fisher and Kelly, 1995). It also provides advance warning of price movements in supply and demand markets that have not yet reached a competitive equilibrium and therefore provides an adjustment dynamic in all experimental markets organized under continuous double-auction trading rules (Plott, 1995). Because the excess bids adjustment dynamic has a Walrasian interpretation, it extends and generalizes the Walrasian hypothesis to markets that are not organized by a Walrasian auctioneer.

Bubbles are not peculiar to the experimental laboratory. They have been found to occur in closed end funds such as the Spain and Iberian fund, as reported in Chapter 18 in this volume. Also noted is the Renshaw (1988) argument that the effect of experience in experimental markets, which is to eliminate bubbles when subjects return for a third time, has an important parallel in security markets: the longer the time that has elapsed since the last crash in market prices, the smaller the number of investors who remember the bubble and crash, and the larger the number of younger inexperienced investors who enter the market to replace more mature investors. Consequently, the greater the time since the previous crash the greater the severity of the current crash.

Financial theorists, and economic theorists, in the rational expectations mold, will tell you privately, and even publicly, that these bubbles should not happen; that "something" is wrong with the experiments, although all specific "somethings," such as the use of student subjects, lack of short selling and margin buying in the first 2–3 dozen experiments, and the like, have all been tested, and the predictions were not borne out. Some have said that the finite horizon, declining value case, is special – the theory, I take it, does not need to hold in such special cases, although Plott (private correspondence) has produced bubbles in an increasing dividend value environment. When you point out that the Spain and Iberian closed end funds (and some other "country" funds) produced massive bubbles, the response is that these were thinly traded, and you could not borrow securities for short sales, which implies that the risk was too high – another special case. But why were people unwilling to loan sufficient shares to enable short selling? Also, why does the theory require short selling? There are thousands of securities that cannot be sold short.

Psychologists (including Richard Thaler) love the bubbles because they see bubbles as violating the rationality of expectations.

Both the theorists and the psychologists, however, are wrong in thinking that rational expectations are falsified by the experiments. The former are wrong to be upset; the latter wrong to be elated. A rational expectations equilibrium, if attained, cannot be instantaneous; there must be a process whereby people go from wherever they start to the ending equilibrium. In the laboratory bubbles, as with the Spain and Iberian funds, we eventually observe convergence to the equilibrium – people are just surprised that it takes so long. In the lab, we are observing the process whereby people gradually become convinced that buying above dividend value and/or selling below dividend value are money-losing strategies. In the first sessions, many nimble traders find these strategies to be profitable, but their profitability withers with time.

As we view it, the experiments provide the theory with a dynamic learning directive. Rational expectations theory does not define a *process* whereby agents come to have rational expectations. The term *rational expectations*, originally used by John Nash, was defined by him as a condition in which a group of agents have common probability beliefs about an event, which is in turn supported by event realizations. In both experimental and financial markets, the provision of common information does not guarantee common expectations (knowledge). The laboratory stock market experiments demonstrate that subjects without common expectations come, through common experience, to achieve common expectations corresponding to fundamental event realizations. Rational expectations models should be interpreted as models of convergent outcomes, not models of the convergence process. This is not to say that there will never be nonconverging environments (e.g., with changing populations of investors), but that conjecture has yet to be demonstrated in experiments.

In the experiments so far, it is experience that eventually squelches the propensity for prices to bubble. Although nothing else succeeds as well, "Figure 18.8" in this volume reports modest success with a futures market on period 8, the midpoint of the 15-period horizon experiments. This suggests that with lots of futures markets, say every second or third period throughout the horizon, the experiential process whereby subjects come to have common expectations might be greatly accelerated.

Of particular significance for future bubbles research is the differential equation system proposed by Caginalp and Ermentrout (1990, 1991), which is based on the interaction between two kinds of traders: fundamentalists, who buy (sell) in proportion to the difference between fundamental value and price (price and fundamental value), and trend-based investors, with finite memories, who buy in a rising market and sell in a declining market. Depending upon how the model is parameterized to reflect the mix of these two types of investors, the equations yield solutions reflecting fundamental value, or substantial boom–bust price bubbles. Caginalp and Balenovich (1993a, b) show how the model can be used to characterize, and forecast, price movements in both experimental and security markets. Current research is concerned with constructing direct tests of the ability of the Caginalp model to predict price changes in experimental markets.

CHAPTER 18

Stock Market Bubbles in the Laboratory

David P. Porter and Vernon L. Smith

Rational expectations models predict that if individuals have common expectations (or priors) as to the value of an asset, and this common value is equal to the dividend value of the asset, then trades, if they occur, will be at prices near intrinsic dividend value (Tirole, 1982). Contrary to this, consider the data in Figure 18.1 which lists the average weekly share price and corresponding net asset value (NAV) for the Spain Fund. The price of the Spain Fund shares from July 1989 to August 1990 begins at a discount from NAV, rises to a premium of 250% over NAV by week 15, and ultimately "crashes" back to a discount by week 61. There is much controversy over the behavior of closed end funds, which still remains a puzzle for a rational expectations theory of asset pricing (see Lee et al., 1991).

Explanations of deviations from NAV rely on models that focus on distinct investor types and their expectations. Instead of entering the debate concerning the interpretation of the price behavior of closed end funds, we shall rely on laboratory methods in economics that allow us to investigate propositions on price formation in a controlled fundamental value environment. In the economy, control over fundamental value and investor information is rarely possible; therefore, minimal conditions for studying the role of expectations in stock market valuations cannot be identified. Smith et al. (1988; hereafter SSW) report the results of laboratory asset markets in which each trader receives an initial portfolio of cash and shares of a security with a dividend horizon of 15 trading periods. Before the tth trading period, the expected dividend value of a share [e.g., $0.24(15 − t + 1)$] is computed and reported to all subjects to guard against any possibility of misunderstanding. Thus, the situation is like that of the stock fund in Figure 18.1 whose net asset value is reported to investors daily or weekly. Each trader is free to trade shares of the security using double-auction trading rules similar to those used on the major stock exchanges. At the end of the experiment, a sum equal to all dividends received on shares, plus initial cash plus capital gains minus capital losses is paid in U. S. currency to the trader.

The data in Figure 18.2 shows a typical result from a laboratory asset

414

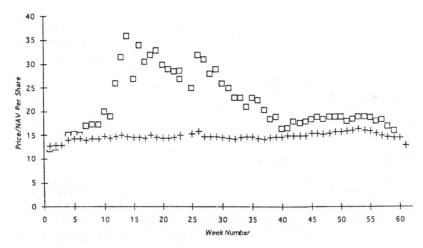

FIGURE 18.1. Share price and NAV: the Spain Fund 6/30/89–8/24/90.
□, price per share; +, NAV per share.

market. With inexperienced traders, bubbles and crashes are standard
fare. However, this phenomenon disappears as traders become experienced. That is, traders who have twice experienced trading in a laboratory asset market will trade at prices that reflect fundamental value.
Figure 18.2 contrasts the mean contract prices and volume for inexperienced traders with those for experienced traders in laboratory asset
markets. The data points show the mean contract for each period and
the numbers next to the price show the number of contracts made in that
period.

Two possible explanations for the existence of bubbles in laboratory
asset markets concern the expectations formation of traders and the
market structure under which they operate. The data from these experiments suggest that a more dynamic model of price formation is required
if one is to try to predict price patterns that have booms and busts or to
develop "policies" that reduce such volatility in asset markets. Recently,
two models have been developed; they focus on investor expectations
and price formation that allow for a wide range of price dynamics.

Day and Huang (1990) have a model that consists of investors who
base their buy and sell decisions either on the long-run investment value
of a security (α-investors) along with a weighting function over possible
estimates of market highs and lows with a fixed horizon, or more adaptive investors (β-investors) who base their decisions on current market
fundamentals. The price adjustment equation is then defined as a

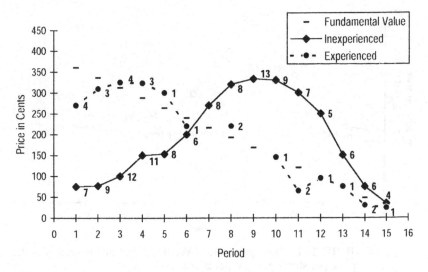

FIGURE 18.2. Mean contract price and volume compared with fundamental value for inexperienced and experienced subjects.

function of market excess demand in which market makers adjust inventory and prices linearly. Specifically, the excess demand equation for α-investors is based on a fixed parameter **a** of α-investor demand along with two parameters that define the support over the market top and bottom for the asset price; a single parameter **b** for β-investor demand; and finally a parameter **c**, which is the speed of price adjustment based on excess market demand. This model can produce dynamic properties with irregular bull and bear markets and short-run chaotic price fluctuations. However, this model is of limited applicability to the experimental asset markets because most of the crucial parameters (**a, b,** and **c**) are exogenous and are unaffected by underlying market variables or structures.

Caginalp and Ermentrout (1990, 1991) have developed a complete dynamical system for investor behavior that results in a system of ordinary differential equations. The model assumes a kinetic reaction among investors that relies on a fundamental value component ζ_2, and an "emotional" component ζ_1. The latter is based on a memory of price history that decays in time, and that captures the tendencies among investors to buy in a recently rising market and sell in a recently declining market.

Given that each unit of asset is either in cash, stock, or in a transition from stock to cash (stock submitted for sale), or cash to stock (buy order placed for a stock), rate equations can be established for these variables as a function of stock price changes. The transition equations, along with the investor sentiment component (ζ_1, ζ_2) equations, can be manipulated to obtain a dynamical system that can be solved numerically to yield a price path for the security. Using data from one of our experiments, Caginalp and Balenovich (1993a) obtain baseline estimates for two parameters in the price change equation. Given the parameter estimates, the price path for any experiment can be determined solely from the intrinsic value of the security and the opening price. They report their predictions of peak prices in nine of our experiments and find errors ranging from 1 to 20%.

The purpose of this chapter is to summarize the results of laboratory asset market bubbles and the effect of proposed changes in the asset market environment and institution that a priori should mitigate bubbles. From these results and the dynamic models alluded to earlier, suggestions for further modeling directions and specific experiments to investigate the robustness of the Caginalp et al. model are provided.

I. Empirical Results from Laboratory Asset Markets

Figure 18.3 supplies the structure of the baseline experiment of SSW where the theory would predict prices that track the fundamental value line. In this environment, inexperienced traders produced high *amplitude*[1] bubbles that are two to three times intrinsic value. In addition, the span of a boom tends to be of long *duration* (10 to 11 periods) with a large *turnover* of shares (five to six times the outstanding stock of shares over the 15-period experiment). In nearly all cases, prices crash to fundamental value by period 15.

Table 18.1 lists the treatments discussed in this chapter along with their hypothesized effect on the bubble characteristics. Table 18.2 lists the mean values of amplitude, duration, and turnover for each treatment compared with the baseline. (For the results listed in this chapter, we have constructed regression models and their parameter estimates that are reported in Appendix A.)

From the values in Table 18.2, we can draw the following conclusions for the baseline asset market:

---

[1] We calculate amplitude as the difference between the highest deviation of mean contract price from its fundamental value and the lowest deviation of mean contract from its fundamental value. This value is then normalized with respect to the expected dividend value over 15 periods.

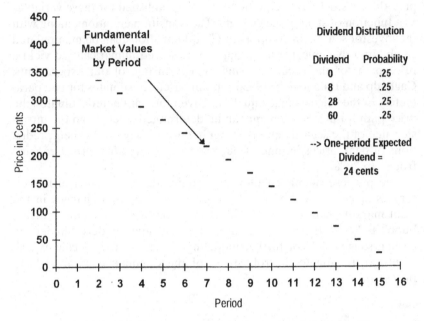

FIGURE 18.3. Parameters for baseline asset market experiment.

Result 1: *Public information on intrinsic dividend (or net asset) value is not sufficient to induce common expectations and trading at fundamental value.*

Result 2: *In replicable laboratory experiments, experience, particularly common group experience, together with common information is sufficient to yield trading near fundamental value.*

The game-theoretic assumption of common knowledge, as a means of finessing the explicit modeling of a pregame or repeated-game learning process, does not appear justified. Certainly common information on dividend value does not imply common knowledge expectations.

Given these results, a natural question to ask is whether these bubbles can be related systematically to individual reported price expectations. In an effort to answer this question, SSW asked subjects to forecast the mean price for the next period with a monetary reward for the best forecaster across all periods. The consensus (mean) forecast results reveal that (1) bullish capital gains expectations arise early in these experiments, (2) the mean forecast always fails to predict price jumps and turning points, and (3) the mean forecasts are highly adaptive (i.e., jumps

Table 18.1. *Stock market treatments and hypotheses*

Treatment	Description	Hypothesis
Baseline	Declining dividend value (see Figure 18.3)	Rational expectations equilibrium has trading at fundamental values
Short-selling	Traders are given the capacity to sell units to be covered by period 15	Traders can leverage sales and counter ebullient expectations
Margin-buying	Traders are given interest-free loan to be paid back by period 15	Purchases can be leveraged to raise prices that are below dividend value
Equal portfolios endowments	Each trader is given identical initial amounts of cash and shares	Traders do not need to use the market to balance portfolios
Brokerage fees	Buyer and seller in a transaction pay 10 cents each for the trade	Should reduce trading to relieve boredom or save costs
Informed insiders	Specially trained traders who are informed of excess bids	Expert traders aware of bubble characteristics engage in arbitrage
Dividend certainty	Security pays a fixed and known amount each period	Trading based on dividend risk avoidance is eliminated
Futures contracting	Traders are given a midhorizon (period 8) security	Futures contracts should give traders a reading on mid-horizon expected value
Limit price change rule	Asset price can only change a fixed percentage amount based on previous period prices	This rule has been recommended by expert advisory groups to moderate bubbles and crashes

in the mean price as well as turning points are only reflected in forecasts after a one-period lag). These observations parallel the performance of professional forecasters (Zarnowitz, 1986).

Result 3: *Subjects have a strong early tendency to develop homegrown expectations of rising prices; their forecasts are adaptive and have a universal tendency to miss price jumps and turning points.*

The dynamics of these price adjustments can be characterized empirically by a Walrasian price adjustment equation, which stipulates that price responds in the direction of the excess demand for the asset.

Table 18.2. *Mean values by stock market treatment (p-values in parentheses)*

Treatment	Inexperienced			Once-experienced			Twice-experienced		
	Amplitude	Duration	Turnover	Amplitude	Duration	Turnover	Amplitude	Duration	Turnover
Baseline	1.21 $n = 19$	9.23	5.79	0.75 (.10) $n = 4$	5.51 (.19)	3.00 (.00)	0.10 (.00) $n = 3$	3.00 (.00)	1.60 (.00)
Short-sell	1.61 (.40) $n = 4$	9.50 (.30)	6.67 (.49)	0.76 (.48) $n = 5$	5.80 (.78)	4.19 (.03)	0.40 (.02) $n = 3$	3.67 (.69)	1.74 (.27)
Margin-buy	3.64 (.00) $n = 2$	8.00 (.66)	5.48 (.59)	1.15 (.09) $n = 1$	2.00 (.21)	2.33 (.58)			
Equal portfolios	1.87 (.12) $n = 4$	10.00 (.44)	6.29 (.84)						
Brokerage fees	0.73 (.00) $n = 2$	10.00 (.44)	5.56 (.67)	0.63 (.62) $n = 3$	4.00 (.90)	4.92 (.10)			
Informed insiders	0.63 (.00) $n = 2$	13.00 (.00)	2.68 (.00)	0.25 (.04) $n = 3$	6.00 (.92)	4.05 (.40)			
Dividend certainty	1.10 (.98) $n = 3$	11.00 (.05)	8.84 (.13)	0.52 (.29) $n = 3$	9.67 (.24)	2.71 (.51)			
Futures contracting	0.92 (.11) $n = 3$	10.00 (.73)	6.85 (.81)	0.60 (.19) $n = 2$	5.50 (.60)	2.63 (.50)			
Limit price change	2.51 (.07) $n = 2$	10.50 (.46)	4.84 (.01)	1.77 (.05) $n = 2$	5.50 (.71)	2.22 (.15)	0.70 (.04) $n = 2$	1.50 (.17)	1.89 (.79)

Specifically, $dp/dt = F[D(p) - S(p)]$ where $F(0) = 0$ and $F' > 0$. The following ordinary least squares (OLS) Walrasian excess demand model (SSW, p. 1142).

$$\bar{P}_{t+1} - \bar{P}_t = \alpha + \beta(B_t - O_t) + \varepsilon_t \tag{1}$$

where $\bar{P}_t$ is the mean price in period t, α is minus the one-period expected dividend value (adjusted for any risk aversion), β is adjustment speed, B_{t-1} is the number of bids to buy tendered in period $t - 1$, and O_{t-1} is the number of offers to sell tendered in period $t - 1$. Price change in this model has three components: (1) the risk adjusted per-period expected dividend payout, (2) an increase (decrease) due to excess demand arising from homegrown capital gains (losses) expectations, a Walrasian measure of which is excess bids $B_{t-1} - O_{t-1}$, and (3) unexplained noise ε_t. The R^2 values range from 0.04 to 0.63. The variances in the estimates are large.

This model explains and predicts price changes better than subjects' forecasts in that it frequently anticipates turning points. A rational expectations prediction for this model is that $\alpha = -24$, the expected one-period dividend and $\beta = 0$. The pooled results over all experiments with treatment effects can be found in Appendix B. The results in Appendix B show that we cannot reject the hypotheses that $\alpha = -24$ and that $\beta > 0$. In addition, experience causes a significant decrease in the capital gains expectations coefficient β. However, this model provides values of R^2 that are much below unity leaving much of the change in prices unexplained.

From the experimental results, which show a dampening of the bubble with experience, Renshaw (1988) hypothesized that the *severity* of price bubbles and crashes depends upon trader experience with extreme market price changes. He examined the relationship between major declines in the Standard and Poor index and the length of time between major declines. The time between crashes is his proxy for investor inexperience. An OLS regression of the measured extent of the index's decline Y on the time since the previous decline X yields the estimate:

$$Y = 5.5 + 0.90X \qquad R^2 = 0.98$$
$$(t = 15.1)$$

The longer it has been since the previous crash in prices, the greater the magnitude of a new crash.

The baseline market developed by SSW omits many institutional features that are present in the field. Because some of these factors may very well dampen bubbles, they have provided the impetus for several new experiments reported in two recent studies: (1) King et al. (1993)

report experiments that introduce short selling, margin buying, brokerage fees, informed "insiders," equal portfolio endowments, and limit price change rules; (2) Porter and Smith (1995; hereafter PS) report new experiments examining the effect of a futures market and the effect of dividend certainty. Table 18.1 lists these structural changes, the associated data, and the predictions of the effect of these treatments on the market. Such structural changes have been suggested by others as an explanation of the bubbles reported in SSW.

Recall that in the baseline experiments individual traders were endowed with different initial portfolios. A common characteristic of first-period trading is that buyers tend to be those with low-share endowments, whereas sellers are those with relatively high-share endowments. This suggests that risk-averse traders might be using the market to acquire more balanced portfolios. If liquidity preference accounts for the low initial prices, which in turn lead to expectations of price increases, then making the initial trader endowments equal across subjects would tend to dampen bubbles.

Result 4: *Observations from four experiments with inexperienced traders show no significant effect of equal endowments on bubble characteristics.*

If risk aversion about price expectations due to dividend uncertainty causes a divergence of common expectations, then the elimination of such uncertainty should reduce the severity of bubbles. The PS experiments demonstrate otherwise (see Figure 18.4 for an example).

Result 5: *When the dividend draw each period is set equal to the one-period expected dividend value, so that the asset dividend stream is certain, bubbles still occur and are not significantly different from the case with dividend uncertainty.*

In Table 18.2 we note that the duration of bubbles is significantly increased with dividend certainty. The results in Appendix B for the Walrasian adjustment equation suggest, however, that dividend certainty does not have a significant effect on the capital gains expectations coefficient β.

Results 4 and 5 are directed at changing the underlying induced value parameters of the baseline experiments but not the basic structure of the market. Stock markets in the field provide margin rules that allow traders to take a position on either side of the market and leverage their sales by taking a short position or leverage their purchases by buying with borrowed funds. Consequently, a small number of traders who have countercyclical expectations would be able to offset the ebullient expectations

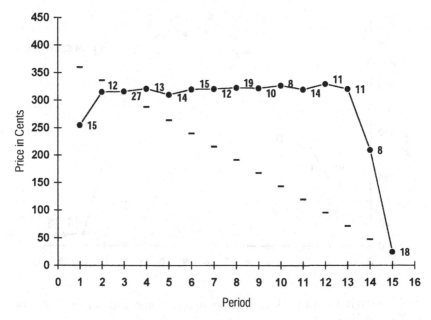

FIGURE 18.4. Mean contract price and volume by period for experiment with certain dividend.

of others. These considerations led to an explanation of the hypothesis that allowing subjects the right to short sell or to buy on margin would dampen bubbles.

Result 6: *Short-selling does not significantly diminish the amplitude and duration of bubbles, but the volume of trade is increased significantly; Figure 18.5 provides an example.*

Result 7: *Margin-buying opportunities cause a significant increase in the amplitude of bubbles for inexperienced ($p < 0.01$) but not for experienced subjects.*

Consequently, if anything, short-selling and margin-buying tend to exacerbate some aspects of observed bubbles.

The laboratory double auction has low participation costs of trading because subjects only have to touch a button to accept standing bids or asks. This, coupled with the conjecture by some critics that laboratory subjects may believe that they are expected to trade may result in laboratory bubbles. (Evidence contrary to this is reported in Chapter 2 in this volume.) However, the claim that subjects trade because they believe

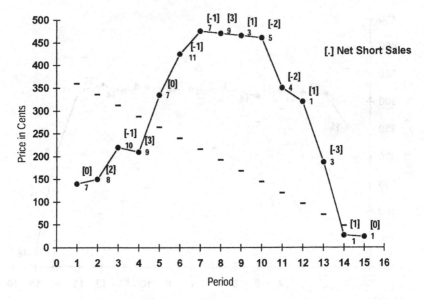

FIGURE 18.5. Mean contract price, volume, and net short sale by period.

they are expected to, merely predicts trade, not bubbles; nor is the claim consistent with the tendency for turnover to fall sharply with experience. One way to test the transactions cost hypothesis is to impose a transaction fee on each trade.

Result 8: *A brokerage fee of 20 cents on each trade (10 cents each on the buyer and seller) had no significant effect on the amplitude, duration, or share turnover.*

These results suggest that bubbles are robust against significant structural and environmental changes. The endogenous process by which expectations are being formed has no difficulty surviving these first-order changes. The observation that individuals do not form common expectations, given common information on asset value, raises the question of whether these bubbles are sensitive to the subject pool. Most of the experiments have been conducted at the University of Arizona and Indiana University, using volunteers from the student population.[2] Could the use of professional traders and business executives eliminate this uncertainty concerning the rationality of other's behavior?

---

[2] Bubbles have been observed with inexperienced student traders in two experiments at the California Institute of Technology and three experiments at the Wharton School.

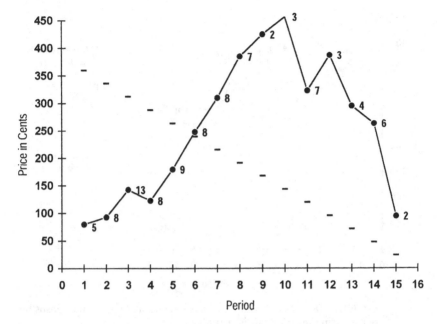

FIGURE 18.6. Mean contract price and volume by period for experiment with corporate executives.

Result 9: *The use of subject pools of small-business persons, midlevel corporate executives, and over-the-counter market dealers has no significant effect on the characteristics of bubbles with first-time subjects.*

In fact the most severe bubble among the original 26 SSW experiments was recorded in an experiment using small businessmen and women from the Tucson, Arizona, community (see Figure 18.6 for a bubble using corporate middle level executives).

Rational expectations theory predicts that if irrational trading patterns create profitable arbitrage, then knowledgeable traders will take advantage of these opportunities and this will eliminate such trading patterns. This hypothesis was tested by having three graduate students read the SSW paper. In addition to seeing past data on laboratory bubbles, these "experts" were given information on the bid and offer count each period. As discovered in SSW, the excess of bids over offers was found to be a leading indicator of average price changes. These informed subjects then participated in a market with six or nine uninformed traders recruited in the usual way.

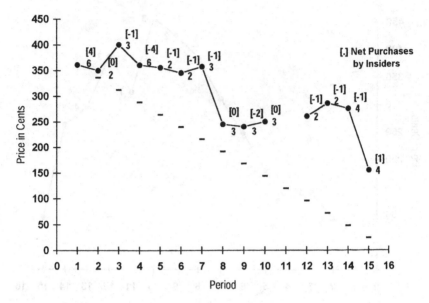

FIGURE 18.7. Mean contract price, volume, and insider purchases by period using informed insider traders.

Result 10: *The results support the rational expectations prediction provided that the informed traders are endowed with a capacity to sell short and the uninformed traders are once experienced. When the uninformed traders are inexperienced, the bubble forces are so strong that the expert traders are swamped by the buying wave; by period 11 they reach their maximum selling capacity, including short sales.*

The failure of the informed traders to eliminate the bubble when the uninformed traders are inexperienced is illustrated by the experiment in Figure 18.7.

It should be noted in Figure 18.7 that because short sales had to be covered by purchases to avoid penalties, when facing inexperienced traders, short-covering by expert traders prevented the market from crashing to dividend value in period 15. Thus, short-selling against the bubble prevented convergence to the rational expectations value at the end.

A futures contract provides a mechanism by which each trader can get a reading on all traders' expectations concerning a future event. In effect, one runs a future spot market in advance. If a price bubble arises because of the failure of common information to induce common

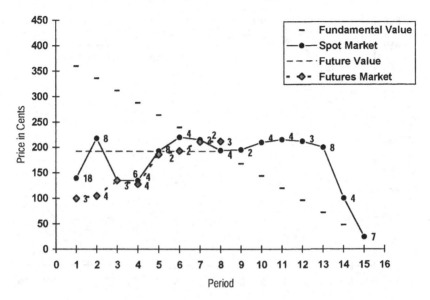

FIGURE 18.8. Mean spot and futures prices and volume by period in futures market experiment.

expectations, but the latter are achieved through repeat experience, then a futures contract should have the effect of speeding up this expectations-homogenizing process. To test this hypothesis, PS ran two sequences of two experiments with the same subjects trained in the mechanics of a futures market. In the new experiments, a future contract due in period 8 was utilized where agents could trade both the spot and futures contracts in periods 1–8; after period 8, only the spot market was active. This market mechanism may help traders focus on their expectations of share value at midhorizon and provide observations (futures contract prices) on the group's period 8 expectations during the first 7 periods of the market. Figure 18.8 shows the results of one of these futures market experiments.

Result 11: *Futures markets dampen, but do not eliminate, bubbles by speeding up the process by which traders form common expectations.*

Appendix B supplies estimates of an ANOVA model on the Walrasian price adjustment equation stated in (1) with treatment effects for futures market and certain dividend experiments. The results clearly demonstrate that the futures market has a significant dampening effect on

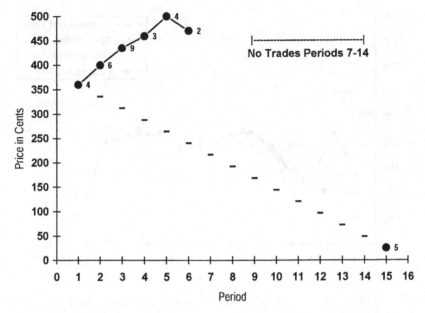

FIGURE 18.9. Mean contract price and volume by period under limit price change rule restriction.

capital gains expectations. In addition, the combination of one-time experience and a futures market significantly reduces the capital gains adjustment coefficient β.

In the wake of the worldwide stock market crash of October 19, 1987, it was widely recommended by various investigatory groups that limit price change rules be implemented on U.S. stock market exchanges. King et al. (1993) report six experiments in which ceiling and floor limits were placed at plus (or minus) twice the expected one-period dividend value.

Result 12: *Price limit change rules do not prevent bubbles; if anything the bubbles are more pronounced.*

King et al. conjecture that bubbles are more severe with limit price change rules because traders perceive a reduced down side risk inducing them to ride the bubble higher and longer. But, of course, when the market breaks, it moves down by the limit and finds no buyers. Trading volume is zero in each period of the crash as the market declines by the limit each period (see Figure 18.9, for an example).

II.   Summary

Laboratory stock markets in which shares have a well-defined expected fundamental (dividend) value, that is common information, exhibit strong price bubbles relative to fundamental value. These bubbles diminish with experience; trades fluctuate around fundamental value when the same group returns for a third trading session. Thus, common information is not sufficient to induce common rational expectations, but eventually through experience in a stationary environment, the participants come to have common expectations. If we suppose that investors are more "inexperienced" the longer it has been since the last stock market crash, the laboratory results are corroborated by a study showing a 98% correlation between the severity of declines in the Standard and Poor index and the length of time since the last crash.

More detailed analysis of the laboratory data shows that expectations of a rising market, as measured by trader price forecasts, occur early in a market. Traders' forecasts invariably miss price jumps and turning points. A more accurate predictor of mean price changes is lagged excess bids: a count of last period's bids minus the offers submitted.

The baseline experiments have been criticized for omitting a number of factors that might account for their propensity to bubble. A new generation of experiments evaluated these factors. Briefly, short-selling does not have a significant impact on bubble characteristics; margin-buying fails to moderate and even increases the amplitude of bubbles for inexperienced subjects; brokerage fees designed to raise transactions cost had no significant effect on bubble characteristics; the use of subjects from pools of small business persons, midlevel corporation executives, and over-the-counter stock dealers had no significant effect on bubbles; the use of subjects who had an opportunity to study SSW, and who were given information on excess bids at the close of each period support the rational expectations equilibrium, but only when the informed traders could leverage their sales with short-selling, and when the uninformed subjects were experienced.

Finally, bubbles seem to be due to uncertainty about the behavior of others, not to uncertainty about dividends, since making dividends certain does not significantly affect bubble characteristics; futures markets help to dampen (but do not eliminate) bubbles by allowing trades in a future spot market to occur in advance and thus speed up the process of creating common expectations; price limit change rules make bubbles worse, apparently by giving traders a perception of reduced downside risk, causing the bubble to carry further and longer.

III.   Further Experimental Tests

How can we use the laboratory to define the environment for an entirely new set of experiments designed to test the Caginalp and Ermentrout (1990, 1991) (also Caginalp and Balenovich, 1993b) differential equation model of stock market price movements? This model requires baseline experiments for calibration. The predictions of the model are then contingent on two conditions for any new experiment: (a) the experiment's specified dividend structure and (b) the experiment's initial trading price level. Therefore, we propose the following experimental testing program.

1. Conduct a new series of baseline experiments with a given uncertain dividend structure. These experiments will serve to parameterize the model including its sampling error characteristics (four experiments).
2. Using the same dividend structure as in step 1, conduct four new experiments in which the first period of trading is bounded by a ceiling and floor plus or minus 10 cents from some selected initial price level P_0. The controlled level of P_0 would be set at one value for two of the experiments and at another value for the remaining two experiments. After the first period of trading in each experiment, the controls would be removed, and prices allowed to move freely for comparison with the predictions of the model.
3. The dividend distribution in step 1 would be doubled in a third series of four experiments. In each experiment the initial period of trading will be constrained by a price floor and ceiling as in step 2.

Given the baseline calibration experiments, the predictive ability of the model would be evaluated using the four distinct prediction paths defined by the controls specified in steps 2 and 3.

Appendix A   ANOVA ESTIMATES OF STOCK MARKET TREATMENT ON AMPLITUDE, DURATION, AND TURNOVER

The following results are based on seemingly unrelated regression estimates of amplitude, duration and turnover simultaneous dummy variable equations.

Equation 1

Dependent variable:		AMPLITUDE	
Valid cases:	72	Missing cases:	0
Total SS:	45.9484	Degrees of freedom:	61
Residual SS:	17.8081	Standard error of estimates:	0.5156
		Log likelihood:	−53.5848

Treatment	Coefficient	Standard error	t-statistic	p-value
Short sales	−0.0481	0.1708	−0.2816	.7791
Certain dividend	0.0626	0.2530	0.2472	.8055
Futures	−0.6796	0.3800	−1.7884	.0782
Limit price rule	0.8843	0.2452	3.6072	.0006
Equal endowments	0.5073	0.2824	1.7960	.0770
Insiders	−0.5646	0.2559	−2.2066	.0308
Transaction fee	−0.3434	0.2628	−1.3066	.1958
Margin buying	0.8375	0.2505	3.3438	.0013
Inexperienced	1.3602	0.1154	11.7849	.0000
Once experienced	0.7889	0.1624	4.8568	.0000
Twice experienced	0.1680	0.2267	0.7410	.4613

Equation 2

Dependent variable:		DURATION	
Valid cases:	72	Missing cases:	0
Total SS:	1034.000	Degrees of freedom:	61
Residual SS:	482.7757	Standard error of estimates:	2.6843
		Log likelihood:	−187.2307

Treatment	Coefficient	Standard error	t-statistic	p-value
Short sales	0.9235	0.8895	1.0382	.3029
Certain dividend	2.7896	1.3175	2.1174	.0379
Futures	−0.3107	1.9785	−0.1571	.8757
Limit price rule	0.1196	1.2764	0.0937	.9256
Equal endowments	0.7583	1.4706	0.5156	.6078
Insiders	1.2659	1.3321	0.9503	.3454
Transaction fee	0.6200	1.3685	0.4530	.6520
Margin buying	0.4967	1.3042	0.3808	.7045
Inexperienced	9.2417	0.6010	15.3779	.0000
Once experienced	5.4722	0.8457	6.4706	.0000
Twice experienced	2.4272	1.1802	2.0567	.0436

Equation 3
Dependent variable: TURNOVER

Valid cases:	72	Missing cases:	0
Total SS:	568.1284	Degrees of freedom:	61
Residual SS:	209.2946	Standard error of estimates:	1.7674
		Log likelihood:	−153.3804

Treatment	Coefficient	Standard error	t-statistic	p-value
Short sales	1.5514	0.5857	0.6488	.0101
Certain dividend	−0.7395	0.8675	−0.8525	.3969
Futures	−2.7666	1.3027	−2.1237	.0374
Limit price rule	−0.1561	0.8404	−0.1858	.8532
Equal endowments	1.0584	0.9683	1.0931	.2783
Insiders	−1.0879	0.8771	−1.2403	.2192
Transaction fee	−0.3911	0.9011	−0.4340	.6656
Margin buying	−0.1470	0.8587	−0.1712	.8646
Inexperienced	5.2291	0.3957	13.2150	.0000
Once experienced	2.6124	0.5568	4.6916	.0000
Twice experienced	1.5769	0.7770	2.0293	.0464

Appendix B   ANOVA ESTIMATES OF TREATMENTS FOR WALRASIAN PRICE ADJUSTMENT

The model that is estimated in this appendix is as follows:

$$P_t - P_{t-1} = \alpha + \omega \cdot X + \delta \cdot C + \phi \cdot Cx + \varphi \cdot F + \gamma \cdot Fx + \eta \cdot S$$
$$+ \lambda \cdot L + \beta \cdot (B_{t-1} - O_{t-1}) + \rho \cdot [X \cdot (B_{t-1} - O_{t-1})]$$
$$+ \mu \cdot [C \cdot (B_{t-1} - O_{t-1})] + v \cdot [Cx \cdot (B_{t-1} - Q_{t-1})]$$
$$+ \theta \cdot [F \cdot (B_{t-1} - O_{t-1})] + v \cdot Fx \cdot [(B_{t-1} - O_{t-1})]$$
$$+ \zeta \cdot [S \cdot (B_{t-1} - O_{t-1})] + \tau \cdot [L \cdot (B_{t-1} - O_{t-1})] + \varepsilon$$

where: P = mean contract price
B = number of bids tendered
O = number of offers tendered
X = experienced baseline
C = Certain dividend treatment dummy

Cx = experienced certain dividend treatment dummy
F = Futures market treatment dummy
Fx = experienced futures market treatment dummy
S = Switch treatment dummy
L = LAN market treatment dummy

Dependent variable: ΔMean contract price by stock market treatment

Certain dividend experienced	Coefficient	Standard error	t-statistic
α	−0.1273	0.0697	−1.8249
Baseline experienced	−0.0118	0.0942	−0.1249
Certain dividend	0.0056	0.1185	0.0477
Certain dividend experienced	−0.0082	0.1229	−0.0674
Futures market	−0.0512	0.1299	−0.3944
Futures market experienced	−0.0188	0.1512	−0.1246
Switch	0.0065	0.1631	0.0399
LAN	0.0041	0.0305	0.1357
β	0.0329	0.0050	6.5923
Baseline experienced	−0.0071	0.0036	−1.9722
Certain dividend	−0.0136	0.0091	−1.4981
Certain dividend experienced	−0.0146	0.0093	−1.5577
Futures market	−0.0237	0.0062	−3.7882
Futures market experienced	−0.0278	0.0095	−2.9072
Switch	−0.0312	0.0135	−2.3012
LAN	−0.0021	0.0946	−0.0211

Number of observations: 364.
R^2: 0.2571.
SSR: 0.0113.
SER: 0.5782.
D-W: 2.0679.

References

Adolphs, R., D. Tanel, H. Damasio, and A. Damasio. 1994. "Impaired Recognition of Emotion in Facial Expressions Following Bilateral Damage to the Human Amygdala." *Nature* 372:669–72.

Alger, D. 1987. "Laboratory Tests of Equilibrium Predictions with Disequilibrium Price Data." *Review of Economic Studies* 54:105–45.

Allen, B., and M. Hellwig. 1986. "Bertrand-Edgeworth Oligopoly in Large Markets." *Review of Economic Studies* 53:175–204.

Allen, V. 1965. "Situational Factors in Conformity." In Leodard Berkowitz, ed., *Advances in Experimental Social Psychology*, Vol. 2. New York: Academic Press.

Allman, J., and L. Brothers. 1994. "Faces, Fear and the Amygdala." *Nature* 372:613–14.

Amihud, Y., and H. Mendelson. 1991. "Volatility, Efficiency and Trading: Evidence from the Japanese Stock Market." *The Journal of Finance* 46:1765–89.

Arrow, K. J. 1982. "Risk Perception in Psychology and Economics." *Economic Inquiry* 20:1–9.

1987. "Rationality of Self and Others in an Economic System." In R. M. Hogarth and M. W. Reder, eds., *Rational Choice: The Contrast between Economics and Psychology*. Chicago: Univ. Chicago Press.

Aumann, R. J. 1987. "Game Theory." In J. Eatwell, M. Milgate, and P. Neuman, eds., *The New Palgrave*, Vol. 2. London: Macmillan.

Axelrod, R. 1984. *The Evolution of Cooperation*. New York: Basic Books.

Axelrod, R., and W. D. Hamilton. 1981. "The Evolution of Cooperation." *Science* 211:1390–6.

Bailey, E. E. 1980. "Contestability and the Design of Regulatory and Antitrust Policy." Mimeo, September 11.

Bailey, E. E., and J. C. Panzar. 1980. "The Contestability of Airline Markets during the Transition to Deregulation." Mimeo, May 6.

Ball, S., and C. Eckel. 1995. "Status and Discrimination in Ultimatum Games: Stars on Thars." Department of Economics, Virginia Tech.

Ball, S., C. Eckel, P. Grossman, and W. Zame. 1996. "Status in Markets." Department of Economics, Virginia Tech.

Baron-Cohen, S. 1995. "Mindblindness: An Essay on Autism and Theory of Mind." Cambridge, MA: MIT Press.

Battalio, R., L. Green, and J. Kagel. 1981. "Income-Leisure Tradeoffs of Animal Workers." *American Economic Review* 71:621–32.

Baumol, W. J. 1982. "Contestable Markets: An Uprising in the Theory of Industry Structures." *American Economic Review* 72:1–15.

Baumol, W. J., and R. D. Willig. 1981. "Fixed Costs, Sunk Costs, Entry Barriers, and Sustainability of Markets." *Quarterly Journal of Economics* 96:405–31.

Baumol, W. J., J. C. Panzar, and R. D. Willig. 1982. *Contestable Markets and the Theory of Industry Structure*. New York: Harcourt-Brace-Jovanovich.

Becker, G. M., M. H. DeGroot, and J. Marschak. 1964. "Measuring Utility by a Single Response Sequential Method." *Behavioral Science* 9:226–32.

Beckman, M. 1965. "Edgeworth-Bertrand Duopoly Revisited." In R. Henn, ed., *Operations Research Verfahren III*. Meisenhein: Verlag Anton Hain.

Benoit, J., and V. Krishna. 1987. "Dynamic Duopoly: Prices and Quantities." *Review of Economic Studies* 54:23–36.

Berg, J. E., and J. W. Dickhaut. 1990. "Preference Reversals: Incentives Do Matter." Univ. Chicago.

Berg, J., J. Dickhaut, and K. McCabe. 1995. "Trust, Reciprocity, and Social History." *Games and Economic Behavior* 10:122–42.

Binger, B., E. Hoffman, and G. Libecap. 1991. "Experimental Methods to Advance Historical Investigation: An Examination of Cartel Compliance by Large and Small Firms." In J. Mokyr, ed., *The Vital One: Essays in Honor of Jonathan R. T. Hughes*. Greenwich, CT: JAI Press.

Binmore, K., J. Swierzbinski, S. Hsu, and C. Proulx. 1992. "Focal Points and Bargaining." Univ. Michigan, mimeo. Forthcoming in the *International Journal of Game Theory*.

Binswanger, H. P. 1980. "Attitudes Toward Risk: Experimental Measurement in Rural India." *American Journal of Agricultural Economics* 62:395–407.

——— 1981. "Attitudes Toward Risk: Theoretical Implications of an Experiment in Rural India." *Economic Journal* 91:867–90.

Blank, R. M. 1991. "The Effects of Double-Blind versus Single-Blind Reviewing: Experimental Evidence from the *American Economic Review*." *American Economic Review* 81(5):1041–67.

Blume, L. E., and D. Easley. 1982. "Learning to Be Rational." *Journal of Economic Theory* 26:340–51.

Bolton, G. E. 1991. "A Comparative Model of Bargaining: Theory and Evidence." *American Economic Review* 81:1096–136.

Bolton, G. E., E. Kator, and R. Zwick. 1993. "Dictator Game Giving: Rules of Fairness versus Random Acts of Kindness." Working Paper, University of Pittsburgh.

Bray, M. M. 1982. "Learning, Estimation and the Stability of Rational Expectations." *Journal of Economic Theory* 26:318–39.

Brewer, M. B., and W. D. Crano. 1994. *Social Psychology*. St. Paul, MN: West Publishing Co.

Brock, W., and J. Scheinkman. 1985. "Price Setting Supergames with Capacity Constraints." *Review of Economic Studies* 52:371–82.

Bronfman, C., and R. Schwartz. 1992. "Price Discovery Noise." Working Paper no. S-92-29, Stern School of Business, New York Univ.

Brown, R. W. 1973. *A First Language: The Early Stages.* Cambridge, MA: Harvard Univ. Press.

Brown-Kruse, J. 1991. "Contestability in the Presence of an Alternative Market: An Experimental Investigation." *RAND Journal of Economics* 22:136–47.

Bull, C., A. Schotter, and K. Weigelt. 1987. "Tournaments and Piece Rates: An Experimental Study." *Journal of Political Economy* 95:1–33.

Burnell, S. J., L. Evans, and S. Yao. 1992. "The Ultimatum Game: Optimal Strategies in the Presence of Rivalry." Preprint, Economics Department, Victoria Univ. Wellington, New Zealand.

Burnham, T., K. McCabe, and V. Smith. 1998. "Friend-or-Foe Priming in an Extensive Form Trust Game." To appear *Journal of Economic Behavior and Organization.*

Burrows P., and G. Loomes. 1989. "The Impact of Fairness on Bargaining." Manuscript in preparation.

Caginalp, G., and D. Balenovich. 1994. "Market Oscillations Induced by the Competition between Value-Based and Trend-Based Investment Strategies." Applied Mathematical Finance 1:129–164.

——— 1993. "Mathematical Models for the Psychology of Oscillations in Financial Markets." Mimeo, Univ. Pittsburgh, Pittsburgh, PA.

Caginalp, G., and G. B. Ermentrout. 1990. "A Kinetic Thermodynamic Approach to the Psychology of Fluctuations in Financial Markets." *Applied Mathematics Letters* 4:17–19.

——— 1991. "Numerical Studies of Differential Equations Related to Theoretical Financial Markets." *Applied Mathematics Letters* 4:35–8.

Calfee, R. C. 1970. "Effects of Payoff on Detection in a Symmetric Auditory Detection Task." *Perceptual and Motor Skills* 31:895–901.

Camerer, C. F. 1987. "Do Biases in Probability Judgment Matter in Markets? Experimental Evidence." *American Economic Review* 77:981–97.

Camerer, C., and K. Weigelt. 1988. "Experimental Tests of a Sequential Equilibrium Reputation Model." *Econometrica* 56:1–36.

Campbell, J., S. LaMaster, V. Smith, and M. Van Boening. 1991. "Off-floor Trading, Disintegration and the Bid-Ask Spread in Experimental Markets." *The Journal of Business,* 64:495–522.

Carmichael, H. L., and W. B. MacLeod. 1995. "Gift Giving and the Evolution of Cooperation." Mimeo, Queens Univ. and Boston College.

Carter, J., and M. Irons. 1991. "Are Economists Different and If So Why?" *Journal of Economic Perspectives* 5:171–7.

Cason, T. N., and A. W. Williams. 1990. "Competitive Equilibrium Convergence in a Posted-Offer Market with Extreme Earnings Inequities." *Journal of Economic Behavior and Organization* 14:331–52.

Cech, P.-A. 1988. "Removal of Regulatory Barriers to Entry." Department of Economics Discussion Paper 88–17, Univ. Arizona.

Chamberlin, E. 1948. "An Experimental Imperfect Market." *Journal of Political Economy* 61:95–108.

Chicago Mercantile Exchange. 1985. *Consolidated Rules*. Chicago: Chicago Mercantile Exchange.

Chu, Y.-P., and R.-L. Chu. 1990. "The Subsidence of Preference Reversals in Simplified and Marketlike Experimental Settings: A Note." *American Economic Review* 80:902–11.

Coase, R. 1960. "The Problem of Social Cost." *Journal of Law and Economics* 3:1–44.

Cohen, K., R. Conroy, and S. Maier. 1985. "Order Flow and the Quality of the Market." In Y. Amihud, T. Ho, and R. Schwartz, eds., *Market Making and the Changing Structure of the Securities Industry*. Lexington, MA: Lexington.

Cohen, K., S. Maier, R. Schwartz, and D. Whitcomb. 1981. "Transaction Costs, Order Placement Strategy, and Existence of the Bidders Spread." *Journal of Political Economy* 89:287–305.

Coleman, J. S. 1987. "Psychological Structure and Social Structure in Economic Models." In R. M. Hogarth and M. W. Reder, eds., *Rational Choice: The Contrast between Economics and Psychology*. Chicago: Univ. Chicago Press.

1990. *Foundations of Social Theory*. Cambridge, MA: Harvard University Press.

Conlisk, J. 1988. "Optimization Cost." *Journal of Economic Behavior and Organization* 9/10:213–28.

Copeland, T. E., and D. Galai. 1983. "Information Effect on the Bid-Ask Spread." *Journal of Finance* 38:1457–69.

Coppinger, V., V. Smith, and J. Titus. 1980. "Incentives and Behavior in English, Dutch and Sealed-Bid Auctions." *Economic Inquiry* 18:1–22.

Cosmides, L. 1985. "The Logic of Social Exchange: Has Natural Selection Shaped How Humans Reason? Studies With the Wason Selection Task." *Cognition* 31:187–276.

Cosmides, L., and J. Tooby. 1987. "From Evolution to Behavior: Evolutionary Psychology as the Missing Link." In J. Dupre, ed., *The Latest and the Best: Essays on Evolution and Optimality*. Cambridge, MA: The MIT Press.

1989. "Evolutionary Psychology and the Generation of Culture, Part II." *Ethology and Sociobiology* 10:51–97.

1991. "Are Humans Good Intuitive Statisticians After All?" Department of Psychology, Univ. California, Santa Barbara.

1992. "Cognitive Adaptations for Social Exchanges." In J. H. Barkow, L. Cosmides, and J. Tooby, eds., *The Adapted Mind: Evolutionary Psychology and the Generation of Culture*. New York: Oxford Univ. Press.

Coursey, D., J. Hovis, and W. Schutze. 1987. "On the Supposed Disparity Between Willingness-To-Accept and Willingness-To-Pay Measures of Value." *Quarterly Journal of Economics* 102:679–90.

Coursey, D., R. M. Isaac, and V. L. Smith. 1983. "Natural Monopoly and Contested Markets: Some Experimental Results." *Journal of Law and Economics* 27:91–113.

Cox, J., and D. Grether. 1996. "The Preference Reversal Phenomenon: Response Mode, Markets and Incentives." *Economic Theory* 7:381–405.

Cox, J., B. Roberson, and V. L. Smith. 1982. "Theory and Behavior of Single Object Auctions." In V. L. Smith, ed., *Research in Experimental Economics*, Vol. 2. Greenwich, CT: JAI Press.

Cox, J., V. L. Smith, and J. Walker. 1988. "Theory and Individual Behavior of First Price Auctions." *Journal of Risk and Uncertainty* 1:61–99.

Dasgupta, P., and E. Maskin. 1986. "The Existence of Equilibrium in Discontinuous Economic Games: Theory and Applications." *Review of Economic Studies* 53:1–26.

Davidson, C., and R. Deneckere. 1986. "Long-Run Competition in Capacity, Short-Run Competition in Price and the Cournot Model." *RAND Journal of Economics* 17:404–15.

——— 1990. "Excess Capacity and Collusion." *International Economic Review* 31:521–41.

Davis, D. D., and C. A. Holt. 1993. *Experimental Economics*. Princeton, NJ: Princeton Univ. Press.

Davis, D., C. Holt, and A. Villamil. 1990. "Supra-Competitive Prices and Market Power in Posted-Offer Experiments." Mimeo, Univ. Virginia.

Dawes, R. M. 1988. *Rational Choice in an Uncertain World*. New York: Harcourt-Brace-Jonanovich.

Day, R. H., and T. Groves. 1975. *Adaptive Economic Models*. New York: Academic Press.

Day, R., and W. Huang. 1990. "Bulls, Bears and Market Sheep." *Journal of Economic Behavior and Organization* 14:299–331.

Demsetz, H. 1968a. "Why Regulate Utilities?" *Journal of Law and Economics* 11:55–65.

——— 1968b. "The Cost of Transacting." *Quarterly Journal of Economics* 82:33–53.

Drago, R., and J. S. Heywood. 1989. "Tournaments, Piece Rates, and the Shape of the Payoff Function." *Journal of Political Economy*, 97:992–8.

Eckel, C. C., and P. Grossman. 1996a. "The Relative Price of Fairness: Gender Differences in a Punishment Game." *Journal of Economic Behavior and Organization* 30:143–58.

——— 1996b. "Altruism in Anonymous Dictator Games." *Games and Economic Behavior* 16(2):181–91.

Edgeworth, F. Y. 1925. "The Pure Theory of Monopoly." In F. Y. Edgeworth, ed., *Papers Relating to Political Economy*, Vol. 1. New York: Burt Franklin.

——— 1932. *Mathematical Psychics*, 1881. London School Reprints of Scarce Works in Economics.

Edwards, W. 1961. "Probability Learning in 1000 Trials." *Journal of Experimental Psychology* 62:385–94.

Einhorn, H. J., and R. M. Hogarth. 1987. "Decision Making Under Ambiguity." In R. M. Hogarth and M. W. Reder, eds., *Rational Choice: The Contrast between Economics and Psychology*. Chicago: Univ. Chicago Press.

Epps, T. W., and K. J. Singleton. 1986. "An Omnibus Test for the Two Sample Problems Using the Empirical Characteristic Function." *Journal of Statistical Computer Simulation* 26:177–203.

Fehr, E., G. Kirchsteiger, and A. Riedl. 1993. "Does Fairness Prevent Market Clearing? An Experimental Investigation." *Quarterly Journal of Economics* 108:437–59.

Fiorina, M. P., and C. R. Plott. 1978. "Committee Decisions Under Majority Rule." *American Political Science Review*, 72:575–98.

Fisher, E., and F. Kelly. 1995. "Experimental Foreign Exchange Markets." Department of Economics, Ohio State Univ., February 24.

Forsythe, R., J. L. Horowitz, N. E. Savin, and M. Sefton. 1994. "Replicability, Fairness and Pay in Experiments with Simple Bargaining Games." *Games and Economic Behavior* 6(3):347–69.

Forsythe, R., F. Nelson, G. Newman, and J. Wright. 1991. "The Iowa Presidential Stock Market: A Field Experiment." In R. M. Isaac, ed., *Research in Experimental Economics*, Vol. 4. Greenwich, CT: JAI Press.

____ 1992. "Anatomy of an Experimental Political Stock Market." *American Economic Review* 82:1142–61.

Forsythe, R., T. Palfrey, and C. Plott. 1982. "Asset Valuation in an Experimental Market." *Econometrica* 50:537–67.

Fouraker, L., and S. Siegel. 1963. *Bargaining Behavior.* New York: McGraw Hill Book Co.

Franciosi, R., P. Kujal, R. Michelitsch, V. Smith, and G. Deng. 1994. "Fairness: Effect on Temporary and Equilibrium Prices in Posted Offer Markets." *Economic Journal* 105:938–50.

Freuchen, P. 1961. *Book of the Eskimos.* Cleveland: World Publishing.

Friedman, D. 1999. "How Trading Institutions Affect Financial Market Performance: Some Laboratory Evidence." Economic Inquiry 31:410–435.

Friedman, J., and A. Hoggatt. 1980. *An Experiment in Noncooperative Oligopoly. Research in Experimental Economics*, Vol. 1. Greenwich, CT: JAI Press.

Fudenberg, D., and J. Tirole. 1993. *Game Theory.* Cambridge, MA: The MIT Press.

Garbade, K., and W. Silber. 1979. "Dominant and Satellite Markets: A Study of Dually-Traded Securities." *Review of Economics and Statistics* 61:455–60.

Gigerenzer, G. 1996. "Rationality: Why Social Context Matters." In P. B. Baltes and U. M. Standinger, eds., *Interactive Minds.* Cambridge: Cambridge Univ. Press.

Glosten, L. R., and P. R. Milgrom. 1985. "Bid, Ask and Transaction Prices in a Specialist Market with Heterogeneously Informed Traders." *Journal of Financial Economics* 14:71–99.

Goodman, B., M. Saltzman, W. Edwards, and D. H. Krantz. 1979. "Prediction of Bids for Two-Outcome Gambles in a Casino Setting." *Organizational Behavior and Human Performance* 24:382–99.

Gordon, H. S. 1954. "The Economic Theory of a Common-property Resource: The Fishery." *Journal of Political Economy* 62:124–42.

Grether, D. M. 1981. "Financial Incentive Effects and Individual Decision

440   **References**

Making." Social Science Working Paper No. 401, California Institute of Technology.

Grether, D., and C. Plott. 1979. "Economic Theory of Choice and the Preference Reversal Phenomenon." *American Economic Review* 69:623–38.

Guth, W., and R. Tietz. 1986. "Auctioning Ultimatum Bargaining Positions." in R. W. Scholz, ed., *Issues in West German Decision Research*. Frankfurt: Lang.

Guth, W., R. Schmittberger, and B. Schwarze. 1982. "An Experimental Analysis of Ultimatum Bargaining." *Journal of Economic Behavior and Organization* 3:367–88.

Halgren, E. 1992. "Emotional Neurophysiology of the Amygdala Within the Context of Human Cognition." In J. Aggleton, ed., *The Amygdala*. New York: Wiley-Liss.

Hamilton, J. 1987. "Off-Board Trading of NYSE-Listed Stocks: The Effects of Deregulation and the National Market System." *Journal of Finance* 42:1331–45.

——— 1988. "Electronic Market Linkages and the Distribution of Order Flow: The Case of Off-Board Trading of NYSE-Listed Stocks." Symposium on Information Technology and Securities Markets Under Stress, Graduate School of Business Administration, New York Univ., May 16–17.

Hanson, N. R. 1969. *Perception and Discovery*, San Francisco: Freeman, Cooper and Co.

Harlow, W. V., and K. Brown. 1990. "Understanding and Assessing Financial Risk Tolerance: A Biological Perspective." *Financial Analysts Journal* 46:50–62.

Harrison, G. 1989. "Theory and Misbehavior in First Price Auctions." *American Economic Review* 79:749–62.

Harrison, G., and K. McCabe. 1992. "Testing Noncooperative Bargaining Theory in Experiments." In R. M. Isaac, ed., *Research in Experimental Economics*, Vol. 5, pp. 137–69. Greenwich, CT: JAI Press.

Harrison G., and M. McKee. 1985. "Experimental Evaluation of the Coase Theorem." *Journal of Law and Economics* 28:653–70.

Hawkes, K. 1992. "Sharing and Collective Auction." In E. A. Smith and B. Winterhalder, eds., *Ecology, Evolution, and Human Behavior*. New York: Aldine de Gruyter.

——— 1993. "Why Hunter-Gatherers Work, An Ancient Version of the Problem of Public Goods." *Current Anthropology* 34:341–61.

Heiner, R. A. 1986. "Uncertainty, Signal Detection Experiments, and Modeling Behavior." In R. Langlois, ed., The New Institutional Economics, pp. 59–115. New York: Cambridge Univ. Press.

Herrnstein, R. J., G. Loewenstein, D. Prelec, and W. Vaughn, Jr. 1991. "Utility Maximization and Melioration: Internalities in Individual Choice." Department of Psychology, Harvard Univ., Draft, 1 April.

Hey, J., and D. Di Cagno. 1990. "Circles and Triangles: An Experimental Estimation of Indifference Lines in the Marschak-Machina Triangle." *Journal of Behavioral Decision Making* 3(4):279–306.

Hoffman, E., and M. Spitzer. 1982. "The Coase Theorem: Some Experimental Tests." *Journal of Law and Economics* 25:73–98.

1985a. "Experimental Law and Economics." *Columbia Law Review* 85:991–1036.

1985b. "Entitlements, Rights, and Fairness: An Experimental Examination of Subject's Concepts of Distributive Justice." *Journal of Legal Studies* 14:259–97.

Hoffman, E., K. McCabe, K. Shachat, and V. Smith. 1994. "Preferences, Property Rights and Anonymity in Bargaining Games." *Games and Economic Behavior* 7(3):346–80.

Hoffman, E., K. McCabe, and V. Smith. 1996a. "On Expectations and the Monetary Stakes in Ultimatum Games." *International Journal of Game Theory* 25(3):289–301.

1996b. "Reciprocity: The Behavioral Foundation of Socio-Economic Games." In W. Albers and W. Guth, eds., *Understanding Strategic Interaction: Essays in Honor of Reinhard Selten*. Berlin: Springer-Verlag.

1996c. "Social Distance and Other-regarding Behavior in Dictator Games." *American Economic Review* 86:653–60.

1996d. "Trust, Punishment, and Assurance: Experiments on the Evolution of Cooperation." Economic Science Association Annual Meeting, October.

Hogarth, R. M., and M. W. Reder, eds. 1987. *Rational Choice: The Contrast between Economics and Psychology*. Chicago: Univ. Chicago Press.

Hoggatt, A. 1959. "An Experimental Business Game." *Behavioral Science* 4:192–203.

Holt, C. 1989. "The Exercise of Market Power in Laboratory Experiments." *Journal of Law and Economics* 32:S107–30.

Holt, C., and F. Solis-Soberon. 1993. "The Calculation of Equilibrium Mixed Strategies in Posted-Offer Auctions." In R. M. Isaac, ed., *Research in Experimental Economics*, Vol. 5. Greenwich, CT: JAI Press.

Homans, G. C. 1967. *The Nature of Social Sciences*. New York: Harcourt, Brace and World.

Hughes, J. R. T. 1982. "The Great Strike at Nushagak Station, 1951: Institutional Gridlock." *Journal of Economic History* 42:1–20.

Hurwicz, L. 1960. "Optimality and Informational Efficiency in Resource Allocation Processes." In K. J. Arrow, S. Karlin, and P. Suppes, eds., *Mathematical Methods in the Social Sciences*. Stanford, CA: Stanford Univ. Press.

1972. "On Informational Decentralized Systems." In C. B. McGuire and R. Radner, eds., *Decisions and Organization*. Amsterdam: North Holland.

Isaac, G. L. 1978. "The Food-sharing Behavior of Protohuman Hominoids." *Scientific American* 238:90–108.

Isaac, R., and C. Plott. 1981. "Price Controls and the Behavior of Auction Markets." *American Economic Review* 71:448–59.

Isaac, R. M., and V. L. Smith. 1985. "In Search of Predatory Pricing." *Journal of Political Economy* 93:320–45.

Isaac, R. M., and J. M. Walker. 1988a. "Group Size Effects in Public Goods Provision: The Voluntary Contributions Mechanism." *Quarterly Journal of Economics* 103:79–200.

442   **References**

1988b. "Communication and Free-Riding Behavior: The Voluntary Contributions Mechanism." *Economic Inquiry* 26:585–608.

1991. "Costly Communication: An Experiment in a Nested Public Goods Problem." In T. Palfrey, ed., *Contemporary Laboratory Research in Political Economy*. Ann Arbor: Univ. Michigan Press.

Isaac, R. M., K. F. McCue, and C. R. Plott. 1985. "Public Goods Provision in an Experimental Environment." *Journal of Public Economics* 26:51–74.

Isaac, R. M., V. Ramey, and A. W. Williams. 1984. "The Effects of Market Organization on Conspiracies in Restraint of Trade," *Journal of Economic Behavior and Organization* 85:191–222.

Isaac, R. M., D. Schmitz, and J. M. Walker. 1989. "The Assurance Problem in a Laboratory Market." *Public Choice* 62:217–36.

Isaac, R. M., J. M. Walker, and S. H. Thomas. 1984. "Divergent Evidence on Free Riding: An Experimental Examination of Possible Explanations." *Public Choice* 43:113–49.

Isaac, R. M., J. M. Walker, and A. W. Williams. 1991. "Group Size and the Voluntary Provision of Public Goods: Experimental Evidence Utilizing Large Groups." Working Paper, Indiana Univ.

Jamal, K., and S. Sunder. 1991. "Money vs. Gaming: Effects of Salient Monetary Payments in Double Oral Auctions." *Organizational Behavior and Human Decision Processes* 49(1):151–66.

Jarecki, H. G. 1976. "Bullion Dealing, Commodity Exchange Trading and the London Gold Fixing: Three Forms of Commodity Auctions." In Y. Amihud, ed., *Bidding and Auctions for Procurement and Allocation*. New York: New York Univ. Press.

Jenness, D. 1957. *Dawn in Arctic Alaska*. Chicago: Univ. Chicago Press.

Joyce, P. 1984. "The Walrasian *Tâtonnement* Mechanism and Information." *RAND Journal of Economics* 15:416–25.

1991. "Differential Behavior in Walrasian Auctions." Mimeo, Department of Economics, Michigan Technological Univ.

Kachelmeier, S. J., and M. Shehata. 1991. "Examining Risk Preferences Under High Monetary Incentives: Experimental Evidence from the People's Republic of China." Draft, Graduate School of Business, Univ. of Texas at Austin.

Kachelmeier, S., S. Limberg, and M. Schadewald. 1991a. "A Laboratory Market Examination of the Consumer Price Response to Information About Producers' Costs and Profits." *The Accounting Review* 66(4):694–717.

1991b. "Fairness in Markets: A Laboratory Investigation." *Journal of Economic Psychology* 12:447–64.

Kahneman, D., and A. Tversky. 1979. "Prospect Theory: An Analysis of Decision under Risk." *Econometrica* 47:263–91.

1982. "The Psychology of Preferences." *Scientific American* 246:160–73.

1996. "On the Reality of Cognitive Illusions: A Reply to Gigerenzer's Critique." Department of Psychology, Princeton Univ.

Kahneman, D., J. Knetsch, and R. Thaler. 1986. "Fairness as a Constraint on Profit Seeking: Entitlements in the Market." *American Economic Review*

76:728–41. Reprinted in R. Thaler, ed., *Quasi Rational Economics*, pp. 199–219. New York: Russell Sage Foundation, 1991.

1987. "Fairness and the Assumptions of Economics." In R. M. Hogarth and M. W. Reder, eds., *Rational Choice: The Contrast between Economics and Psychology*. Chicago: Univ. Chicago Press.

1990. "Experimental Tests of the Endowment Effect and The Coase Theorem." *Journal of Political Economy* 98:1325–48. Reprinted in R. Thaler, ed., *Quasi Rational Economics*, pp. 167–88. New York: Russell Sage Foundation.

Kalai, E., and E. Lehrer. 1993. "Rational Learning Leads to Nash Equilibrium." *Econometrica* 61:1019–45.

Kaplan, A. 1964. *The Conduct of Inquiry*. New York: Chandler Publishing Co.

Kaplan, H., and K. Hill. 1985a. "Hunting Ability and Reproductive Success Among Male Ache Foragers: Preliminary Results." *Current Anthropology* 26:131–3.

1985b. "Food Sharing Among Ache Foragers: Tests of Explanatory Hypotheses." *Current Anthropology* 26:233–45.

Ketcham, J., V. Smith, and A. Williams. 1984. "A Comparison of Posted Offer and Double Auction Pricing Institutions." *Review of Economic Studies* 51:595–614.

King, R. R., V. L. Smith, A. Williams, and M. Van Boening. 1993. "The Robustness of Bubbles and Crashes in Experimental Stock Markets." In I. Prigogine, R. H. Day, and P. Chen, eds., *Nonlinear Dynamics and Evolutionary Economics*. Oxford: Oxford Univ. Press.

Knetsch, J. L., and J. A. Sinden. 1984. "Willingness to Pay and Compensation Demanded: Experimental Evidence of an Unexpected Disparity in Measures of Value." *Quarterly Journal of Economics* 99:507–21.

Kormendi, R. C., and C. R. Plott. 1982. "Committee Decisions Under Alternative Procedural Rules: An Experimental Study Applying New Non-monetary Methods of Payment." *Journal of Economic Behavior and Organization* 3:175–95.

Kreps, D. 1990a. *Game Theory and Economic Modelling*. Oxford: Clarendon.

Kreps, D. M. 1990b. *A Course in Microeconomic Theory*. Princeton, NJ: Princeton Univ. Press.

Kreps, D., P. Milgrom, J. Roberts, and R. Wilson. 1982. "Rational Cooperation in the Finitely Repeated Prisoners' Dilemma." *Journal of Economic Theory* 27:245–52.

Kroll, Y., H. Levy, and A. Rapoport. 1988. "Experimental Tests of the Separation Theorem and the Capital Asset Pricing Model." *American Economic Review* 78:500–19.

Kruskal, W. A. 1957. "Historical Notes on the Wilcoxon Unpaired Two-Sample Test." *Journal of the American Statistical Association* 52:356–60.

Lee, C., A. Scheilfer, and D. Thaler. 1991. "Investor Sentiment and the Closed-End Fund Puzzle." *Journal of Finance* 46:75–109.

Leffler, G. L., and L. C. Farwell. 1963. *The Stock Market*, 3rd. ed. New York: The Ronald Press.

Levine, M., and C. Plott. 1977. "Agenda Influence and its Implications." *Virginia Law Review* 61:561.

Levitan, R., and M. Shubik. 1972. "Price Duopoly and Capacity Constraints." *International Economic Review* 13:111–22.

Lichtenstein, S., and P. Slovic. 1971. "Reversals of Preference Between Bids and Choices in Gambling Decisions." *Journal of Experimental Psychology* 89:46–55.

Lohr, S. 1992. "Lessons from a Hurricane: It Pays Not to Gouge." *New York Times*, September 22.

Lucas, R. E., Jr. 1987. "Adaptive Behavior and Economic Theory." In R. M. Hogarth and M. W. Reder, eds., *Rational Choice: The Contrast between Economics and Psychology*. Chicago: Univ. Chicago Press.

Marburg, T. 1951. "Domestic Trade and Marketing," In H. Williamson, ed., *Growth of the American Economy*, pp. 511–33. Englewood Cliffs, NJ: Prentice-Hall.

Marr, D. 1982. *Vision*. San Francisco: Freeman.

Maskin, E., and J. Tirole. 1988. "A Theory of Dynamic Oligopoly II: Price Competition, Kinked Demand Curves, and Edgeworth Cycles." *Econometrica* 56:571–600.

McAfee, P. 1992. "A Dominant Strategy Double Auction." *Journal of Economic Theory* 56:434–50.

McCabe, K. 1989. "Fiat Money as a Store of Value in an Experimental Market." *Journal of Economic Behavior and Organization* 12(2):215–31.

McCabe, K. A., S. J. Rassenti, and V. L. Smith. 1991. "Testing Vickrey's and Other Simultaneous Versions of the English Auction." In R. M. Isaac, ed., *Research in Experimental Economics*, Vol. 4. Greenwich, CT: JAI Press.

1992. "Designing Call Auction Institutions: Is Double Dutch Best?" *Economic Journal* 102:9–23.

1993. "Designing a Uniform Price Double Auction: An Experimental Evaluation." In D. Friedman and J. Rust, eds., *The Double Auction Market Institutions, Theories, and Evidence*. Reading, MA: Addison-Wesley.

1995. "Institutional Design for Electronic Trading." In R. Schwartz, ed., *Global Equity Markets*. Chicago: Irwin.

1996. "Game Theory and Reciprocity in Some Extensive Form Experimental Games." *Proceedings National Academy of Science* 93:13421–8.

1998. "Reciprocity, Trust and Payoff Privacy in Extensive Form Bargaining." *Games and Economic Behavior* 24:10–24.

McCabe, K., V. Smith, and M. LePore. 1998. "Intentionality Signaling: Why Game Form Matters." Economic Science Laboratory, Univ. Arizona, March.

McClelland, G., M. McKee, W. Schulze, E. Beckett, and J. Irwin. 1991. "Task Transparency versus Payoff Dominance in Mechanism Design: An Analysis of the BDM." Laboratory for Economics and Psychology, Univ. Colorado, June.

McCloskey, D. 1985. "The Loss Function Has Been Mislaid: The Rhetoric of Significance Tests." *American Economic Review* 75:201–5.

McElroy, M. B. 1987. "Additive General Error Models for Production Cost and Derived Demand or Share Systems." *Journal of Political Economy* 95:737–57.

McKelvey, R. D., and T. R. Palfrey. 1992. "An Experimental Study of the Centipede Game." Econometrica 60:803–836.

Mendelson, H. 1987. "Consolidation, Fragmentation, and Market Performance." *Journal of Financial and Quantitative Analysis* 22:189–207.

Messick, S., and A. H. Brayfield. 1964. *Decision and Choice.* New York: McGraw-Hill.

Miller, R. G., Jr. 1981. *Simultaneous Statistical Inference*, 2d ed. New York: Springer-Verlag.

Miller, R., C. R. Plott, and V. L. Smith. 1977. "Intertemporal Competitive Equilibrium: An Empirical Study of Speculation." *Quarterly Journal of Economics* 91:599–624.

Nelson, R. R., and S. G. Winter. 1982. *An Evolutionary Theory of Economic Change.* Cambridge, MA: Harvard Univ. Press.

New York Stock Exchange. 1987. *Constitution and Rules.* Chicago: Commerce Clearing House.

North, D. 1990. Institutions, *Institutional Change and Economic Performance.* Cambridge: Cambridge Univ. Press.

Noussair, C. 1992. "A Theoretical and Experimental Examination of Auctions in Multi-unit Demand Environments," Ph.D. dissertation, California Institute of Technology.

Ochs, J., and A. E. Roth. 1989. "An Experimental Study of Sequential Bargaining." *American Economic Review* 79:355–84.

Okun, A. 1981. *Prices and Quantities: A Macroeconomic Analysis.* Washington, DC: The Brookings Institution.

Osborne, M., and C. Pitchik. 1986. "Price Competition in a Capacity-Constrained Duopoly." *Journal of Economic Theory* 38:238–60.

Otani, Y., and J. Sicilian. 1990. "Limit Properties of Equilibrium Allocations of Walrasian Strategic Games." *Journal of Economic Theory* 51:295–312.

Pinker, S. 1994. *The Language Instinct.* New York: William Morrow and Co.

Plott, C. R. 1982a. "Industrial Organization Theory and Experimental Economics." *Journal of Economic Literature* 20:1485–527.

1982b. "A Comparative Analysis of Direct Democracy, Two Candidate and Three Candidate Elections in an Experimental Environment." Social Science Working Paper 457, California Institute of Technology, Pasadena.

1986. "Laboratory Experiments in Economics: The Implications of Posted-Price Institutions," *Science* 232:732–8.

1987. "Rational Choice in Experimental Markets." In R. M. Hogarth and M. W. Reder, eds., *Rational Choice: The Contrast between Economics and Psychology.* Chicago: Chicago Univ. Press.

1988. "Research on Pricing in a Gas Transportation Network." Technical Report No. 88-2. Washington, DC: Federal Energy Regulatory Commission, Office of Economic Policy, July.

1995. "Properties of Disequilibrium Adjustment in Double Auction Markets."

446   **References**

Mimeograph, Division of Humanities and Social Sciences, California Institute of Technology, December.

Plott, C. R., and G. Agha. 1983. "Intertemporal Speculation with a Random Demand in an Experimental Market." In R. Tietz, eds., *Aspiration Levels in Bargaining and Economic Decision Making*. Berlin: Springer-Verlag.

Plott, C. R., and V. L. Smith. 1978. "An Experimental Examination of Two Exchange Institutions." *Review of Economic Studies* 45:133–53.

Plott, C. R., and J. T. Uhl. 1981. "Competative Equilibrium with Middlemen." *Southern Economic Journal* 47:1063.

Plott, C., A. Sugiyama, and G. Elbaz. 1994. "Economies of Scale, Natural Monopoly, and Imperfect Competition in an Experimental Market." *Southern Economic Journal* 61:261–87.

Porter, D., and V. L. Smith. 1995. "Futures Contracting and Dividend Certainty in Experimental Asset Markets." *Journal of Business* 68:509–41.

Rapoport, A. 1987. "Prisoner's Dilemma." In J. Eatwell, M. Milgate, and P. Newman, eds., *The New Palgrave*, Vol. 3, pp. 973–6. London: Macmillan.

Renshaw, E. 1988. "The Crash of October 19 in Retrospect." *The Market Chronicle* 22:1.

Rice, W. R. 1996. "Sexually Antagonistic Male Adaptation Triggered by Experimental Arrest of Female Evolution." *Nature* 379:232–4.

Robinson, J. 1977. "What Are the Questions?" *Journal of Economic Literature* 15:1318–39.

Robinson, J. P., P. R. Shaver, and L. S. Wrightsman. 1991. "Measures of Personality and Social Psychological Attitudes." New York: Academic Press.

Roth, A. E. 1990. "Bargaining Experiments." In J. Kagel and A. Roth, eds., *Handbook of Experimental Economics*. Princeton: Princeton Univ. Press.

Roth, A. E., V. Prasnikar, M. Okuno-Fujiwara, and S. Zamir. 1991. "Bargaining and Market Behavior in Jerusalem, Ljublkana, Pittsburgh, and Tokyo: An Experimental Study." *American Economic Review* 81:1068–95.

Sauermann, H., and R. Selten. 1959. "Ein oligolpolexperiment." *Zeischreft for die Gesante Staatswissenschaft* 115:427–71.

Savage, L. J. 1962. "Bayesian Statistics." In R. E. Machol and P. Grey, eds., *Recent Developments in Information and Decision Processes*, New York: Macmillan.

Scherer, F. 1970. *Industrial Pricing*. Chicago: Rand McNally.

Schotter, A., K. Wiegelt, and C. Wilson. 1994. "A Laboratory Investigation of Multiperson Rationality and Presentation Effects." *Games and Economic Behavior* 6:445–68.

Schwartz, M., and R. Reynolds. 1983. "Contestable Markets, an Uprising in the Theory of Industry Structure: Comment." *American Economic Review*, 73:488–90.

Schwartz, R. A. 1988. *Equity Markets*. New York: Harper and Row.

Schwartz, T., and J. S. Ang. 1989. "Speculative Bubbles in the Asset Market: An Experimental Study." Paper presented at the American Finance Association meeting, Atlanta, December.

Selten, R. 1975. "Re-examination of the Perfectness Concept for Equilibrium Points in Extensive Games." *International Journal of Game Theory* 4(l):25–55.

Selten, R., and R. Stoecker, R. 1986. "End Behavior in Sequences Of Finite Prisoner's Dilemma Supergames." *Journal of Economic Behavior and Organization* 7:47–70.

Shogren, J. F., S. Y. Shin, D. J. Hayes, and J. B. Kliebenstein. 1994. "Resolving Differences in Willingness to Pay and Willingness to Accept." *American Economic Review* 84:255–70.

Shubik, M. 1959. *Strategy and Market Structure: Competition, Oligopoly, and the Theory of Games.* New York: Wiley.

Siegel, S. 1959. "Theoretical Models of Choice and Strategy Behavior: Stable State Behavior in the Two-Choice Uncertain Outcomes Situation." *Psychometrika* 24:303–16.

1961. "Decision Making and Learning Under Varying Conditions of Reinforcement." *Annals of the New York Academy of Science* 89(5):766–83.

Siegel, S., and J. Andrews. 1962. "Magnitude of Reinforcement and Choice Behavior in Children." *Journal of Experimental Psychology* 63(4):337–41.

Siegel, S., and L. Fouraker. 1960. *Bargaining and Group Decision Making: Experiments in Bilateral Monopoly.* New York: McGraw-Hill.

Siegel, S., and D. A. Goldstein. 1959. "Decision-Making Behavior in a Two-Choice Uncertain Outcome Situation." *Journal of Experimental Psychology* 57(1):37–42.

Siegel, S., A. Siegel, and J. Andrews. 1964. *Choice, Strategy, and Utility.* New York: McGraw-Hill.

Simon, H. A. 1955. "A Behavioral Model of Rational Choice." *Quarterly Journal of Economics* 69:99–118.

1956. "A Comparison of Game Theory and Learning Theory." *Psychometrika* 3:267–72.

1987. "Rationality in Psychology and Economics." In R. M. Hogarth and M. W. Reder, eds., *Rational Choice: The Contrast between Economics and Psychology.* Chicago: Univ. Chicago Press.

Slovic, P., and S. Lichtenstein. 1983. "Preference Reversals: A Broader Perspective." *American Economic Review* 73:596–605.

Slovic, P., B. Fischoff, and S. Lichtenstein. 1982. *New Directions for Methodology of Social and Behavioral Science: Question Framing and Response Consistency,* No. 11. San Francisco: Jossey-Bass.

Smith, A. 1776; 1937. *The Wealth of Nations,* New York: The Modern Library, Random House.

Smith, V. L. 1962. "An Experimental Study of Competitive Market Behavior." *Journal of Political Economy* 70:111–37.

1964. "Effect of Market Organization on Competitive Equilibrium." *Quarterly Journal of Economics* 78:181–201.

1965. "Experimental Auction Markets and the Walrasian Hypothesis." *Journal of Political Economy* 73:387–93.

448   **References**

1976a. "Experimental Economics: Induced Value Theory." *The American Economic Review* 66:274–9.

1976b. "Bidding and Auctioning Institutions: Experimental Results." In Y. Amihud, ed., *Bidding and Auctioning for Procurement and Allocation*, pp. 43–64. New York: New York Univ. Press.

1977. "The Principle of Unanimity and Voluntary Consent in Social Choice." *Journal of Political Economy* 85:1125–40.

1980. "Relevance of Laboratory Experiments to Testing Resource Allocation Theory." In J. Kmenta and J. Ramsey, eds., *Evaluation of Econometric Models*, pp. 345–77. San Diego: Academic Press.

1981. "An Empirical Study of Decentralized Institutions of Monopoly Restraint," In G. Horwich and J. P. Quirk, eds., *Economic Essays in Honor of E. R. Weiler*. West Lafayette, IN: Purdue Univ. Press.

1982. "Microeconomic Systems as an Experimental Science." *American Economic Review*, 72:923–55.

1985. "Experimental Economics: Reply." *American Economic Review* 85:265–72.

1986. "Experimental Methods in the Political Economy of Exchange." *Science* 234:167–73.

1991. "Rational Choice: The Contrast Between Economics and Psychology." *Journal of Political Economy* 99:877–97.

Smith, V. L., and J. M. Walker. 1993a. "Rewards, Experience and Decision Costs in First Price Auctions." *Economic Inquiry* 31:237–44.

1993b. "Monetary Rewards and Decision Cost in Experimental Economics." *Economic Inquiry* 31:237–44.

Smith, V. L., and A. Willlams. 1981. "On Nonbinding Price Controls in a Competitive Market." *American Economic Review* 71:467–74.

1982. "The Effects of Rent Asymmetries in Experimental Auction Markets," *Journal of Economic Behavior and Organization* 3:99–111.

1983. "An Experimental Comparison of Alternative Rules for Competitive Market Exchanges." In M. Shubik, ed., *Auctioning and Bidding*. New York: New York Univ. Press.

1990. "The Boundaries of Competitive Price Theory: Convergence, Expectations and Transactions Costs." In L. Green and J. Kagel, eds., *Advances in Behavioral Economics*, Vol. 2, pp. 3–35. New York: Ablex.

1992. "Experimental Market Economics." *Scientific American* 267(6):116–21.

Smith, V. L., G. L. Suchanek, and A. W. Williams. 1988. "Bubbles, Crashes, and Endogenous Expectations in Experimental Spot Asset Markets." *Econometrica* 56:1119–51.

Smith, V. L., A. W. Williams, W. K. Bratton, and M. G. Vannoni. 1982. "Competitive Market Institutions: Double Auctions vs Sealed Bid-Office Auctions." *American Economic Review* 72:58–77.

Smith, V. L., and F. Szidarovszky. 1999. "Monetary Rewards and Decision Cost in Strategic Interactions." Submitted to *American Economic Review*.

Stigler, G. J. 1957. "Perfect Competition, Historically Contemplated." *Journal of Political Economy* 65:1–17.

Stoecker, R. 1980. "Experimentelle Untersuchung des Entscheidungsverhaltens im Bertrand-Oligopol." In *Wirtschaftstheoretische Entscheidungsforschung*, Vol. 4. Bielefeld, Germany: Pfeffersche Buchhandlung.

Stoll, H., and R. Whaley. 1990. "Stock Market Structure and Volatility." *Review of Financial Studies* 3:37–71.

Sunder, S. 1995. "Experimental Asset Markets: A Survey." In A. Roth and J. Kagel, eds., *Handbook of Experimental Economics*, pp. 445–500. Princeton: Princeton Univ. Press.

Swensson, R. G. 1965. "Incentive Shifts in a Three-Choice Decision Situation." *Psychonomic Science* 2:101–2.

Swets, J. A., and S. T. Sewell. 1963. "Invariance of Signal Detectability Over Stages of Practice and Levels of Motivation." *Journal of Experimental Psychology* 66:120–6.

Telser, K. G. 1993. "The Ultimatum Game: A Comment." Mimeo, Department of Economics, Univ. Chicago.

Thaler, R. 1980. "Toward a Positive Theory of Consumer Choice." *Journal of Economic Behavior and Organization* 1:39–60.

1987. "The Psychology and Economics Handbook: Comments on Simon, on Einhorn and Hogarth, and on Tversky and Kahneman." In R. M. Hogarth and M. W. Reder, eds., *Rational Choice: The Contrast between Economics and Psychology*. Chicago: Univ. Chicago Press.

Thaler, R., and E. Johnson. 1990. "Gambling with the House Money and Trying to Break Even: The Effects of Prior Outcomes or Risky Choice." *Management Science* 36:643–60.

Theil, H. 1971. "An Economic Theory of the Second Moments of Disturbances of Behavioral Equations." *American Economic Review* 61:190–4.

Tirole, J. 1982. "On the Possibility of Speculation Under Rational Expectations." *Econometrica* 50:1163–81.

Tooby, J., and I. De Vore. 1987. "The Reconstruction of Hominoid Behavioral Evolution Through Strategic Modeling." In W. G. Kinzey, ed., *Primate Models of Human Behavior*. Ithaca, NY: SUNY Press.

Trivers, R. 1971. "The Evolution of Reciprocal Altruism." *Quarterly Review Biology* 46:35–7.

Tversky, A., and W. Edwards. 1966. "Information Versus Reward in Binary Choice." *Journal of Experimental Psychology* 71:680–3.

Tversky, A., and D. Kahneman. 1983. "Extensional versus Intuitive Reasoning: The Conjunction Fallacy in Probability Judgment." *Psychological Bulletin* 90(4):293–315.

1987. "Rational Choice and the Framing of Decisions." In R. M. Hogarth and M. W. Reder, eds., *Rational Choice: The Contrast between Economics and Psychology*. Chicago: Univ. Chicago Press.

Vickrey, W. 1961. "Counterspeculation, Auctions, and Competitive Sealed Tenders." *Journal of Finance* 16:8–37.

1976. "Auctions, Markets, and Optimal Allocation." In Y. Amihud, ed., *Bidding and Auctions for Procurement and Allocation*. New York: New York Univ. Press.

450   References

Vives, X. 1986. "Rationing Rules and Bertrand-Edgeworth Equilibria in Large Markets." *Economics Letters* 21:113–16.

Walras, L. 1871; 1954. *Elements of Pure Economics: Or the Theory of Social Wealth*. Homewood, IL: Irwin.

Wason, P. 1966. "Reasoning." In B. M. Foss, ed., *New Horizons in Psychology*. Harmondsworth: Penguin.

Wellford, C. P. 1990. *Takeovers and Horizontal Mergers: Policy and Performance*. Ph.D. dissertation, Univ. Arizona.

Wilcox, N. T. 1989. "Well-Defined Loss Metrics and the Situations That Demand Them." Economic Science Association Meetings, Tucson, AZ, October 28–29.

1992. "Incentives, Complexity, and Time Allocation in a Decision-Making Environment." Public Choice/Economic Science Association Meetings, New Orleans, March 27–29.

Williams, A. A. 1979. "Intertemporal Competitive Equilibrium: On Further Experimental Results." In V. L. Smith, ed., *Research Experimental Economics*, Vol. 1. Greenwich, CT: JAI Press.

1980. "Computerized Double-Auction Markets: Some Initial Excremental Results." *Journal of Business* 53:235–57.

Williams, A. A., and V. L. Smith. 1984. "Cyclical Double-Auction Markets With and Without Speculators." *Journal of Business* 57:1–33.

Williams, A. A., V. L. Smith, and J. Ledyard. 1986. "Simultaneous Trading in Two Competitive Markets: An Experimental Examination." Manuscript, Indiana Univ., Bloomington.

Williams, F. 1973. "Effect of Market Organization on Competitive Equilibrium: The Multiunit Cases," *Review of Economic Studies* 40:97–113.

Wilson, R. 1985. *Game-Theoretic Analyses of Trading Processes*. Stanford, CA: Stanford Business School.

Winterfeldt, D. von, and W. Edwards. 1986. *Decision Analysis and Behavioral Research*. New York: Cambridge Univ. Press.

Wolf, C., and L. Pohlman. 1983. "The Recovery of Risk Preferences from Actual Choice." *Econometrica* 51:843–50.

Zajac, E. 1985. "Perceived Economic Justice: The Example of Public Utility Regulation." In H. P. Young, ed., *Cost Allocation: Methods, Principles and Applications*. Amsterdam: North-Holland.

Zarnowitz, V. 1986. "The Record and Improvability of Economic Forecasting." NBER Working Paper 2099.

Zeckhauser, Richard. 1987. "Comments: Behavioral versus Rational Economics: What You See Is What You Conquer." In R. M. Hogarth and M. W. Reder, eds., *Rational Choice: The Contrast between Economics and Psychology*. Chicago: Univ. Chicago Press.

Index

451